LAW IN A CHANGING WORLD

Law in a Changing World

The Climate Crisis

EDITED BY JUTTA BRUNNÉE,
BRENDA COSSMAN, ANDREW GREEN,
AND BENJAMIN ALARIE

UNIVERSITY OF TORONTO PRESS
Toronto Buffalo London

Toronto Buffalo London
utppublishing.com
Printed and bound by CPI Group (UK) Ltd, Croydon, CR0 4YY

ISBN 978-1-4875-6332-5 (cloth) ISBN 978-1-4875-6334-9 (EPUB)
ISBN 978-1-4875-6333-2 (PDF)

Library and Archives Canada Cataloguing in Publication

Title: Law in a changing world : the climate crisis / edited by Jutta Brunnée, Brenda Cossman, Andrew Green, and Benjamin Alarie.
Names: Brunnée, Jutta, editor | Cossman, Brenda, 1960–, editor | Green, Andrew (Andrew James), editor | Alarie, Benjamin, editor.
Description: Includes bibliographical references.
Identifiers: Canadiana (print) 20250124955 | Canadiana (ebook) 20250125013 | ISBN 9781487563325 (paper) | ISBN 9781487563332 (PDF) | ISBN 9781487563349 (EPUB)
Subjects: LCSH: Climatic changes – Law and legislation.
Classification: LCC K3585.5 .L39 2025 | DDC 344.04/6 – dc23

Cover design: John Beadle
Cover image: Envato Elements

We wish to acknowledge the land on which the University of Toronto Press operates. This land is the traditional territory of the Wendat, the Anishnaabeg, the Haudenosaunee, the Métis, and the Mississaugas of the Credit First Nation.

University of Toronto Press acknowledges the financial support of the Government of Canada, the Canada Council for the Arts, and the Ontario Arts Council, an agency of the Government of Ontario, for its publishing activities.

Canada Council for the Arts Conseil des Arts du Canada

ONTARIO ARTS COUNCIL
CONSEIL DES ARTS DE L'ONTARIO
an Ontario government agency
un organisme du gouvernement de l'Ontario

Funded by the Government of Canada Financé par le gouvernement du Canada | Canada

Contents

Figures

LAW IN A CHANGING WORLD

Introduction: How Climate Change Is Affecting Law and What to Do about It

JUTTA BRUNNÉE, BRENDA COSSMAN, ANDREW GREEN, AND BENJAMIN ALARIE

Climate change is here. It is here in wildfires and heat, in floods and drought, in ocean currents and hurricanes. It is impacting people and species around the world and its harms are likely to get worse. Law holds a central part in the story of climate change. Much of the academic, policy, and public discussion around the law and climate change has been focused on what role law can, or has failed to, play in reducing emissions of greenhouse gases. From the binding emission reduction targets of the Kyoto Protocol (2005), and the non-binding emission reduction pledges of the Paris Agreement (2015), to national policies such as Canada's 2030 Emissions Reduction Plan, to community and local activism to reduce carbon emissions, the public and policy discussions have been focused primarily on mitigating climate change. With the increasing frequency, severity, and scale of climate-induced weather disasters, questions of adaptation and compensation for loss and damage have assumed growing importance. While these issues of mitigation and adaptation are crucial, they do not exhaust the ways climate change is altering the law. From investment law to constitutional law, housing law to health law, changing climate is exacerbating or reshaping the challenges we face and the solutions that we must seek.

In 2023, scholars from the University of Toronto Faculty of Law came together to explore the implications of climate change for the law. With very few exceptions, the participants were not climate law experts, and deliberately so. Each of the authors engaged with the implications of climate change for their areas of expertise. The goal was to grapple with the effect of climate change on virtually all areas of law, and the challenges its impacts pose both for law and for those working with law. We asked our colleagues to rise to the challenge that climate change presents to all of us, to move beyond our comfort zones, to challenge ourselves to tackle what we may have thought of as someone else's area of expertise. The here and now of climate change demands that we recognize the ways it is affecting all areas of law. It requires a rethinking of who, what, and how law regulates. The conference provided an opportunity to experiment with new ideas to inject into one of the fundamental challenges of our times.

This volume provides the fruits of this exploration. It is not just another book on climate change law, rather it seeks to broaden the field by examining how climate change is affecting law, and in turn, how law might help address and mitigate climate change. The chapters explore a wide array of issues from the role of different levels of government, to insurance, to the assessment of risk, to the differential impact of climate change and disaster on vulnerable populations. Despite, or perhaps because, of this diversity of issues, several interesting themes have emerged.

I. Legal Institutions Are Central to Addressing Climate Change

It has been suggested that climate change represents the ultimate tragedy of the commons.[1] Everyone seeks to benefit from the use of fossil fuels while allowing others to bear the costs of reducing emissions. Climate change, however, is a particularly pernicious, some say a "super wicked," problem because it has layers of uncertainty, collective action, and intergenerational equity added to it.[2]

Many of the chapters point to the central role of institutions in how we address such a problem. A key dynamic that connects a number of contributions is the interplay of the legislature, the executive, and the courts. One, at times seemingly appealing, approach to addressing climate change is to ignore democracy and lean into whatever science provides as an appropriate solution. Democracy could be seen as an obstacle to timely, effective action. However, legitimacy, effectiveness, and fairness depend not only on expertise but also on legality and political accountability.[3] The balance implicates both administrative law and constitutional law.[4] Commitments to legality are essential in the face of emergencies, including the climate emergency.[5]

A second set of institutional questions lay around the line between markets and state action. One clear dispute about the appropriate line lies in actuating the innovation necessary to base the massive transformation needed to address climate change. Both large scale government action and private markets have some advantages in bringing about the necessary technological change, but some synthesis between them will likely be necessary.[6] However, climate change implicates this line in other areas as well. One stark example is the area of housing.[7] Building houses is increasingly seen as necessary to accommodate a growing population, and a crisis of homelessness seems to demand a public response. Yet any positive obligation on the part of the state to house individuals seems to run up against the need to limit climate change – both the building and the use of homes have serious implications for whether we meet our climate commitments. In such a situation, thinking about the proper role of government potentially points to a new approach to balancing rights and public policy and to the state's role in what otherwise has been seen as primarily a private market issue. Another example is the move by states to take on the role of insurer – even potentially on a very large scale such as insuring against future harms from climate change.[8]

But this centrality of institutions to addressing climate change also puts these institutions at risk, which has implications not only for climate law but also more broadly. Two cases help explain this point.[9] The US Supreme Court's decision in *West Virginia* shows how courts are attempting to rebuild administrative and constitutional law in part in response to an attempt by the federal government to impose controls on emissions from electricity generators. The court expanded the "major questions doctrine," which will not only potentially limit the government's ability to address climate change but also have implications in other areas of law from health care to labour law. In Canada, a constitutional challenge to the federal government's carbon pricing scheme gave rise to a dispute among Supreme Court of Canada justices about the appropriate constraints on the discretion granted to administrative decision makers. As in the United States, the divisions exposed by this debate may affect the ability of the executive to make policy in a range of areas.[10]

However, while institutions are exposed to change in the face of climate action, the chapters in this collection present a range of interesting innovations or features which would improve not only climate action but also policy in other areas. These include sophisticated discussions on forms of accountability for policy such as the enduring power of concepts of legality,[11] the surprising accountability benefits of non-binding international agreements,[12] and the formidable political underpinnings of administrative law.[13] They encompass new roles for old institutional forms such as royal commissions,[14] innovative tools to enhance incentives for action,[15] and institutional bypasses that allow action in the face of political immobility.[16] These innovations also advocate for an openness to Indigenous ideas and values that have been undervalued and dismissed in the past but provide the seeds for change.[17]

II. Climate Change Exacerbates Vulnerabilities That the Law Must Come to Grips With

Justice, not surprisingly, is central to how we should address climate change and to discussions on how climate change is impacting law and legal institutions more generally. Climate change will inflict its harms particularly harshly on the vulnerable – those without resources, those who live on the margins, or those who have been marginalized by mainstream society. Our solutions may be more or less just – we can, for example, reach the much-vaunted goal of "net zero" in ways that ameliorate inequality or that exacerbate it. Moreover, climate change impacts on our laws and institutions more generally can move us towards or away from a more just society.

The calls for a "just transition" are the most obvious manifestations of the mixing of justice and climate law. While "just transition" is at times narrowly interpreted as the impact of climate laws on workers, it also needs to account for other vulnerable individuals such as the disabled, but more often than not fails to do so.[18] Moreover, a "just" transition must include not only the transition to a "net zero" economy but also to a world that has adapted to climate change. Developing countries in particular are struggling with the need to finance adaptation and to repair or recover from past harms and we are only beginning to develop means of addressing these struggles fairly.[19]

However, the chapters in this book point to other, more nuanced ways in which law should consider the vulnerable and the need for justice. Having youth front litigation against governments to force action on climate change seems a pragmatic and effective route, but it raises a myriad of questions about using youth, who are vulnerable in so many ways, as a means.[20] Their vulnerability is enhanced in the era of climate change where anxiety about the future can foster mental health challenges.[21]

Not surprisingly, given its broad-ranging impacts, climate change intertwined with many justice claims. Climate action is consistent with a view of animal rights as eating less meat can lead to much lower greenhouse gas emissions.[22] We have tools that can foster this connection and lead to broader, overlapping impacts such as on sustainable agriculture. However, some of the links create more significant problems. A clash of rights, such as between a right to housing and a right to stable climate, will demand new approaches to mediating the claims for fairness.[23]

The need to think about relationships and ethics will be key to addressing climate change and to adapting law and legal institutions to the new reality. Law and lawyering must be open to such pressures. How should lawyers think about a tension between effective climate action and the impact of that action on vulnerable individuals? Should legal ethics be altered in the face of a climate emergency, away from its purported neutrality?[24] Do we need to alter some of our core decision-making structures to account for our obligations to future generations or to the disabled or to Indigenous Peoples?[25]

III. Responsibility and Risk at Every Level

One approach to solving a tragedy of the commons is centralized control. Global climate change has eluded such control. While international law has developed new, promising tools, the paramountcy of state sovereignty has hindered centralized international action.[26] However, the chapters in the volume bring a "polycentric" sentiment to legal regulation – that mitigating and adapting to climate change demands attention at all levels of governance. A more decentralized, localized, polycentric approach was advanced by Nobel Prize winning economist Elinor Ostrom, who argued that multilateral policies are necessary, but not sufficient, to address the global collective-action problem of climate change.[27] She argued instead for "a multi-scale approach to the problem of climate change would be more effective and encourage experimentation and learning."[28]

Climate change cannot be tackled by any one policy, action, actor, or institution alone. Societies should pull all the levers at their disposal. The chapters in this collection aim to contribute to exploring the various impacts, risks, and responsibilities across levels of governance. International law and institutions have a role to play in promoting cooperation between states, in setting national targets for carbon reduction, and in harmonizing national approaches. The Paris Agreement provides some hope for a structured approach to reciprocal action by states. However, many past attempts to limit emissions through international agreements have failed, and current demands for payments for loss and damage are facing challenges. New visions of the role of international law and new legal institutions are necessary to meet these challenges.[29]

But many of the legal challenges addressed within this collection point to action at other levels. Domestic laws and state governance are clearly implicated and raise complicated challenges. What are the relative roles of the executive, the legislature, and the judiciary? Which institutions are best placed to combine expertise with the voices of different domestic actors? Delving deep in terms of governance, the chapters in this collection raises other issues: what level of governance should develop ethical rules for lawyering?; what role can different levels of government usefully play in promoting innovation or fostering sustainable agriculture? Many chapters go even deeper – to the role of and impact on individuals as citizens, consumers, and even lawyers.[30]

This collection explores the multiple legal levers that need to be pulled as we struggle to address, redress, and mitigate the profound consequences of climate change. Of course, not all the levers may be compatible with one another, and political resources are not unlimited, so difficult choices and priorities are required. Notwithstanding the shared impulse of the chapters to seek potential legal levers, the chapters are not without tensions. Some suggest that climate change may force us to revise fundamental or settled legal principles, while others place more emphasis on applying them more consistently and strictly. There are also differences in emphasis on whether climate change should be, or needs to be, addressed by the actions of some powerful organization – either the state or a private organization, centralized or decentralized – or whether the most important actions are those of ordinary individuals, even if the state needs to guide them in making those changes. Rather than resolving these and other tensions, we hope to contribute to a deeper discussion of the multilayered challenges of legal responses to climate change.

IV. Outline

Part 1 of the collection explores governance: who governs climate change? It addresses questions of the rule of law and governance in times of crisis, including the challenges that climate change presents to some of the very conceptual foundations of law. How might the climate crisis require fundamental transformations in the roles of local, Indigenous, national, inter, and transnational governance? Are law and democratic participation "sustainable?" This first part addresses both the normative foundations of international and domestic law and the institutions needed to undergird effective policy. The chapters in this part come from scholars located within very different legal approaches. From Indigenous legal traditions to law and philosophy to law and economics, each chapter approaches the question of governance through a unique theoretical lens, reflecting the polycentric challenges of and responses to climate change.

In the first chapter, Jutta Brunnée considers the role of international law. As she notes, our window for averting dangerous climate change is rapidly closing. In "International Climate Law in Precarious Times," she considers the potential role of international law in ensuring ambitious collective action in the context of a complex challenge like climate change. She argues that international law's most important role is to provide a normative framework with which national policy debates can engage. She suggests that, counter-intuitively, the non-binding nature of states' emission reduction commitments under the Paris Agreement should be seen as a strength rather than a weakness of the current UN climate regime. Bringing about deep emissions cuts is ultimately up to us; law's role is to help shape solutions, not impose collective action.

In his chapter, "Indigenous Law and Climate Change," John Borrows argues that Indigenous laws are an important source in thinking about and redressing climate change. Indigenous Peoples have experienced climate change through deep time, human time, colonial time, and in our lifetimes. Throughout these experiences, Indigenous Peoples have grappled with not only climate change but also handling its adverse effects. They have done this through Indigenous measures, standards, principles, criteria, precedent, tradition, signposts, benchmarks, tenets, procedures, and conventions and customs. Borrows argues that, as a result, Indigenous Peoples already *have* laws to address climate governance. Indigenous Peoples' laws, flowing from their experiences with climate change over time, must be part of the discussion on climate governance. These laws contain intellectual and cultural resources to help us make decisions, regulate our affairs, and resolve disputes related to climate justice in the present and future.

The role of the rule of law in responding to emergencies caused by civil unrest is extensively discussed. David Dyzenhaus has developed a theory of how such a response can occur productively through a coordination of legal institutions, which permits a "virtuous cycle of legality" to unfold. In such a cycle, institutions – the legislature, the judiciary, and the executive – learn, from past experience, how to achieve an appropriate balance between rights protection, furthering legislative objectives, and the need to defer to the expert judgment of officials in specialized agencies. In their chapter, "Legality's Place in a Changing World," David Dyzenhaus and Megan Pfiffer consider the applicability of the theory of legality to a very different kind of emergency situation – that created by climate change. With climate change, the emergency is ongoing and increasing in intensity, and the problem is often the state's inaction rather than action. Dyzenhaus and Pfiffer explore the problem of maintaining legality while addressing the climate emergency through a reading of the Supreme Court of Canada decision in *References re Greenhouse Gas Pollution Pricing Act*, particularly, in the dissents concerned with the delegation of discretionary authority.

While much scholarship has addressed the challenges of formulating and implementing effective climate change policy, Edward Iacobucci and Michael Trebilcock turn to a prior question that has received much less attention: how should we design institutions to address climate change? In their chapter, "Confronting the Institutional Challenges at the Heart of Climate Change Policy," Iacobucci and Trebilcock offer a law and economics perspective to the challenges of designing climate policymaking institutions. A host of challenges confront institutional design in this context, including scientific and technological uncertainty, cognitive biases, collective action and coordination problems, and polycentric goals. The chapter reviews these challenges, and their interaction, and considers practical responses in the context of Canadian institutional design. While no institution can possibly address all concerns simultaneously, Iacobucci and Trebilcock argue in favour of suggestions for a commission of inquiry that balances the competing considerations and that provides a public forum for a national debate on climate change policy.

Part 2 of this collection addresses questions of justice in times of climate change. Climate change is acting as an accelerant of inequality and injustice locally, nationally, and internationally. The concept of climate justice focuses on the disproportionate impact of climate change on low-income and racialized communities around the world, and seeks a more equitable distribution of the burdens of climate change and its mitigation. The drive to decarbonize raises questions of who bears the costs of transition and who is benefiting from it, including the call for efforts to promote a "just transition," within and among countries. Adaptation to climate change similarly gives rise to questions about who has to adapt, who will pay for the adaptation, who is included in our concerns about adaptation (both in terms of different people as well as other species and the natural environment), and how we should think about the health effects of climate change. The chapters in this part address questions of climate justice and injustice in three distinct legal areas.

In their chapter, "Reconciling the State's Obligation in Respect of the Climate and Housing Crises," Olivia O'Connor and Christopher Essert explore the conflicting pressures of climate and housing justice. The need to lower greenhouse gas emissions quickly and sharply is well known. But Canada also desperately needs more housing, both to alleviate homelessness and to make housing more affordable. Residential construction (or construction generally), however, is a major source of greenhouse gas emissions. It appears that addressing the housing crisis head-on will make the climate crisis worse; conversely, while ceasing all construction would make a major difference on the climate front, it would obviously do nothing to address the housing crisis, and likely would make that worse. In their chapter, O'Connor and Essert approach this apparent conflict by describing the two crises in terms of justice and public law rights against the state and discussing a model for reconciling competing rights of that form.

In their chapter, "Shifting Appetites: The Impact of Animal Agriculture on Climate Change and Plant-Based Diets as a Solution," Angela Fernandez and Krystal-Anne Roussel explore the role of animal agriculture as a contributor to climate change and argue for a transition to plant-based diets. They explore the challenges governments face in embracing diet as a strategy to mitigate climate change, but argue that changing public opinion, developments in science and technology, increasing concern with animal welfare, and political events may be creating the opportunity for change. Fernandez and Roussel suggest concrete measures that could be enacted, including amendments to the Environmental Farm Plan program, incorporating national principles for sustainable agriculture and shifting subsidies from animal products to plant-based ones. They advocate in favour of a "just transition" approach that takes into account the needs and interests of affected communities and workers.

The contribution by Gabrielle Peters and Trudo Lemmens addresses both the devastating impact of climate change on disabled people and the ways in which disability rights are being marginalized in climate change discussions. In their chapter, "Climate Change, Vulnerability Theory, and the BC Heat Dome: From Inclusion to Responsive Government," they address the need for greater inclusion of disabled people in developing climate change adaptation, mitigation, and emergency response planning. Current failures in policy reflect a lack of awareness and understanding around issues of disability among those involved in planning, and disabled people's knowledge and needs to be included moving forward. But Peters and Lemmens question whether "inclusion" alone will be sufficient to produce better policy outcomes. Through the lens of vulnerability theory and the case study of the 2021 heat dome in British Columbia, they argue that inclusion without more significant restructuring of the state's role will do little to mitigate climate injustice for disabled people.

Part 3 of this collection considers the challenges that climate change presents to institutions of governance. How might responding to climate change require a transformation in existing modes of governance? Within government, does climate change require a renegotiation of the balance of powers between the executive, legislative, and judicial branches? Between federal, provincial, and local governance? More broadly, might it require a recalibration of the relative roles of markets, private actors, governments, and transnational organizations? These issues speak both to our capacity to slow climate change and to how we might fairly adapt governance to transcend the current failures in policy, which reflect a lack of awareness and understanding among those involved in planning to its impacts.

Climate change has the potential to alter many landscapes – literally and metaphorically. These landscapes include the ground under the main institutions of government. In their chapter, "The Most Dangerous Branch?," Andrew Green and Albert Yoon examine the shifting role of supreme courts and the implications for climate policy. They focus on the dividing lines between the courts, the legislature, and the executive primarily through two recent cases: the US Supreme Court's decision in *West Virginia v EPA* and the Supreme Court of Canada's decision in *Reference re Greenhouse Gas Pollution Pricing Act*.[31] Green and Yoon examine how the balance between expertise, political accountability, and legality is being changed through doctrines around deference and the limits of judicial review. They argue for an approach that provides the executive with sufficient flexibility to act in the face of changing concerns and the existential threat of climate change, while tying it to the exercise of expertise and accountability for its decisions.

The issue of climate justice returns in a global context in Mariana Mota Prado and Patricia Galvão Ferreira's chapter, "Who Is Paying for the Costs of Climate Change? The Insuresilience Global Partnership as an Institutional Bypass." Developed countries historically have contributed the most to the genesis of the climate crisis but strongly resist the idea that they should have an obligation to compensate for climate-related loss and damage caused by extreme weather events in other countries. Climate insurance has been proposed as one alternative to compensation. Prado and Ferreira analyse how climate insurance has been treated inside the UN system through the Warsaw International Mechanism on Loss and Damages associated with Climate Change Impacts (WIM) and in an outside initiative the InsuResilience Global Partnership (IGP), arguing that the latter may be operating as an international institutional bypass of the former. IGP tries to overcome some of WIM's shortcomings and avoid the political stalemate that characterizes climate change politics regarding loss and damage in the UN. Yet, they warn that IGP could reduce incentives to strengthen either WIM or other new and potentially more promising multilateral solutions.

Eco-anxiety – the fear of environmental damage, climate change, and ecological disaster – has been recognized by The American Psychiatric

Association as a growing threat to mental health. Studies have shown that individuals are experiencing extreme or chronic anxiety because they feel unable to control environmental problems, particularly climate change. In "Climate Anxiety and Youth Activism," Brenda Cossman explores a different kind of regulation: self-governance. More specifically, the chapter considers the role of eco-anxiety in projects of self-governance produced in part by a pervasive sense of regulatory failure. Cossman has previously explored the role of anxiety in self-governance: the way that free-floating discourses of anxiety produce anxious subjects, who with the help of experts then undertake a range of self-governing projects to manage, mitigate, and reduce unpleasant emotions. In this chapter, she considers how climate anxiety is now animating the political and legal actions of youth activists. It may now be politicizing rather than depoliticizing.

Part 4 of the collection contains two reflections on lawyering in times of climate change. How does the here and now of climate change affect what we do as lawyers, judges, and legal educators? Does the existential threat human societies face require a reconsideration of legal ethics? What are the ethics of climate change lawyering? What is the relationship between lawyering and civil disobedience? How do we think about legal standing and who gets to be represented? What types of strategies are likely to be successful in raising concerns about climate change?

In "Vulnerable Litigants and Movement Lawyering in Climate Justice Litigation," Cheryl Milne considers the ethical and strategic issues raised by climate change litigation on behalf of children and youth. Many climate change advocacy groups representing children and youth have launched court challenges around the world, advancing arguments that risk little chance of success given the complexity of the cases and the innovative legal foundations for the claims. While one aim is to draw attention to the issue, are these cases ethically suspect? What are the ethical issues that lawyers need to consider when representing children who participate as test case litigants? While it might be argued that the climate crisis warrants radical tactics, this chapter explores the legal and ethical issues involved in movement lawyering for vulnerable litigants as a response to the existential crisis that is climate change.

Lawyers are deeply implicated in the climate crisis, yet the mechanisms we have for regulating lawyer behaviour – legal ethics regimes – are conspicuously absent from discussions about appropriate responses to global warming's existential threat. Against this backdrop, Abdi Aidid, in his chapter "Ethical Lawyering and Existential Threats," considers two questions. The first is whether legal ethics regimes can play a role in responding to the climate crisis. He argues that because of lawyers' involvement in everything from abetting corporate carbon emissions to pursuing climate justice to drafting legislation, legal-ethical rules are an underexplored lever for climate interventions. Second, he considers whether the *discipline* of legal ethics is capable of responding to challenges on the scale of the ongoing climate crisis. Aidid argues that challenges of an existential nature should motivate a reconsideration of some of legal ethics' more narrow and provincial frameworks, namely the centrality of the lawyer-client relationship and the constraint of jurisdiction.

The final part of this collection explores law, technology, and climate change. The chapters in this part consider law's role in promoting climate change innovation and encouraging adoption of new mitigation measures. Benjamin Alarie and Andrew Green, in their chapter "Markets, Mobilization, and Transformation: Approaches to Innovation in Addressing Climate Change," consider the relative roles of state- and market-oriented approaches to climate change innovation. They explore two main policy postures to address climate change: (1) an incremental and experimental approach, dominated by market forces and private-sector investment in innovative technologies; and (2) large-scale nation-state emergency mobilization, emphasizing government coordination and direction of investment in clean energy. Recognizing the merits and limitations of both strategies, they argue for a synthesized approach that leverages the strengths of each. They illustrate their claims with two examples. First, the *Inflation Reduction Act* offers an example of such a synthesis through its ambitious public commitments to support clean energy development through tax incentives and loan programs. Second, they analyse public and private fusion energy research efforts and emphasize the importance of innovation, cost-benefit analysis, and diverse mitigation strategies. Alarie and Green argue that policies that harness both incremental and nation-state mobilization approaches, such as public-private partnerships, can foster more effective and collaborative climate change mitigation strategies.

Anthony Niblett explores how governments can incentivize new technologies to either mitigate climate change (such as carbon sequestration) or develop efficient, clean alternatives to harmful activities. In his chapter, "A Cautiously Optimistic View of Innovation and Climate Change," Niblett argues that the markets will not solve the problem by themselves. Markets fail to incentivize investment in innovation because knowledge is a public good. But the archetypal legal solution – assigning property rights to innovations – also fails. Mitigating climate change, like knowledge, is a public good. The free rider problem is pervasive. Niblett explores alternatives, focusing on government "prizes." Should governments offer prizes for general innovation in climate change, or would it be optimal to offer prizes for solutions to specific problems such as carbon sequestration? Should prizes be offered for potential solutions (grants) or the realization of successful solutions? Perhaps most importantly, how do we ensure international cooperation between governments to mitigate the free rider effect across jurisdictions?

V. Climate Change, Law, and Relationships

The issues raised by climate change cut across areas of expertise, jurisdiction, levels of governance, and disciplines. Climate change is a complex, multifaceted problem that does not fit neatly into our existing legal categories. It challenges our familiar modes of thinking and approaches to problem solving. The intersecting and interacting problems that make up the climate crisis demand that we take up the challenge. Climate experts cannot remain in their silos, and those working in seemingly unrelated areas of expertise must explore the connections between their work and climate change. The climate crisis demands that we reach across categories and approaches, that we inject new ideas into long running debates, and that we ignite new debates.

This collection is the result of an effort to take these propositions seriously by asking colleagues, most of whom had not previously engaged with climate change, to do so in the context of their areas of expertise. The project is animated by the idea that we need to think about climate change at its most quotidian: its impact on the everyday world. As legal scholars, we need to interrogate our respective areas of law, from our many scholarly perspectives to understanding the profound transformations and considering how we might best respond and mitigate the most devastating effects. In this respect, this collection seeks to heed John Borrows' warnings of the danger of telling a single story,[32] offering instead many stories of potential sources of legal regulation.

The collection is by no means a comprehensive sweep of the issues raised by climate change, or even the areas of law and expertise it touches. Our goals are more modest: we hope to illustrate the importance of engaging beyond familiar terrain and to contribute to an increasingly urgent conversation about how climate change is affecting virtually everything we do. We hope that the contributions in this collection will engage an audience of academics and students, as well as the wider legal community and the public, to spark imagination on how to grapple with the all-encompassing impact of climate change on the world – in this case the legal world.

A strong undercurrent flows through much of the book – that the response of law and legal institutions both shapes and is a function of our relationships with each other. We are seemingly becoming more polarized politically all the time. Climate change policy is no exception. Yet, as Jutta Brunnee noted, law "must be grounded in a society's shared understandings."[33] Law and legal institutions are central to both creating and reflecting those shared understandings. It expresses our commitments to each other. In discussing the need for Canadian climate law to incorporate Indigenous perspectives, John Borrows pointed to one particular example from Anishinaabe teachings of the importance of understanding "how human beings can be more loving to one another and the earth."[34] It is in finding the proper relationship with and responsibilities for each other that the path forward lies.

NOTES

1 The term was initially coined in Garrett Hardin, "The Tragedy of the Commons" (1968) 162:3859 Science 1243, online: <https://doi.org/10.1126/science.162.3859.1243>, to describe degradation of all resources used in common by rational, utility-maximizing individuals rather than conserved for the benefit of all. The climate change crisis has often been described through the lens of the commons. See Jouni Paavola, "Climate Change: The Ultimate 'Tragedy of the Commons'?" in Daniel H. Cole & Elinor Ostrom, eds, *Property in Land and Other Resources* (Cambridge, MA: Lincoln Institute of Land Policy, 2011) 417; Maebh O'Gorman, "Global Warming: A Tragedy of the Commons" (2010) Osgoode Hall Law School Comparative Research in Law & Political Economy Series Research Paper No 32/2010.

2 See Edward Iacobucci & Michael Trebilcock, "Confronting the Institutional Challenges at the Heart of Climate Change Policy" in this volume discussing the nature of super-wicked problems and the obstacles presented by climate change.

3 Andrew Green & Albert Yoon, "The Most Dangerous Branch?" in this volume on the balance between expertise, legality, and political accountability.

4 In a fascinating presentation, Alan Brudner discussed how the US Supreme Court's decision in *West Virginia* striking down federal climate regulation implicates core questions of constitutional form.

5 Megan Pfiffer & David Dyzenhaus, "Legality's Place in a Changing World" in this volume.

6 Benjamin Alarie & Andrew Green, "Markets, Mobilization, and Transformation: Approaches to Innovation in Addressing Climate Change" in this volume; Anthony Niblett, "A Cautiously Optimistic View of Innovation and Climate Change" in this volume.
7 Olivia O'Connor & Christopher Esser, "Reconciling the State's Obligations in Respect of the Climate and Housing Crises" in this volume.
8 Mariana Mota Prado & Patricia Galvão Ferreira, "Who is Paying for the Costs of Climate Change? The InsuResilience Global Partnership as an Institutional Bypass" in this volume.
9 Green & Yoon, *supra* note 3.
10 Pfiffer & Dyzenhaus, *supra* note 5; Green & Yoon, *supra* note 3.
11 Pfiffer & Dyezenhaus, *supra* note 5.
12 Jutta Brunnée, "International Climate Law in Precarious Times" in this volume.
13 Green & Yoon, *supra* note 3.
14 Iacobucci & Trebilcock, *supra* note 2.
15 See Niblett, *supra* note 6 advocating for prizes to enhance incentives for innovative climate action.
16 See Prado & Ferreira, *supra* note 8.
17 John Borrows, "Indigenous Law and Climate Change" in this volume.
18 Gabrielle Peters & Trudo Lemmens, "Climate Change, Vulnerability Theory, and the BC Heat Dome: From Inclusion to Responsive Government" in this volume.
19 Prado & Ferreira, *supra* note 8; Brunnée, *supra* note 12.
20 Cheryl Milne, "Vulnerable Litigants and Movement Lawyering in Climate Justice Litigation" in this volume.
21 Brenda Cossman, "Climate Anxiety and Youth Activism" in this volume.
22 Angela Fernandez & Krystal-Anne Roussel, "Shifting Appetites: The Impact of Animal Agriculture on Climate Change and Plant-Based Diets as a Solution" in this volume.
23 O'Connor & Essert, *supra* note 7.
24 Abdi Aidid, "Ethical Lawyering and Existential Threats" in this volume.
25 Iacobucci & Trebilcock, *supra* note 2; Peters & Lemmens, *supra* note 18.
26 Brunnée, *supra* note 12.
27 Elinor Ostrom, *Governing the Commons: The Evolution of Institutions for Collective Action* (Cambridge: Cambridge University Press, 1990) at 14, online: <https://doi.org/10.1017/CBO9780511807763>; Daniel H. Cole, "Advantages of a Polycentric Approach to Climate Change Policy" (2015) 5 Nature Climate Change 114, online: <https://doi.org/10.1038/nclimate2490>. See also Elinor Ostrom, "Beyond Markets and States: Polycentric Governance of Complex Economic Systems" (2010) 100:3 Am Econ Rev 641, online: <https://doi.org/10.1257/aer.100.3.641>; Elinor

Ostrom, "A Polycentric Approach for Coping with Climate Change" (2009) World Bank Policy Research Series Working Paper No 5095, online: <https://doi.org/10.1596/1813-9450-5095>.

28 Elinor Ostrom, "A Multi-Scale Approach to Coping with Climate Change and Other Collective Action Problems" (2010) 1:2 Solutions 27.

29 Brunnée, *supra* note 12; Prado & Ferreira, *supra* note 8.

30 See e.g., Brunnée, *supra* note 12; Borrows, *supra* note 17; Aidid, *supra* note 24; Fernandez & Roussel, *supra* note 22.

31 *West Virginia v EPA*, 142 S. Ct. 2587 (2022); *Reference re Greenhouse Gas Pollution Pricing Reference*, 2021 SCC 11.

32 Borrows, *supra* note 17.

33 Brunnée, *supra* note 12.

34 Borrows, *supra* note 17.

PART ONE

Law in Times of (Climate) Change: Who Governs?

1 International Climate Law in Precarious Times

JUTTA BRUNNÉE

I. Introduction

Our time is marked by the convergence of numerous complex challenges: tense geopolitics and shifting international power dynamics, increasingly inward-looking domestic politics, the rise of autocratic tendencies in Western democracies, the global pandemic, the Russian invasion of Ukraine, global economic slowdown and inflation, the exponential development of artificial intelligence, accelerating climate change … and the list goes on.[1] What is the role of law in such precarious times? I consider this question with a focus on the role international law in the context of the climate crisis.

I begin by canvassing different perspectives on how international law should respond to the climate crisis. I suggest that, in the absence of strongly shared substantive values or goals, international law is most likely to furnish procedural frameworks that order interaction and decision-making, create space for dialogue and for work towards common ground and collective action. I then show that providing a stable yet adaptable international framework for encouraging domestic climate action is the main role international climate law plays today. The Paris Agreement,[2] which is now at the centre of the global climate regime, plays precisely that role. Perhaps counter-intuitively, the fact that states' emission reduction commitments are non-binding is a strength rather than a weakness of the agreement. Ultimately, whether we bring about the deep emission cuts and other transitions climate change demands, and what role law plays to these ends, is up to us – our societies, political actors, and individuals. At least for the time being, law's role is to help shape solutions. It can facilitate and coordinate, but cannot impose, collective action.

II. What Role *Should* International Climate Law Play, and Why Doesn't It?

Since the 1950s, when the world began to rebound from the Second World War, human impacts on the environment have expanded to such an extent that the socio-economic system and the biophysical earth system are now inextricably linked.[3] Through this "great acceleration," human activity has pushed Earth to a series of tipping points – thresholds beyond which significant and irreversible changes may occur. Humanity has become a "planetary-scale geologic force," such that the world is said to have entered a new geologic epoch – the "Anthropocene."[4] In a recent book, Oxford philosopher Toby Ord went so far as to suggest that we have arrived at a "precipice." For the first time in our history, he observes, humanity "is at high risk of destroying itself."[5] While "our choices can still make all the difference,"[6] it is imperative that we grapple with the existential risks we face.[7]

The climate crisis is emblematic of human development pushing against planetary boundaries and racing towards the "precipice."[8] The window for averting dangerous or even catastrophic climate change is rapidly closing. Climate change is driven by concentrations of carbon dioxide (CO_2) in the Earth's atmosphere. The "Keeling Curve" provides a sobering visual representation of the precipitous rise in CO_2 concentrations in the second half of the twentieth century.[9] Humanity's impact is even more starkly evident when one zooms out to see current atmospheric CO_2 concentrations in a longer-term context: the steep increase from the 1950s onward and the current concentrations are unprecedented – in over 800,000 years.[10]

In short, given its potential to disrupt natural, economic, and social systems on Earth, climate change represents a grave threat to humanity that demands a determined response at all levels. There is a range of perspectives on what international law's role should be in this response. One might be inclined to say, for example, that international law's priority task is to impose stringent obligations on states to rapidly reduce their greenhouse gas emissions and to provide for their enforcement.[11] Some have imagined an international organization taking charge, advocating for future generations and working with states to mitigate the effects of climate change.[12] Others have suggested that the Anthropocene demands much more radical change in international law. It must transcend its current moorings in state sovereignty and focus instead on the limits of what our planet can sustain.[13] Likewise, international law must overcome the enduring inequality that stems from the ravaging of nature during industrialization and colonialism, as well as its embrace of the growth-oriented logic of the international economic order.[14]

Each of these perspectives highlights important dimensions of the role that international law could, and eventually might, play in addressing climate change. But law does not operate in a vacuum. It must be grounded in a society's shared understandings.[15] Yet more dramatic calamities than the heatwaves, droughts, floods, or storms we are already experiencing may well ignite the emergence of new normative understandings and approaches.[16] For now, however, we remain mired in the complexities of climate change,[17] a "super-wicked" problem, as some have put it.[18]

As it stands, finding shared ground around ambitious climate action and what constitutes a "just transition" has proven difficult even at the domestic level – the protracted and polarized debates here in Canada underscore this point.[19] At the international level, on account of states' different histories, outlooks, and priorities, as well as starkly unequal capacities, contributions to the climate crisis and exposure to its harmful impacts, shared understandings are yet harder to come by. Moreover, the domestic and international challenges are intertwined. Domestic climate policy disagreements further complicate international lawmaking in a system that requires the agreement of sovereign states.

Indeed, state sovereignty remains the most widely shared and deeply entrenched understanding in international society. Such is the centrality of sovereignty in the international legal order that it has proven highly resistant to the development of norms that would constrain states or impose ambitious requirements on them. This dynamic has hampered the development of international environmental law. International environmental law grew out of and remains anchored in principles that define sovereign rights and duties.[20] Sovereignty's enduring sway is evident in the exceedingly slow and incremental evolution of rules that limit state freedom by imposing obligations to prevent environmental harm.[21] To be sure, environmental harm prevention obligations are now firmly established and applicable to all states as "general international law."[22] A recent uptick in initiatives to seek judicial opinions on the content of these harm prevention duties in relation to climate change suggests that they could play an important role in providing parameters for climate action.[23]

Various principles have emerged that aim to place additional limits on state sovereignty, or even to extend international law's normative purview beyond the inter-state paradigm, such as common concern for the global environment, precaution, sustainable development, or intergenerational equity. However, although these principles have exerted some influence on international discourse and policy choices,[24] they have not been established as binding constraints on state sovereignty. The same is true for the emergence of norms that would better address the fraught history of North–South relations and recalibrate states' responsibilities for global environmental protection in light of different contributions, impacts, and capacities.[25] Given industrialized and developing states' shared commitment to state sovereignty, the emergence of rules that prioritize earth systems and their boundaries, rather than international law's current territorial logic, seems even less likely at this stage.[26]

Instead of developing generally applicable rules, states have tended to tackle international environmental challenges through multilateral environmental agreements (MEAs). A treaty-based approach enables states to circumscribe the issues they agree to tackle. MEAs also reflect the insight that, in many situations, shared ground must be developed before law can take hold. At the outset, shared understandings are often procedural in nature, focused on providing stable, long-term settings for the exchange of views and the gradual development mutually agreed priorities and goals. Hence, the most common design for MEAs, the framework-protocol model, emphasizes procedures for engagement and the incremental development of commitments over time.[27]

The first step is a framework treaty that identifies the issue of concern and sets out an agreed objective, basic principles for and commitments to action, procedural obligations designed to promote information sharing and engagement, as well as rules and institutions for decision-making and subsequent treaty development. Supplementary treaties, often referred to as protocols, allow for a larger problem to be broken down into more manageable sub-issues, facilitating agreement on binding obligations. Early examples include regional agreements that tackle different aspects of marine environmental protection through individual protocols,[28] or long-range transboundary air pollution on a pollutant-by-pollutant basis.[29] The framework-protocol approach has also been deployed in the context of global problems. The 1985 Vienna Convention on the Depletion of the Ozone Layer was supplemented by the 1987 Montreal Protocol, which was then repeatedly amended and adjusted to regulate a growing range of ozone depleting substances and to speed up the elimination of these substances.[30] The ozone regime is often referred to as the most successful of all international environmental regimes,[31] and it has set the ozone layer on the path to full recovery.[32]

The UN climate regime initially emulated the approach of the ozone regime. The adoption of a UN Framework Convention on Climate

Change in 1992 (UNFCCC) was followed by the adoption of the Kyoto Protocol in 1997.[33]

The UNFCCC outlined the nature of the climate challenge in remarkably forthright fashion. The treaty's objective was the prevention of dangerous human interference with the climate system.[34] It declared climate change to be a "common concern of humankind" and acknowledged "that the global nature of climate change calls for the widest possible cooperation by all countries and their participation in an effective and appropriate international response."[35] Moreover, it specifically acknowledged that parties ought to cooperate "in accordance with their common but differentiated responsibilities and respective capabilities" and that developed country parties ought to "take the lead in combating climate change."[36] The convention also embraced precaution, intergenerational equity, and sustainable development as principles to guide parties' efforts.[37]

The relatively speedy development of the Kyoto Protocol was possible in part because new commitments for developing countries were specifically excluded from the negotiations,[38] thereby bracketing the charged questions of burden sharing between industrialized and developing countries.[39] The Kyoto Protocol reflected the convention's premise that developed countries should take the lead in climate action and the insistence of developing countries that their commitments ought to be differentiated from those of developed countries. Accordingly, it established binding emission reduction targets only for industrialized countries.[40] It was this very feature that ultimately prompted the United States of America to step away from the Kyoto Protocol.[41] The result was that some of the main emitters of greenhouse gases, major developing countries like China and India on the one hand and the world's leading industrialized country on the other were not bound by the Protocol. Although all protocol parties met their targets, the treaty ended up covering countries that accounted for a mere 24 per cent of global emissions.[42]

Furthermore, the Kyoto Protocol imposed emission reduction targets only for a five-year period, running from 2008 to 2012. In the negotiations for post-2012 emission reductions, the parties had to confront the difficult burden sharing issues head-on.[43] In view of the emissions trajectories of emerging economies like China and India,[44] industrialized countries insisted that any post-2012 regime had to include emissions targets for developing countries. In turn, developing countries insisted that the Kyoto Protocol, with binding emission reduction obligations for only industrialized countries, was the appropriate model and ought to be extended for an additional commitment period.[45]

Earlier I noted that state sovereignty has proven resistant to the development of international law that would limit sovereignty, let alone transcend, it. The centrality of state sovereignty also shapes, and constrains, treaty-based lawmaking processes. After all, states must consent to be bound by a treaty. In other words, states must agree to binding emission targets, and equally, they must agree to new or more ambitious targets under an existing treaty.[46] Moreover, a threshold number of states must agree to be bound before any treaty, or changes to it, can enter into force at all.[47] Given the entrenched disagreements between states, notably industrialized countries and countries in the Global South, the climate regime ended up being hamstrung by the need for state consent to new obligations. The 2015 Paris Agreement changed tack.[48]

III. What Role *Does* International Climate Law Play?

At the beginning of this chapter, I suggested that in the absence of strongly shared substantive values or goals, international law is most likely to provide procedural frameworks that order interaction and facilitate collective action. The Paris Agreement plays precisely this role.

Since its inception, the climate regime wrestled with the challenges of reconciling starkly different positions to enable more ambitious commitments in a consent-based system. Building on the framework-protocol model, the UNFCCC sought to forge common ground while the Kyoto Protocol introduced binding emission targets. However, because states must opt into obligations, it proved impossible to develop a long-term regime that would be binding on all major emitters. The Paris Agreement was designed to avoid this dilemma by introducing a new approach. It adopted what observers have described as a "bottom-up" approach,[49] relying on non-binding goals and principles to guide similarly non-binding national commitments to climate action. At first glance, this might seem like an improbable way out of the climate crisis. But the Paris Agreement's non-binding elements should not be equated with weakness.

The Paris Agreement calls upon states to strengthen the global response to climate change by mitigating emissions so as to hold global temperature increases "to well below 2° C above pre-industrial levels and pursuing efforts to limit the temperature increase to 1.5° C."[50] To this end, all states are to undertake progressively more ambitious efforts.[51] States' contributions to "the global response to climate change" are to be "nationally determined."[52] Parties are required to make such "nationally determined contributions" (NDCs),[53] but the specifics are up to each state.

While parties are free to determine the content of their NDCs, it is important to note that their freedom is not unfettered. The Paris Agreement constrains states in several ways. To begin with, individual parties are obligated not only to make nationally determined contributions to global climate action but also to "pursue domestic mitigation measures, with the aim of achieving the[ir] objectives."[54] Furthermore, in joining the Paris Agreement, states consent to maintaining consecutive NDCs,[55] such that they are committed to climate action over the long term.

Aside from these obligations, states' freedom to determine their contributions is constrained by a series of understandings and requirements. First, the Paris Agreement sets out a series of normative expectations, including that each successive NDC "will represent a progression beyond" the party's current NDC and will "reflect its highest possible ambition," as well as "its common but differentiated responsibilities and respective capabilities, in the light of different national circumstances."[56] The parties' NDCs are also to be pursued "with a view to achieving the purpose" of the Paris Agreement, notably the temperature goals it sets out to guide mitigation efforts.[57] Second, the parties are subject to a range of reporting and other procedural requirements, designed to ensure accountability for performance.[58] The Paris Agreement's transparency framework provides for a publicly accessible tracking of parties' progress in the achievement of their NDCs.[59] Third, while individual parties "may at any time adjust" their existing NDCs, the Paris Agreement specifies that an NDC may be adjusted "with a view to enhancing its level of ambition, in accordance with the guidance" adopted by the parties.[60] In other words, the Paris Agreement's direction of travel is towards greater ambition; back-sliding is not permitted.[61] Finally, every five years, parties are to "assess the collective progress towards achieving the purpose of this Agreement and its long-term goals."[62] The outcome of this "Global Stocktake," which was undertaken for the first time this year,[63] is intended to inform parties in updating and enhancing their NDCs, as well as in enhancing international cooperation.[64]

The approach of the Paris Agreement does not guarantee success, of course. One might be sceptical that non-binding commitments can in fact inspire countries to adopt costly policies and achieve deep cuts in greenhouse gas emissions.[65] A recent empirical study suggests there is some reason for optimism. It found support for the idea animating the Paris Agreement's design – that "by making pledges non-binding … national governments would be more flexible to reveal what they are willing and able to implement."[66] Indeed, the study suggests that "[n]on-binding commitments, with the right supporting institutions, can elicit greater adjustment by countries."[67]

For now, we can say that the Paris Agreement has garnered near-universal participation,[68] in large part by side-stepping the entrenched positions on differentiation, notably between the Global South and North.[69] Instead of trying to resolve a perhaps unresolvable debate, the agreement effectively provides for self-differentiation, bounded by its principles and procedures. Furthermore, in abandoning the quest for binding obligations, the Paris Agreement has liberated climate action from the shackles of formal international lawmaking.[70] By leaving states the freedom to make national policy choices and enabling adjustment without the delays and blockages inherent in the negotiation of binding requirements, the agreement promises more dynamic development of global climate action. Moreover, the Paris Agreement has a range of features designed to "ratchet up" states' ambition over time. Chief among these are its temperature goals, the expectation that NDCs become successively more ambitious, and a procedural framework that ties parties into continuous engagement with the internationally agreed goals and expectations. Transparency requirements expose all parties to public scrutiny, and the Global Stocktake will serve to shine the spotlight on shortfalls in collective action.

IV. Conclusion

Climate change is an urgent crisis. It is also a highly complex policy challenge. In this chapter, I have focused principally on the need to rapidly reduce the greenhouse gas emissions that drive global warming. However, I have also suggested that reducing emissions engages a host of other issues and considerations, which earned climate change the moniker of "super-wicked" problem.

International law could develop in a variety of ways to measure up to the climate crisis, ranging from imposing deep emission reduction obligations on states to much more fundamental changes in its normative fabric. The latter seem unlikely at this juncture, given both the lack of agreement on what ought to be done and state sovereignty's hold on international law's normative assumptions and consent-based lawmaking processes. It may seem unsatisfying to conclude that international law's role in dealing with perhaps the most profound crisis that humanity has faced is to provide a stable yet adaptable international framework for encouraging domestic climate action. Yet, such a flexible approach may be the only way to come to grips with the complexity of the climate crisis.

The UN climate regime was established in 1992 to prevent dangerous human interference with the climate system. Thirty years later, greenhouse gas emissions are still on the rise and climate change has entered the danger zone.[71] One's first inclination might be to say that international law has failed to avert the crisis. But international law as such is not the problem. *We* are.[72] International law's role is to help create the circumstances in which we can find our way out of this crisis of our making. Whereas the Kyoto Protocol turned out to be a dead end, the Paris Agreement has provided at least a pathway towards the urgently needed collective action. In the final analysis, then, the answer to the question about the role of international law in times of climate change is sobering: it is up to us.

Acknowledgments

I am grateful to my colleagues Benjamin Alarie and Andrew Green for their helpful comments on an earlier version of this chapter.

NOTES

1 See e.g., World Economic Forum, *The Global Risks Report 2023*, 18th ed (Geneva: World Economic Forum, 2023), online (pdf): <https://www3.weforum.org/docs/WEF_Global_Risks_Report_2023.pdf>.

2 *Paris Agreement to the United Nations Framework Convention on Climate Change*, 3156 UNTS (adopted 12 December 2015; entered into force 4 November 2016) [*Paris Agreement*].

3 Will Steffen et al, "The Trajectory of the Anthropocene: The Great Acceleration" (2015) 2:1 Anthropocene Rev 81 at 93, online: <https://doi.org/10.1177/2053019614564785>. See also Eva Lövbrand, Malin Mobjörk & Rickard Söder, "One Earth, Multiple Worlds: Securing Collective Survival on a Human-Dominated Planet" in Eva Lövbrand & Malin Mobjörk, eds, *Anthropocene (In)securities: Reflections on Collective Survival 50 Years After the Stockholm Conference* (Oxford: Oxford University Press, 2021) 1 at 3.

4 Steffen et al, *supra* note 3.

5 Toby Ord, *The Precipice: Existential Risk and the Future of Humanity* (New York: Hachette Books, 2020) at 31, 33.

6 *Ibid* at 9.

7 Note that Ord defines "existential risk" as "a risk that threatens the destruction of humanity's longterm potential," stressing that the concept applies "only to threats against the whole of humanity." See *ibid* at 37, 39.

8 *Ibid* at 103–13.

9 For the curve, see "The Keeling Curve" online: *Scripps Institution of Oceanography* <https://keelingcurve.ucsd.edu>. Charles Keeling initiated the measurement of atmospheric CO_2 concentrations. Measurements have been taken on Mauna Loa since 1958. See Rob Monroe, "The History of the Keeling Curve," *Scripps Institute of Oceanography* (3 April 2013), online: <https://keelingcurve.ucsd.edu/2013/04/03/the-history-of-the-keeling-curve/>.

10 See NASA, "The Relentless Rise of Carbon Dioxide" (29 August 2013, accessed 21 February 2023), online: <https://science.nasa.gov/resource/graphic-the-relentless-rise-of-carbon-dioxide/> (noting that historical measurements are based on ice-core data)

11 See generally Johan G. Lammers, "What Is Wrong with International Environmental Law?" in Cedric Ryngaert et al, eds, *What's Wrong with International Law: Liber Amicorum A.H.A. Soons* (Leiden: Brill, 2015) 214, online: <https://doi.org/10.1163/9789004294585_017>. From a political science perspective, see e.g., Scott Barrett, "Climate Treaties and the Imperative of Enforcement" (2008) 24:2 Oxford Rev Econ Policy 239, online: <https://doi.org/10.1093/oxrep/grn015> (proposing separate agreements on aspects of the problem, each with enforcement options).

12 See Kim Stanley Robinson, *The Ministry for the Future* (New York: Hachette Book Group, 2020).

13 See e.g., Louis J. Kotzé et al, "Earth System Law: Exploring New Frontiers in Legal Science" (2022) 11 Earth Syst Gov 1, online: <https://doi.org/10.1016/j.esg.2021.100126>.

14 See e.g., Louis J. Kotzé, Louise du Toit & Duncan French, "Friend or Foe? International Environmental Law and its structural complicity in the Anthropocene's climate injustices" (2021) 11:1 Oñati Socio-Leg Ser 180, online: <https://doi.org/10.35295/OSLS.IISL/0000-0000-0000-1140>; Sarah Riley Case & Julia Dehm, "Redressing Historical Responsibility for the Unjust Precarities of Climate Change in the Present" in Benoit Mayer & Alexander Zahar, eds, *Debating Climate Law* (Cambridge: Cambridge University Press, 2021) 170, online: <https://doi.org/10.1017/9781108879064.014>. Yet others suggest that change in international law must go beyond decolonization, bringing about a "radical break from the past in the spheres of production, spatial organization and law" and the emergence of a post-imperial and post-capitalist international law. See B.S. Chimni, "The Grotian Tradition, Grotian Moment, and Decolonization: A TWAIL Perspective" (2021) 42 Grotiana 252 at 266, 276, online: <https://doi.org/10.1163/18760759-42020001>. And see, in this volume, John Borrows, "Indigenous Law and Climate Change" (arguing that "to address climate change we should

recognize and revitalize Indigenous legal principles, processes, criteria, measures, indicia, benchmarks, precedents, and guides that are related to the earth, water, and air").

15 See Jutta Brunnée & Stephen J. Toope, "International Law and the Practice of Legality: Stability and Change" (2018) 49:4 VUWLR 429, online: <https://doi.org/10.26686/vuwlr.v49i4.5334>.

16 See Robinson, *supra* note 12 at 1–12 (depicting a heatwave that leaves 20 million people dead and prompts countries to ramp up efforts to grapple with climate change).

17 Climate change is not merely an "environmental" problem, but it has scientific, political, economic, social, security, as well as inter- and intra-generational equity dimensions, to name but a few.

18 See e.g., Richard Lazarus, "Super Wicked Problems and Climate Change: Restraining the Present to Liberate the Future" (2009) 94 Cornell LR 1153; Kelly Levin et al, "Overcoming the Tragedy of Super Wicked Problems: Constraining Our Future Selves to Ameliorate Global Climate Change" (2012) 45 Policy Sci 123 at 127–9, online: <https://doi.org/10.1007/s11077-012-9151-0> (identifying features that render complex problems "super wicked": time is running out; those seeking to end the problem are also causing it; no central authority; and policies discount the future irrationally). See also Edward Iacobucci & Michael Trebilcock, "Confronting the Institutional Challenges at the Heart of Climate Change Policy" in this volume.

19 See e.g., Andrew Green, *Picking Up the Slack: Law, Institutions and Canadian Climate Policy* (Toronto: University of Toronto Press, 2022), online: <https://doi.org/10.3138/9781487553319>.

20 For a detailed tracing, see Jutta Brunnée, "Procedure and Substance in International Environmental Law" (2020) 40 Rec des Cours 75 at 118–29, online: <https://doi.org/10.1163/9789004444386>.

21 See Jutta Brunnée, "International Environmental Law: Of Sovereignty, Complexity, and Grotian Moments" (2022) 43 Grotiana 3 at 8–12, online: <https://doi.org/10.1163/18760759-43010002>.

22 See *Legality of the Threat or Use of Nuclear Weapons*, Advisory Opinion, [1996] ICJ Rep 226 at 242; *Gabčíkovo-Nagymaros Project (Hungary v. Slovakia)* [1997] ICJ Rep 7 at 1; *Pulp Mills on the River Uruguay (Argentina v Uruguay)* [2010] ICJ Rep 14 at 55–6, 78; *Certain Activities Carried out by Nicaragua in the Border Area (Costa Rica v Nicaragua) and Construction of a Road in Costa Rica along the San Juan River (Nicaragua v Costa Rica)* [2015] ICJ Rep 665 at 705–7. See also *Responsibilities and Obligations of States Sponsoring Persons and Entities with Respect to Activities in the Area*, Advisory Opinion, ITLOS Rep 10 [2011] at 43, 46–7, online: <https://www.itlos.org/en/main/cases/list-of-cases/case-no-17/>.

23 See International Tribunal for the Law of the Sea, *Request for an Advisory Opinion Submitted by the Commission of Small Island States on Climate Change and International Law*, 21 May 2024, no 31, online: <https://www.itlos.org/fileadmin/itlos/documents/cases/31/Advisory_Opinion/C31_Adv_Op_21.05.2024_orig.pdf>. See also UNGA, *Request for an Advisory Opinion of the International Court of Justice on the Obligations of States in Respect of Climate Change*, 29 March 2023, Resolution 77/276, online: <https://www.icj-cij.org/sites/default/files/case-related/187/187-20230412-app-01-00-en.pdf>.

24 See Daniel Bodansky Jutta Brunnée & Lavanya Rajamani, *International Climate Change Law* (Oxford: Oxford University Press, 2017), online: <https://doi.org/10.1093/law/9780199664290.001.0001>, for an example.

25 Brunnée, *supra* note 21 at 12–17.

26 See also Giovanna M. Frisso & Elizabeth A. Kirk, "Changing Role of Law-Making in Responding to Planetary Boundaries" in Duncan French & Louis J. Kotzé, eds, *Research Handbook on Law, Governance and Planetary Boundaries* (Cheltenham, UK: Edward Elgar, 2021) 147, online: <https://doi.org/10.4337/9781789902747.00016> (for a broad exploration of the challenges of developing law that would reflect interconnected Earth systems processes).

27 For an overview see Jutta Brunnée & Christopher Campbell-Duruflé, "Environment, Multilateral Agreements" in Rüdiger Wolfrum, ed, *Max Planck Encyclopedia of Public International Law* (Oxford: Oxford University Press, November 2022), online: <https://doi.org/10.1093/law:epil/9780199231690/e1760>.

28 See e.g., *Convention for or the Protection of the Marine Environment and the Coastal Region of the Mediterranean*, 1102 UNTS 27 (adopted 16 February 1976; entered into force 15 April 1988; amended 10 June 1995). On the related protocols, see United Nations Environment Programme (UNEP), "Barcelona Convention and Protocols" (accessed 24 February 2023), online: <https://www.unep.org/unepmap/who-we-are/barcelona-convention-and-protocols>.

29 See *Convention on Long-Range Transboundary Air Pollution*, 1302 UNTS 217 (adopted 13 November 1979; entered into force 16 March 1983) [*LRTAP*]. For the related protocols, see UN Economic Commission for Europe (UNECE), "Protocols" (accessed 23 February 2023), online: <https://unece.org/protocols>.

30 See *Vienna Convention for the Protection of the Ozone Layer*, 1513 UNTS 293 (adopted 22 March 1985; entered into force 22 September 1988); *Montreal Protocol on Substances that Deplete the Ozone Layer*, 1522 UNTS 3 (adopted 16 September 1987; entered into force 1 January 1989).

31 See e.g., Frederike Albrecht & Charles F. Parker, "Healing the Ozone Layer: The Montreal Protocol and the Lessons and Limits of a Global Governance Success Story" in Paul t'Hart & Mallory Compton, eds, *Great Policy Successes* (Oxford: Oxford University Press, 2019), 304 at 304, online: <https://doi.org/10.1093/oso/9780198843719.003.0016>.

32 See UNEP, "Ozone Layer Recovery Is on Track, Helping Avoid Global Warming by 0.5°C" (9 January 2023), online: <https://www.unep.org/news-and-stories/press-release/ozone-layer-recovery-track-helping-avoid-global-warming-05degc>.

33 *United Nations Framework Convention on Climate Change*, 1771 UNTS 107 (adopted 9 May 1992; entered into force 21 March 1994) [*UNFCCC*]; *Kyoto Protocol to the United Nations Framework Convention on Climate Change*, 2303 UNTS 162 (adopted 10 December 1997; entered into force 16 February 2005) [*Kyoto Protocol*].

34 *UNFCCC*, *supra* note 33, art 2.

35 *Ibid*, preamble.

36 *Ibid*, preamble, art 3.1.

37 *Ibid*, preamble, art 3.

38 UNFCCC, "The Berlin Mandate: Review of the Adequacy of Article 4, Paragraph 2(a) and (b), of the Convention, Including Proposals Related to a Protocol and Decisions on Follow-up," FCCC/CP/1995/7/Add. 1, 4 (6 June 1995).

39 See Bodansky, Brunnée & Rajamani, *supra* note 24 at 105–9.

40 See *Kyoto Protocol*, *supra* note 33, art 3.1. Each party's target was set out in an Annex B to the protocol.

41 See Bodansky, Brunnée & Rajamani, *supra* note 24 at 107.

42 *Ibid* at 108, 173.

43 See *ibid* at 109.

44 For example, by 2005, China had overtaken the United States as the single largest national emitter of greenhouse gases. See *ibid* at 8, 354.

45 See *ibid* at 108.

46 For a detailed exploration, see Jutta Brunnée, "State Consent in the Evolving Climate Regime: Individual and Collective Aspects" in Samantha Besson, ed, *Consenting to International Law* (Cambridge: Cambridge University Press, 2023) 215, online: <https://doi.org/10.1017/9781009406444.012>.

47 See e.g., *Kyoto Protocol*, *supra* note 33, arts 20, 21, and 25.

48 *Paris Agreement*, *supra* note 2.

49 See e.g., Jessica F. Green, Thomas Sterner & Gernot Wagner, "A Balance of Bottom-up and Top-down in Linking Climate Policies" (2014) 4 Nat Clim Chang 1064, online: <https://doi.org/10.1038/nclimate2429>.

50 *Paris Agreement*, *supra* note 2, art 2.1(a).

51 *Ibid*, art 4.3.
52 *Ibid*, art 3.
53 *Ibid*, art 4.2.
54 *Ibid*.
55 *Ibid*.
56 *Ibid*, art 4.3.
57 *Ibid*, arts 2, 3, 4.1.
58 *Ibid*, arts 13–15.
59 See UNFCCC, "Introduction to Transparency" (accessed 26 February 2023), online: <https://unfccc.int/Transparency>
60 See *Paris Agreement*, *supra* note 2, art 4.11.
61 For a detailed assessment, see Lavanya Rajamani & Jutta Brunnée, "The Legality of Downgrading Nationally Determined Contributions under the Paris Agreement: Lessons from the US Disengagement" (2017) 29: J Envtl L 537, online: <https://doi.org/10.1093/jel/eqx024>.
62 *Paris Agreement*, *supra* note 2, art 14.1.
63 See UNFCCC, *Outcome of the First Global Stocktake*, UN Doc FCCC/PA/CMA/2023/L.17 (13 December 2023), online: <https://unfccc.int/sites/default/files/resource/cma2023_L17_adv.pdf>.
64 *Ibid*, arts 14.2 and 14.3 (the "global stocktake").
65 For a sceptical view, see Cary Coglianese, "Pledging, Populism, and the Paris Agreement: The Paradox of a Management-Based Approach to Global Governance" (2019) 34 Md J Intl L 139.
66 See David G. Victor, Marcel Lumkowsky & Astrid Dannenberg, "Determining the Credibility of Commitments in International Climate Policy" (2022) Nat Clim Chang at 1, online: <https://doi.org/10.1038/s41558-022-01454-x>; the study draws on the insights of over 800 diplomatic and scientific experts with decades of climate policy experience (at 6).
67 *Ibid*.
68 The Paris Agreement has 195 parties. See United Nations Treaty Collection, "Paris Agreement" (accessed 26 February 2023), online: <https://treaties.un.org/Pages/ViewDetails.aspx?src=TREATY&mtdsg_no=XXVII-7-d&chapter=27&clang=_en>.The United States, as the leading developed country emitter, has a complicated history with the Paris Agreement. It had joined the agreement under the Obama Administration, withdrew from it during the Trump Administration, and rejoined under the Biden Administration. See Anthony J. Blinken, "The United States Officially Rejoins the Paris Agreement" (21 February 2021), online: *US Department of State* <https://www.state.gov/the-united-states-officially-rejoins-the-paris-agreement/>.

69 In some respects, the Paris Agreement might be akin to an "institutional bypass" along the lines explored in the development literature. See Mariana Mota Prada & Michael Trebilcock, *Institutional Bypasses: A Strategy to Promote Reforms for Development* (Cambridge: Cambridge University Press, 2018). See also Mariana Mota Prado & Patricia Galvão Ferreira, "Who is Paying for the Costs of Climate Change? The InsuResilience Global Partnership as an Institutional Bypass" in this volume.

70 See generally Joost Pauwelyn, Ramses A. Wessel & Jan Wouters, "When Structures Become Shackles: Stagnation and Dynamics in International Lawmaking" (2014) 25:3 Eur J Intl L 733, online: <https://doi.org/10.1093/ejil/chu051>.

71 See UNEP, *Emissions Gap Report 2022* (17 October 2022), online: <https://www.unep.org/resources/emissions-gap-report-2022>; Intergovernmental Panel on Climate Change, Press Release, 2021/17/PR, "Climate Change Widespread, Rapid, and Intensifying," (9 August 2021), online (pdf): <https://www.ipcc.ch/site/assets/uploads/2021/08/IPCC_WGI-AR6-Press-Release_en.pdf>.

72 I am reminded of Karin Mickelson invoking Murray Bookchin's description of an exhibit on environmental issues at the New York Museum of Natural History. She notes: "The very last item was a huge mirror with a sign over it that read 'The Most Dangerous Animal on Earth'." See Karin Mickelson, "South, North, International Environmental Law, and International Environmental Lawyers" (2000) 11 YB Intl Env L 52 at 77, online: <https://doi.org/10.1093/yiel/11.1.52> (citing to Murray Bookchin, *Remaking Society: Pathways to a Green Future* [Boston: South End Press, 1990] at 23).

2 Indigenous Law and Climate Change

JOHN BORROWS

I. Introduction

We need all the help we can get in addressing climate change. We need wisdom from multiple angles and many sources.[1] Indigenous knowledge is one of those sources.[2] Like all other humans, Indigenous Peoples are affected by climate change, and they have experiences that can help us appreciate the nature of the problem and its solutions. For example, historic and contemporary encounters with environmental collapse and upheaval have generated insight for the Indigenous Peoples. Even though the causes of climate change were different in the past, we should not ignore how they responded to these earlier events. Moreover, Indigenous Peoples' present experiences with rising waters, degraded landscapes, and fouled air reveals the nature and scope of climate change. Indigenous Peoples' knowledge, laws, and traditions inherently contain the reasons for taking our present crisis seriously, and their perspectives also contain resources to help us reverse its progression and effects.[3]

While this chapter highlights the need to draw on Indigenous Peoples' experiences and laws in dealing with climate change (understanding that some climatic change is part of the earth's natural cycles), it is also clear that the current climatic changes we are experiencing are not natural; they are the result of human action (and inaction).[4] Earth-wide climate change due to human causes is unprecedented. Despite the truth and devastating impacts of human-caused climate change, some claim that we should accept it, or perhaps even embrace it, because climate change is older than human life. This is not a wise approach; accepting or embracing climate change caused by human forces would minimize responsibility for those who could do something about it. Failing to address climate change will also cause tremendous suffering for those least able to bear its burdens. Finally, failing to address climate change would also mean failing to respect and activate Indigenous Peoples' law and experience related to such change.

This is my thesis: Indigenous Peoples' observations about the past, and their laws relative to the present, are pertinent to changing our relationship with climate change. This approach can enhance Indigenous law's role in understanding how we deal with ever-present changes around us. This chapter examines Anishinaabe perspectives and laws relative to climate change and provides a few other, select examples from Indigenous Peoples using their law to address environmental restoration, which is necessary for reversing climate change.

II. Anishinaabe Perspectives on Climate Change: Deep Time, Human Time, Colonial Time, Elder Time

Anishinaabe Peoples live around the North American Great Lakes, woodlands, and prairies.[5] I am an Anishinaabe citizen of the Chippewa of the Nawash First Nation on the Saugeen Peninsula, in what is now Ontario, Canada. Our home is called Neyaashiinigmiing, or portage point, and it lies between Lake Huron and Georgian Bay. Our perspectives related to climate change might be considered in four layers: deep time, human time, colonial time, and within our Elders' lifetimes.[6] We are constantly reminded of the earth's dynamism and dramatic movement through epochs of time in our territories.[7]

Deep Time: In my traditional territory, the Niagara Escarpment, which runs through our reserve, reminds us of a time when our part of the earth was flooded.[8] The Escarpment was formed over 440 million years ago when, what we now call Ontario, was at the equator. At that time, the area was a shallow, warm sea teeming with aquatic life.[9] When life perished, these creatures' spent bodies were layered on the ocean floor. Through vast ages, they travelled on tectonic plates until they reached their current latitude, which is where we now have our reserve. Today, throughout our territory, you find evidence of this earlier time. Fossils are buried in the rocks and are piled loosely at your feet as you walk along the shore. The geological evidence embedded in the escarpments on our reserve, and the stories Anishinaabe tell about these rocks, demonstrates the earth's climatic volatility through deep time.

Human Time: We also see evidence of the earth's dynamism within a human time scale.[10] About 12,000 years ago, the lands where we currently live were covered with ice shields several kilometres high. The earth's surface moved under their weight in world-altering ways. When the glaciers retreated, the ground rebounded. Melting waters quickly flooded each hollow forming the Great Lakes as we know them. Our creation stories flow from the challenges experienced during this time, as the climate radically changed. Skywoman and Nanaboozhoo (a trickster), formed a council with the beaver, loon, otter, and others to determine how to survive the flood.[11] Eventually, a small muskrat pulled soil from under the deep water, which was deposited on a turtle's back to form terrestrial life. Evidence of climate change is woven through our constitutional stories and clearly written on the earth that surrounds us. Anishinaabe governance, laws, and ethics would not exist without these formative experiences.

Colonial Time: Anishinaabe and other Indigenous Peoples of the Great Lakes have also had to grapple with human-caused regional climate change over the past 400 years.[12] Our territories have been paved over and planted with cities like Toronto, Chicago, Milwaukee, Duluth, Ottawa, Detroit, Buffalo, Ottawa, and Montreal, as well as places in between. Urban heat sinks change the weather in these cities, in unusual and sometimes life-threatening ways. Indigenous lifeways have also been pushed aside and replaced with political, social, and economic systems that marginalize environmental care. Indigenous Peoples are prevented from re-establishing our governance, law, and ethics as guiding forces in these spaces. Furthermore, our fields, forests, and lakes have been transformed through agriculture, mining, forestry, recreation, and factories, along with the infrastructure designed to facilitate these activities. Irreversible loss and widespread death have followed for many species of plants, insects, birds, animals, and (Indigenous) humans. Pesticides, tailing ponds, garbage dumps, erosion, and invasive species have contributed to air, water, and noise pollution to contaminate the primary sources of life in our territories. All of this is to say that Indigenous Peoples have lived with human-caused climate change for the past 400 years, and we have been devastated.

Elder time: Significant change has also happened within recent human memory. I know family stories from great-great-great, great-great, and first great-grandparents chronicling the losses we sustain as air, water, and land have been changed by human activity. Within the lives of my own immediate ancestors, scientists in Ontario have chronicled the extirpation of the passenger pigeon, greater prairie chicken, least shrew, eastern elk, blue walleye, gravel chub, shortnose cisco, black cisco, paddlefish, eastern tiger salamander, spring salamander, Blanchard's cricket frog, frosted elfin, Karner blue, Persius duskywing, timber rattlesnake, russet-tipped clubtail, incurved grizzled moss, Macoun's shining moss, dwarf umbrella-sedge, yellow-fringed orchid, Commons's panic grass, wild-rye, and black oat-grass.[13] Moreover, many other species are now extinct in local regions, and the list of endangered species grows each year. According to our Elders, these changes are accelerating in their intensity.[14] In most ways, we are still living in a colonial time that disrupts and sometimes destroys relationships with our territories. Environmental changes were wrought by vast numbers of people that relate differently to our lands. Their activities have changed the air, water, and earth's temperature, which influences the reactions of plants, insects, fish, birds, and animals to these shifting conditions. This has made some of the effects of climate change visible within our short lifetimes. Anishinaabe Elders say that fish run at unusual times, the sap flows from the trees in unpredictable ways, and the strawberry, blueberry, and wild rice harvest does not follow cycles from merely 40 or 50 years ago. For many Anishinaabe Elders and knowledge keepers, climate change is a very personal experience.[15]

III. Anishinaabe Law and Climate Change

In considering perspectives related to these different eras, Anishinaabe Peoples have made observations about how to deal with climate change and how to challenge its adverse effects. They do so through measures, standards, principles, criteria, precedent, tradition, signposts, benchmarks, tenets, procedures, conventions, and customs. In other words, Anishinaabe Peoples, along with other Indigenous Peoples, have laws to address climate governance. Law does not just flow from parliaments or legislators, or get interpreted by courts with the assistance of lawyers, or get enforced by police. Law can also be approached from a functional perspective by considering its operative role and social effect on a society. From this perspective, Indigenous Peoples' law, flowing from their experiences with climate change, holds important lessons for climate governance.

For example, when considering deep time, Anishinaabe law teaches that humans are late arrivals and that life can develop and go on without us. Thus, we must be careful not to put humans at the centre of our decisions. Lessons from the time of human arrival in the Great Lakes are about legal process and principles, as the muskrat and turtle story demonstrates. This story contains standards such as, *inter alia*, the necessity of counselling together, including different perspectives in decision-making (including the smallest beings), and finding solutions in the elements at hand. Anishinaabe law through colonial time teaches that violating treaties destroys environments, devastates animals, destabilizes Indigenous populations, and degrades the land, water, and air. Finally, Anishinaabe law as practiced in our Elders' recent lifetimes (which seeks environmental restoration) demonstrates how burning fossil fuels, cutting down forests, and the factory farming of livestock devastates life's sustainability.

To address climate change, we should take lessons from these experiences. We should recognize and revitalize Indigenous legal principles, processes, criteria, measures, indicia, benchmarks, precedents, and guides that are related to the earth, water, and air. Indigenous law contains intellectual and cultural resources to help us make decisions, regulate our affairs, and resolve disputes in the present day. As we extend this recognition, we must also acknowledge that, while Indigenous law can be environmentally sound, Indigenous Peoples can also act in ways that destroy life's very possibilities. Like all humans, appetites can be insatiable and Indigenous Peoples can act in gluttonous, voracious, and immoderate ways.[16] Many of our trickster and wiindigok stories chronicle such misuses and show what happens when we forget that the environment is not limitless[17] These stories also contain lessons for climate governance. Indigenous Peoples can act contrary to their norms, ethics, and values, and our laws contain powerful cautions and restraints against such behaviour. Therefore, we need to apply Indigenous laws that respect and connect to Indigenous environmental kinship norms, as opposed to rules that would facilitate water, land, and air use without reference to sustainability.

Indigenous law is the product of complex forces.[18] It develops in both moments of harmony and rupture. Law does not merely arise from agreement; it is also forged in moments of conflict. Indigenous Peoples grapple with both agreement and disagreement, in both historic and contemporary settings. It should go without saying that Indigenous Peoples do not all see the world in the same way. We strive for the freedom to be different from other Canadians. We also work to advance the freedom to be different from one another too. Indigenous law exists to help us act with a degree of cohesion in the face of internal difference. It should also function as a check on our own worst excesses. In addition, it should also restrain broader Canadian laws to ensure that constitutional balances contain and constrain ecological overreach. The application of Indigenous Peoples' environmental laws, ethics, and perspectives is an important tool for helping us deal with profound climate change questions.

As Indigenous Peoples' laws are extended, we must recognize that they come from many sources.[19] Some are rooted in stories about deep time, human time, colonial time, and Elder time, as I have discussed earlier. Some Indigenous laws are considered to be sacred and living (aadizoonakag), while others are more routine (dibaajimowinan) yet significant for the principles and processes they contain. Most of our laws are formed through deliberation and operate through discussion, negotiation, persuasion, and debate. Human interpretation is the proximate cause of their application. Other laws are positivistic or declaratory and can be found in legislation, resolutions, codes, and chronicles. In these declarative forms, they often contain "do's and don'ts" and might involve fines, restrictions, incentives, and other consequential factors related to their being upheld or broken. Some Indigenous laws come from customary ways of interacting with one another, which incentivizes behaviour that is productive, such as having good relationships, and disincentivizes conduct that damages our relationships with one another.[20] The distinctions between the different sources of law outlined earlier should not be approached too formalistically. Moreover, they are not exhaustive. The practice of Indigenous law usually involves the interaction of many sources, including laws rooted in other legal systems. We should always acknowledge that Indigenous Peoples have choices when they formulate law. Further, we must always recognize that Indigenous Peoples hold many different views about law's character and practice, within and across categories, which facilitates and frustrates participation, freedom, agency, and choice.

IV. Learning Law from the Earth: Akinomaagewin

There is another source of Anishinaabe law that requires further elaboration in dealing with climate change. This source flows from reasoning through analogy by looking to the earth (i.e., the biosphere) and how it functions in its interactions between plants, animals, fish, insects, water, air, and humans.

This process of reasoning by looking to the earth for analogies and criteria to guide our relationships is called akinomaagewin.[21] Aki is the first syllable, which means earth in Anishinaabe. Nomaage, in the middle of the word, means "to point towards and take direction from." I learned this word and practice from an Elder from my reserve, Basil Johnston. Akinomaagewin is the word for the process that analogizes or distinguishes human obligation and opportunity by reference to the natural world. In this way, the earth and its constituents can be regarded as a legal archive. Reading this law requires a literacy that would allow us to read the earth through language, experience, stories, deliberation, customs, song, dance, discussion, and observation through long periods of time. It can also be called an environmentally derived law. This kind of law looks to the natural world as the precondition for the subsequent work and life that humans enjoy. It posits that we cannot be reconciled with one another unless we are also reconciled with the earth.[22] It understands that law must respect planetary boundaries. This has significant implications for addressing climate change.

One way we reference akinomaagewin is through our seven ancestral teachings. I discuss this process through my book, *Law's Indigenous Ethics*, published with the University of Toronto Press in 2019.[23] I discussed Anishinaabe legal ethics as constitutional obligations, and these grandmother and grandfather teachings are identified as Zaagi'idwin (love), Debwewin (truth), Nibwaakaawin (wisdom), Manaaji'idiwin (respect), Zoongide'ewin (courage), Gwayakwaadiziwin (honesty), and Dabaadendiziwin (humility). I will briefly focus on one of these words to illustrate my point by taking guidance and our laws from the earth.

Zaagi'idwin is our word for love.[24] Elder Basil Johnston taught and wrote that love is related to the Anishinaabe word for river mouth, Zaagiing. The Zaagiing River flows through Grey and Bruce counties and eventually empties into Lake Huron. As the river flows, it captures energy from the land through the various tributaries and delivers that microbial life and nutrients through this channel at the mouth of the Zaagiing. About 300 years ago, it was the richest site throughout our territory. As river mouths convey such high nutrient content, we would have witnessed an exceptionally significant diversity of life. For example, as a result of the microbial life, there would be many insects living in relationship with this diversity. Then, as a result of those insects' presence, many fish would surge in and out of the river, feasting on those insects. With a variety of insects and fish, birds would gather in profusion to feast on the fish and insects. All this activity produces death and decay, which feeds the riverbanks and bottoms, thereby producing excellent conditions for a rich mixture of plant life. As a result of the abundance of fish, insects, plants, and birds, animals gather at river mouths in significant numbers. With all this activity, it should come as no surprise that human communities treat river mouths as a desirable place to live.

You might wonder how the ecology of a river mouth relates to law. In describing Zaagiing, I have given you an example of love. Love involves gathering beneficial energy and delivering this through defined channels to others, including the more-than-human world. This energy generates the abundance and diversity necessary for the very conditions of life. If you want to practice Anishinaabe law, as I learned it from Basil Johnston, then you should immerse yourself in the river's lessons to understand how human beings can be more loving to one another and to the earth. The idea is to do what the river does but within a human form.

Anishinaabe law can have many sources and objectives because it is ultimately the product of human deliberation. However, if we follow our strands of law, which reason in relation to rivers and other more-than-human forces, they can nurture the conditions for healthier climates, including the air we breathe. This approach to constitutionalism is, fortunately, taking hold as Anishinaabe Peoples translate their laws into written form. The natural world and the seven ancestral teachings are prominent in these developments. For example, the preamble to the Anishinabek Nations ChiNaaknigewin Constitution references law's Indigenous ethics in the following manner.

> Ngo Dwe Waangizid Anishinaabe. Debenjiged gii'saan anishinaaben akiing giibi dgwon gaadeni mnidoo waadiziwin. Shkode, nibi, aki, noodin, giibi dgosdoonan wii naagdowendmang maanpii shkagmigaang. Debenjiged gii miinaan gechtwaa wendaagog Anishinaaben waa naagdoonjin ninda niizhwaaswi kino maadwinan. Zaagidwin, Debwewin, Mnaadendmowin, Nbwaakaawin, Dbaadendiziwin, Gwekwaadziwin miinwa Aakedhewin. Debenjiged kiimiingona dedbinwe wi naagdowendiwin. Ka mnaadendanaa gaabi zhiwebag miinwaa nango megwaa ezhwebag, miinwa geyaabi waa ni zhiwebag.[25]

Through these commitments, the Anishinaabe peoples highlight the seven ancestral laws, and they are putting them into written form. In English, the Constitution reads:

> One Anishinaabe family. Creator placed the Anishinaabe on the earth along with the gift of spirituality. Here on Mother Earth, there were gifts given to the Anishinaabe to look after fire, water, earth, and wind. The Creator also gave the Anishinaabe seven sacred gifts to guide them. They are: Love, Truth, Respect, Wisdom, Humility, Honesty, and Bravery. The Creator gave us sovereignty to govern ourselves. We respect and honour the past, present, and future.[26]

The climate is very prominently included as a part of this type of constitutionalism.

It should be acknowledged that the Anishinabek Nation's constitution sets high goals. You might wonder how ideas like love, truth, humility, wisdom, honesty, courage, or respect could be constitutional standards. They may appear to be too vague, too ambiguous, and too broad to do the work of law.[27] However, the Canadian constitution also contains ambiguity and has lofty goals. In Canada's *Constitution Act 1867*, we read about the desire for Peace, Order, and Good

Government.[28] In Canada's *Constitution Act 1982*, the Charter purports to "guarantee" the rights and freedoms set out in it, such as life, liberty, security, and equality.[29] In considering Canada's broad constitutional objectives, we recognize these are broad aspirations too. Nevertheless, clans, kin, citizens, legislatures, and courts give meaning to these laws in the stories we tell ourselves. They come to life as we interpret these words through innumerable cases as people try to hold our governments to account on those principles. Anishinaabe Peoples, in some of their legal activities such as constitutional drafting, are merely trying to achieve the same goal. They reinforce their underlying commitments to and with the natural world.

I hope you can see the climate governance implications in this strand of Anishinaabe law, which attempts to operationalize love in specific contexts. If love was understood as flowing from and to the earth, our sacred, customary, deliberative, and declarative laws would reflect these principles. Practising law by nesting ourselves within the more-than-human world and promulgating interdependence is one way to strengthen our relationships with our rivers, plants, insects, birds, fish, animals, humans, and other beings. Anishinaabemowin functions through animacy and sees the earth as living, as a relative with whom you can communicate.[30] Anishinaabe Peoples do not hear audible words emanating from the earth, but they have resources to deliberate about what various components of the earth require by listening to its changes and the interactions of its different features. Language has been developed to facilitate these relationships.[31] Anishaabemowin's nouns are not gendered by male and female, as you might find in French, for example. They are gendered by animacy and inanimacy. Some of the nouns that are animate in the Anishinaabe language would be surprising to English speakers. Anishinaabe teachings, combined with observation, to which is added language, help people to see the earth as a dynamic living entity that can teach us about its governance. It is also the case that our world is very verb-oriented. Verbs are action-oriented. About 70 per cent of Anishinaabe words are verbs. Thus, when you speak Anishaabemowin, you are heavily involved in conjugation rather than categorization. There are many words for law itself, and they are all verbs. They indicate what people do and participate in. If we thought of law itself as a verb, something we all do, something we all participate in, something we can all conjugate, then perhaps we would see an opportunity to enhance its participatory elements. The practice of law in relationship to the climate places a premium on governing ourselves in relationship with other life forms.

V. Anishinaabe and Indigenous Treaties and the More-than-Human World

Anishinaabe Elder Basil Johnston taught me that the first treaties the Anishinaabe Peoples had were with the natural world, including the plants, animals, rocks, rivers, fish, deer, moose, caribou, and others more than human beings.[32] Mutual obligations exist that all have a place and territory where all can sustain themselves. Earth's climate flows from the waters, rocks, plants, animal, human, and other life. It would be wrong to see climate governance as being limited to monitoring and adjusting air quality. We will not have a healthier climate without healthy grasslands, trees, animals, birds, and other living beings. To enhance our climate, we need to make and respect treaties with the natural world.

For example, Indigenous Peoples on the western prairies and eastern slope of the Rocky Mountains have entered into treaties with bison, often known as the buffalo.[33] Article 1 of the *Buffalo Treaty* expresses a commitment to a direct relationship with these beings:

> Recognizing BUFFALO as a practitioner of conservation, WE, collectively, agree to: perpetuate conservation by respecting the interrelationship between us and 'all our relations' including animals, plants, and Mother Earth; to perpetuate and continue our spiritual ceremonies, sacred societies, sacred languages, and sacred bundles to perpetuate and practice as a means to embody the thoughts and beliefs of ecological balance.

Indigenous communities in Canada and the United States have become party to this treaty. They have legally pledged to work to see the buffalo run again from Yellowstone to the Yukon, "as a wild free-ranging animal and as an important part of the ecological system; to provide a safe space and environment across our historic homelands, on both sides of the United States and the Canadian border, so together WE can have our brother, the BUFFALO, lead us in nurturing our land, plants and other animals to once again realize THE BUFFALO WAYS for our future generations."[34] The treaty can be read online. You can attend ceremonies related to its promulgation. You can hear the songs attached to it and you can participate in its pipe ceremonies. Buffalo have now been put into the back country of Banff National Park as a result of this treaty, with the hope that there can be a reinvigoration of this landscape.[35]

Another example of the holistic possibilities of Indigenous climate governance comes from the Skeetchestn and Tk'emlups Peoples in British Columbia's interior, who used their own laws to decide whether to allow a gold mine to proceed in their territory.[36] They gathered in clans, with families across different bands, with Elders, and youth family Councils. They took account of the water, the fisheries, the fauna, the flora, the sky world, water world, and health, in their own legal terms. They practiced what Caroline Hilton calls Indigenomics.[37] In so doing, they concluded not to pursue a mining project. In other cases, they did allow other development to occur in their territory. Throughout the country, you can find examples of environmental assessments that are either being run by Indigenous Peoples or required by them when the Crown consults with them about development.

These examples show how Indigenous Peoples are searching for places where their laws can be revitalized.[38]

VI. Canada's Indigenous Treaty Traditions and Climate Change

The attempt to follow laws related to the natural world, which respects both specific ecological niches and broader planetary boundaries, is good for climate governance. When laws grow from broader ecologic relationships there is a greater incentive to be mindful of life's sources. Of course, mindfulness is not sufficient to create mutual obligations between the human and the more-than-human world. Laws must be strengthened through pledges that hold consequences for nations who are non-compliant, particularly important when creating co-governance regimes between peoples with different world views. Indigenous Peoples have attempted to do so through treaties. Anishinaabe and many Indigenous Peoples entered into treaties with the Crown in our early years to try and create a multi-juridical legal engagement. In 1764, for example, Indigenous Peoples and the Crown pledged to link arms together and to support one another.[39] The wampum belts woven to record these agreements signal the importance of rooting relationships between nations in the earth. Other belts contain environmental images, such as rivers, lands, plants, and animals.

In 1701, another important treaty memorialized terms that ended a 50-year war between the Haudenosaunee and Anishinaabe.[40] This treaty is represented by a purple circle in the middle of a white belt, and on the middle of the purple circle is a rectangle. This "Dish with One Spoon" treaty places the parties in a shared relationship with the living earth, which teaches and nourishes them. White beads mark the dominant theme of the agreement, which means peace. There are seven rows of white beads sewn into these hides, which can represent the seven ancestral teachings, but also the seven directions of east, south, west, north, up, down, and centre. The belt could be interpreted as incorporating the entire environment in engaging the parties, while taking care to ensure that the treaty is not interpreted as opening the land to all nations beyond the Haudenosaunee and Anishinaabe.[41] In the middle of the belt, as mentioned, is a purple object that represents a bowl, or a dish, which means the earth is a common bowl, and we all eat out of the same dish. The small white rectangular object on the middle of the purple bowl (in the middle of the belt) reminds the parties that when they eat out of the earth's bowl, they must bring a spoon, rather than a knife or fork, which means that we must create peaceful conditions.

Though limited to particular parties, the concept underlying this treaty has significant implications for climate governance. We all eat out of one bowl – the biosphere. In sustaining our climate, we must find pathways of peace that include love, humility, respect, and honesty to ensure that we are not threatening one another or our relations.

My own great-great grandfather entered into a treaty dealing with land in Ontario.[42] Our traditional territory is bounded by what is now Goderich on the east coast of Lake Huron, to Arthur in the middle of the province, to Collingwood on the shores of Georgian Bay. When our ancestors made treaties, they put their clan markers on treaty documents to share our land with people coming from other parts of the world. In marking participation as otters, bears, pike, eagles, and other ancestral relatives, we were inviting people from other parts of the world to live in accordance with the Anishinaabe law.[43] We wanted to teach our laws to the settlers, so they would see the rivers as places of love, so they would see the fish and animals as our teachers and our kin. As we entered into treaties with one another, we extended a governance pattern that could protect the environment and thus pass along our experiences regarding the land, water, and airs dynamic climate.

VII. Indigenous Law, Legal Education, and Climate Change

Law schools must do more to teach how Indigenous law holds implications for climate action. These initiatives are slowly developing.[44] The University of Victoria Law School teaches Indigenous law alongside common law (JID/JD), through comparison and contrast. Professors teach in the classroom and on the land throughout this degree, frequently emphasizing Indigenous Peoples' relationship to their environments and the changing climate.[45] I have often taught these issues to first-year law students in my trans-systemic Anishinaabe/onstitutional law class. My colleagues have followed similar patterns, teaching Cree/criminal law, Gitksan/property law, Tsilhqot'in/contract law,

Hul'q'umi'num'/tort law, etc. I have also taught Anishinaabe law on reserves in Ontario to students at Western, Windsor, Osgoode Hall, and McGill Law School.[46] The environment and climate change is also an important aspect of this work.[47] My colleagues have also been involved in these land-based courses, including Professors Valarie Waboose, Jeff Hewitt, Heidi Stark, Kekek Stark, Hannah Askew, and Lindsay Borrows. Indigenous Elders, knowledge keepers, leaders, and community members have joined us in these land-based experiences.

I have also taught Anishinaabe law courses in the city of Toronto at the University of Toronto law school. One of these classes was a land-based course, taught outdoors, and it was listed in the catalogue with the following description: "Anishinaabe laws are a proud of part of Toronto's natural landscape, and the class will facilitate student understanding of Anishinaabe law by teaching and learning about how law is reflected in natural features within the city. Reference to the sources of law is a vital resource for regulating behaviour and resolving disputes. Students will hear and work with sources of Anishinaabe law found in traditional stories, the environment, treaties, declarations, customs, etc." During this class, we discussed Anishinaabe deep time, human time, colonial time, and Elder time in various places around the university. We did this through visits to the site of an ancient stream buried under what is now called Philosophers' Walk, at the heart of the University of Toronto campus.[48] We spoke about the river as a gathering site for Anishinaabe and other Indigenous Peoples. Its degradation, like many urban watercourses, holds implications for climate change mitigation and adaptation.[49] In this context, the students talked about our relationship to water throughout the region and beyond. Along the way, I taught law by discussing Anishinaabe kinship principles and processes related to the cedar and maple trees, and with the plants that were waiting for new life in an Indigenous garden outside of the Hart House Student Centre.[50] We subsequently visited the anthropology building and viewed the material evidence of the Haudenosaunee and the Anishinaabe's relationship with the natural world, which drew our attention back to Indigenous climate governance.[51] Afterwards, we visited the Royal Ontario Museum and further discussed this issue with reference to historic clothing, transportation, household implements, and ceremonial items, and the changes in these technologies throughout the years.[52] During this course, we also visited Massey College's Gi-Chi-Twaa Gimaa Nini Mississauga Anishinaabek AName Amik (The King's Anishinaabek Sacred Place), or Chapel Royal, which is a Chapel of the Queen in the middle of the city, dedicated to reconciliation between the Crown and Indigenous Peoples.[53] A few of our wampum belts are housed there, and we discussed the laws we advanced to address the more-than-human world as Indigenous Peoples and Europeans encountered one another. This course was partially designed to help the students understand that one does not require pristine spaces to understand the connection between climate governance and Indigenous law. This information is available in urban spaces, and my goal was to help students to see these connections more clearly.

Furthermore, at the law schools of the University of Victoria, University of British Columbia, and Queen's University, there are upper-year courses in Indigenous Peoples and Environmental Governance, which devote growing attention to climate change issues.[54] The professors from the respective schools are Cree (Darcy Lindberg), W̱SÁNEĆ (Robert Clifford), and Anishinaabe (Lindsay Borrows). These courses focus on the interaction between Indigenous laws' revitalization and the climate crisis, with the goal of addressing climate crisis mitigation in intertwined and mutually reflective ways.[55] These courses build upon and generate student projects, faculty scholarship, and community-based service by focusing on Indigenous law and its potential to address climate change in varied and innovative ways.[56] While these efforts are nascent, as Indigenous law has only been taught in law schools for a very short period, they nevertheless show the potential for Indigenous perspectives related to climate governance to continue to grow throughout the land.

VIII. Conclusion

Indigenous Peoples across the land have extensive experience and laws to respond to climate change. These laws need to be broadcast, extended, and developed on their own terms to strengthen our relationships with the earth, waters, and skies. Further, Canadian law must incorporate Indigenous and common law perspectives.[57] Indigenous perspectives and laws on climate governance are necessary for implementing constitutional rights involving their Aboriginal Peoples. This area of law has been described as a bridge between legal cultures.[58] The Supreme Court has held that the purpose of constitutional Aboriginal and treaty rights is reconciliation.[59] This includes Indigenous Peoples' relationships to the more-than-human world, reinforcing the point that reconciliation with one another is premised on reconciliation with the earth. In this regard, Indigenous law's implications for climate governance are an important part of our future dealings with this issue.

Acknowledgments

I thank Fenner Stewart for initially prompting this piece, which in a varied form appears as "Indigenous Law and Canadian Climate Governance" in Fenner Stewart & Janis Sarra, eds., *Reflections on Connecting Canada's Climate Policy Network* (Canada Climate Law Initiative: Vancouver, 2023). Thanks also go to Dean Jutta Brunnée for her invitation to further develop this work and for her helpful editorial suggestions.

NOTES

1 There are also resources in many traditions and disciplines for addressing climate change. For a discussion of how religious approaches discuss this issue see Katherine Hayhoe, *Saving Us: A Climate Scientist's Case for Hope and Healing in a Divided World* (New York: Simon & Schuster, 2021). For a discussion on how culture influences views about climate change, see Giuseppe Feola, Hilary Geoghegan & Alex Arnall, eds, *Climate and Culture: Multidisciplinary Perspectives on a Warming World* (Cambridge: Cambridge University Press, 2019), online: <https://doi.org/10.1017/9781108505284>. For a discussion of how behavioural economics addresses climate change, see Cass R. Sunstein et al, "How People Update Beliefs about Climate Change: Good News and Bad News" (2017) 102 Cornell L Rev 1431, online: <https://doi.org/10.31228/osf.io/qn5wp>; George Marshall, *Don't Even Think about It: Why Our Brains Are Wired to Ignore Climate Change* (New York: Bloomsbury, 2014). To illustrate the role of poetry and prose in addressing climate change, see Ayana Johnson & Katharine Wilkinson, *All We Can Save: Truth, Courage, and Solutions for the Climate Crisis* (New York: One World, Random House, 2020); Kim Stanley Robinson, *The Ministry for the Future* (New York: Orbit Books, 2020).

2 Julie Koppel Maldonado, Benedict Colombi & Rajul Pandya, eds, *Climate Change and Indigenous Peoples in the United States: Impacts, Experiences and Actions* (New York: Springer, 2014), online: <https://doi.org/10.1007/978-3-319-05266-3>; Douglas Nakashima, Igor Krupnik & Jennifer Rubis, eds, *Indigenous Knowledge for Climate Change Assessment and Adaptation* (Cambridge: Cambridge University Press, 2018), online: <https://doi.org/10.1017/9781316481066>; Randall Abate & Elizabeth Ann Kronk, eds, *Climate Change and Indigenous Peoples: The Search for Legal Remedies* (Cheltanham: Edward Elgar, 2013), online: <https://doi.org/10.4337/9781781001806>.

3 Álvaro Fernández-Llamazares et al, "'Scientists' Warning to Humanity on Threats to Indigenous and Local Knowledge Systems" (2021) 41:2 J Ethnobiol 144, online: <https://doi.org/10.2993/0278-0771-41.2.144>.

4 IPCC, *The Ocean and Cryosphere in a Changing Climate: A Special Report of the Intergovernmental Panel on Climate Change* (Cambridge: Cambridge University Press, 2022) at 45, online: <https://doi.org/10.1017/9781009157964>: "Evidence and understanding of the human causes of climate warming, and of associated ocean and cryosphere changes, has increased over the past 30 years of IPCC assessments (very high confidence). Human activities are estimated to have caused approximately 1.0°C of global warming above pre-industrial levels (SR15). Areas of concern in earlier IPCC reports, such as the expected acceleration of sea level rise, are now observed (high confidence). Evidence for expected slow-down of AMOC [Atlantic Meridional Overturning Circulation] is emerging in sustained observations and from long-term palaeoclimate reconstructions (medium confidence), and may be related with anthropogenic forcing according to model simulations, although this remains to be properly attributed. Significant sea level rise contributions from Antarctic ice sheet mass loss (very high confidence), which earlier reports did not expect to manifest this century, are already being observed."

5 Anishinaabe Peoples are the fourth largest Indigenous Nation in North America, after the Navajo, Cherokee, and Lakota Nations. They live within the Great Lakes watershed, surrounding, in large part, Lakes Superior, Huron, and Michigan and occupying the farmlands and woodlands north of Lake Ontario and Lake Erie. They also have reservations in the forests and prairies of Manitoba, northern Minnesota, and North Dakota; see Helen Hornbeck Tanner, *Atlas of Great Lakes Indian History* (Norman, OK: University of Oklahoma Press, 1982) at 58–9.

6 Anishinaabe professors Melissa Nelson and Kyle Whyte remind us that Indigenous Peoples have experienced climate change through these different periods. See Melissa Nelson, "The Hydromythology of the Anishinaabeg: Will Mishipizhu Survive Climate Change or Is He Creating It?" in Jill Doerfler, Niigaanwewidam James Sinclair & Heidi Kiiwetinepinesiik Stark eds, *Centering Anishinaabeg Studies: Understanding the World through Stories* (Lansing: Michigan State University Press, 2013) 213; Kyle Whyte, "Indigenous Science (Fiction) for the Anthropocene: Ancestral Dystopias and Fantasies of Climate Change Crises (2018) 1 Environ Plan E: Nat Space 224, online: <https://doi.org/10.1177/2514848618777621>. Professor Whyte also highlights how Indigenous Peoples experience climate change through spiraling time, which considers the duration, span, and movement of relationships within the natural and human world.

7 Kyle Whyte also writes of kinship time, as follows: "Kinship time, as opposed to linear time, reveals how today's climate change risks are already

caused by peoples' not taking responsibility for one another's safety, well-being, and self-determination. Any solutions to climate change will be enacted within a state of affairs that's already rife with irresponsibility. Kinship, as an ethic of shared responsibility, focuses attention on how responsible relationships must first be established or restored for it to be possible to have renewable energy projects that respect Indigenous safety, well-being, and self-determination." See Kyle Whyte, "Time as Kinship" in Jeffrey Jerome Cohen & Stephanie Foote, eds, *The Cambridge Companion to Environmental Humanities* (Cambridge: Cambridge University Press, 2021) at 39–40, online: <https://doi.org/10.1017/9781009039369.005>.

8 The Bruce-Grey Geology Committee, *Geology and Landforms of Grey & Bruce Counties* (Owen Sound: Field Naturalists and Stan Brown Printers, 2014) at 17.

9 During this period, often called Silurian Period, the climate was generally warm and stable, in contrast to the glaciers of the late Ordovician and the extreme heat of the Devonian, see Adam D. Sproson, "Pacing of the Latest Ordovician and Silurian Carbon Cycle by a ~4.5 Myr Orbital Cycle," (2020) 540 Palaeogeogr Palaeoclimatol Palaeoecol.

10 Ron Morton & Carl Gawboy, *Talking Rocks: Geology and 10,000 Years of Native American Tradition in the Lake Superior Region* (Minneapolis: University of Minnesota Press, 2003); M. Calner, "Silurian Global Events – At the Tipping Point of Climate Change" in Ashraf M.T. Elewa, ed, *Mass Extinction* (Berlin: Springer, 2008).

11 See Nicolas Perrot, "Memoir on the Manners, Customs, and Religion of the Savages of North America" in Emma Helen Blair, ed, *The Indian Tribes of the Upper Mississippi Valley and Region of the Great Lakes* vol 1 (Cleveland: Arthur H. Clark, 1911) at 37:

"After the creation of the earth, all the other animals withdrew into the places which each kind found most suitable for obtaining therein their pasture or their prey. When the first ones died, the Great Hare caused the birth of men from their corpses, as also from those of the fishes which were found along the shores of the rivers which he had formed in creating the land. Accordingly, some of [them] derive their origins from a bear, others from a moose, and others similarly from various kinds of animals.... You will hear them say that their villages each bear the name of the animal which has given its people their being – as that of the crane, or the bear, or of other animals."

12 John Riley, *The Once and Future Great Lakes Country: An Ecological History* (Montreal: McGill-Queen's Press, 2014); Dan Egan, *The Death and Life of the Great Lakes* (New York: W.W. Norton, 2017), online: <https://doi.org/10.1515/9780773589810>.

13 For further information see *Species at Risk Ontario List*, O Reg 230/08 c. 6; to see pictures of these species consult "Species at Risk in Ontario,"

Government of Ontario (accessed 3 October 2024), online: <https://www.ontario.ca/page/species-risk-ontario>; "Nature Rarities of Southwestern Ontario," *Carolinian Canadian* (accessed 3 October 2024), online: <https://caroliniancanada.ca/sar/nature-rarities>.

14 A.K. Menzies et al, ""I See My Culture Starting to Disappear": Anishinaabe Perspectives on the Socioecological Impacts of Climate Change and Future Research Needs" (2022) 7 FACETS 509, online: <https://doi.org/10.1139/facets-2021-0066>.

15 See Robin Clark et al, "Gathering Giizhik in a Changing Landscape" (2022) 27:4 Ecol Soc at 29, online: <https://doi.org/10.5751/ES-13605-270429>.

16 Calvin Martin, *Keepers of the Game: Indian-animal Relationships and the Fur Trade* (Los Angeles: University of Los Angeles Press, 1982).

17 Robin Wall Kimmerer, "Windigo", in Simmons Buntin, Elizabeth Dodd & Derek Sheffield, eds, *Dear America: Letters of Hope, Habitat, Defiance, and Democracy* (San Antonio, Texas: Trinity University Press, 2020); Robin Wall Kimmerer, *Braiding Sweetgrass* (Minneapolis: Milkweed, 2013) at 374–9.

18 See, generally, John Borrows, *Canada's Indigenous Constitution* (Toronto: University of Toronto Press, 2010).

19 *Ibid.*

20 *Ibid.*

21 John Borrows, "Earth-Bound: Indigenous Resurgence and Environmental Reconciliation" in Michael Asch, John Borrows & Jim Tully, eds, *Resurgence and Reconciliation* (Toronto: University of Toronto Press, 2018) 49, online: <https://doi.org/10.3138/9781487519926-004>.

22 "Reconciliation between Aboriginal and non-Aboriginal Canadians, from an Aboriginal perspective, also requires reconciliation with the natural world. If human beings resolve problems between themselves but continue to destroy the natural world, then reconciliation remains incomplete. This is a perspective that we as Commissioners have repeatedly heard: that reconciliation will never occur unless we are also reconciled with the earth. Mi'kmaq and other Indigenous laws stress that humans must journey through life in conversation and negotiation with all creation." The Truth and Reconciliation Commission of Canada, *Honouring the Truth, Reconciling for the Future, Summary of the Final Report of Truth and Reconciliation Commission of Canada* (Ottawa: TRC Commission, 2015) at 18.

23 John Borrows, *Law's Indigenous Ethics* (Toronto: University of Toronto Press, 2019), online: <https://doi.org/10.3138/9781487531140>.

24 This thought is developed in more detail, see Borrows, *supra* note 21.

25 Anishinaabe-Chi-Naaknigewin, online (pdf): <https://www.anishinabek.ca/wp-content/uploads/2016/05/Anishinaabe-Chi-Naaknigewin-modified.pdf>.

26 *Ibid.*

27 This point is developed more in Borrows, see *supra* note 23.
28 *Constitution Act, 1867 (UK)*, 30 & 31 Vict, c 3.
29 *Canadian Charter of Rights and Freedoms*, Part I of the *Constitution Act, 1982*, being Schedule B to the *Canada Act 1982* (UK), 1982, c 11, s 91(24).
30 Basil Johnston, *Honour Mother Earth: Mino-audiaduah Mizzu-Kummik-Quae* (Cape Croker: Kegedonce Press, 2003); Robin Wall Kimmerer, "Learning the Grammar of Animacy (2017) 28:2 Anthropol Conscious 128, online: <https://doi.org/10.1111/anoc.12081>.
31 See, generally, Great Lakes Fish and Wildlife Commission, *Dibaajimowinaan: Anishinaabe Stories of Culture and Respect* (Odahana, WI: Great Lakes Indian Fish and Wildlife Commission, 2013); Wendy Makoons Geniusz, *Our Knowledge Is Not Primitive: Decolonizing Botanical Anishinaabe Teachings* (Syracuse: Syracuse University Press, 2009), online: <https://doi.org/10.1353/book.109810>.
32 John Borrows, *Recovering Canada: The Resurgence of Indigenous Law* (Toronto: University of Toronto Press, 2002), as discussed in chapters 1 and 2. Heidi Kiiwetinepinesiik Stark, "Marked by Fire: Anishinaabe Articulations of Nationhood in Treaty Making with the United States and Canada" (2012) 36:2 Am Indian Q 119, online: <https://doi.org/10.5250/amerindiquar.36.2.0119>.
33 The Buffalo: A Treaty of Cooperation, Renewal and Restoration, online: <https://www.buffalotreaty.com/treaty>.
34 *Ibid.*
35 Helen Pike, "Banff Bison Herd Should Remain on the Landscape, Parks Canada Says in Draft Pilot Report," *CBC News* (10 November 2022), online: <https://www.cbc.ca/news/canada/calgary/bison-herd-banff-photos-parks-canada-stewards-1.6646728>.
36 Stk'emlúpsemc te Secwepemc Nation (SSN), *Honouring the Vision of Our Ancestors*, online (pdf): <https://stkemlups.ca/wp-content/uploads/2013/11/SSN_4Pager-v13-12.02-WEB.pdf>. Illustration drawn from Carol Anne Hilton, *Indigenomics: Taking a Seat at the Economic Table* (Gabriola Island Publishers, British Columbia: New Society Publishers, 2021).
37 Illustration drawn from Hilton, *supra* note 36.
38 For example, potlatch system built on feasts that place reciprocity at their centre are growing on the west coast. They speak to the environment, including the sky world, in strong ways. People dance their laws. Masks, totem poles, button blankets, and other physical representations of the natural world show their relationships with the fish, killer whales, cedar, and other more than human beings. Laws are pursued in feast halls, which embody the broader climate, as people make decisions about harvesting, land use, water allocation, and many other issues related to the changing world that surrounds them.

39 For further discussion of this treaty see Alan Corbiere, *Anishinaabe Treaty-Making in the 18th- and 19th-Century Northern Great Lakes: From Shared Meanings to Epistemological Chasms* (PhD Dissertation, York University, September 2017), online (pdf): <https://core.ac.uk/download/pdf/322837923.pdf>; Amelia Healey, "Treaty of Niagara," *Great Lakes Research Alliance* (18 February 2022), online: <https://grasac.artsci.utoronto.ca/?p=1636>; John Borrows, "Constitutional Law From a First Nation Perspective: Self-Government and the Royal Proclamation" (1994) 28 UBC L Rev 1; Nathan Tidridge, *The Queen at the Council Fire: The Treaty of Niagara, Reconciliation, and the Dignified Crown in Canada* (Toronto: Dundurn, 2015).

40 See Victor Lytwyn, "A Dish with One Spoon: The Shared Hunting Grounds Agreement in the Great Lakes and St. Lawrence Valley Region," in David Pentland, ed, *Papers of the Twenty-Eighth Algonquian Conference* (Winnipeg: University of Manitoba Press, 1997) 210.

41 Dean Jacobs & Victor Lytwyn, "Naagan ge bezhig emkwaan: A Dish with One Spoon Reconsidered" (2020) 112 Ont Hist 191, online: <https://doi.org/10.7202/1072237ar>.

42 This history is described in John Borrows, "A Genealogy of Law: Inherent Sovereignty and First Nations Self-Government" (1992) 30 Osgoode Hall LJ 291, online: <https://doi.org/10.60082/2817-5069.1724>.

43 *Chippewas of Saugeen First Nation v. Town of South Bruce Peninsula et al.*, 2023 ONSC 2056 (CanLII) at paras 71–75, 96. For parallel arguments see *Restoule v. Canada (Attorney General)*, 2018 ONSC 7701 at paras 412–23. For a general discussion of Anishinaabe perspectives related to treaty formation see Heidi Stark, "Respect, Responsibility, and Renewal: The Foundations of Anishinaabe Treaty Making with the United States and Canada" (2010) 34 Am Indian Cult Res J 145, online: <https://doi.org/10.17953/aicr.34.2.j0414503108l8771>.

44 See e.g., John Borrows, "Making Meaning: Indigenous Legal Education and Student Action" (2022) 67:4 McGill LJ 493, online: <https://doi.org/10.7202/1098594ar>.

45 Sara Ramshaw, "Against Exclusion: Teaching Transsystemically, Learning in Community" (2019) 30 Law Crit 131, online: <https://doi.org/10.1007/s10978-019-09245-8>.

46 For brief descriptions of these courses, see Meena Sundararaj, "A Student Writes: Indigenous Law in Context at Neyaashiinigmiing Cape Croker Reserve," *University of Toronto Faculty of Law* (13 October 2017), online: <https://www.law.utoronto.ca/news/student-writes-indigenous-law-in-context-neyaashiinigmiing-cape-croker-reserve>; Serena Dykstra Zachary Donofrio Jasleen Johal, "Anishinaabe Law Camp," *Obiter* (29 September, 2014), online: <https://obiter-dicta.ca/2014/09/29/anishinaabe-law-camp/>;

"Anishinaabe Law Class: Law as a Human Experience," *McGill Focus Law/Droit* (1 November 2017), online: <https://focuslaw.mcgill.ca/anishinaabe-law/>; Michael Coyle, "Anishinaabe Law Camp," *Michael Coyle* (28 March 2017), online: <https://michaelcoyle.com/anishinaabe-law-camp/>; Valarie Waboose & Gemma Smyth, "Reflections on the Anishinabe Law Camp (Bkejwanong Territory)," *Reconciliation Syllabus* (25 October 2016), online: <https://reconciliationsyllabus.wordpress.com/2016/10/25/reflections-on-the-anishinabe-law-camp-bkejwanong-territory/>; David P. Ball, "He Spent His Life Immersed in Indigenous Law. Now He's Helping Canada's Next Generation of Lawyers Change its Course," *Toronto Star* (15 November 2018), online: <https://www.thestar.com/vancouver/2018/11/15/he-spent-his-life-immersed-in-indigenous-law-now-hes-helping-canadas-next-generation-of-lawyers-change-its-course.html>.

47 See John Borrows, "Learning from the Land: Indigenous Law and Outdoors Legal Education" 33 Windsor YB Access Just 1.

48 For further discussion of this site see John Borrows, *Recovering Canada: The Resurgence of Indigenous Law* (Toronto: University of Toronto Press, 2002) at ix-xii, 159–62.

49 Karl Wantzen et al, "Back to the Surface – Daylighting Urban Streams in a Global North–South Comparison (2022) 10 Front Ecol Evol 1, online: <https://doi.org/10.3389/fevo.2022.838794>. More research is needed to understand the connections between climate change and urban ecosystems; see Rebecca L. Hale et al, "Effects of Climate on the Expression of the Urban Stream Syndrome" (2016) 35:1 Freshw Sci 421, online: <https://doi.org/10.1086/684594>; Nasrin Alamdari & Terri S. Hogue, "Assessing the Effects of Climate Change on Urban Watersheds: A Review and Call for Future Research" (2021) 30:1 Environ Rev 61, online: <https://doi.org/10.1139/er-2021-0003>.

50 The garden is replanted each year, for example see Hannah James, "U of T Opens Traditional Medicine Garden for the Summer," *University of Toronto News* (16 June 2017), online: <https://www.utoronto.ca/news/u-t-opens-traditional-medicine-garden-summer>. Further insight on Indigenous law and plant knowledge is found in Nancy Turner, ed., *Plants, People, and Places: The Roles of Ethnobotany and Ethnoecology in Indigenous Peoples' Land Rights in Canada and Beyond* (Montreal: McGill-Queen's Press, 2020), online: <https://doi.org/10.1515/9780228003175>.

51 "First Nations in Toronto: Permanent Exhibit," *University of Toronto Department of Anthropology*, online: <https://www.anthropology.utoronto.ca/about-us/our-department/first-nations-toronto-exhibit>.

52 For a discussion of Anisinaabe art at the Royal Ontario Museum, see Ruth B. Phillips, "The Issue Is Moot: Decolonizing Art/Artifact" (2022) 27:1 J Mat Cult 48, online: <https://doi.org/10.1177/13591835211069603>.

53 See "The Chapel Royal at Massey College, Gi-Chi-Twaa Gimaa Kwe Mississauga Anishinaabek AName Amik: The Queen's Anishinaabek Sacred Place, St. Catherine's Chapel," Massey College online (pdf): <https://www.masseycollege.ca/wp-content/uploads/2020/11/MASSEY-CHAPEL-Art-Booklet-v6-7inchspreads-web-email.pdf>.

54 The course description for Queen's Law School, Law 398, Indigenous Ecological Governance, reads:

> This transsystemic course examines ecological governance through Indigenous laws, and Canadian law by comparison. It is a central condition of being human that we must take from the earth to survive, yet the extractive narratives and practices within Canadian law stand in contrast to Indigenous legal orders which conceptualize extraction in a different set of legal foundations. These differences uniquely animate decision-making obligations, processes, and principles related to the more-than-human world (plants, animals, fungi, water, rocks etc.). This course proposes that the essential work of reconciliation between Indigenous and non-Indigenous legal orders includes reconciling ourselves with the earth and confronting the "lifeworlds" we both explicitly and implicitly uphold. We will explore legal approaches, tools, and practices available to Indigenous peoples for stewarding their homelands in contemporary contexts, possibilities for working across legal orders, and consider questions of environmental justice from various perspectives.

On file with author.

55 See "Mar. 16: Indigenous Worldviews, Indigenous Law Revitalization and Self Determination as Critical Responses to CNE," *Peter Wall Institute* (16 March 2023), archived online: *Wayback Machine* <https://web.archive.org/web/20240214170717/pwias.ubc.ca/events/march-16-panel-discussion-robert-clifford-and-jocelyn-stacey/>.

56 Examples of these professors' researches related to these fields include Darcy Lindberg, *Nêhiyaw Âskiy Wiyasiwêwina: Plains Cree Earth Law and Constitutional/Ecological Reconciliation* (PhD Dissertation, University of Victoria, 2022), online: <https://hdl.handle.net/1828/11985>; Robert Clifford, "Saanich Law and the Trans Mountain Pipeline Expansion," *Centre for International Governance Innovation* (4 July 2019), online: <https://www.cigionline.org/articles/saanich-law-and-trans-mountain-pipeline-expansion/>; Lindsay Borrows, "The Land Is Our Casebook Revitalizing Indigenous Law in Relation with the Living World" (LLM Thesis, University of Alberta Faculty of Law, 2021) [unpublished].

57 *R. v. Vanderpeet*, [1996] 2 SCR at para 42.

58 *Delgamuukw v. British Columbia*, [1997] 3 SCR 1010 at para 81.

59 *Mikisew Cree First Nation v. Canada (Governor General in Council)*, [2018] 2 SCR 765 at para 22.

3 Legality's Place in a Changing World

MEGAN PFIFFER AND DAVID DYZENHAUS

Liberal democracies operate on the assumption that the state will use its power lawfully, within the constraints not only of the law but also of the rather more elusive idea of the rule of law. Emergencies put pressure on that assumption since they are exceptional situations for which, or so it is often claimed, no advance legal solution is possible. It would follow that in an emergency situation, it is legitimate for the executive – the only organ of state capable of acting swiftly and effectively – to act outside of the law or even against the law if it wishes effectively to restore the normal order.

The German fascist jurist Carl Schmitt argued that this phenomenon showed the liberal state's commitment to the rule of law to be a sham. He claimed to find empirical evidence for this argument in the fact that liberal states will try to address emergencies by creating a legal framework that authorizes the executive to take the measures necessary to deal with them in a way that maintains the constraints of the rule of law. However, he argued, if the scheme successfully addresses the emergency, the measures to protect the rule of law will fail, since a true emergency – a state of exception – cannot be regulated by the rule of law. Thus, to the extent that measures succeed, they will pay only lip service to the rule of law.

One of us has developed a theory of how a response to emergencies can productively happen within the "rule-of-law project" through the coordination of legal institutions, which permits a "virtuous cycle of legality" to unfold. In such a cycle, institutions – the legislature, the judiciary, and the executive – learn from past experience how to achieve an appropriate balance between rights protection, furthering legislative objectives, and the need to defer to the expert judgment of officials in specialized agencies.[1] However, the theory also acknowledges that an "empty cycle" of legality may unfold: one in which there is a "thin veneer of legality" over the "reality" of "executive decision-making, untrammeled by any prospect of effective judicial supervision."[2]

Here we ask whether that theory applies to the emergency situation presented by climate change. If an empty cycle is inevitable when a liberal state attempts to respond to the climate emergency, it might appear both franker and lot more efficient to fully embrace "climate authoritarianism," as Schmitt would suggest. Precisely such an argument has recently been published in the flagship journal of American political science, the *American Political Science Review*.[3] There, Ross Mittiga argues that the climate crisis could become so serious that a turn to authoritarian rule will be legitimate.

Canada has already made a start at addressing the climate emergency. A central pillar of its strategy is carbon pricing, which involves putting a price on greenhouse gas (GHG) emissions to induce people and businesses to reduce their reliance on GHG emitting substances. In 2018, Parliament enacted the *Greenhouse Gas Pollution Pricing Act* (*GGPPA*),[4] which established a nation-wide carbon pricing scheme that operates in provinces where a scheme is not in effect, or where the one in effect is insufficiently stringent. Several provinces, including Saskatchewan, Ontario, and Alberta, challenged the constitutionality of the *Act* on the ground that it violated the federal division of powers. In *References re Greenhouse Gas Pollution Pricing Act*,[5] the majority of the Supreme Court of Canada upheld the act under the national concern branch of Parliament's residual power to legislate for the peace, order, and good government of the nation. It described climate change as "an existential challenge … a threat of the highest order to the country."[6] Three judges dissented on grounds of division of power and rule of law, and as we will show, this division starkly raises the issue of whether there can be a rule-of-law response to the climate emergency.[7]

Section I assesses the statutory framework of the *GGPPA*, and the contested views of its legality in the Supreme Court of Canada in light of the challenge. In Section II, we argue that the weaknesses in the statutory framework exposed by the dissents indicate the need for better design, not that we should succumb to the challenge. Section III returns to Schmitt and Mittiga, bringing to light the normative underpinnings of this debate, which the Schmittean challenge obscures under the pretense that its main claims are empirical. Section IV provides a conclusion.

I. The GGPPA in the Supreme Court

As we just mentioned, in *References re Greenhouse Gas Pollution Pricing Act*, a majority of the Supreme Court of Canada held that the *GGPPA* was constitutional. However, the three dissenters – Justices Côté, Brown, and Rowe – had rule of law concerns arising from provisions that delegate authority to the Governor in Council over significant aspects of the carbon pricing scheme. This includes the power to determine which provinces the scheme applies to, which substances fall within the scheme's ambit, the amount of the fuel charge, who pays it, and who is exempt from it.[8] Part 2 of the *Act*, which is a complex exemption to the fuel charge that establishes a pricing system for industrial enterprises, allows the Governor in Council to determine which facilities benefit from the exemption and to determine the details of the system.[9] The *Act* also includes "Henry VIII" clauses that provide that regulations prevail over the text of the *Act* in the event of a conflict.[10] This means that the Governor in Council effectively has the power to amend the *Act* via regulations.

There are good reasons why Parliament might choose to delegate discretionary authority to the executive in a scheme like this. Carbon pricing is a polycentric issue, one that requires government to respond to changing and unpredictable environmental, economic, and industrial conditions. The executive has access to expert advisors who understand how to adapt to these conditions. Further, regulation-making authority provides the executive with a swift and effective tool to address changes in these conditions that render existing provisions obsolete. If the legislature were unable to delegate discretionary authority over a scheme like this, the scheme would likely be less effective, thus negatively impacting both the environment and the economy.

Although Justice Côté acknowledged these benefits in her dissenting reasons, she objected to the provisions that delegate authority to the Governor in Council. She argued that in general "excessive" delegation reduces the degree of public awareness and scrutiny of important policy issues because courts and executive bodies lack the open and deliberative character of the legislature.[11] Additionally, she would have struck down the Henry VIII clauses as independently unconstitutional. The main thrust of her critique was that "Henry VIII clauses endow the executive with authority to act arbitrarily. They do so by permitting the executive to act contrary to the empowering statute, creating an authority without meaningfully enforceable limits and thus an absolute discretion."[12] As a result, although she agreed with the majority that Parliament has the authority to enact minimum national standards of GHG price stringency to reduce GHG emissions, she refused to uphold the *Act* as it is currently drafted.

These arguments should be taken seriously for at least three reasons. First, the Governor in Council's discretion under the *Act* has the potential to affect a range of significant interests. Justice Côté and her dissenting colleagues were clearly motivated by a concern that the Governor in Council would use its discretion to target certain provinces or emissions-intensive industries.[13] However, unfettered discretion could also be used to undermine the efficacy of the Act, thereby impairing Canada's efforts to address climate change. If, for example, industry lobbyists could influence the exercise of discretion to secure lower fuel charges or higher emissions limits, the *Act* would be less effective than it would have otherwise been at reducing GHG emissions. Second, if Justice Côté is right that the provisions of the *Act* that delegate authority to the Governor in Council cannot be reconciled with the rule of law, the majority's position to the contrary lent the legitimacy of a judgment of the highest court of the land to a thin veneer of legality covering a situation where the rule of law appears to operate but in substance does not. Third, and perhaps most importantly, if Justice Côté is correct, and the provisions that she and her colleagues objected to are necessary features of the *Act*, Schmitt's challenge seems to be vindicated. In other words, if the relevant provisions of the *Act* cannot be reconciled with the rule of law, and they are necessary features of legislation that addresses climate change, this supports the proposition that we must choose between legality and averting the climate emergency.

There are hints in two of the dissenters' judgments that they might be willing to sacrifice fundamental constitutional principles, including the rule of law, to address such an emergency. Justice Côté argued that the leading Canadian case upholding the constitutionality of Henry VIII clauses did not apply because that case involved the emergency circumstances of World War I.[14] Her view was that because Parliament had not framed the *GGPPA* as emergency legislation, standards of legality could not be justifiably relaxed like they were in that case. Further, Justice Brown's reasoning signals that he would have been more willing to uphold the *Act* as emergency legislation. He cited with approval the idea that in the case of an emergency, "[i]nvocation of exceptional measures is typically justified on the basis that the ordinary system is not up to handling the threat and that, once the crisis passes, the usual state of affairs can and will return."[15] He only declined to uphold the law as emergency legislation because the Attorney General had "not done the necessary (or any) work to show that Parliament justifiably relied upon its emergency power as a source of its authority."[16] The logic underlying both of these positions is that had Parliament framed the *Act* as emergency legislation, Justices Côté and Brown might have been willing to accept the relaxation of ordinary constitutional principles. The GGPPA and the references thus appear to take us headlong into Schmitt's challenge. We now consider whether Justice Côté was correct in her assessment that the *Act* cannot be reconciled with the rule of law.

II. The Rule-of-Law Response

The answer to this question depends, at least in part, on the theory of law one adopts. Underlying Justice Côté's judgment are assumptions about law, mainly the idea that the text of an act is the sole source of limitations on discretionary authority. In reviewing the provisions that delegate authority, she describes textual limits as "the only limit[s] whatsoever" on the executive's discretion under the Act. Delegations not subject to textual limitations are described in her judgment as "wholly-unfettered" grants of discretion.[17] It is easy to see why this assumption makes Henry VIII clauses appear so problematic from a rule-of-law perspective. If it were true that the only limitations on delegated authority come from the text of an act, then a clause that permitted the executive to alter the text would provide the executive completely unbridled power to legislate.

However, if one rejects that assumption, it becomes possible to reconcile such provisions with the rule of law. An alternative to that assumption was most famously articulated by Justice Rand's in *Roncarelli v. Duplessis*.[18] Curiously, Justice Côté quoted the following passage from his reasons in her analysis:

> … there is no such thing as absolute and untrammelled "discretion," that is that action can be taken on any ground or for any reason that can be suggested to the mind of the administrator; no legislative Act can, without express language, be taken to contemplate an unlimited arbitrary power exercisable for any purpose, however capricious or irrelevant, regardless of the nature or purpose of the statute.[19]

Justice Côté took this passage to constitute a warning against absolute discretion.[20] However, it is better understood as part of a conception of law that entails more substantial limits on any delegation of discretionary authority than Justice Côté's conception allows. On this conception, discretionary authority is limited not only by the text of the Act, but by the "nature or purpose of the statute." That is why, on Justice Rand's conception of law, no statutory provision can be taken to delegate unlimited power.[21]

If Justice Rand were on the bench for the reference, he might have relied directly on this passage to rebut Justice Côté's conclusion that any of the provisions of the GGPPA provide the executive the wholly unfettered authority she insisted they do. Because the provisions were enacted within a statute with a specific nature and purpose, the discretion they delegate is always so limited. This argument applies with no less force to Henry VIII clauses, which are situated in the context of an overarching statutory scheme just like any ordinary grant of discretionary authority. Though they provide the executive the power to modify specific provisions of the Act, the discretion they afford remains limited by the purposes for which the power was granted. Contrary to Justice Côté's suggestion, they do not "endow the executive with authority to act arbitrarily."[22] Any exercise of authority under such a clause would need to be undertaken in accordance with that purpose.

In response to an argument along those lines advanced by the majority, Justice Côté held that the *Act* empowers the Governor in Council to set "variable and inconsistent standards on an industry-by-industry basis,"[23] and that the statutory purpose of reducing GHG emissions through pricing does not place meaningful limitations on this power. To draw out the ramifications of this issue, she relied on the following hypothetical:

> ...the executive could decide to impose such strict limits on the fossil fuel or potash industries, both heavy emitters of GHG emissions, that the industries would be decimated. According to the majority's reasoning, this example, regardless of its improbability, would fulfill the statutory purpose of reducing GHG emissions through GHG pricing and therefore be a valid use of the executive's regulatory powers accorded by the GGPPA.[24]

There are two ways to read this passage. The first is rooted in a concern that the Governor in Council will target certain industries in pursuit of purposes that are irrelevant to the scheme, and those exercises of discretion will be validated because they are consistent with the statutory purpose of reducing GHG emissions through GHG pricing. However, a reply to this reading can also be found in Justice Rand's reasons in *Roncarelli*. There, he held that officials who exercise discretionary authority under a statute are bound by an implied public duty to act "with a rational appreciation of [its] intent and purpose and not with an improper intent and for an alien purpose."[25] This is a corollary of the idea that discretionary authority is limited by the nature and purposes of the statute. It entails that the pursuit of an irrelevant purpose itself will take an exercise of discretion beyond the confines of the statute, thereby rendering it unlawful. In this way, Justice Rand's conception of law in *Roncarelli* provides the resources to address concerns that otherwise improper exercises of discretion will be validated by the scheme's admittedly broad purpose.

The second interpretation of the hypothetical does not worry that the Governor in Council might act for improper motives. Rather, it worries that the Governor in Council, in exercising its discretion in pursuit of the *Act*'s purposes, will do so overzealously or unreasonably in respect of certain industries, to an extent that threatens their viability. This reading is more cause for concern, as there is some grounding in the law for the idea that so long as an exercise of discretion is exercised in pursuit of the relevant statutory purpose and is consistent with it, courts cannot intervene. In *Katz Group*, the Supreme Court of Canada set out a series of principles that apply to the review of regulations.[26] Most significantly, regulations are subject to a presumption of validity. This places the burden on the applicant for judicial review to demonstrate that an impugned regulation is invalid, rather than requiring the executive body to justify it. Further, courts are only permitted to intervene if the regulation is "irrelevant," "extraneous," or "completely unrelated" to the statutory purpose.[27] Conspicuously absent from the decision is the idea that regulations are subject to review for reasonableness, which applies to all other forms of administrative decision-making. If this were the framework that applies to the review of regulations under the *GGPPA*, then Justice Côté's rule of law concerns could come to fruition.

Moreover, even if more robust limits apply in principle to the exercise of regulation-making authority, there is still the issue of the enforceability of those limits. The reality is that the kind of "smoking gun" evidence necessary to prove that a public official acted unreasonably or for an irrelevant purpose is difficult to come by. The *Act* fails to assist affected parties on that front because it does not afford them any procedural rights. Consequently, there is no guarantee that a body of extrinsic evidence will be created, which is sufficient to permit courts to review exercises of regulation-making authority in a meaningful way. As Justice Rowe explained in his dissenting reasons, "[t]his problem is particularly pernicious where the Governor in Council is empowered to make regulations. As Cabinet deliberates in secret, submissions to it are protected from disclosure and it gives no reasons for its decisions. It is very nearly a total black box."[28] Because a duty of fairness that would impose these obligations is unlikely to be implied by the common law under the *Act*,[29] affected parties could be left dependent on voluntary practices to flesh out a record for judicial review.

These are genuine weaknesses of the legality of the scheme. But, in our view, rather than vindicating Schmitt's challenge, they highlight the need for better institutional design on at least two fronts. First is the design of the framework for judicial review of regulations. As we saw earlier, the principles set out in *Katz Group* have the potential to leave courts powerless in the face of regulations that are unreasonable but nonetheless not "irrelevant," "extraneous," or "completely unrelated" to the statutory purpose. Fortunately, the Supreme Court of Canada has already articulated a more robust framework for the review of administrative decisions that requires decisions to be justified, transparent, and intelligible to their subjects. Indeed, in *Canada (Minister of Citizenship and Immigration) v. Vavilov*, the court expressed its aim to develop a "coherent and unified approach to judicial review" based on these principles to promote a "culture of justification" among those who wield public power.[30] In our view, an important next step in the development of such a culture is an explicit ruling that the promulgation of regulations by the executive is subject to the same framework for review as any other public administrative decision.[31]

The second front concerns measures to ensure that a record is produced that is sufficient to make the limits on discretionary authority under the *Act* meaningfully enforceable. This could include a duty to hear the submissions of affected parties, a duty to give reasons for regulatory decisions, and a duty to disclose relevant information for the purposes of judicial review. Not only would these types of procedural rights contribute to the production of a record, but they would contribute towards addressing the democratic deficit associated with delegated regulation-making authority highlighted by Justice Côté in this case. We recognize that there is a fine balance to be struck here, as affording procedural rights to affected parties would encumber the Governor in Council, cutting against their ability to respond quickly to changing conditions. However, we also note that some steps are already taken by the executive on a voluntary basis to consult with affected parties and to justify regulations as they are made.[32] Further, courts have discretionary powers to order the production of information necessary to conduct judicial review, even where privilege is asserted.[33] Accordingly, affording these procedural rights under the *Act* would not encumber the executive substantially more than it already does in practice. Instead, it would prevent the parties from expending time and resources fighting over preliminary procedural issues before meaningful judicial review can even take place.

We do not offer these suggestions under the pretense that they provide a complete solution to the problem of maintaining legality while addressing the climate emergency. Addressing the climate emergency within the confines of the rule of law is an ongoing project that will require persistence, creativity, and a willingness to challenge orthodox approaches to regulation on many fronts. It is for this reason that we are encouraged by the work of public lawyer Jocelyn Stacey. In a compelling argument covering the vast terrain of Canadian environmental law, she demonstrated that the climate emergency not only can but also must be addressed within a rule-of-law framework, much like the one sketched here.[34] In doing so, she reminds us that the rule-of-law project has always been a kind of experimental one in which we should expect updates and revisions in light of recalcitrant experience.

We offer these suggestions merely to point out that we can and should do better. Our emphasis here is on the "can" because, as we pointed out in section I, the Schmittean challenge is composed of both a theoretical argument that emergencies cannot in principle be dealt within the constraints of the rule of law, and an empirical claim that attempts to deal with them will fail, either because they operate within the rule of law or succeed, but only by a pretense that they are so operating. Ultimately, then, the contest between the liberal rule-of-law project is a matter of normative argument – a contest over "should" rather than "can" – and so not plain empirics. It is to that contest that we now turn.

III. Authoritarianism: Drift or Embrace?

In "Political Legitimacy, Authoritarianism, and Climate Change,"[35] Ross Mittiga argues that the climate crisis could become so serious that authoritarian rule will be legitimate. To elaborate this argument, Mittiga draws a distinction between foundational legitimacy and contingent legitimacy. Foundational legitimacy "requires that citizens' essential safety needs are met" and is "foundational in the sense that no government can be legitimate unless it satisfies this demand."[36] Contingent legitimacy "requires that the power used by the government… be in principle, 'acceptable' to all those who are subjected to it."[37] In Mittiga's view, "a core feature of all [contingent legitimacy] standards is that they shift over time, across cultures, and in light of new circumstances."[38] He argues that under normal conditions, foundational legitimacy operates as an unacknowledged background condition of contingent legitimacy. However, in moments of crisis, tensions emerge between foundational legitimacy and contingent legitimacy.[39] In those circumstances, preserving or restoring foundational legitimacy should take priority over satisfying any particular demand of contingent legitimacy.

Interestingly, Mittiga pays scarcely any attention to the rule of law and sometimes seems oblivious to its relevance. Instead, he focuses on when it might become justifiable to abandon democracy, referring only in passing to the accompanied abandonment of other "constitutional limits on power"[40] that a turn to climate authoritarianism would involve. Such lack of attention is especially striking in his footnote discussion of Stacey's work, where he says that she has "persuasively argued that all environmental issues should be approached through the "perspective of an ongoing emergency"[41] and that the epistemic issues that these issues raise "suggest that the emergency governance framework may be enduringly relevant to environmental policies."[42] He thus completely neglects the main thrust of her book – that it is a rule-of-law answer to Schmitt's challenge. In short, her "emergency governance framework" for the climate emergency is fully on side with the rule-of-law project.

Mittiga's neglect is best explained by the fact that he follows Schmitt in supposing that even liberal democracies recognize the need to resort to authoritarianism in that they enact statutes that make advance provision for a state of emergency to be declared so that the state may operate for a time outside of the ordinary legal framework. In addition, he claims that in Germany, the emergency powers provision of the Weimar Constitution – Article 48 – "provided a fully legal route for the … government's descent into fascist totalitarianism."[43] In support of this last claim, he cites one newspaper article and seems oblivious to the body of work that points out that to assume that the descent was "fully legal" is to adopt the view of legality advocated most prominently by Schmitt in the 1930s in a bid to legitimize the turn to authoritarian rule.

On that view, the rule of law is a sham. The sovereign is a political entity that stands outside of the law and not only can but also may legitimately intervene at any time in the "normal" legal order. The state of exception to the normal order of things is just the most vivid evidence of this fact, which is not merely a correct description of the world, but also freighted normatively, in that the sovereign has absolute authority both to declare a state of emergency and to determine appropriate measures to deal with it. Schmitt's view of legitimacy is not an alternative to a liberal democratic one but a rival constructed with deadly intent. As a Nazi lawyer observed in 1935, all of Schmitt's works are "from the ground up trained on one target: the unmasking and destruction of the liberal, rule-of-law state and the conquest of the legislative state."[44]

In making his arguments, Mittiga purports to rely on philosopher Bernard Williams's critique of liberal theories of legitimacy and in particular on the place of Thomas Hobbes's political theory in that account.[45] In fact, as some scattered references in the footnotes and one in the text reveal, his argument owes more to Schmitt than to either Williams or Hobbes.[46] In particular, his distinction between foundational and contingent legitimacy, and his claims about the primacy of foundational legitimacy, are no more than a restatement of Schmitt's theory of the exception. Foundational legitimacy is *foundational*, and hence, the authentic form of legitimacy that ever lurks behind the veneer of the contingent "normal," and which will be given concrete expression when the political sovereign breaks through the veneer, including the veneer of legality. Mittiga's willingness to countenance illiberal measures echoes in the dissents in *References re Greenhouse Gas Pollution Pricing Act* insofar as they cast doubt on the ability of states to craft a rule-of-law response to emergencies and suggest that measures outside of the constraints of the rule of law may thus be required.

IV. Conclusion

Our analysis of the virtues and vices of Canada's efforts to address the climate emergency through the GGPPA suggests not only that hard work is needed to ensure both the success of such measures and that they conform to the rule of law, but also that such work is a task we cannot shirk, especially when the context of the climate emergency is far from the only one in which support is being voiced for a return to authoritarian rule. Confronting the climate crisis requires unwavering dedication and adherence to liberal democratic principles and to the rule of law, as well as vigilant resistance against any resurgence of authoritarianism, to safeguard the future of our planet, protect the rule of law, and, consequently, uphold the values of a just society.

NOTES

1 David Dyzenhaus, "Preventive Justice and the Rule-of-Law Project" in Andrew Ashworth, Lucia Zedner & Patrick Tomlin, eds, *Prevention and the Limits of the Criminal Law* (Oxford: Oxford University Press, 2013) 91 at 91, online: <https://doi.org/10.1093/acprof:oso/9780199656769.003.0006>.

2 *Re MB* [2006] EWHC 1000 (Admin), [2006] H.R.L.R. 29 (2006) 150 at para 103, Sullivan J.

3 Ross Mittiga, "Political Legitimacy, Authoritarianism, and Climate Change" (2021) 116:3 Am Pol Sci Rev 998, online: <https://doi.org/10.1017/S0003055421001301>.

4 *Greenhouse Gas Pollution Pricing Act*, SC 2018, c 12, s 186 [*GGPPA*].

5 *References re Greenhouse Gas Pollution Pricing Act* 2021 SCC 11 [*References re: GGPPA*].

6 *Ibid* at para 167.

7 We do not deal with the division of power issue. It may be that the strategy behind this reasoning is similar to that of the majority of the US Supreme Court in *Dobbs*, which overruled *Roe v. Wade*. The matter is said to be in

the jurisdiction of the federal sub-units in the knowledge that several will prohibit abortion, or, in the climate matter, not address climate change.

8 See *GGPPA, supra* note 4, ss 3, 40–1.

9 *Ibid* s 5.

10 See *ibid* at s 168(4). The name of these clauses refers to Henry VIII's penchant for ruling by proclamation rather than through Parliament. For further discussion of such clauses, and the institutional concerns they raise, see Andrew Green and Albet Yoon, "The Most Dangerous Branch?" in this volume.

11 *References re: GGPPA, supra* note 5 at para 237.

12 *Ibid* at para 274.

13 For Justice Brown's reasoning on this point, see e.g., *ibid* at paras 337, 339, 412; for Justice Rowe's, see *ibid* at paras 595, 599, 609, 614.

14 *Re George Edwin Gray* (1918), 57 SCR 150.

15 *References re: GGPPA, supra* note 5 at para 400, citing Sarah Burningham, "'The New Normal': COVID-19 and the Temporary Nature of Emergencies," *Centre for Constitutional Studies* (4 June 2020), online (blog): <https://www.constitutionalstudies.ca/2020/06/the-new-normal-covid-19-and-the-temporary-nature-of-emergencies/>.

16 *References re: GGPPA, supra* note 5 at para 401.

17 *Ibid* at paras 229–30.

18 *Roncarelli v. Duplessis* [1959] SCR 121 [*Roncarelli*].

19 *Ibid* at 140.

20 *References re: GGPPA, supra* note 5 at para 275.

21 See David Dyzenhaus, "Rand's Legal Republicanism" (2010) 55 McGill LJ 491, online: <https://doi.org/10.7202/1000621ar>.

22 *References re: GGPPA, supra* note 5 at para 274.

23 *Ibid* at para 238.

24 *Ibid.*

25 *Roncarelli, supra* note 18 at para 143.

26 *Katz Group Canada Inc. v. Ontario (Health and Long-Term Care)*, 2013 SCC 64 [2013], SCR 810 at paras 24–28 [*Katz Group*].

27 *Ibid* at para 28.

28 *References re: GGPPA, supra* note 5 at para 606.

29 On this point, see *Attorney General of Canada v. Inuit Tapirisat of Canada et al.*, [1980] 2 SCR 735.

30 *Canada (Minister of Citizenship and Immigration v. Vavilov* 2019 SCC 65 [2019] 4 SCR 653 at paras 88 and 2 [*Vavilov*].

31 Currently there is a debate among appellate courts regarding whether *Vavilov* or *Katz Group* applies to the judicial review of regulations. Compare *Portnov v. Canada (Attorney General)*, 2021 FCA 171, where the Federal Court of Appeal held that *Vavilov* is the governing framework with *Auer v. Auer*, 2022 ABCA 375 where the Court of Appeal of Alberta held that *Katz Group* applies.

32 For example, the Governor in Council voluntarily releases Regulatory Impact Analysis Statements when it implements or changes regulations under the Act. Such a statement was relied upon by the court in the only judicial review proceedings concerning a challenge to regulations under the act that have occurred so far. See generally, *Manitoba v. Canada (Attorney General)*, 2021 FC 1115.
33 See *Canada (Citizenship and Immigration) v. Canadian Council for Refugees*, 2021 FCA 72 at paras 101–22.
34 See Jocelyn Stacey, *The Constitution of the Environmental Emergency* (Oxford: Hart Publishing, 2018).
35 Mittiga, *supra* note 3.
36 *Ibid* at 999.
37 *Ibid*.
38 *Ibid*.
39 *Ibid* at 1003.
40 *Ibid* at 998.
41 *Ibid* at 1006.
42 *Ibid*.
43 *Ibid* at 1005, relying on Jeffrey Herf, "Emergency Powers Helped Hitler's Rise. Germany Has Avoided Them Ever Since," *The Washington Post* (19 February 2019), online: <https://www.washingtonpost.com/outlook/2019/02/19/emergency-powers-helped-hitlers-rise-germany-has-avoided-them-ever-since/>.
44 F.A. Hayek, *Law, Legislation and Liberty*, vol 1 (London: Routledge, 1990) at 161, quoting from a review by Georg Dahm, my translation. Dahm was a member of the "Kiel school" of law, which had the reputation of being a "shock troop university" for the construction of National Socialist law – see Michael Stolleis, *A History of Public Law in Germany: 1914–1945* (Oxford: Oxford University Press, 2004) at 291–5, online: <https://doi.org/10.1093/acprof:oso/9780199269365.001.0001>. Dahm, of course, meant his observation to be laudatory. See David Dyzenhaus, "The Concept of the Rule-of-Law State in Carl Schmitt's *Verfassungslehre*" in Jens Meiherhenrich and Oliver Simons, eds, *The Oxford Handbook of Carl Schmitt* (Oxford: Oxford University Press, 2016) 480 at 490.
45 Bernard Williams, "Realism and Moralism in Political Theory" in Williams, *In the Beginning Was the Deed* (Princeton, NJ: Princeton University Press, 2005) 1 at 3.
46 We cannot here discuss why Mittiga's understanding of both Williams and Hobbes distorts their theories so as to make them surrogates for Schmitt. But see David Dyzenhaus, "Emergencies and Human Rights" in Bardo Fassbender & Knut Traisbach, eds, *The Limits of Human Rights* (Oxford: Oxford University Press, 2019) 89 at 89, online: <https://doi.org/10.1093/oso/9780198824756.003.0007>.

4 Confronting the Institutional Challenges at the Heart of Climate Change Policy

EDWARD IACOBUCCI AND MICHAEL TREBILCOCK

I. Introduction

Formulating and implementing effective climate change policies has often been described as a "super-wicked problem."[1] It presents a daunting set of challenges to policymakers seeking to formulate substantive strategies for combatting climate change and its impacts. Aside from thorny questions about optimal public policy, there is a prior issue that is, in our view, understudied: rather than considering the optimal substantive approach to climate change policy, we consider the challenges climate change presents to designing domestic institutions established to formulate climate change policy. While we leave to others the equally formidable challenge of designing effective global institutions to address global collective action problems, we are sensitive to the interactions between the two sets of institutional challenges (domestic and global). The scope of the considerations that are relevant to climate change policy present not just substantive complexity but institutional design complexity as well. We review the distinctive challenges that climate change policy poses for institutional design, and we propose a Canadian institutional response to address these challenges.

II. Climate Change Policy Challenges

1. Scientific Uncertainty

Climate science has made remarkable progress over the past two decades. As reflected in regular UN Intergovernmental Panel reports on climate change, there is a broad consensus among hundreds of scientists from around the world that significant levels of global warming are likely to induce severe climatic consequences. However, the precise causes and effects of different degrees of global warming, and their timing in different parts of the globe, can never be more than probabilistic in nature.[2] Climate change predictions typically fall within a zone of genuine uncertainty as to time and space, making it all the more challenging to address plausible but remote concatenation of circumstances or "tipping points" that could conceivably lead to a global human catastrophe.[3]

2. *Technological Uncertainty*

Since the advent of the industrial revolution, fossil fuels, beginning with coal and then later oil and natural gas, have played a central role in advances in standard indicators of economic and social well-being. Fossil fuels are centrally implicated in many of the major sectors of our economies, including electricity generation, transportation, food production (including red meat and fertilizers), and are a major input into manufacturing processes in various key industries such as steel, cement, and plastics. Dramatically reducing the role of fossil fuels in these sectors over a foreseeable timeframe without massively disrupting or undermining economies poses enormous technological challenges. Yet the path of innovation to reduce reliance on fossil fuels is unpredictable. While some technological innovations that will reduce global carbon emissions and global warming are at hand, others are uncertain both in their timing and in their feasibility.[4]

3. *Cognitive Biases*

Much recent scholarship in behavioural economics and moral and social psychology has documented the extent to which we as individuals in our mental processes face a constant tension between emotions or gut instincts and rational analytical processes, leading us to succumb in various contexts to a wide variety of psychological heuristics or biases.[5] Partly because of these biases, and partly because of radical scientific and technological uncertainty, many will find it difficult to think about policy in the climate change context rationally. As a consequence, forging anything like a strong general social and political consensus faces formidable challenges.[6] It is true that in the past, citizens in many countries were able to support broad-based mobilization of efforts to support a major national cause, such as the two world wars or the Great Depression, or even to some extent the recent global pandemic. However, in all these cases, the threats to human welfare were imminent and tangible (and even then, public consensus on appropriate mitigation strategies was often tenuous). In the case of climate change, the effects of global warming are likely to seem remote for many citizens. It may be that the increasing frequency of extreme weather events will engender a broader public sense of immediacy of the crisis, but these events are still likely to be unevenly distributed in time and space, and causation issues are likely to be complex. The interaction of cognitive biases and genuine technological and scientific uncertainty presents an obstacle to consensus about the optimal response to climate change.

4. *Collective Action*

Formidable collective action problems arise in several related contexts with respect to climate change policy: intergenerational collective action challenges, contemporary collective action challenges, and coordination challenges. The first two challenges concern externalities and the sub-optimal incentives facing individuals or individual political entities to address climate change. The third set of challenges concern the difficulties that arise even on the assumption that individuals and political entities want to address climate change.

I. INTERGENERATIONAL COLLECTIVE ACTION PROBLEMS

At least in liberal democracies, governments are typically elected for four- or five-year terms, and politicians seeking election or re-election will be highly sensitive to the temporal distribution of costs and benefits of policies that they espouse. Policies that impose substantial costs on present generations of voters in the interests of future generations of citizens who are not currently voters will often seem politically irrational. While Alan Jacobs in his book, *Governing for the Long-Term,*[7] argues that governments in liberal democracies are often able to invest in policies that generate long-term benefits, such as investments in infrastructure, health and education, and public pensions, in these cases a broad cross-section of current voters see these policies as of benefit to themselves or at least their children.

Intergenerational collective action problems in a climate change context pose daunting normative and political challenges. Current generations are asked to bear costs that may only provide benefits several generations later. This raises clear political challenges for contemporary policymakers, but it also raises philosophical questions about the value of future versus current lives and well-being.[8] As Joseph Heath has pointed out in a recent book, many of the philosophical debates that these issues have prompted are institution-free and unhelpful in canvassing politically realistic policy options in the here and now.[9]

II. CONTEMPORARY COLLECTIVE ACTION PROBLEMS

Climate change presents a commons problem on an unprecedented scale. The presence of carbon dioxide and other gases in the atmosphere, a commons, is creating upheavals in the earth's climate that affect all of its inhabitants to a greater or lesser extent. Such a commons problem also presents acute collective action problems. A decision by an individual to burn fossil fuels may bring private benefits to the person, but it creates externalities by contributing gases to the atmosphere and degrades the commons in a manner that imposes costs on all inhabitants of the earth. Even if it would be collectively rational for individuals not to burn the fuel – that is, the costs of burning the fuel and contributing to climate change exceed the benefits from burning the fuel – it may nevertheless be individually rational for the person to make the decision: they realize all the private benefits from the fuel, while the costs are dispersed across billions. Collective action problems not only afflict decisions to act in a manner that results in socially excessive emissions but also undermine incentives to invest in mitigation and abatement. Privately costly investment in pollution-reducing technology, for example, produces benefits that extend well beyond the decision-maker, benefits that the decision-maker will predictably care less about.

The collective action problems arise at the level of the individual, but similarly arise at the level of government. Domestically, decisions by one local government, be it a province, state, or municipality, to adopt regulations or other policies that implicate climate change have an impact on other domestic jurisdictions. As Andrew Green points out in his recent book, *Picking up the Slack: Law, Institutions, and Canadian Climate Policy*,[10] even where costly climate change policies are initially adopted by domestic governments, there will be strong political temptations for current or future governments to engage in low visibility backsliding from commitments through exceptions, dispensations, weak enforcement, or inadequate budgetary appropriations. Moreover, different regions of the country or different sectors of the economy will seek to shift the burden of policies onto other regions of the country or sectors of the economy – a contemporary domestic collective action problem in the formulation and implementation of climate change policies rendered particularly acute in Canada's case by the concentration of fossil fuel production and emission sources in two provinces (Alberta and Saskatchewan) and an important element in the national economy.

Finally, of course, any decision by a domestic government in turn has international effects. If national governments are motivated to act in the interests only of their constituents, there will predictably be too little effort to resist climate change, just as individuals predictably make decisions to burn fossil fuels at a socially excessive rate because of their failure to internalize the total social costs of their activity. For example, Canada contributes about 2 per cent of total global greenhouse gas emissions. Even if Canada were to reduce its emissions to zero, this would have a minimal impact on climate change. From a purely self-interested perspective, Canada has an incentive not to incur costs to avoid emissions and instead free ride on others' costly emission reductions. Other countries may all reason similarly, and little will be done to combat climate change.

III. COORDINATION PROBLEMS

Externalities and collective action problems afflict decision-makers' incentives to address climate change optimally. But even assuming that decision-makers wanted to address climate change optimally, there are severe coordination challenges at the governmental level (let alone at the individual level). In federal systems such as those adopted in Canada and the United States, the division of powers between the national, provincial/state, and municipal governments poses major coordination problems in yielding coherent national policies, particularly in contexts such as climate change policy that implicate directly or indirectly a wide range of policy domains. In the Canadian context, provinces are constitutionally assigned jurisdiction over their electricity and other energy sectors. All provinces regulate, and some own, their electricity utilities. In turn, municipal governments are typically responsible for building codes, land use planning, and public transit systems. While the Supreme Court of Canada has upheld the constitutionality of a national carbon tax under the national concern head of power, subject to provincial ability to determine their own compliance policies,[11] generating coherent and effective climate change policies even within the federal government is likely to implicate a wide range of ministries whose policies are likely to be engaged, directly or indirectly, by effective climate change policies but whose traditional interministerial coordination mechanisms may not be robust enough to yield coherent policies. While Canada lacks the elaborate system of checks and balances at the federal level as the United States,[12] problems of effective policy coordination at the national level in Canada in the climate change context are not trivial. Thus, coordination problems may arise both between levels of government and within the same level of government.

Coordination problems are also acute at the international level but are critical in achieving meaningful policy to address climate change.[13]

Without coordination, domestic efforts to reduce emissions would risk a flood of imports from countries that have not adopted similar policies, would risk exports being uncompetitive in these and third countries' markets, and would risk domestic investment and jobs migrating to these countries. This would be tantamount to political and economic self-harm and would have no significant impact on climate change.

To avoid this catastrophe/futility scenario, one possibility is that countries around the world would negotiate an internationally binding treaty that enshrines some common, or at least minimum, emission reduction commitments, but to date, despite decades of efforts, such a treaty remains elusive.[14] Coordination problems help explain this failure.

A more modest interim strategy may be for countries unilaterally to impose carbon tariffs at the border on imports from countries that have not adopted similarly stringent climate change policies to the importing countries (as the EU has recently done). One can also imagine that a subset of countries might coordinate such policies with a view to presenting a common front to non-compliant countries, in the hope that such a climate club would over time induce the negotiation of a more comprehensive international treaty.[15] But as a purely interim measure, such coordinated policies on border carbon tariffs may not address purely domestic emissions in non-traded goods and services sectors. Such coordinated policies may also not address reduced competitiveness of export-oriented industries in countries adopting such measures in foreign markets where governments have not adopted similar domestic climate change measures. Critically, any such climate club, to be effective, must include countries or regions that are major sources of greenhouse gas emissions, such as China, the United States, the European Union, the United Kingdom, Brazil, Russia, and India. In the current fraught geopolitical environment, such a club may seem a daunting prospect.

The Paris Agreement, perhaps reflecting the substantive complexities of climate change policy, perhaps reflecting coordination challenges, does not impose binding commitments on signatory countries.[16] Rather, it sets out a framework that encourages national governments to take steps to combat climate change. Jutta Brunnée argues that this framework appropriately provides a stable but adaptable procedure for encouraging action, without attempting to impose binding substantive commitments that would be unsuccessful.[17] Such an argument gains persuasive force in the shadow of the acute coordination challenges that afflict international efforts to address climate change.

5. Polycentrism

Formulating policy responses to climate change is not a technocratic exercise that turns on normatively uncontestable values. On top of scientific and technological challenges, there is a range of values at stake in something as profoundly affecting as climate change. There are a host of trade-offs in climate change policy, many of which entail potentially incommensurable values. For example, how much economic cost should society bear to avoid the non-birth of a future generation? How should we trade off important questions about improving the quality of life of the impoverished in one part of the world today versus the imminent extinction of a species owing to climate change? How should we weigh the loss of entire nation-states, and their associated cultures, in low-lying waters against economic growth in the rest of the world? Glib corner solutions, with an all-or-nothing view of the values at stake in climate change policy, are inappropriate; . optimal policy requires sensitivity to a range of values. Institutions charged with formulating policy to deal with climate change require a breadth of expertise, along with political and public credibility, that is unusually wide.

III. Institutional Design and Interactions between Climate Change Policy Challenges

We have reviewed several considerations that present impediments to progress on climate change. In this section, we elaborate on the *interaction* between the considerations with a focus on institutional design. We show that it is often the case that designing an institution to address one kind of impediment aggravates, or at least fails to address, a different kind of concern. In particular, without attempting to be comprehensive, we consider in a pairwise fashion a number of the challenges and elaborate on the tension that the pairing suggests for institutional design. Even this incomplete survey of the tensions illustrates the daunting degree of complexity in the design of climate change institutions.

1. Scientific and Technological Uncertainty: Cognitive Biases

On the one hand, there is considerable scientific and technological uncertainty about the path of climate change, as well as the prospects for innovation that would reduce the risks of catastrophic change. On the other hand, those subject to climate change policy are vulnerable to cognitive biases that make it difficult to respond rationally to complicated problems. This is a toxic combination for an institution contemplating climate change policy. Such an institution would, certainly in a democracy but also in many autocracies, be sensitive to the buy-in of those affected by the policy that it formulates. An unpopular policy may have a limited life and may not be effective while it exists. Yet communications strategies designed to elicit buy-in on something that has considerable uncertainty about the costs and benefits of inaction and action, including accounting for uncertain future technological developments, are fraught. Given the scale of the issue, and the fluidity of information about science and technology, reasonably well-informed and purely rational thinkers will have difficulty assessing the merits of a climate change strategy. If one then considers the cognitive biases that may be brought to bear, exacerbated by social media where fact, fiction, and fabrication freely intermingle unmediated, institutions seeking to persuade citizens to accept costly (but not apocalyptic) strategies face a daunting task.[18]

2. *Contemporary Collective Action Problems: Coordination Challenges*

Collective action problems require concerted action among the parties affected by them. In the case of climate change, all states – and all citizens of those states – are affected by climate change. This presents an extraordinarily difficult coordination problem. Democracies and autocracies must coordinate. Low-lying coastal states must coordinate with inland states. Hot climate countries must coordinate with cold climate countries. Poor countries must coordinate with rich countries. Given the disparity of the particular interests at stake in climate change, even if ultimately there is a shared understanding of the risks of climate change to life on Earth, coordination efforts will confront challenges in getting all relevant stakeholders – that is, all people on the planet – to agree to a course of action. It is not surprise that getting countries to agree on meaningful strategies to combat climate change has proven to be elusive.

The fact that the collective action and coordination problems are international raises a related, yet conceptually distinct, problem for institutional design. Even if countries agree to a particular benchmark or set of strategies for combatting climate change, there is a distinct problem of enforcing that agreement. International agreements often lack effective legal enforcement mechanisms; it is up to domestic authorities to ensure compliance. As a consequence, what may appear to be breakthroughs in the coordination problem in the form of international agreements may be entirely Potemkin progress, with individual jurisdictions following the logic of collective action in failing to live up to their ostensible commitments.

3. Scientific and Technological Uncertainty: Contemporary Collective Action Problems

The considerable uncertainty that exists about optimal climate change policy interacts uncomfortably with collective action problems. At the very least, successful responses to collective action problems require buy-in and cooperation among the parties affected by it. In the case of climate change, this involves states and their citizens. Yet the scientific and technological uncertainty surrounding climate change, including the possibility of future technological innovations in clean energy, will inevitably and reasonably engender disagreement about optimal climate change policy. Good faith disagreement may interact uncomfortably with self-interest: citizens (or countries) who are motivated by self-interest rather than the collective good may invoke uncertainty as a justification for taking a lighter touch in adopting or enforcing costly climate change strategies, which may exacerbate collective action problems. Alternatively, uncertainty may generate the opposite reaction: proposals for apocalyptic policy responses.

4. Intergenerational Collective Action Problems/Polycentrism: Contemporary Collective Action Problems

The relationship between intertemporal and contemporary collective action problems, as well as the confounding role of polycentricity, present further difficulties for the path forward on climate change policy.

Intertemporal collective action problems raise profound philosophical and ethical challenges. For example, should policy choose to lift an existing person out of crushing poverty even if it comes at the expense of a potential future life that is never lived because of climate change? The tradeoffs that this entails raise conceptual questions that are far from straightforward to answer. Thoughtful people may have entirely different views about the best answers to the tradeoffs. Any meaningful approach to climate change policy requires attention to the multifaceted nature of the problems with climate change, yet polycentricity presents another series of profoundly difficult institutional questions. The values to be weighed are often incommensurable, which makes any kind of trade-off much more than a technocratic exercise.

In the face of highly contestable questions that ultimately turn on the values of the decision-maker, there are advantages of decentralizing decision-making to more local institutions. Rather than having a monolithic policy approach to an issue that may invite a very wide range of reasonable reactions, decentralized decision-making allows local communities to formulate policy that better reflects local values and norms. However, decentralized institutions, while appropriate in the face of polycentricity, do not sit well with the collective action problems surrounding climate change. The decisions made by local communities may reflect local values, but they may also be shaped by local recognition that locally costly efforts to mitigate climate change may in themselves be irrelevant to resolving climate change. In other words, decentralizing decision-making to reflect polycentric values collides with the imperative of centralized decision-making institutions and international cooperation to overcome collective action problems.[19]

IV. Canadian Institutional Design

As we observed at the outset, while there has been a veritable outpouring of scholarly literature on climate change and climate change policies in recent years (scientific, technological, philosophical, and economic), much of this literature is largely institution-free. Yet, as the previous sections have demonstrated, there are vexing challenges in designing appropriate institutions to take the lead in formulating climate change policy. In this section, we turn from the principles underlying institutional design to a canvass of the literature, such as it is, on comparative institutional design and to Canadian institutional design.

1. The Literature

Dubash et al., in a synopsis of case studies of national climate institutions in the United States, the United Kingdom, Germany, Australia, China, India, Brazil, and South Africa, principally writing from a political science or public administration perspective, state that "the study of climate institutions is in its infancy, compared with the study of targets and policies."[20] They argue that the interplay between institutions and politics shapes what countries put forward as their Nationally Determined Contributions in international agreements such as the Paris Agreement. Institutions determine who sits at the table, how decisions are made and by whom, and the cognitive priors carried into decision-making. The authors then insightfully address how states in their eight case studies have addressed three core climate governance challenges: coordination, building consensus, and strategy development.

With respect to coordination challenges, the scale and scope of mitigation and adaptation challenges require coordination across policy domains as diverse as energy, industry, agriculture, and urbanization. One option that emerges from the case studies is to layer climate coordination responsibilities onto existing environmental ministries, but this approach has proven to be relatively ineffective in producing muscular climate change policy, in part because environmental ministries are often relatively weak. Another option is for countries to reorganize their bureaucracies and allocate climate change responsibilities to new institutions (displacement rather than layering). A further option has been to develop new interministerial coordination committees, which have had mixed success, while a yet further approach has been creating climate laws, subsuming the coordination challenge within a framework of target setting and compliance.

With respect to building consensus, institutions are needed to mediate low and high carbon interests and ideally build consensus towards low carbon futures. Ideally, institutions can provide credible information and analysis that shifts politics, creates new narratives, and creates credible spaces for bargaining among interests, as exemplified by the UK Climate Change Committee, instituted on a non-partisan basis in 2008. The Committee sets authoritative five-year carbon budgets for various sectors, which are non-binding on the government of the day but require public explanations of divergences from the committee's recommendations.

With respect to strategy development, decarbonization requires transformational rather than incremental change and while many countries have mechanisms to set targets, these mechanisms are frequently ad hoc, unstable over time, and not rooted in domestic climate processes aimed at long-term strategic transformation. Dubash et al. acknowledge that climate institutions are underdeveloped in part because countries do not start with a blank slate in creating institutions and the existing configuration of institutions and institutional traditions create a form of path dependence that defies universal best practice formulations.[21] Because of such path dependence, and because the Paris Agreement encourages countries to establish their own means of achieving their climate commitments, institutional design questions are appropriately answered at the national level at the present time; we focus on institutions in Canada.

Turning to Canada, Andrew Green charts the unpromising trajectory of climate change policy in Canada over the past 25 years, with successive federal governments setting and then missing or abandoning various greenhouse gas emission reduction targets.[22] Currently, the federal government has committed itself under the Paris Agreement to a target of 40–45 per cent reductions of greenhouse gas emissions below 2005 levels by 2030, and achieving net zero emissions by 2050. To that end, it has enacted an incrementally increasing carbon tax of $50 per ton of

CO_2 as of 2022 that provides latitude for provinces to adopt alternative measures of equivalent efficacy.

Green is not optimistic that these targets are robust and argues that Canadian climate change policy has been beset by three sources of infirmity: executive discretion in the setting, modification, and enforcement of targets; diffusion of responsibilities across national, provincial, and municipal governments; and deference by courts to often opaque forms of executive decision-making. These infirmities result from the Canadian institutional framework to date.

2. Institutional Design in Canada

In addressing institutional design in Canada, we note as an initial matter the existence of some important constraints. Canada is but one small player in a global crisis. For the purposes of this section, we take global institutions as given and focus instead on Canadian institutions. On the one hand, such a focus on domestic institutions clearly leaves critical issues to the side. On the other hand, recent history of domestic adherence to international agreements has been abysmal. While there are many possible explanations for this record, including collective action problems, weak domestic institutions appear to be one factor. Moreover, the Paris Agreement leaves considerable discretion with individual countries to determine their own objectives and means to achieve those objectives. It follows that better institutional design in Canada justifies closer examination despite the importance of international institutions.

Canada's federal structure creates another set of constraints on institutional design. Jurisdiction over climate change policy is divided in Canada across federal, provincial, and municipal governments. Given the national (and indeed international) scope of climate change, there is constitutional authority for federal powers over laws addressing climate change. As noted earlier, the Supreme Court concluded that imposing charges on carbon emissions was within the federal government's authority to act in the face of a national concern, which climate change is.[23] On the other hand, laws and policies that fall within provincial authority are also highly relevant to climate change policy. Provincial energy policy, including provincial gasoline taxes, and the regulation of electricity production, will also influence the provinces' progress towards emissions goals. Municipalities may also contribute to Canadian emissions, through zoning by-laws for example, or through public transportation infrastructure.

Federalism and consequential fragmentation of authority creates challenges, especially from a collective action and coordination perspective, as Green suggests. But there are easily overlooked advantages from decentralization for climate change institutions. Most importantly, decentralized institutions may better respond to local values in making trade-offs between competing values. Federalism is a constraint in Canada, but ought not to be regarded as unambiguously negative.

As a final preliminary observation, we articulate a distinction that we find helpful in designing institutions dealing with scientifically grounded public policy questions: the distinction between risk assessment and risk management.[24] In a climate change context, this requires adopting institutional arrangements that are relatively deferential to climate scientists in projecting potential impacts in a Canadian context of climate change at various levels of global warming, while recognizing that choices among policy instruments for mitigating the risks of climate change and abating the consequences of those that cannot be mitigated require complex normative and empirical judgments and trade-offs across sectors of the economy and regions of the country. Institutional design should take seriously the distinction between risk assessment and risk management. In thinking about a Canadian climate change institution, this distinction has various dimensions of importance, one of which is that much of the risk assessment action takes place at a supra-national level. Canada has joined the international consensus on climate change and has adopted targets accordingly. It follows that for Canadian institutions, considerable focus will be on risk management; that is, how best to achieve the commitments set in the shadow of the Paris Agreement.

We turn next to a proposal to establish a commission of inquiry.

3. *Commission of Inquiry*

It is clear from our review of the challenges confronting climate change institutional design that no institution can be optimal on all dimensions at the same time. Just as substantive climate change policy requires a balancing of competing values, the same is true for institutional design. Any proposed institutions will reflect a compromise. Drawing on a time-honoured and distinctive Canadian institutional tradition for addressing major and intractable policy challenges, we propose the creation of a commission of inquiry into climate change policy, which would become the major national focal point for public debates over climate change policy, a focal point presently sorely lacking. A total of 450 federal inquiries have been commissioned under the Inquiries Act between Confederation and 2014, and many more at the provincial level. These commissions of inquiry have addressed a vast range of policy issues, including federal–provincial fiscal relations, taxation law and policy, trade policy, health care, bilingualism and biculturalism, the status of women, and Indigenous Peoples in Canada. While it is true that these commissions have had a mixed record in influencing subsequent public policy, at their best they can be a major catalyst for policy change. Moreover, by adopting an institutional framework that Canada has relied on many times, our recommendation avoids attempting to create new institutional forms to address climate change, an approach that has been consistently unsuccessful in international experience.[25]

To justify our recommendation, consider again the challenges that climate change institutions confront. There are significant collective action and coordination problems that, on their own, tend to push for centralized institutions. At the same time, there are polycentric trade-offs that, all things equal, push for local authorities to make decisions that reflect local preferences. There is scientific and technological uncertainty that calls for reliance on experts, but cognitive biases on the part of citizens that push for institutions that are perceived broadly as trustworthy. Moreover, a scientific expert may be attuned to risk assessment but may not necessarily be an expert sensitive to the polycentric trade-offs necessary for managing that risk. A commission, with an appropriate mandate and appropriate membership, responds to these challenges.

With respect to mandate, the commission should be charged with identifying mitigation and abatement policies that reduce emissions and meet existing targets at least economic cost. In other words, given the existence of international agreements and associated commitments, the commission would not be charged with risk assessment but rather risk management. The commission would be responsible for identifying a fair distribution of these costs across regions of the country and sectors of the economy, especially with respect to subclasses of disadvantaged consumers who are ill-equipped to bear any additional costs from these policies and subsets of workers whose employment security may be prejudiced by these policies. Dealing fairly with the adverse impact of climate change policies on our least advantaged citizens will be crucial to forging public and political consensus on effective policies moving forward.[26] Relatedly, the commission ought to pay close heed to communications strategies, attempting to overcome biases that will affect reactions to its recommendations.[27] The commission's mandate would also include a review of appropriate divisions of policy responsibilities between national, provincial, and municipal governments within the flexibilities permitted by the current Canadian Constitution. These recommendations should take seriously the trade-offs between the need for coordination to address collective action problems and the desirability of having different regions settle the vexing trade-offs inherent in climate change management according to local preferences.[28]

As to the composition of the commission, we favour a commission of 10–12 members serving in their personal capacities but reflecting regional, sectoral, and Indigenous sensitivities and broad prior experience in the policymaking process. Reflecting the tension between sensitivity to regional preferences over polycentric policy questions and the importance of coordination, we recommend that the members reflect geographical diversity across Canada; that is, while we contemplate a federal structure, it ought to be representative geographically. We also regard it as necessary, but far from sufficient, to have climate expertise on the commission. A climate change expert would be welcome, but the balance of the commission ought to reflect different perspectives. For example, economic, labour, and business expertise would be helpful. Political expertise and experience in government or civil service would also be helpful, in part to ensure that communications are politically savvy in addressing citizens' cognitive biases, and in part to ensure that there is commission expertise in the choice of policy instrument and design.

We would impose one important constraint on such appointees: that they are all committed to the view that climate change poses a serious social and economic problem and warrants serious governmental policy responses, but does not warrant closing down the economy and most of us returning to living off the land, reflecting an extreme view of the potential impacts of climate change espoused by some environmentalists.[29] At the same time, members ought not to believe that anthropogenically driven climate change is a hoax of one kind or another and should be ignored, or left to future unspecified technological innovations to address if and when such innovations emerge. Both these extreme views are not helpful to real-world climate change policymaking.[30]

While identifying specifics regarding process is beyond the scope of this chapter, drawing on a recent book on public inquiries by one of us,[31] including personal involvements in such inquiries and lessons learned from such involvements, certain process considerations are important to the success of the commission. The commission should be given clear timelines (such as a short discussion paper focusing on the issues under deliberation within three months of creation, public submissions within six months, and an interim report within a year) and clear expectations of deliverables. Experience shows that leadership of commissions is crucial. We favour the appointment of a chair of the commission with a long and highly respected record of public service and close familiarity with both the domestic and international dimensions of climate change policy. We imagine supporting the commission with a small but seasoned multidisciplinary research staff reflecting expertise in climate change science; choice of policy instruments; political science/public administration in terms of the practicalities of policy implementation, to provide syntheses, or to commission syntheses, of relevant literature and comparative experience; and a public communications specialist.

While a commission provides an impetus for policy and legal reform, it cannot implement change. That is appropriate: the political nature of decision-making on climate change policy requires political authority and accountability. Recognizing the importance of political accountability for polycentric, political policy choices, and building on the United Kingdom experience with its Climate Change Committee, we propose that the federal government through its elected representatives would be free to reject or modify the recommendations of the commission (which we envisage would be reporting to the Prime Minister), but would be required to provide public reasons for rejections or modifications. While we envision a national commission of inquiry, we recommend that provincial authorities also be invited to respond to its recommendations, which will include an allocation of responsibility across jurisdictions. We envisage that the commission's mandate would extend beyond the first year or so of its initial report, which might accord high priority to policy interventions required progressively to meet the federal government's 2030 targets, but would thereafter focus primarily on progressively meeting the government's longer-term 2050 net zero emissions target. It would also periodically re-evaluate the implementation and efficacy of prior recommendations, as well as the realism of the government's near-term and long-term targets currently reflected in Canada's Nationally Determined Contributions under the Paris Agreement. It would also monitor closely the evolution of effective international cooperative agreements and the case for unilateral or coordinated border measures with respect to imports from countries that have failed to commit to effective measures to achieve comparable emission reduction targets.

V. Conclusion

Canada's record to date in moving forward effectively on the climate change policy agenda is somewhere between weak and abysmal, and a business-as-usual approach to future policymaking in this context is an almost certain guarantee of failure. Our proposal draws on a substantial scholarly literature on the role and efficacy of commissions of inquiry in Canada, as well as work by one of the authors on such inquiries and lessons learned from his personal involvement. While our proposal is no doubt open to refinement, improvement, or counterproposals, the time for handwaving, handwringing, and vacuities in effective Canadian climate change policy is over.

NOTES

1 Richard Lazarus, "Super-Wicked Problems and Climate Change" (2009) 94 Cornell L Rev 1153.
2 For short and accessible accounts of climate change science, see Lawrence Krauss, *The Physics of Climate Change* (New York: Boot Hill Press, 2021) and Kerry Emanuel, *What We Know about Climate Change* (Boston: MIT Press, 2018). See also Michael Mann, *Our Fragile Moment: How Lessons from Earth's Past Can Help Us Survive the Climate Crisis* (New York: Public Affairs, 2023). For a more sceptical view of mainstream understandings of climate science, see Steven Koonin, *Unsettled? What Climate Change Science Tells Us, What It Doesn't, Why It Matters* (Dallas: Ben Bella Books, 2020). Rather than making certain predictions one way or the other, the Intergovernmental Panel on Climate Change assigns various degrees of confidence in its predictions that range from virtually certain to extremely unlikely: see IPCC, *Climate Change 2021: The Physical Science Basis*, Valérie Masson-Delmotte et al, eds (Geneva: IPCC, 2021), online (pdf): <https://www.ipcc.ch/report/ar6/wg1/downloads/report/IPCC_AR6_WGI_SPM_final.pdf>.
3 Cass Sunstein, *Averting Catastrophe* (New York: NYU Press, 2021), online: <https://doi.org/10.18574/nyu/9781479808502.001.0001>; Toby Ord, *The Precipice: Existential Risk and the Future of Humanity* (New York: Hachette Books, 2020); Gernot Wagner & Martin Weitzman, *Climate Shock* (Princeton, NJ: Princeton University Press, 2015).
4 Bill Gates, *How to Avoid a Climate Catastrophe* (New York: Alfred Knopf, 2021); Vaclav Smil, *How the World Really Works* (Toronto: Viking, 2022). For a more optimistic view, see Mark Jacobson, *No Miracles Needed* (New York: Cambridge University Press, 2023).
5 For an extensive review of this literature see Joseph Heath, *Enlightenment 2* (Toronto: Harper Collins, 2014); see also e.g., Daniel Kahnemann, *Thinking Fast and Slow* (New York: Farrar, Strauss & Giroux, 2013); Jonathan Haidt, *The Righteous Mind* (New York: Random House, 2013); David Moscrop, *Too Dumb for Democracy?* (New Brunswick: Goose Lane, 2019).
6 See Andrew Hoffman, *How Culture Shapes the Climate Change Debate* (Palo Alto: Stanford University Press, 2015).
7 Alan Jacobs, *Governing for the Long Term* (Cambridge: Cambridge University Press, 2011).
8 See William MacAskill, *What We Owe the Future* (New York: Hachette Books, 2022).

9 Joseph Heath, *Philosophical Foundations of Climate Change Policy* (New York: Oxford University Press 2021), online: <https://doi.org/10.1093/oso/9780197567982.001.0001>.
10 See Andrew Green, *Picking Up the Slack* (Toronto: University of Toronto Press, 2022), online <https://doi.org/10.3138/9781487553319>.
11 *References re Greenhouse Gas Pollution Pricing Act* 2021 SCC 11.
12 Fukuyama describes the US system as a "vetocracy" that preclude many major policy initiatives at the national level: Francis Fukuyama, *Liberalism and Its Discontents* (New York: Farrar, Strauss and Giroux, 2022).
13 See, e.g., Jutta Brunnée, "International Climate Law in Precarious Times" in this volume; Scott Barrett, *Why Co-operate? The Incentive to Supply Global Public Goods* (New York: Oxford University Press, 2007), online: <https://doi.org/10.1093/acprof:oso/9780199211890.003.0001>.
14 See Brunnée, *supra* note 13.
15 See William Nordhaus, "The Climate Club" May/June 2020 Foreign Aff 1.
16 *Paris Agreement to the United Nations Framework Convention on Climate Change*, 3156 UNTS (adopted 12 December 2015 and entered into force 4 November 2016).
17 Brunnée, *supra* note 13.
18 See Hoffman, *supra* note 6.
19 John Kay and Mervyn King, *Radical Uncertainty: Decision-Making for an Unknowable Future* (London: Bridge Street Press, 2021).
20 Dubash et al, "National Climate Institutions to Complement Targets and Policies" (2021) 374:6568 Science 690, online: <https://doi.org/10.1126/science.abm1157>.
21 These summary observations are helpfully elaborated on in some detail by the lead author in an introduction to a special issue of Environmental Politics comprising the eight case studies: Navroz Dubash, "Varieties of Climate Governance: The Emergence and Functioning of Climate Institutions" (2021) 30 Environ Pol 1–25, online: <https://doi.org/10.1080/09644016.2021.1979775>.
22 Green, *supra* note 10; see also William Leiss, *Canada and Climate Change* (Montreal: McGill-Queen's Press, 2022), online: <https://doi.org/10.1515/9780228009856>.
23 *References re Greenhouse Gas Pollution Pricing Act*, *supra* note 11.
24 See Edward Iacobucci & Michael Trebilcock, *Existential Threats: Climate Change, Pandemics and Institutions* (2022) 65:4 Can Pub Adm 1, online: <https://doi.org/10.1111/capa.12504>.
25 Dubash et al., *supra* note 20.
26 See Michael Trebilcock, *Dealing with Losers: The Political Economy of Policy Transitions* (New York: Oxford University Press, 2014), online: <https://doi.org/10.1093/acprof:oso/9780199370658.001.0001>.

27 See Hoffman, *supra* note 6.

28 In addition to focusing on mitigation policies, the Commission's mandate should include abatement policies given that past and current greenhouse emissions are "baked in" for several more decades, implying that effective responses to severe weather events that cannot now be avoided must be an important element in the policy menu. See Alice Hill & Leonardo Martinez-Diaz, *Building a Resilient Tomorrow* (New York: Oxford University Press, 2020), online: <https://doi.org/10.1093/oso/9780190909345.001.0001>.

29 See Wes Jackson & Robert Jensen, *An Inconvenient Apocalypse* (Notre Dame, IN: University of Notre Dame Press, 2022).

30 See, e.g., Alessio Terzi *Growth for Good: Reshaping Capitalism to Save Humanity from Climate Catastrophe* (Cambridge: Harvard University Press, 2022), online: <https://doi.org/10.4159/9780674276338>; Wagner & Weitzman, *supra* note 3.

31 Michael Trebilcock, *Public Inquiries: A Scholar's Engagements with the Policy-Making Process* (Toronto: University of Toronto Press, 2022), online: <https://doi.org/10.3138/9781487553975>.

PART TWO

Law and Justice in Times of (Climate) Change

5 Reconciling the State's Obligations in Respect of the Climate and Housing Crises

OLIVIA O'CONNOR AND CHRISTOPHER ESSERT

I. Conflict

One feature of the climate crisis is its pervasive impact: there seems to be almost no area of law or politics (or life more generally) that will remain untouched by this unprecedented challenge. In this chapter, we begin to explore a framework for thinking about an instance of this broader phenomenon – the conflict between the climate crisis and the housing crisis. Canada, along with many other jurisdictions, is facing a severe shortage of housing. Given the plausible thought that the state has a duty to ensure that each of its subjects has a home, this housing shortage is something that the state is obligated to address, possibly by ensuring that more homes are built. But building homes – like building more of anything in general – is a major source of greenhouse gas (GHG) emissions. An unconstrained program to build all the units of housing that Canada currently needs has the potential to generate GHG emissions far above any reasonable assessment of our "climate budget" and, consequently, to put the state's obligations in respect of the climate out of reach. We thus appear to have a conflict between two different and pressing state duties. Our goal here is not to solve this problem – that will take several different steps, some of which we consider elsewhere[1] – but to propose a framework for thinking about it. We hope that this framework will, in addition to its benefits in this context, be of broader application, because this is not the only context in which the state's duties in respect of the climate might be at odds with its other duties. This chapter proceeds as follows: in section II, we present our understanding of the nature of the state's duties in relation to the climate; in section III, we do the same with respect to housing. We then show, in section IV, how we can draw from an important developing strand in constitutional theory to approach the problem generated by the tension between these duties.

II. Climate

Our first step is to clarify what we mean when we refer to the climate, not as a scientific matter, but as a legal matter, that is, as a subject matter in respect of which we have legal rights and duties. The climate can be understood as a condition on collective human existence that engages questions about what it means to live together in a just society: a healthy and stable climate is a requirement for, and a part of the shared condition that is partly constitutive of, a rights-based liberal democracy like Canada. Because of this, we think that the climate can be thought of as a public good – like public transportation, public parks, public rights of way, or herd immunity – in respect of which we all have distinctly public rights and duties.

Public goods, as we understand them here, have a couple of important features.[2] First, they are necessary to and partially constitutive of the possibility of our living together in a democratic society, a society that takes seriously an idea of equal standing, according to which no person is subordinated to any other. In other words, we cannot have a liberal democracy without them because without a given public good, the members of the society would be faced with some problem of subordination. For example, without public rights of way – roads, sidewalks, and so on – there would be a problem about the possibility of getting from one place to another without the leave of private owners of land[3]; without parks and other forms of public space, important egalitarian elements of democratic societies (involving expression and association, for instance) would be unavailable.[4]

In our context, we already introduced the basic thought: without a healthy climate, human existence itself becomes, at the limit, impossible. Furthermore, environmental degradation and climate change continue to threaten the integrity of our institutions, the infrastructure we rely upon, and our society more generally. Liberal democracies concerned with sustaining themselves must respond. Germany's Federal Constitutional Court acknowledged this insight in a landmark 2021 decision that recognized climate protection as a necessary "precondition" to freedom in a liberal democratic society.[5] The Supreme Court of Canada (SCC) recently upheld the Federal government's GHG pricing scheme as a matter of national concern falling under the federal legislature's power to legislate for the "peace, order, and good government" of Canada (the "POGG" power).[6] The SCC acknowledged that climate change poses a grave existential threat to Canada as a whole. Unlike in the German decision, the SCC did not state that the government must take particular action vis-à-vis climate change. It only stated that the government *could* do so and, further, was silent as to the place of the climate in Canadian democracy. Nevertheless, it is possible to understand the POGG power as a response to a problem about rightful coexistence and public goods, which arises in our particular federal context, allowing the federal legislature jurisdiction to address serious issues of national importance that cannot be addressed by the provinces acting individually or together. POGG, so understood, entitles the Parliament to provide for certain public goods, one of them being a national, unified approach to GHG regulation (in the form of a carbon price).

The second important feature of public goods is their publicness. Public goods must be provided by public authorities because the nature of the good in question is inconsistent with its being provided privately (that is, provided as a contingent result of individual choices and preferences). The entitlements we hold as members of a public cannot be conditional upon exercises of private choice if they are to actually solve the problems of subordination justifying and necessitating those entitlements in the first place. In the cases of public rights of way and other public spaces, it is up to private landowners how others may use their land. There is nothing objectionable, as a matter of private law, in a private landowner saying that others may not cross their land, but when that same unobjectionable refusal is made by every other private landowner, everyone is left with no way to get to where they want to go without the leave of another. The problem here is not just that you cannot get where you want to go but also that your going anywhere at all is dependent on what others are willing to permit.[7] Recourse to the level of the public is necessary to solve this problem. And just as people's basic ability to move around in space is not the sort of thing that should be left up to the choices of others, but rather is a public good that must be guaranteed by the state, we might similarly think that the climate's role in a liberal democracy means that the state must take responsibility for ensuring it is healthy and stable.

Another consideration going to the distinctly, and exclusively, public nature of public goods is that the problem to which any given public good is a solution often arises out of the cumulative effects of the otherwise unobjectionable acts of individual private persons. We can assume for our purposes that there is nothing objectionable about the emission of GHGs as such. However, as experience is demonstrating with a vengeance, when everyone emits GHGs at high levels, we end up with a cumulative level of emissions that is unsustainable. This situation must be understood structurally, or perhaps systematically: it is a situation that can be understood somehow at the same time as nobody's fault and everybody's fault. Legal regulation of GHG emissions needs to account for this structure by recognizing the climate as something fundamentally public in the relevant sense. In other words, the rightness or wrongness of our actions with respect to the climate as a public good is not a question of a particular harm that occurs between individual persons: the clearest way to understand the wrongfulness of an individual's excessive GHG emissions does not seem to refer to a discrete, particular harm that can be meaningfully linked to those emissions. Rather, we should think about our legal situation here in terms of our status as members of an institutionally constituted public that currently permits individual contributions whose cumulative effects demand a response. Because the problem arises at the systemic level – at the level of the public – the solution does, too. Hence, we need public rules about permissible GHG emissions, including, potentially, at something like a per-person level. The justification for setting per-person GHG entitlements in a relatively direct way flows from the climate's status as a public good: each person's right to "use" the climate by, *inter alia*, emitting GHGs, is set and constrained by a public determination as to the proper scope of that entitlement.

Within this structure of the climate as a public good, we can see that the state has an obligation to solve the problem. The problem is fundamentally public, and so cannot properly be solved by regulating private persons. This generates an obligation on the state, embodying the public, to set rules that instantiate – whether in process or outcome – its overall mandate of ensuring rightful coexistence between equal citizens. We can helpfully think of these rules in terms of our holding a public right or owing a public duty. An important extension of this idea is that the rightness or wrongness of our actions vis-à-vis the climate is not a question of whether we impose some benefit or burden on some person or persons in particular, but rather of whether we follow the rules that constitute our entitlements as members of the public. In a democratic society, the rules that constitute an entitlement regarding a public good ought to represent public determinations arrived at according to what is a process of broadly democratic rulemaking. Understood in this way, these rules have a close (arguably, partially constitutive) relationship with liberal democracy. Adherence to them is not just required because, by stipulation, one's legal interaction with a public good can only be public, but also because following public rules in respect of distinctly public goods is essential to rightful coexistence.

Understanding the legal structure of the climate as a public good allows us to understand how the state has an obligation to do its part in protecting a stable and healthy climate. There is a lot of room here for institutional discretion as to the right way to accomplish this public purpose. In actual practice, one possible option is the state's enacting rules that set limits on the GHG emissions any person, or organization, could have.[8] These rules could restrict, compel, or incentivize behaviour in various ways (as with, for instance, Canada's federal GHG pricing system). More specific to our present context, it seems as though it would be within the state's purview, pursuant to something like a general society-wide climate budget, to set rules around how much housing space people could possess, given the environmental impacts of construction and the fact that construction of larger homes generates more GHGs than construction of smaller homes.[9] But we should notice that setting such rules – as either a lower or upper bound – could engage the right to housing and that such a limit would need to be justified.

III. Housing

In this section, we explain the nature and justification of a right to adequate housing or, as we prefer to think of it, the right to a home. We will be brief in this section because our concern is ultimately the reconciliation of this right with its climate implications.[10]

The essence of the idea of a right to adequate housing begins from the recognition that a home is a legally constituted thing: what makes your home yours is, first and foremost, the legal entitlements that you have in it, the fact that, in your home, it is up to you how others can act. One way to see this is by noting that someone can be housed in a space that belongs to another but still homeless: the "hidden homeless," who live with friends or relatives (legally as licensees rather than tenants), are homeless precisely because what they do in the space where they live is subject to the control of someone else. When we talk about providing homes, to the homeless or in general, we are talking about providing legal control over a space. This legal control is important because it is constitutive of the possibility of doing the sorts of things we do at home, and standing as a full member of a liberal egalitarian democracy requires the capacity to do these things without the leave of another.

Our homes are the site of many important and valuable parts of our social world: they are where we eat, sleep, bathe, and engage in ways of doing and being associated with one's more intimate life, whatever that might look like; they are where we host friends and family, in casual settings and for important cultural and religious rituals; they are where we study, where we engage in hobbies, where we surf the internet, where (lately, for better or worse) many of us work. The reason that homelessness is such a pressing social problem is that to be homeless is to lack a place where one can do any of these things without being under the control of someone else.[11] The value of a home from the viewpoint of the legal system is that it is a space that one has a legal right to control, and this legal control makes it into a space in which one can choose if or when to engage in these activities, with whom, and under what conditions. In a slogan: homes are constitutive of a broad and important set of activities and relations that make up our social world. A right to a home is a right to be able to participate in those activities and relations as an equal member of society, in other words, to not be subordinated with respect to them.

A full elaboration of the right to a home might be divided into three distinct elements. The first is the nature of the legal control over the space: here is where questions about the scope of private rights of action in trespass and nuisance or about the rights of tenants versus owners would be broached. We say nothing about that here, except what we said already: a home requires sufficient legal rights over the space such that one can understand it as, in fact, one's own home.[12] The second is about the nature of the state's duty to end homelessness and provide homes to all of its subjects. This is a complex issue that we cannot explore in detail here. But the basic idea can be stated as follows: an institution of private property, as the only way that can ensure that we can relate to one another on morally acceptable terms in respect of activities in space, including those activities constitutive of a home, brings with it as a part of its own justification a duty on the state to ensure that the institution does not subordinate any of those subject to it by ensuring that each has a home of their own. The justification of a system of property demands that the state strive to ensure that the operation of the system does not itself subordinate anyone in respect of property, and part of the way to do so is to ensure that everyone has an adequate home.[13]

The third element of the elaboration of the right to a home concerns the physical characteristics of a home: what, as a matter of architecture and engineering, are we talking about when we talk about an adequate home?[14] The abstract idea provides the starting point. A home needs to be a space that is sufficiently large and sufficiently well-organized to allow its inhabitants to participate as an equal in a sufficiently wide range of the kinds of activities and relations that are constituted by this idea of a home.[15] It is clear that the empirical criteria cannot stand on their own: no matter how strong the legal protections involved, a 2 m^2 space simply could not count as a sufficient home in our social world given the extremely limited uses that could be made of it; to similar effect, a hallway 1 m wide and 200 m long would have the area of a large home, but would not provide its "residents" much, if anything, of the central value of a home, because it would not really be possible to do very much in that space.

But while this normative legal idea of a home can rule out certain proposals, it does, importantly, leave a significant scope for institutional discretion. The idea of a home cannot tell us that a home for a single adult needs to be 18 m^2 rather than 17 m^2: if one of those is an available option, the other must surely be, too. Moreover, notice that the kind of space that can count as a home is surely something that depends on the relevant social and historical conditions of the society in question: a home sufficient to stand as an equal means something different in Canada than in Singapore, something different in 2022 than it did in 1822. Importantly, the egalitarian character of a home – the way that homes allow us to relate as equals – suggests that the way that the social and historical context is relevant in determining adequacy is at least partly comparative: if everyone else has a home of x m^2, we might be entitled to assume that a home of that size would enable an appropriate range of activities and relations, such that a home of 0.1x m^2 would, as a social matter, be inferior, as the range of activities and relations possible for this tiny home's inhabitants would be significantly constrained as compared to the social norm, such that possessing such a space would not give them what, in their society, counted as the central egalitarian value of a home. At the same time – and especially in our present context, where the whole point of our inquiry is to recognize the climate impacts of residential construction – we cannot allow equality here to generate an inexorably one-way ratchet: there is a sort of a problem of expensive tastes here, one that plausibly is at the root of the very problem we are trying to solve. But the historical and social contingency of the content of the right to a home does mean that what counts as adequate will be, to some extent, a function of what is generally available.

More positively, we can see how the abstract normative idea of a home can be brought to bear on otherwise normatively inert social facts to help us generate a more-or-less determinate specification of what a home needs to be in the context of a particular social setting. In other words, if we begin with the idea that a home needs to be a space in which its inhabitants can participate in the sorts of activities and relations that homes are for in our specific historical and social context, then we can look around and gather a reasonable conception of what those activities and relations are. A home, here and now, is a space for eating and sleeping and watching I Love Lucy and having dinner parties and celebrating birthdays and playing Monopoly and having Zoom calls. Human beings, naturally and socially constituted as we are, need certain kinds of spaces and spatial arrangements to do those things: an appropriate number of bedrooms and bathrooms, a kitchen, some common space, and so on. As in many other areas of the law, these social facts are always subject to the oversight of the abstract normative value: the mere fact that everyone is doing something cannot on its own make doing that thing acceptable, but the fact that everyone is doing something might be a helpful clue in our search for what is acceptable and, fundamentally, what we must be able to do to relate as equals in our particular societies.[16]

Therefore, we can see that what counts as an adequate home is in part a socially constituted idea.[17] This is a central part of our account. What the state is obligated to provide in terms of adequate homes is something that needs to be reconciled with the state's duties in terms of the climate. The benefit of our understanding of the right to a home is in part its inherent malleability. The characteristics of adequacy can only be spelled out in the "here and now," and our present "here and now" is a world in climate crisis. This leads us to the question of reconciliation.

IV. Reconciliation

We saw that the state is obligated to take urgent steps to address the climate crisis, as the climate can be understood as a public good partly constitutive of the very possibility of such a society, and that the state has an obligation to ensure that its members are adequately housed, but that this obligation leaves a relatively wide scope for what sizes and types of physical spaces are required. We know that larger spaces generally generate larger climate impacts. This seems to put the two obligations so far considered in tension. Determining how much housing should be built will require a justified, proportionate response to the apparently conflicting rights engaged.

The kind of rights people ought to have in terms of housing and the climate require that the state take positive action to ensure them. Where one right is limited in apparent furtherance of the other – as would be the case if housing space entitlements were curtailed to reduce climate impacts, or if housing construction occurs beyond the bound of what is ideal from the climate perspective – this limitation needs to be, all things considered, necessary from the perspective of rightful coexistence. We can further understand permissible state action vis-à-vis housing and climate rights as constrained by two duties. The first is an obligation not to do *too little* in respect of each right: the state must neither actively damage the possibility of our living together rightfully nor, by omission, fail to see to its realization.[18] On this account, states including Canada have engaged in egregious violations of the public's right to a healthy and stable climate, in failing to act on climate change. Housing rights have also been violated as the state has failed to ensure that homes are available to everyone in our society. Clearly, much more must be done in respect of both these rights.[19]

Difficulties arise, of course, where the world as we find it permits the possibility and then the actuality of conflict between the more determined instances of rightful coexistence to which we are entitled.[20] Here enters the second duty constraining the state: a (more familiar) obligation not to introduce unjustifiable limitations on the rights engaged by state action – that is, to not do *too much* by introducing limitations that are not in pursuit of a legitimate end or that infringe the right in question more than is necessary.[21] Fundamentally, when we understand the question of conflicting rights as an exercise in articulating, as best as possible, the terms of existence that will realize a society of equals, these two obligations are just the same duty approached from different directions: the overarching idea is simply the idea of rightful coexistence in a society of equals.

Understanding when a certain limitation is justified necessitates a process of reasoning whereby the rights in question – here, the right to housing and the right to a safe and healthy climate – are read together.[22] Rather than weighing the rights against one another and aiming to find a middle ground, or trying to determine which interest preponderates in a given instance, an idea of reconciliation aims to bring the rights into accord,[23] thus understanding them as each being partly constitutive of rightful coexistence a society of equals. With this in view, we can now mention a few points about what a proportionate reconciliation between housing and climate rights might look like. As with any question of rights limitation, context is everything. This is not the forum to examine in detail the kind of information required for context-sensitive analysis of reconciliation. But something can be said about the form of the problem, along with some preliminary observations about the status quo and some possible future scenarios.

In thinking through the apparent tension between the state's obligations in respect of housing and the climate, it is helpful to notice that whereas it seems quite hard to arrive at a non-arbitrary quantitative metric of adequate housing space, climate change is a very numbers-friendly issue; it lends itself well to (and requires) the setting of quantitative rules. Further, it is instructive to notice that while the right to a home does not generate much by way of hard numerical limits, there are ascertainable upper bounds vis-à-vis the climate, beyond which lies something like unmitigable catastrophe.[24] Because of this, if we want to arrive at a quantitative minimum for space entitlements, we might do well to work from the great many quantitative things the climate has to say on the matter.

It is possible that in determining total and individual climate-impact entitlements, the state would articulate rules setting out per-person ceilings and allocate resources among areas (e.g., housing, transit, infrastructure, etc.) according to a determination of policy. In doing so, it would be open to the state to set maximum housing space entitlements and, in accounting for individual rights to adequate housing, to also set minimums (which may or may not be set partially according to climate considerations). An inquiry into whether such a minimum was justified would begin by asking whether, given the minimum in question, a conflict actually arises. It may well be the case that such a figure allows for totally adequate homes.[25]

In between two extremes – one an unjustifiable infringement of housing rights, the other an unjustifiable infringement of public rights in the climate – there should be some point, though not necessarily one that falls squarely between them, where housing and climate rights can be proportionately reconciled. At this point of reconciliation, each right would stand in the fullest expression that could be achieved while minimally impacting the other, and each deviation from the total fulfillment of one right would be necessary to the furtherance of the other.[26] The relations between the rights would be the one that best articulated and instantiated the determining ideal of how best we can coexist as equals in a liberal democracy.

That said, we should be careful not to collapse the two distinct rights at play into one broad inquiry. The rights are both analytically and normatively distinct, and we should further notice that assessing whether a given state of affairs constitutes a proportionate reconciliation involves two technically discrete, though closely enmeshed, proportionality inquiries. For each limitation, we would ask whether the incursion is necessary, or if there is another, milder way of giving effect to the promoted right. We might inquire into whether what the state aims to provide or do overshoots what is necessary to fulfill the right, and whether the state's chosen means impact the relevant right to the least extent possible. Because the aim is to bring both rights into their fullest possible expression, we would also want to ask if the state had failed to take advantage of opportunities for positive synergies between housing and climate (for example, by requiring housing to be built using the most GHG efficient materials available). If, for each of housing and climate rights, the respective limitation was necessary, as mild as possible, and sufficiently in furtherance of the other right, the limitation would be justified. Again, this would be a very context-heavy inquiry. For instance, poorly designed homes might be needlessly large and thus needlessly productive of GHG emissions, where better-designed but smaller homes could be just as adequate from the viewpoint of the right to housing and productive of fewer GHGs: the suggestion here that the two rights need to be approached together shows how the second option would be preferable.[27] A related idea is that imposing an upper-bound on the amount of housing that could be built for or inhabited by a single person would have significant positive impacts on the state's ability to give effect to the right to housing while also pursuing climate targets. Prohibiting the construction of needlessly large homes (or perhaps imposing a prohibitive tax on those who choose to inhabit existing ones) would not infringe the right to housing but would allow the state to set a higher minimum housing entitlement. It may well be the case that the state is obliged to set such maximums to proportionately reconcile the right to housing and the public's right to a healthy and stable climate.

Our purpose here has not been to engage in such an inquiry in detail. We do that elsewhere, in stages, and in collaboration with others. But the legal-theoretic problem we have aimed to work through here is an essential part of the story. Climate change is an existential threat, to be sure, but we remain convinced that it is one that can, and should, be approached using the tools appropriate to a liberal democracy. Our hope is that the foregoing provides some assistance in that difficult but essential task.

Acknowledgments

This chapter arose out of some work done with Shoshanna Saxe, of the Department of Civil and Mining Engineering, and Gabriel Eidelman, of the Munk School of Global Affairs and Public Policy. For comments on earlier drafts and discussion of these issues, we're grateful to Saxe and Eidelman, as well as Andrew Green, Steve Lorteau, Jacob Weinrib, and the editors of this volume.

NOTES

1 Olivia O'Connor et al, "Adequate Housing Size as an Element of the Right to Housing" (2024) Intl J Housing Policy, online: <https://doi.org/10.1080/19491247.2024.2417320>.
2 There may be some overlap here with "public goods" as understood by economists (non-excludable, non-rivalrous), but we understand the concept in a different sense.

3 See Arthur Ripstein, *Force and Freedom* (Cambridge: Harvard University Press, 2009) at 243–50, online: <https://doi.org/10.4159/9780674054516>.
4 See Christopher Essert, "The Nature and Value of Public Space (With Some Lessons from the Pandemic)" (2022) 50 Fordham Urb LJ 61.
5 Federal Constitutional Court, Karlsruhe, 24 March 2021 (2021) Order of 24–04–21, 1 BvR 2656/18 (Germany).
6 *References re Greenhouse Gas Pollution Pricing Act*, 2021 SCC 11.
7 This is why a "private" solution to this problem, whereby landowners would bargain for the right to pass over others' land, can never solve the problem of subordination to which public rights of way are a response. See Ripstein, *supra* note 3 at 249.
8 To be clear, the claim here is that this is an available option for a state. We make no claims about how this option compares to or interacts with others that have (or have not) been tried, including various forms of taxation, except to say that, surely, an effective climate policy will require many different and complementary elements.
9 Aldrich Arceo et al, "Capturing Variability in Material Intensity of Single-Family Dwellings: A Case Study of Toronto, Canada" (2021) 175 Resour Conserv Recycl 105885, online: <https://doi.org/10.1016/j.resconrec.2021.105885>.
10 For an expansion of the arguments here (and replies to various objections we do not have space to consider), see Christopher Essert, "Homeless as a Legal Phenomenon," in Nicole Graham, Margaret Davies & Lee Godden, eds, *The Routledge Handbook of Property, Law and Society* (New York: Routledge, 2022) 137, online: <https://doi.org/10.4324/9781003139614-14>; Christopher Essert, "What Makes a Home: A Reply" (2022) 41 Law & Phil 469, online: <https://doi.org/10.1007/s10982-021-09438-2>; Christopher Essert, "Property and Homelessness" (2016) 44 Philos Public Aff 266, online: <https://doi.org/10.1111/papa.12080> [Essert, "Property and Homelessness"].
11 And we can say the same thing, adjusted appropriately, about housing that is inadequate in the sense described below: someone with inadequate housing has, at best, a home that is defective in the relevant respect.
12 Ownership and legal tenancy both count as control in the relevant sense. See Essert, "Property and Homelessness," *supra* note 10 at 285.
13 This is the argument in Christopher Essert, *Property Law in the Society of Equals,* (Oxford University Press, 2024).
14 Questions about location are relevant under this heading, too, but we lack space to address them here.
15 Notably, a well-designed space can reduce the need for size in absolute terms, to a certain extent.

16 This is a familiar point in the law of torts, exemplified by Learned Hand's judgment in *The TJ Hooper*, 60 F (2d) 737 (1932).

17 And in part, it is straightforwardly *not* socially constituted: whatever the social context, a home is a place over which one has legal control.

18 Dieter Grimm, "The Protective Function of the State" in Georg Nolte, ed, *European and US Constitutionalism* (Cambridge: Cambridge University Press, 2005) 137, online: <https://doi.org/10.1017/CBO9780511493904.011>.

19 An important question that we mostly set aside here asks about the possibility that climate goals require the imposition of maximum home sizes for homes built through market processes. It is likely that they do, but this situation raises a different kind of problem than the one that confronts us here, since it involves (roughly) a conflict between private rights and public purposes. Our intuition here is that such maximums would be uncontroversially permissible from the perspective of a right to housing, so long as they did not prevent the construction of adequate homes.

20 The analytical sequence of possibility to actuality to proportionality is drawn from Jacob Weinrib, *Dimensions of Dignity: The Theory and Practice of Modern Constitutional Law* (Cambridge: Cambridge University Press, 2016) ch 7, online: <https://doi.org/10.1017/CBO9781316026663>.

21 Grimm, *supra* note 18.

22 These thoughts are inspired by the German constitutional doctrine of "Practical Concordance" (Praktische Konkordanz). See Thilo Marauhn & Nadine Ruppel, "Balancing Conflicting Human Rights: Konrad Hesse's Notion of 'Praktische Konkordanz' and the German Federal Constitutional Court" in Eva Brems, ed, *Conflicts between Fundamental Rights* (Cambridge: Intersentia, 2018) 273.

23 Frank Iacobucci, "'Reconciling Rights': the Supreme Court of Canada's Approach to Competing Charter Rights" (2003) 20 SCLR 137, online: <https://doi.org/10.60082/2563-8505.1038>; Marauhn & Ruppel, *supra* note 22.

24 IPCC, *Climate Change 2022: Mitigation of Climate Chane (Working Group III Contribution to the Sixth Assessment Report of the Intergovernmental Penal on Climate Change)* (Geneva: Intergovernmental Panel on Climate Change, UN, 2022).

25 At this initial stage of asking whether there is a conflict between the rights in actuality, the way that homes are designed will be important. Depending on the gross amount of space, good design can make the difference between realizing and not realizing the right to housing. On our account, the state has an obligation not just to justify infringements, but, of course, to prevent them before they arise, including by ensuring housing is well designed.

26 Grimm, *supra* note 18; Heiner Bielefeldt, "Limiting Permissible Limitations: How to Preserve the Substance of Religious Freedom" (2020) 15 Relig Human Rights 3, online: <https://doi.org/10.1163/18710328-BJA10001>.

27 Understanding conflicts of rights in this way has the added benefit of possibly revealing positive synergies between the rights as they interact in the world. Hence, for instance, legislators might mandate that new housing be constructed in a way that reduces the urban heat-island effect, facilitates meaningful access to public transit, or efficiently uses the vertical space available to a building. Where such synergies in a situation of conflicting rights are identifiable and go unpursued, the state has gone too far in that it has provided for an unjustified infringement (as the infringement is not, all things considered, the mildest way of achieving the sought-after objective) *and* has done too little in failing to bring the involved rights into the fullest possible accord. In a more ideal world – one without the myriad constraining contextual factors that make conflicts of rights possible in our own – the best articulation of any and all rights would just be something like a total fulfilment. This is quite simply what each right, read alone, demands. Any deviation, then, from complete fulfillment of each conflicting right needs to be justified. This is, of course, just another way of saying that both rights need to be brought into the fullest possible accord.

6 Shifting Appetites: The Impact of Animal Agriculture on Climate Change and Plant-Based Diets as a Solution

ANGELA FERNANDEZ AND KRYSTAL-ANNE ROUSSEL

We have to live, we have to give this place to the kids with the animals still alive and a chance to make a living. That's not too much to ask.

– Kim Stanley Robinson, *The Ministry for the Future* (2020)[1]

I. Introduction

Despite its considerable environmental consequences, the role of animal agriculture in contributing to climate change has received little attention in policy discussions, and it is rarely (only 7 per cent of the time) included in media discussion of climate change.[2] While Canada has committed to achieving a 40–45 per cent reduction in greenhouse gas (GHG) emissions by 2030 and net zero emissions by 2050 in the *Canadian Net-Zero Emissions Accountability Act*, the focus has primarily been on limiting emissions from sectors such as transportation, housing, manufacturing, and oil and gas industries.[3] Achieving Canada's emission reduction targets will require not only substantial cuts in emissions but transformative changes in the food system, particularly in the area of animal agriculture.[4] This chapter outlines the problem animal agriculture creates and recommends a shift to plant-based diets.

The evidence is clear: current levels of animal production and consumption are unsustainable within the global food system.[5] Globally, the most conservative estimates suggest that raising livestock accounts for nearly 15 per cent of all human-induced GHG emissions emitted each year, while the most comprehensive assessments put that number somewhere between 20 and 51 per cent.[6] Land degradation to support livestock grazing and feed crop production also contributes significantly to air pollution, water pollution, and biodiversity loss, all of which affect our ability to adapt to and mitigate the impacts of climate change. Animal agriculture is also highly inefficient, consuming about 83 per cent of the earth's farmland and about 56 per cent of its fresh water while producing only 18 per cent of all calories.[7] This is not a sustainable way of feeding people.

Regrettably, current climate policies in Canada inadequately address the impact of animal agriculture, despite the existence of viable measures that can be implemented. In fact, the impacts of animal agriculture on the environment could be addressed quite quickly if people in the Global North would embrace changes to the way that they eat. Extensive research indicates that reducing meat consumption and shifting to a plant-based food system – focused on fruits, vegetables, grains, and beans – represents the single most effective strategy for reducing our emissions.[8] This is because livestock farming is a major source of methane, a GHG that is many times more powerful and harmful than carbon dioxide, and remains in the atmosphere for a much shorter amount of time – around twelve years compared with centuries.[9]

A global shift towards plant-based diets can potentially reduce diet-related emissions by up to 70 per cent and do so much more rapidly than reductions in any other sector.[10] Unfortunately, relying on individuals to make a substantial dietary shift is difficult and governments have been slow to push for dietary change in any comprehensive strategies to mitigate climate change.[11]

Nevertheless, the Canadian government can play a crucial role in promoting plant-based eating aligned with Canada's Food Guide and providing support to farmers transitioning to more sustainable, plant-based alternatives. These initiatives would significantly contribute to achieving Canada's emission reduction targets. Addressing the growth of industrial animal agriculture is crucial in ongoing efforts to effectively tackle carbon emissions reduction.

In this chapter, we explore the barriers and potential solutions to encouraging a transition to plant-based diets by means of climate change law and policy. As awareness of the environmental impacts of animal agriculture is increasing and plant-based foods are growing in availability and popularity, it is time for policymakers to get creative and take seriously the need for a food system transformation.

II. Overview of the Role of Animal Agriculture in Climate Change

Animal agriculture is a major contributor to climate change. Animal production contributes a significant share of all three major GHGs: (i) carbon dioxide (CO_2); (ii) methane (CH_4); and (iii) nitrous oxide (N_2O). In brief, the animal agriculture industry accounts for approximately 9 per cent of global anthropogenic CO_2 emissions, between 35 and 40 per cent of all global anthropogenic CH_4 emissions, and roughly 65 per cent of all anthropogenic N_2O emissions.[12] These last two trap heat at much higher rates than CO2 and stay in the atmosphere for less time, which is why their reduction can have a dramatic and immediate impact on GHG emissions.[13] This means that reductions in the animal agriculture industry can mitigate climate change much more rapidly than reductions in CO_2 from any other sector.[14] Methane specifically has garnered increased attention and awareness for the immediate impacts of its reduction.[15]

The animal agriculture sector has both direct and indirect impacts on climate change. Direct emissions refer to emissions released from animal sources including enteric fermentation and manure management.[16] Approximately 86 million tons of methane are released globally each year from enteric fermentation alone, and this number is on the rise due to an increase in poor feed quality on farms.[17] Methane is also released as a result of poor manure management, especially where manure is stored wet or as a slurry.[18] This is significant because methane emissions have increased drastically over the past twenty years due to a shift towards the use of liquid manure management systems rather than dry ones.[19] Together, digestion and manure represent approximately 80 per cent of all agricultural methane emissions.[20]

Indirect emissions refer to those derived from farm operations, livestock products processing, fertilizer and feed grain production, transportation, and land use changes.[21] Farm operations and maintenance alone account for approximately 90 million tons of CO_2 per year in electricity, ventilation, heating, and cooling.[22] Further, approximately 3 million tons of CO_2 are emitted each year as a result of fertilizer production for feed crops, and 73 per cent of all grain produced in Canada is fed to livestock.[23] The transportation of animals to slaughterhouses and retailers, transportation of animal by-products, and transportation of feed to livestock farms also contribute significant amounts of GHG emissions. Unfortunately, these emissions are not typically calculated or included in the data as part of the industry's GHG emissions contributions.[24] This means that the role of animal agriculture in climate change could be significantly higher than many estimates suggest.[25] This fact also helps explain why animal agriculture is sometimes reported to be responsible for up to 51 per cent of human-induced GHG emissions.[26]

A disproportionate share of the climate impact of food waste can also be attributed to meat and animal products (including dairy), according to a report by World Wildlife Fund.[27] The report, which recommends reducing how frequently we eat other animals, found that meat and animal products account for 40 per cent of CO_2 equivalent emissions associated with global farm stage food waste, despite only comprising 13 per cent of food waste tonnage.[28]

While this chapter will focus on GHG emissions, the animal agriculture industry is also responsible for several other environmental harms, including air and water pollution, deforestation, land degradation, and biodiversity loss – all of which affect the ability to adapt to and mitigate the impacts of climate change.[29] The practices involved in animal agriculture also cause harm to animals, workers, and public health, including inhumane treatment of animals, occupational risks to workers, and the emergence of antibiotic-resistant bacteria from the overuse of antibiotics in factory farming.[30] Reducing reliance on animal agriculture would also reduce these harms and risks.

III. We Cannot Rely on Magic or Silver Bullets

It is very understandable that when faced with something as overwhelming and intractable as the real risk of catastrophic climate change, people will reach for solutions that perform an anxiety-reduction function.[31] Even better if those solutions do not require individuals or societies to change what they are currently doing. Believing that a miraculous technological fix or "magic bullet" will save us can be reassuring.

Various technological solutions have been proposed to mitigate the impact of animal agriculture, including the use of manure digesters. Manure digesters are designed to capture methane produced by animal waste and convert it into biogas for energy production. While this approach seems promising, research suggests the disadvantages of manure-to-energy projects far outweigh the benefits.[32] For instance, they require significant energy inputs to operate and maintain, and they can only capture a small portion of the methane emissions produced by animal waste. Moreover, the requirement to build new and expand existing natural gas distribution lines to accommodate manure digesters will increase high-impact infrastructure and impose a risk of accidental leaks or spills of liquid manure. Lastly, since small and medium-sized farms often cannot afford the cost of setting up and maintaining manure digesters, this technology is primarily available to large-scale industrial animal production, a trend that raises concerns about animal welfare and environmental justice.

Geoengineering is also a topic that often appears in the context of fixes that do not require behaviour change. This form of technology plays an important role in the 2020 climate change thriller *The Ministry for the Future*, a quote from which introduces this chapter. It states something that one would not think requires an argument, namely, that we must leave the planet and its animals to future generations who will need it to live. The book's author delivered the keynote address at the University of Toronto Faculty of Law conference from which the present volume arises.[33] Geoengineering plays an important role at the beginning of the novel as a short-term fix unilaterally deployed by India after that country suffers a horrendous heat wave. This "casting of dust" (aerosol particulates, mostly sulfur dioxide) jetted up high in the atmosphere mimics a volcanic eruption, deflecting the sun's rays for a three-to-four-year period.[34] Talk of such technologies, known collectively as "solar radiation management," has been around for a long time. In his book, *Reason in a Dark Time*, philosopher and environmental ethicist Dale Jamieson recounts how as long ago as 1965, a scientific advisory committee to US President Johnson included an appendix to a report chaired by Al Gore's teacher at Harvard, Roger Ravelle, warning about the effects of too much carbon dioxide in the atmosphere.[35] "Not a word was said about reducing carbon emissions."[36] Instead it offered a geoengineering solution: scattering small reflective particles over large ocean areas, thousands of square miles.[37]

One can understand a penchant in Robinson's novel for the complex over the simple, as befits the "science" side of science fiction.[38] However, the obvious objection to a focus on geoengineering is that we cannot afford to adopt a "wait and see" attitude towards what develops in this sector, which has seen promising (what usually sound like pretty far-fetched) solutions as far back as 1965 (and seriously proposing ideas like "painting roofs white, injecting reflective aerosols into the atmosphere, or even […] launching space shields to protect us from solar radiation" since the 1990's[39]). The other danger is distraction from the basic challenge of reducing emissions, counting on "a hypothetical technology" that promises to solve all our problems, a "silver bullet."[40] As Jamieson puts it, "many of us find technological solutions to urgent problems almost irresistibly attractive."[41] Human psychology being what it is, "[w]e will avert our eyes from reality as long as a simple solution seems just over the horizon."[42] We want a solution that requires no lifestyle change at the moment, promising "gain without pain," a "Plan B" akin to "the 'morning after pill' for societies who do not practice safe consumption."[43]

Geoengineering solutions tend to carry with them what Jamieson calls "an attitudinal marker of suspicion" that "in the opinion of the speaker, requires a heightened level of scrutiny."[44] That is probably a correct way to view them, that is, with suspicion. Even those who support these solutions acknowledge that they are "a last resort."[45] However, they should not be dismissed simply because they are, as Jamieson puts it, "novel, weird, exotic, unfamiliar, or untested."[46] These and other climate change strategies directed towards abatement, mitigation, and adaptation should, in Jamieson's view, be thought about as "portfolios of responses rather than simple sweeping solutions."[47] Andrew Green notes in his book *Picking Up the Slack: Law Institutions and Canadian Climate Policy* that Nobel prize-winning economist Elinor Ostrom called this a "polycentric approach," involving actors at all levels.[48] In a world of country-specific "pledge and review," "climate change policy for the foreseeable future will largely reflect the motley collection of policies and practices adopted by particular countries."[49] This leaves us with what Jamieson describes as "a portfolio of policies without a single, effective portfolio manager."[50]

Should not this climate change portfolio, like any portfolio, be diversified? It certainly should *not exclude* strategies that can be used to move along emissions-reducing behaviour change *now*, the "Plan A," not the "Plan B" emergency-response kind. These are crucial realistic components of an overall emissions-lowering response. Jamieson writes: we all "have a shot at making a difference in what enters the portfolio. A lot could happen, though it may all seem drunk and disorderly."[51] Yet there are orderly ways of making shifts in consumption, which would have large impacts, especially so in animal agriculture, given the enormous amount it contributes to anthropogenic climate change.

IV. Plant-Based Diets as a Solution to the Climate Crisis

Extensive literature demonstrates the environmental benefits of shifting towards a more plant-based food system, including significantly reducing GHG emissions, conserving natural resources, and mitigating the impacts of climate change.[52] According to scientists from Stanford and the University of California, Berkeley, reducing or eliminating animal agriculture and shifting to a plant-based diet "is our best and most immediate chance to reverse the trajectory of climate change."[53]

A 2018 study by the University of Oxford published in the journal *Science* found that adopting a vegan diet could reduce an individual's carbon footprint by up to 73 per cent.[54] A more recent study suggested that making global dietary changes, such as substituting 50 per cent of the main animal products (pork, chicken, beef, and milk), could lead to significant environmental benefits by 2050.[55] These changes could result in a substantial reduction in global environmental impacts, including a 31 per cent decline in agriculture and land use GHG emissions compared to 2020 levels.[56] While individual action is hardly sufficient to lead to a drastic reduction in emissions, it is important not to *underestimate* the impact a personal choice to abstain from using animal products (or reducing them) can have, both in terms of the number of animals creating emissions and the influence individuals can have over the dietary choices of others in their lives.[57] "Be the change" is a powerful idea.[58] Nevertheless, structural and institutional responses are required to really deal with a problem of this magnitude.[59] There are also unanticipated costs to focusing only on individual change and individualizing responsibility for carbon emissions when systemic change is required.[60]

Unfortunately, current environmental protection legislation in most Canadian jurisdictions is woefully inadequate to deal with the environmental impacts of the animal agriculture sector. This is especially distressing because Canada is warming twice as quickly as the global average and three times faster in the North with already very noticeable extreme weather events that have taken place such as the 2021 British Columbia Heat Dome and the 2023 Canadian wildfires.[61]

Despite the rapidly deteriorating situation, government policy is not poised to address the contributions of animal agriculture to climate change. Most notably, the Government of Canada has effectively exempted animal agriculture from the federal *Greenhouse Gas Pollution Pricing Act* (GGPPA).[62] The GGPPA implements Canada's federal carbon pollution pricing system. During the course of its development, the animal agriculture industry lobbied heavily for "primary agriculture and meat and food processing [to] be exempt from carbon pricing."[63] Under section 36 of the act, farmers may use an exemption certificate and benefit from relief of the fuel charge if: the location at which the fuel is delivered is a farm; the fuel is for use exclusively in the operation of eligible farming machinery; and all or substantially all of the fuel is for use in the course of eligible farming activities.[64] At the UN Secretary General's Climate Ambition Summit in September 2023, Canada pledged to reduce methane emissions through the implementation of new regulations.[65] However, both the announcement and the regulations concentrate solely on the oil and gas sector, while disregarding the substantial methane emissions stemming from animal agriculture.

A similar pattern emerges in provincial legislation across the country. Ontario's *Environmental Protection Act*, for example, does not generally apply to the discharge of contaminants if it is in accordance with "normal farming practices."[66] Green notes that in 2012, the agricultural industry in British Columbia asked for and was granted relief from the province's carbon tax despite the fact that the agricultural industry faced no harm from the tax.[67]

In addition to exempting animal agriculture from climate and environmental protection laws and policies, the Government of Canada continues to actively promote, develop, and subsidize the growth of the animal agriculture industry. It is estimated that "the federal government provides subsidies of somewhere between $6 and $8 billion annually to the agriculture sector, with the bulk of those subsidies going to the dairy, egg, and chicken industries."[68] Unfortunately, these subsidies are geared towards helping the animal agriculture industry become more competitive and economically viable, rather than being tailored towards meaningful climate change mitigation and adaptation.[69] For example, in their recent "2030 Emissions Reduction Plan," the federal government allocated incentives for producers to adopt on-farm practices.[70] This includes $470 million for the Agricultural Climate Solutions: On-Farm Climate Action Fund, $150 million for a resilient agricultural landscapes program aimed at encouraging farmers to adopt on-farm practices like nitrogen management and rotational grazing, as well as $330 million to triple funding for the Agricultural Clean Technology program.

The Government of Canada recently pledged more than $7.5 million to support the Dairy Farmers of Canada (DFC) in advancing sustainable development within the dairy industry.[71] This funding is specifically designated to assist the DFC in conducting research aimed at finding solutions to enhance both the environmental and economic sustainability, as well as the resilience, of the Canadian dairy sector. In August 2023, the Ontario government also announced its commitment to provide over $300,000 to strengthen the Dairy Herdsperson Apprenticeship program at the University of Guelph Ridgetown Campus, in collaboration with the Dairy Farmers of Ontario.[72] This initiative aims to equip young individuals for "lucrative" careers in the dairy industry.[73] Regrettably, these funding opportunities primarily focus on improving the industry's competitiveness and helping farmers adapt to the challenges posed by climate change, rather than reducing GHG emissions or promoting a shift towards more sustainable food production practices.

A similar phenomenon appears to be happening in the US with the $2.8 billion in funding the USDA is handing out to big agricultural companies via its "climate smart commodities," a program that has been criticized for its lack of transparency and oversight.[74] The Union of Concerned Scientists worries that "[t]he lack of any published evaluation criteria [for the so far seventy projects who have been awarded funding] makes us question whether the USDA's standards for climate-smart projects will end up supporting the current monolithic agricultural model, which perpetuates existing inequities by leaving out smaller-scale farmers and underserved producers."[75] Meat, dairy, and livestock were involved in fifty-five out of the seventy funded projects. Others involve corn and soybeans, commodities overwhelmingly used to feed agricultural animals. Without more oversight, the concern is that the money will be absorbed by these big incumbents, who have created the problems in the first place and have ample profits to direct towards emission-lowering solutions.[76] Additionally, the 2018 Farm Bill, which establishes how the government will prioritize and allocate funding for the American food system, increased the amount of government assistance and tax breaks available to the largest factory farms.[77]

On a global scale, world leaders have also been criticized for their failure to address the impacts of animal agriculture on climate change. Animal agriculture has never been seriously discussed at any of the major climate change conferences around the world, nor is it widely featured in the Nationally Determined Contributions of countries that have ratified the Paris Agreement.[78]

In the lead up to the United Nations' latest climate change conference (COP28), for example, environmentalists and animal rights organizations urged world leaders to recognize the environmental impact of animal agriculture and set clear and tangible targets for transition towards sustainable, plant-based food systems.[79] While COP28 did include a day dedicated to food system change for the first time in the nearly three-decade history of the climate regime, the event still failed to address the urgent need to reduce industrial meat and dairy production to limit global warming.[80] COP28 also once again drew criticism for the inclusion of unsustainable meat and dairy items on menus.[81] In 2021, nearly 60 per cent of the meals served at COP26 included meat or dairy, which campaign group Animal Rebellion described as the equivalent of "serving cigarettes at a lung cancer conference."[82]

Why have governments failed to embrace diet change as a strategy to mitigate climate change?

V. Nudging/Forcing the Shift

The decision not to more actively encourage plant-based food production and consumption through climate change policy may be explained, in part, by a concept known as the "Overton window." Named after American policy analyst Joseph Overton, the "Overton window" is a term used to describe "the range of policies politically acceptable to the mainstream population at a given time."[83] As meat and dairy consumption is still the norm, governments may believe that plant-based diets have not achieved the degree of social acceptability to be considered a legitimate solution to climate change. This is supported by the fact that, for much of Western history, vegetarianism and veganism were often considered too "extreme" or even "radical" to be adopted by the mainstream population.[84] However, the Overton window can shift over time due to various factors, such as changes in public opinion, new developments in science and technology, and political events.[85] In this instance, several factors may be forcing the window to shift.

First, there has been a growing acceptance of plant-based diets in recent years. A 2021 study conducted by Leger Research found that consumer demand for plant-based foods is growing in Canada and around the world.[86] Recent data from 2021 shows that two-thirds of Canadians consume plant-based foods frequently, and 31 per cent of Canadians plan to eat more plant-based foods within the next year.[87] In Toronto specifically, a poll conducted by Angus Reid found that almost two-thirds of residents are interested in reducing meat consumption and 21 per cent have taken steps to do so.[88] In the same poll, 94 per cent support plant-based foods in public spaces and 86 per cent are aware of the environmental impact of animal agriculture.[89] A 2023 poll of 803 people in the lower mainland of British Columbia (that is, Vancouver and its environs) found that two thirds of those surveyed (65 per cent) have reduced their meat consumption, primarily motivated by the following fours factors: health (46 per cent); economics (38 per cent); environmental concern (38 per cent); and animal rights/welfare (29 per cent).[90]

Second, in keeping with these polls, there has been increasing public awareness of the environmental impacts of animal agriculture. In 2006, the UN Food and Agriculture Organization published the report, *Livestock's Long Shadow*, which concluded that animal agriculture is one of the leading causes of climate change.[91] That same year, *An Inconvenient Truth*, an American documentary film about former US Vice President Gore's campaign to educate people about global warming, was released.[92] This was a time when people were still debating whether climate change was real, and the film was very much geared towards providing incontrovertible proof using graphs and other dramatic visuals.[93] When pressed by advisors to make the methane arguments relating to animal agriculture in the film, apparently his response was "it is hard enough to get people to think about CO2; don't confuse them."[94] Nearly two decades on, President Biden continues to ignore the role animal agriculture plays in methane production, creating what Yale

Law School's Law, Ethics and Animals Program's executive director Viveca Morris has called a "cow-shaped hole" in his methane plan.[95]

Since 2006, several popular documentary films, including *Cowspiracy: The Sustainability Secret* (2014) and *#ForNature* (2021)[96] have explored the role of animal agriculture in climate change. Studies are focusing on the methane impact of livestock, including one from 2022.[97] Another in February 2023 found that if worldwide dietary eating patterns do not change, this could amount to nearly a one degree Celsius increase in warming driven by high methane foods by 2100, with these foods making up more than 80 per cent of future warming from food consumption.[98] The Intergovernmental Panel on Climate Change's (IPCC) Special Report on "climate change and land" in 2019 described plant-based diets as a major opportunity for mitigating and adapting to climate change – and included a policy recommendation to reduce meat consumption.[99] Increasing accessibility of this information can shift public opinion about the environmental cost of our dietary choices and influence consumer decision-making and public policymaking.[100]

However, the animal agriculture industry is actively working to keep the public uninformed about the environmental impacts of the sector. For example, the latest IPCC Report in 2023 watered down its original draft wording that "plant-based diets can reduce GHG emissions by up to 50 per cent compared to the average emission-intensive Western diet." The final wording was changed to a recommendation to adopt "balanced, sustainable healthy diets acknowledging nutritional needs." It did not directly mention beef and dairy or that wealthy countries should urgently reduce meat consumption. This change was pushed by Brazil and Argentina, countries with powerful cow production industries.[101] Further, in advance of COP28, leaked documents brought to light a pro-meat communications plan developed by industry giants such as JBS and the Canadian Cattle Association to promote a "pro-meat" message to policymakers during the summit.[102]

New developments in science and technology may also be shifting the window. In 2020, a comprehensive review of the literature outlined the most prominent perceived and objective barriers preventing people from switching to plant-based diets.[103] The most prominent barrier identified was the perceived difficulty in abstaining from meat consumption. Arguably, the development of high-quality plant-based meat/dairy alternatives, and cultivated meat, provides an opportunity to overcome this barrier.[104] Many plant-based products have been developed to visually resemble meat and match the taste, structure, and nutritional value preferences of meat eaters, which could make the shift to plant-based diets less difficult and more appealing.[105] For example, researchers at the University of Guelph recently used corn protein called zein (a waste product of corn meal) to replicate meat texture in plant-based alternatives.[106]

The second most prominent barrier identified in the study was health concerns, specifically nutrient deficiencies such as protein and calcium. New developments in public health and education could help to break down this barrier. In 2019, for example, Canada introduced a new Food Guide that encourages individuals to eat plant-based food, noting that "the regular intake of plant-based foods – vegetables, fruit, whole grains, and plant-based proteins – can have positive effects on health."[107] Again, a popular documentary, *The Game Changers* (2021), following athletes who use plant-based diets, focused on demonstrating that the diet is suited to building strength and promoting health.[108] A new book, *Let the Plant-Based Games Begin* (2023), similarly reveals Olympic athletes' secrets to enhanced performance and recovery with plant-based diets.[109]

Growing awareness of the other links between human health and plant-based diets may also help to overcome these concerns. For example, a doctor named Michael Greger has written a provocatively titled book, *How Not to Die*, which recommends a plant-based diet for everyone but especially those suffering from or with a family history of certain diseases.[110] Since the COVID-19 pandemic, for example, many scholars and animal activists have worked to emphasize how the emergence of new zoonotic infectious diseases from human interactions with wildlife are connected to changes in ecosystems and land use and intensification of agriculture, including animal agriculture.[111]

The "One Health" paradigm has also gained momentum as a way to bootstrap concern for animals (whether wild or domestic) to concern for human health as well as the climate and environment in light of the Pandemic.[112] The One Health Institute at the University of California at Davis defines their approach as working to "ensure the well-being of people, animals, and the environment through collaborative problem solving – locally, national, and globally."[113] While links between human health and animal health go back to the nineteenth century and principles of veterinary public health date to the mid-twentieth century, "One Health, One World" was coined by a conference organized by the Wildlife Conservation Society in 2004.[114]

The term was first used in 2003–2004 in association with the emergence of severe acute respiratory disease (SARS) and H5N1, the highly pathogenic avian influenza.[115] A range of international organizations have since adopted the framework and November 3 has been designated as "One Health Day."[116] Since the rise of COVID-19 in 2020, several major health organizations have highlighted the importance of adopting a One Health approach to stop the spread of infectious diseases.[117] For example, the World Bank's report, "Putting Pandemics Behind Us: Investing in One Health to Reduce Risks of Emerging Infectious Diseases," acknowledges that "[g]rowing demand for animal-sourced foods has increased the number of livestock on farms, creating more opportunities for crossover of pathogens."[118] The Centers for Disease Control and Prevention also states that "[o]ne of the lessons learned from COVID-19 is that emerging zoonotic infectious diseases are here to stay and fighting new disease threats such as COVID-19, Ebola, and Zika requires One Health collaboration across human, animal, and environmental health organizations."[119]

While the COVID-19 pandemic has reinforced the relevance of One Health principles, the general idea of linkages between human, animal, and planetary welfare is not necessarily limited to the issue of pandemics and zoonotic disease. This is important because as memories of the pandemic fade, so too might an awareness of these issues. Soon enough it may be difficult to begin any conversation with "remember how that pandemic started (or may have started) with live animal markets in China and how unprepared the world was to handle it."[120] As Jeff Sebo writes, "there is a risk that, as we overcome COVID-19, these lessons will fade from our memories, and our sense of urgency around pandemics, climate change, and other such threats will fade as well."[121]

Another example of growing understanding of the interconnections between human well-being, animal welfare, and environmental conservation can be found in the emerging "One Welfare" paradigm, which is less focused on wild animals and infectious disease.[122] One Welfare promotes key global objectives such as supporting food security, sustainability, reducing human suffering, and improving productivity within the farming sector through a better understanding of the value of high welfare standards. It extends the approach of (and partially overlaps) the One Health theme used for human and animal health. In explaining their choice to use the "One Welfare" paradigm rather than "One Health" a program manager at the Vancouver Humane Society (VHS) explained: "Ultimately, it comes down to whether one sees health as part of welfare, or welfare as part of health. The VHS sees health as part of welfare generally, but we are very supportive of the one health lens."[123]

While it seems unlikely that politicians and other leaders will do what needs to be done until there is widespread public acceptability of plant-based diets as a mitigation solution, the aforementioned analysis shows that this point may not be as far off as people might think. Ultimately, exactly how far along things have come does not matter, as governments should act even if transitioning is not popular. Reducing meat and dairy consumption is essential to combat the climate crisis, so it is time to move beyond controversy over the desirability of intervention and towards practical policy discussions about how we can transition to more sustainable diets.

VI. Policy Options to Increase the Consumption of Plant-Based Foods in Canada

It is time for policymakers to leverage the growing awareness of the harmful impacts to health, the environment, farmed animals, and human workers of animal agriculture, along with the rising popularity of plant-based foods, and take seriously the need for a major food system transformation.

This section of the chapter outlines several steps policymakers can take to successfully encourage a shift to more plant-based food consumption and production. The United States, for example, is talking about measures that Canada should also be contemplating.

1. Alter Choices through Incentives and Shifting Subsidies

On 19 February 2021, California Assembly Bill 1289 – the "Smart Climate Agriculture Program: Plant-Based Agriculture" – was introduced.[124] If passed, the bill would establish the Smart Climate Agriculture Program, which would require the Department of Food and Agriculture to provide grants to persons farming on small to midsize farms to transition the use of the land from raising livestock or growing feed crops to plant-based agriculture and to provide technical assistance to those persons with regard to the program.

In 2020, the United Kingdom introduced the *Agriculture Act*, which similarly incentivizes a shift away from intensive animal agriculture by offering payments that reward farmers for managing "land or water in a way that protects or improves the environment," "managing water or livestock in a way that mitigates or adapts to climate change," and promoting animal welfare.[125]

In Canada, this could be achieved through amendments to the Environmental Farm Plan (EFP). An EFP is a voluntary planning tool meant to educate farmers about the climate and environmental impacts of agriculture, help them identify areas in which they can improve their own environmental performance, and promote best management practices. Financial incentives and cost-share programs are often available to assist farmers in implementing projects under their EFPs. Based on research by Dr. Heather McLeod-Kilmurray and Dr. Nathalie Chalifour, a recent report by AEL Advocacy recommends two key changes to the EFP program that could help farmers transition to plant-based production:

1. The federal government should establish national principles for sustainable agriculture to guide the direction of EFPs. Much like the European Commission's "Farm to Fork Strategy," these principles should be based on the Guiding Principles for Sustainable Healthy Diets developed by the Food and Agriculture Organization of the United Nations and the World Health Organization, which highlight the combined health and environmental benefits of shifting towards a more plant-based diet.
2. The amount of funding farmers receive for creating and implementing an action plan based on an EFP should be considerably increased to encourage participation in the program.[126]

Shifting subsidies from animal products to fruits, vegetables, beans, and grains meant for human consumption could also help fight climate change. Because "agricultural subsidies are an important factor influencing production and consumption choices, reducing and restructuring government subsidies would likely have a profoundly positive impact on the environment."[127] Indeed, one might ask why, morally and politically, individuals who oppose animal agriculture should accept their tax dollars going to subsidies that support animal producers.[128] Attention is being paid to how to push for reform of these subsidies.[129] The Vancouver Humane Society found that 58 per cent of their respondents supported shifting subsidies.[130]

A recent report finds that both the European Union and the United States award livestock farmer about 1,000 times more public funding than plant-based and cultivated meat.[131] This amounts to a massive differential in the funding of the incumbent sector as against new more environmentally and animal friendly alternatives. The same study found that the amount of lobbying by meat producers was also many times higher than for alternatives.[132] This creates a missed opportunity, especially in Canada, where consumers are curious about alternatives such as cultivated meat, more so than Americans.[133] The beef industry spends large amounts of money sowing confusion about its climate change impacts.[134] Dairy has launched a very public attack on plant-based milks.[135] These massive disparities in funding pose a challenge to the idea that just getting the facts out there is enough.[136] Funds should be devoted to countering those misleading messages.

An additional argument in Canada is the substantial reductions in health care costs governments can achieve by redirecting subsidies away from the meat and dairy sectors. According to the Academy of Nutrition and Dietetics, adopting a plant-based diet can lead to significant health cost savings by reducing the risk of chronic diseases such as heart disease, type 2 diabetes, and certain cancers.[137]

2. Restrict Factory Farming

Governments can also restrict the ability of farmers and consumers to engage in perpetuating the worst climate culprits in the animal agriculture sector. Approaches involving moratoria on large factory farms, known as concentrated animal feeding operations (CAFOs), are being proposed in the United States.[138] In 2020, a senator from New Jersey, Cory Booker, introduced the *Farm System Reform Act* (co-sponsored by Bernie Sanders and Elizabeth Warren), which would place a moratorium on new large factory farms and close all such farms by 2040.[139] The Bill was reintroduced on 2 February 2023.[140]

On 18 February 2022, California Assembly Bill 2764 was introduced in the California State Legislature.[141] This bill would have placed a moratorium on the construction and expansion of CAFOs in California, which would apply to any sort of commercial animal farm that makes over $100,000 in revenue. The original version of the bill also included a moratorium on the expansion and construction of slaughterhouses, but the bill was amended in March 2022 to exclude this provision. Unfortunately, the bill did not receive a hearing in the Assembly Agriculture Committee before a legislative deadline and consequently did not proceed in the California Assembly.

Similarly, Senate Bill 85–1 in Oregon would prohibit the construction and expansion of CAFOs as defined by the Oregon Departments of Environmental Quality and Agriculture by the large numbers of animals they confine.[142] Data from the American Society for the Prevention of Cruelty to Animals confirms that 83 per cent of Oregonians support a moratorium on new and expanding factory farms, and a public hearing of the Senate Natural Resources Committee showed overwhelming support for the bill.[143]

3. Guide Choice by Changing the Default

Canadian federal and provincial governments could also implement institutional "soft solutions" that could help people transition, such as "Default Veg,"[144] "Greener by Default,"[145] "Meatless Mondays,"[146] or

"Plant-Powered Fridays"[147] at all public institutions by means of procurement policies. The first two programs make plant-based food the default, while giving diners the choice to opt into meat/dairy, thereby "preserving choice."[148] Studies have shown that serving plant-based meals by default increases their selection by an average of 60 per cent, thus reducing food's greenhouse gas emissions by 40 per cent and water footprint by 24 per cent.[149] The 2023 Vancouver Humane Society survey showed that 60 per cent of those polled support reduction of animal products in government strategies.[150]

Canadian municipalities are in a favorable position to facilitate the shift towards plant-based diets. Municipal governments can use their purchasing power and set policies to reduce food waste, support eco-friendly food producers, and decrease carbon-intensive products. Municipal governments can also encourage other community members, including schools, health care institutions, businesses, and restaurants, to adopt similar measures.

A policy brief published by the Guarini Center on Environmental, Energy, & Land Use Law in the United States could help guide local policymakers in this regard.[151] The policy brief outlines a range of existing policy options for municipalities to reduce animal-based food consumption and promote plant-based alternatives, such as reducing procurement of animal-based foods, setting standards for food procurement, and offering subsidies for plant-based food. In 2020, the Vancouver Humane Society conducted a cost-benefit analysis and found that the City of Vancouver could save up to $99,000 in procurement costs, reduce over 500 tons of GHG emissions, and save nearly 400 farmed animal lives annually by implementing policy recommendations to increase plant-based purchasing at the municipal level.[152]

Municipal government could also leverage novel policy options, such as divesting from animal agriculture investments, using securities regulations to disclose risks, implementing eco-friendly food establishment certifications, requiring private establishments to offer vegan/vegetarian options, levying targeted taxes on animal-based food products, and requiring restaurants to provide environmental information and vegetarian options.[153]

Food choices are often shaped more by unconscious adherence to habit and situational cues than by conscious motivation and so setting plant-based "defaults" especially in public and institutional settings can have a big impact.[154] From a human psychology perspective, much of the literature has focused on social norms.[155] Green defines these as "what people feel is right or appropriate" and emphasizes their importance to making progress on climate action.[156] Given how social humans are, we are very sensitive to what is or is not considered to be "normal" in a given situation. The authors of a recent report by Mercy for Animals point out that "[m]any people may be ready to change but fear being perceived as outliers and underestimate how many people are like them."[157] Much depends on the social setting and what people see others doing. They write:

> Fifty years ago, many of us would never have conceived of a world where same-sex marriage and nonbinary gender identity were (generally) accepted and normal. Today, that is the world many of us live in. Alternative practices become normalized, older ones are jettisoned. We can escape the "normalization trap."[158]

Because people are typically highly social, they also care about what others think and also how behaviour is changing over time.[159] Smoking is perhaps the best case in point, having moved from being perceived as "a matter of personal preference to an object of danger and disgust" for how it impacts others (e.g., second-hand smoke and, in Canada, the burden smoking-related illnesses place on a public health care system).[160] Convenience will also be key, as has been learned with recycling programs.[161] Policies need both carrots and sticks.[162] Photojournalist Jo-Anne McArthur writes "[p]erhaps one day meat will be sold with a warning similar to those on cigarette packets: 'eating meat can cause forest fires, climate change, and pandemics.'"[163] A recent study published in the journal *Appetite* supports this idea, indicating that graphic warning labels on food, akin to those on tobacco products, could reduce meat consumption by 7–10 per cent.[164] The study involved showing over a thousand meat-eating adults images of meals with health, climate, and pandemic warnings, or no labels.[165] Pandemic warnings proved most effective, leading to a 10 per cent reduction in meat selection, followed by health warnings at 8.8 per cent, and climate warnings at 7.4 per cent.[166]

VII. Conclusion

Shifting to a plant-based food system presents a unique and exciting opportunity for governments and policymakers, as it offers the triple benefit of rapid and dramatic climate change mitigation, reducing environmental degradation, and lowering human health costs, thereby playing a pivotal role in securing a sustainable future for Canadians.

Public institutions and governments have responsibilities towards human health, the environment, and animal welfare, as well as towards those who work in animal industries. Governments need to think critically about the methods of food production they choose to subsidize with our tax dollars. Plant-based options, which would go a long way towards helping Canada meet GHG reduction targets, need much more support than they are currently receiving.

Encouraging the transition to a plant-based food system may be met with objections, such as job losses in the animal agriculture industry and resistance to changing long-standing cultural and dietary habits. These concerns are legitimate and require attention to achieve a fair and equitable transition. A just transition approach is needed to address these concerns, which involves considering the needs and interests of affected communities and workers, and providing support for their transition to new employment and livelihood opportunities. By taking a just transition approach, we can ensure that the transition to a plant-based food system is inclusive and equitable for all, while also addressing the urgent need to reduce the environmental impact of animal agriculture.[167]

Issues relating to animal agriculture and what food we should be investing in need to be included in any future conversations about Canada's domestic climate change policy.[168] As Dean Brunnée put it at the first panel of the University of Toronto Faculty of Law Climate Change conference, which produced this volume, we must "pull all the levers."[169] This is consistent with the "everyone's responsible" message from the Supreme Court of Canada and its recent decision on the constitutionality of the federal government's carbon price to establish minimum standards for pricing GHG emissions.[170] Questioning animal agriculture and promoting plant-based options are well within the realm of the politically feasible.[171] Indeed, as the excellent plant-based food at this conference demonstrated, key to this feasibility and shifting the Overton window is food being delicious.[172] The people who prepared and ate that food and found it to be so are among those regular people who will decide, because as Dean Brunnée said "We all have to decide."[173]

Acknowledgments

The authors wish to thank the audience at the Canadian Animal Law Conference at the University of Toronto, Faculty of Law (1 October 2023), participants in the Brooks Institute for Animal Rights, Law & Policy, Brooks Annual Workshop for Scholars held in Nashville TN (8 July 2023) attended by Delci Winders, Jessica Eisen, Sara Schindler, Justin Marceau, Kristen Stilt, Doug Kysar, Maneesha Deckha, Dale

Jamieson, Lori Gruen, Emma LeBlanc, and Thomas Poston, as well as Viveca Morris, Jeff Sebo, Andrew Green, Jutta Brunnée, and Heather McLeod-Kilmurray for their invaluable comments on earlier drafts.

NOTES

1 Kim Stanley Robinson, *The Ministry for the Future* (London: Orbit, 2020) at 248.

2 Constanza Arévalo, Jenny Splitter & Jo Anderson, "Animal Agriculture Is the Missing Piece in Climate Change Media Coverage" *Faunalytics* (31 May 2023), online: <https://faunalytics.org/animal-ag-in-climate-media/> [https://perma.cc/3CEC-HJ9Z]. See also Núria Almiron & Milena Zoppeddu, "Eating Meat and Climate Change: The Media Blind Spot – A Study of Spanish and Italian Press Coverage" (2015) 9:3 Environ Commun 307, online: <https://doi.org/10.1080/17524032.2014.953968>.

3 *Canadian Net-Zero Emissions Accountability Act*, SC 2021, c 22. See Andrew Green, *Picking Up the Slack: Law, Institutions and Canadian Climate Policy* (Toronto: University of Toronto Press, 2022) at 28, online: <https://doi.org/10.3138/9781487553319> (on the Canadian pattern since 1992 of setting targets, missing them, and setting lower targets that are further out into the future), 174–5 (explaining that this legislation requires the government to set national GHG emissions strategies every five years, starting in 2030 and how the statute is modelled on the *UK Climate Change Act*).

4 The Government of Canada's latest climate plan demonstrates that agriculture is responsible for 10 per cent of Canada's total emissions and is also one of the main sources of methane emissions, contributing 29 per cent to Canada's total methane emissions in 2019. See Canada, *2030 Emissions Reduction Plan* (Ottawa: Government of Canada, 2022) at 59, online (pdf): <https://publications.gc.ca/collections/collection_2022/eccc/En4-460-2022-eng.pdf> [https://perma.cc/7E4L-QZDP].

5 Intergovernmental Science-Policy Platform on Biodiversity and Ecosystem Services, *The Global Assessment Report on Biodiversity and Ecosystem Services: Summary for Policymakers* (Bonn: IPBES, 2019), online (pdf): <https://files.ipbes.net/ipbes-web-prod-public-files/2020-02/ipbes_global_assessment_report_summary_for_policymakers_en.pdf> [https://perma.cc/J2A6-YDHC]; Alan Espinosa-Marrón et al, "Environmental Impact of Animal-Based Food Production and the Feasibility of a Shift Toward Sustainable Plant-Based Diets in the United States" (2022) 3 Front Sustain 1, online: <https://doi.org/10.3389/frsus.2022.841106>.

6 Estimates range considerably based on various factors, including the year used for estimates, emissions sources considered, and the Global

Warming Potential (GWP*) values used for methane and nitrous oxide. See e.g., Michael B Eisen & Patrick O Brown, "Rapid Global Phaseout of Animal Agriculture has the Potential to Stabilize Greenhouse Gas Levels for 30 Years and Offset 68 Percent of CO_2 Emissions This Century" (2022) 1:2 PLOS Clim, online: <https://doi.org/10.1371/journal.pclm.0000010>; Pierre Gerber et al, *Tackling Climate Change through Livestock: A Global Assessment of Emissions and Mitigation Opportunities* (Rome: Food and Agriculture Organization of the UN, 2013); Xiaoming Xu et al, "Global Greenhouse Gas Emissions from Animal-Based Foods Are Twice those of Plant-Based Foods" (2021) 2 Nat Food 724, online: <https://doi.org/10.1038/s43016-021-00358-x>; Robert Goodland & Jeff Anhang, "Livestock and Climate Change: What if the Key Actors in Climate Change Are … Cows, Pigs, and Chickens?," *World Watch* (November/December 2009), online (pdf): <https://awellfedworld.org/wp-content/uploads/Livestock-Climate-Change-Anhang-Goodland.pdf> [https://perma.cc/7NTN-TZZP]; Matthew N. Hayek, "The Carbon Opportunity Cost of Animal-Sourced Food Production on Land" (2021) 4 Nat Sustain 21, online: <https://doi.org/10.1038/s41893-020-00603-4>; Richard Twine, "Emissions from Animal Agriculture – 16.5% Is the New Minimum Figure" (2021) 13:11 Sustain 6276, online: <https://doi.org/10.3390/su13116276>. For a discussion about the problems with using GWP* to calculate emissions from animal agriculture, see Matthew N. Hayek & Scot M. Miller, "Underestimates of Methane from Intensively Raised Animals Could Undermine Goals of Sustainable Development" (2021) 16:6 Enviro Res Lett 16, online: <https://doi.org/10.1088/1748-9326/ac02ef>; Matthew N. Hayek et al, "Research Needs for a Food System Transition" (2023) 41 Clim Chang 176, online: <https://doi.org/10.1007/s10584-023-03507-2>.

7 Jeff Sebo, *Saving Animals, Saving Ourselves: Why Animals Matter for Pandemics, Climate Change, and Other Catastrophes* (Oxford: Oxford University Press, 2022) at 50, online: <https://doi.org/10.1093/oso/9780190861018.001.0001> (citing the 2018 *Science* magazine Oxford study by J. Poore & T. Nemecek discussed below in text at note 54 and Isabell Weindl et al, "Livestock Production and the Water Challenge of Future Food Supply: Implications of Agricultural Management and Dietary Choices" (2017) 47 Glob Environ Change 121 at 121–32, online: <https://doi.org/10.1016/j.gloenvcha.2017.09.010>).

8 Damian Carrington, "Avoiding Meat and Dairy Is 'Single Biggest Way' to Reduce Your Impact on Earth", *The Guardian* (18 May 2018), online: <https://www.theguardian.com/environment/2018/may/31/avoiding-meat-and-dairy-is-single-biggest-way-to-reduce-your-impact-on-earth> [https://perma.cc/P2HB-LS8D]; United Nations Framework Convention

on Climate Change (UNFCCC), "We Need to Talk about Meat" (19 May 2021), online (blog): <https://unfccc.int/news/we-need-to-talk-about-meat> [https://perma.cc/2S3V-7BLF]. See also Eisen & Brown, *supra* note 6; Brianne Riehl & Aurora Marstokk, *Animal-Sourced Food Consumption and Canada's Emission Targets*, (Vancouver, Navius Research, 2022), online (pdf): <https://www.worldanimalprotection.ca/siteassets/reports-pdfs/Animal-sourced-food-consumption-and-Canadas-emissions-targets-Navius-Research-22-08-30/> [https://perma.cc/3HCR-T2QT].

9 International Energy Agency, "Global Methane Tracker 2022: Methane and Climate Change" (2022), online: <https://www.iea.org/reports/global-methane-tracker-2022/methane-and-climate-change> [https://perma.cc/6UKL-3MDS].

10 Marcho Springmann et al, "Analysis and Valuation of the Health and Climate Change Co-Benefits of Dietary Change" (2016) 113:15 Proc Natl Acad Sci 4146, online: <https://doi.org/10.1073/pnas.1523119113>. See also Peter Scarborough et al, "Vegans, Vegetarians, Fish-Eaters and Meat-Eaters in the UK Show Discrepant Environmental Impacts" (2023) 4 Nat Food 565, online: <https://doi.org/10.1038/s43016-023-00795-w>.

11 Eisen & Brown, *supra* note 6.

12 Henning Steinfeld et al, *Livestock's Long Shadow: Environmental Issues and Options* (Rome: Food and Agriculture Organization of the United Nations, 2006) at 112. See also Sebo, *supra* note 7 at 50.

13 See Sebo, *supra* note 7; M. Melissa Rojas Downing et al, "Climate Change and Livestock: Impacts, Adaptation, and Mitigation" (2017) 16 Clim Risk Manag 145 at 152, online: <https://doi.org/10.1016/j.crm.2017.02.001> (referring to the Intergovernmental Panel on Climate Change report suggesting that the global warming potential of methane is thirty-four times that of CO2, while the global warming potential of nitrous oxide is 310 times that of CO_2).

14 The livestock sector emits much larger shares of methane and nitrous oxide than any other individual sector, and these two GHGs have much higher potentials to warm the atmosphere than CO_2. See David Cassuto, "The CAFO Hothouse: Climate Change, Industrial Agriculture and the Law" (2010) Anim Soc Insti Policy Pap at 1.

15 See Patricia (Trish) Fisher, *The 'Dark Horse' of Climate Change: Agricultural Methane Governed in the United States and Canada*, (North American Climate Policy, 2022), online (pdf): <https://fordschool.umich.edu/sites/default/files/2022-04/NACP_Fisher_final.pdf> [https://perma.cc/B39V-VZLW]. In 2021, Canada confirmed its support for the Global Methane Pledge, which aims to reduce global methane emissions by 30 per cent below 2020 levels by 2030. Canada, Environment and Climate Change Canada, News Release, "Canada Confirms Its Support for the Global

Methane Pledge and Announces Ambitious Domestic Actions to Slash Methane Emissions," (11 October 2021), online: <https://www.canada.ca/en/environment-climate-change/news/2021/10/canada-confirms-its-support-for-the-global-methane-pledge-and-announces-ambitious-domestic-actions-to-slash-methane-emissions.html> [https://perma.cc/X4WT-LDYL]. The Pledge recognizes that "reducing methane emissions from energy, agriculture, and waste can achieve near-term gains in our efforts in this decade […] and is regarded as the single most effective strategy to keep the goal of limiting warming to 1.5°C within reach while yielding co-benefits including improving public health and agricultural productivity." See Global Methane Pledge, "About the Global Methane Pledge" (accessed 6 April 2023), online: <https://www.globalmethanepledge.org/#about> [https://perma.cc/4PEF-TS2K].

16 Steinfeld et al, *supra* note 12.

17 *Ibid.*

18 Agriculture and Agri-Food Canada, "Methane" in "Greenhouse Gases and Agriculture" (last modified 9 December 2022), online: <https://agriculture.canada.ca/en/environment/greenhouse-gases#b> [https://perma.cc/228E-YHNZ].

19 Humane Society International, "An HSI Report: The Impact of Animal Agriculture on Global Warming and Climate Change" (2008) 2 HSI Reports 1 at 9, online: <https://www.wellbeingintlstudiesrepository.org/hsi_reps_fap/2> [https://perma.cc/6SJB-G9J3].

20 Gerber et al, *supra* note 6 at 1.

21 Downing et al, *supra* note 13 at 152.

22 *Ibid* at 154.

23 Michael Appleby, *Eating Our Future: The Environmental Impact of Industrial Animal Agriculture* (London: World Society for the Protection of Animals International, 2008) at 12, online: <https://wildbeimwild.com/wp-content/uploads/2015/08/eating-our-future_english_tcm46-28198.pdf>.

24 Humane Society International, *supra* note 19 at 5.

25 *Ibid.*

26 Goodland & Anhang, *supra* note 6.

27 World Wildlife Fund, *Driven to Waste: The Global Impact of Food Loss and Waste on Farms* (Woking, UK: WWF, 2021), online (pdf): <https://wwfint.awsassets.panda.org/downloads/wwf_uk__driven_to_waste___the_global_impact_of_food_loss_and_waste_on_farms.pdf> [https://perma.cc/8VQL-XYY8].

28 *Ibid* at 9.

29 See AEL Advocacy, *Animal Agriculture and Environmental Protection: A Multi-Jurisdictional Legislative Review* (Ottawa: AEL Advocacy in

collaboration with World Animal Protection, 2023), online (pdf): <https://www.aeladvocacy.ca/_files/ugd/c883e8_f53399310b88483f9162831fe61bb606.pdf [https://perma.cc/X6KW-6NVM]. One of the authors, Krystal-Anne Roussel, co-founder of AEL Advocacy, co-wrote this report in collaboration with World Animal Protection.

30 See Farm Forward, "Factory Farming: Impact on Animals, Workers, Environment, & More" (accessed 11 April 2023), online: <https://www.farmforward.com/issues/climate-and-the-environment/factory-farming-impact-animals-enivronment/> [https://perma.cc/4GEA-B453]; Ranya Mulchandani et al, "Global trends in antibiotic use in food-producing animals: 2020 to 2030" (2023) 3:2 PLOS Glob Public Health e0001305, online: <https://doi.org/10.1371/journal.pgph.0001305>; United Nations Environment Programme, *Bracing for Superbugs: Strengthening Environmental Action in the One Health Response to Antimicrobial Resistance* (Geneva: UN Environment Programme, 2023), online: <https://www.unep.org/resources/superbugs/environmental-action> [https://perma.cc/UFE9-TPTJ]; World Animal Protection, Global Public Health Cost of Antimicrobial Resistance Related to Antibiotic Use on Factory Farms" (New York: World Animal Protection, 2023), online (pdf): <https://www.worldanimalprotection.us/siteassets/reports-programmatic/global-public-health-technical-report.pdf>.

31 See Brenda Cossman, "Climate Anxiety and Self Governance" in this volume.

32 Patty Keough, "Manure-to-Energy Projects – Greenwashing or a Real Solution to Reducing Methane Emissions from Livestock Production?," *Environmental, Natural Resources, & Energy Law Blog* (23 January 2023), online (blog): <https://www.lclark.edu/live/blogs/216-manure-to-energy-projects-greenwashing-or-a-real> [https://perma.cc/N59E-DF73]. See also Jenny Splitter, "America Has a Manure Problem and the Miracle Solution Being Touted Isn't All That It Seems," *The Guardian* (20 January 2022), online: <https://www.theguardian.com/us-news/2022/jan/20/manure-natural-gas-pipeline-factory-farms-greenwashing>; Phoebe Gittelson et al, "The False Promises of Biogas: Why Biogas Is an Environmental Justice Issue" (2022) 15:6 Environ Just 352, online: <https://doi.org/10.1089/env.2021.0025>.

33 "Law in a Changing World: Welcome and Keynote Address," Faculty of Law, University of Toronto, *YouTube* (2 Mar 2023), online: <https://youtu.be/WcR2dVfGkFI>.

34 See Robinson, *supra* note 1 at 18–20, 31–4, 37–9.

35 Dale Jamieson, *Reason in a Dark Time* (Oxford: Oxford University Press, 2014) at 20, 16, online: <https://doi.org/10.1093/acprof:oso/9780199337668.001.0001> (noting Revelle's relationship to Al Gore).

36 *Ibid* at 204.
37 *Ibid* at 20, 204.
38 See Robinson, *supra* note 1, cover carrying the blub by Jonathan Lethem: "The best science fiction nonfiction novel I have ever read."
39 Jamieson, *supra* note 35 at 204.
40 *Ibid* at 224 (quoting economist William Nordhaus), 220.
41 *Ibid* at 204.
42 *Ibid* at 224.
43 *Ibid* at 219.
44 *Ibid* at 207. The title of one subsection at 219 is "The Category Formerly Known as Geoengineering," because it has come under such criticism. Russ George, for example, refused to use the term because fertilizing the ocean with iron is a proposed method for reducing carbon dioxide. In an interview, in answering the question "Would you call this geoengineering?" he replied: "Geoengineering is an entirely derogatory spin term. If they can put that to you, you've lost already." David Biello, "Pacific Ocean Hacker Speaks Out," *Scientific American* (24 October 2012), online: <https://www.scientificamerican.com/article/questions-and-answers-with-rogue-geoengineer-carbon-entrepreneur-russ-george/> [https://perma.cc/J2GZ-GFEK]. See Green, *supra* note 3 at 60 (who says he will not talk about geoengineering except to say that while it is a potential option, it comes with considerable uncertainty given the problems of unintended consequences and an appropriate regulatory framework, and he dearly hopes that those who say it may be all we have left are wrong).
45 Jamieson, *supra* note 35 at 207.
46 *Ibid* at 207, 219.
47 *Ibid* at 201.
48 Green, *supra* note 3 at 156.
49 Jamieson, *supra* note 35 at 227 (in the current "world of 'pledge and review,'" all we have are "reviewable public pledges regarding emissions reductions and climate finance. The hope is that the publicity of the process will motivate states to make pledges that are fair and adequate to addressing climate change, and then to live up to them") at 201. This is even more true since the Paris Agreement was adopted at COP21 in 2015. See Jutta Brunnée, "Between Stability and Change: International Climate Law in Precarious Times," in this volume (arguing that the "bottom up" country-specific approach created by the Paris Agreement is a positive in the wake of the Kyoto agreement, which had more teeth insofar as it was binding but failed due to rejection by the United States and not including India and China. With the Paris Agreement and its "nationally determined contributions," each country commits itself "to doing at least something"). See also "Panel 1: Law in Times of Climate Change: Who Governs?,"

Faculty of Law, University of Toronto, *YouTube* (9 March 2023), online: <https://youtu.be/QeiQQsswRME> [https://perma.cc/VAL7-XX79] at approximately 10–13 minutes and in the Q&A at approximately 50–51 minutes.

50 Jamieson, *supra* note 35 at 228.

51 *Ibid.*

52 See AEL Advocacy, *supra* note 29; Riehl & Marstokk, *supra* note 8; Joshua Gibbs & Francesco P Cappucio, "Plant-Based Dietary Patterns for Human and Planetary Health" (2022) 14:8 Nutrients 1614, online: <https://doi.org/10.3390/nu14081614>; Bingli Clark Chai et al, "Which Diet Has the Least Environmental Impact on Our Planet? A Systematic Review of Vegan, Vegetarian and Omnivorous Diets" (2019) 11:15 Sustainability 4110, online: <https://doi.org/10.3390/su11154110>.

53 Ker Than, "Replacing Animal Agriculture and Shifting to a Plant-Based Diet Could Drastically Curb Greenhouse Gas Emissions, According to New Model," *Stanford News* (1 February 2022), online: <https://news.stanford.edu/stories/2022/02/new-model-explores-link-animal-agriculture-climate-change> [https://perma.cc/58MZ-VKDZ].

54 J. Poore & T. Nemecek, "Reducing Food's Environmental Impacts through Producers and Consumers" (2018) 360:6392 Science 987, online: <https://doi.org/10.1126/science.aaq0216>.

55 Marta Kozicka et al, "Feeding climate and biodiversity goals with novel plant-based meat and milk alternatives" (2023) 14 Nat Commun 5316, online: <https://doi.org/10.1038/s41467-023-40899-2> [https://perma.cc/XSJ7-MTGY].

56 *Ibid* at 3.

57 Vegetarian Calculator puts the number of farmed animals consumed in the lifetime of an average person eating animal products in a developed country at 7,000. See Jo-Anne McArthur & Keith Wilson, *Hidden* (New York: Lantern Books, 2020) at 268. See also Vegetarian Calculator (accessed 6 April 2023), online: <https://vegetariancalculator.com/> [https://perma.cc/BN5X-M2TR].

58 See James Tully, "Sustainable Democratic Constitutionalism and Climate Crisis" (2020) 65:3 McGill LJ 545 at 560–61, 564, online: <https://doi.org/10.7202/1075601ar>. See also Jamieson, *supra* note 35 at 8 (our individual actions matter to the world and ourselves: "Our thoughts and actions can inspire others, change their lives, and even affect the course of history"), 182. The phrase "be the change" is usually attributed to Mahatma Gandhi. See Joseph Ranseth, "Gandhi Didn't Actually Ever Say 'Be the Change You Want to See in the World.' Here's the Real Quote…" (27 August 2015), online (blog): <https://josephranseth

.com/gandhi-didnt-say-be-the-change-you-want-to-see-in-the-world/> [https://perma.cc/DPK4-UGAZ].

59 See Jamieson, *supra* note 35 at 61 ("climate change can be seen as presenting us with the largest collective action problem that humanity has ever faced"). See also 99, 105, 162. It is the very definition of a "wicked" problem with both vertical and horizontal coordination challenges. See Edward Iacobucci & Michael Trebilcock, "Confronting the Institutional Challenges at the Heart of Climate Change Policy" in this volume.

60 See David Hagmann et al, "Costly Distractions: Focusing on Individual Behavior Undermines Support for Systemic Change" (2023) online: <https://doi.org/10.31219/osf.io/z2vwb> [https://perma.cc/9FSK-3A6V]. In this study, researchers found that people exposed to policies targeting individual behaviour become "less likely to propose systemic policy reforms, hold governments less responsible for solving the policy problem, and are less likely to support organizations that seek to promote systemic reform."

61 "Canada's 2021 Nationally Determined Contribution Under the Paris Agreement" (2021) 1 at 2, online (pdf): <https://cuspnetwork.ca/wp-content/uploads/2021/07/Canada's_Enhanced_NDC_Submission_EN.pdf> [https://perma.cc/AZ8R-PHF9]; Green, *supra* note 3 at 20–1. See Gabrielle Peters & Trudo Lemmens, "Inequitable Resilience to Climate Change and Policy Failure: Disability and Collective Responsibility During B.C.'s Heat Dome" in this volume. On 25 June 25 2023, the Canadian Interagency Forest Fire Centre declared the 2023 wildfire season was the worst in Canada's history. See Morgan Lowrie, "Forest Fire Centre Declares 2023 Already Worst Year Ever for Canadian Wildfires," *CTV News Montreal* (26 June 2023), online: <https://montreal.ctvnews.ca/forest-fire-centre-declares-2023-already-worst-year-ever-for-canadian-wildfires-1.6456879> [https://perma.cc/L3DF-6P3T]. See also Danielle Celermajer, *Summertime: Reflections on a Vanishing Future* (North Sydney, Australia: Penguin Random House, 2021) on the Australian bush fires in "the Black Summer" of 2019–20.

62 *Greenhouse Gas Pollution Pricing Act*, SC 2018, c 12 [*GGPPA*].

63 House of Commons, Standing Committee on Agricultura and Agri-Food (Chair: Pat Finnegan), *Toward a Resilient Canadian Agriculture and Agri-Food System: Adapting to Climate Change* (Ottawa: House of Commons, 2018) at 22–23, online (pdf): <https://www.ourcommons.ca/Content/Committee/421/AGRI/Reports/RP9814809/agrirp11/agrirp11-e.pdf> [https://perma.cc/9GM9-83QH].

64 *GGPPA*, *supra* note 62 at s 36.

65 Environment and Climate Change Canada, News Release, "Minister Guilbeault Supports Advancing Climate Ambition in New York City,"

Cision (22 September 2023) online, <https://www.newswire.ca/news-releases/minister-guilbeault-supports-advancing-climate-ambition-in-new-york-city-809661268.html> [https://perma.cc/62Y2-TTXZ].

66 *Environmental Protection Act*, RSO 1990 c E 19; Ontario's primary legislation governing the storage and applications of nutrients to farmlands, *Nutrient Management Act, 2002*, SO 2002, c 4, has also been shown to be inadequate for protecting the environment from the impacts of animal agriculture. See a report by the Environmental Commissioner of Ontario, *Back to Basics: Respecting the Public's Voice on the Environment* (Toronto: Environment Commissioner of Ontario, 2018), online (pdf): <https://www.auditor.on.ca/en/content/reporttopics/envreports/env18/Back-to-Basics.pdf> [https://perma.cc/A3VL-XGK6].

67 Green, *supra* note 3 at 73.

68 Animal Protection Party of Canada, "Animal Agriculture Is Destroying the Earth and Our Government Is Subsidizing It" (15 June 2019), online: <https://www.animalprotectionparty.ca/animal-agriculture-is-destroying-the-earth-and-our-government-is-subsidizing-it/> [https://perma.cc/DQS6-GMGV].

69 Natalie Chalifour & Heather McLeod-Kilmurray, "The Carrots and Sticks of Sustainable Farming in Canada" (2016) 17 VJEL 303 at 306.

70 Environment and Climate Change Canada, *2030 Emissions Reduction Plan* (Gatineau, QC: Environment and Climate Change Canada, 2022) at 61–2, online (pdf): <https://publications.gc.ca/collections/collection_2022/eccc/En4-460-2022-eng.pdf> [https://perma.cc/AHZ6-XYNE].

71 Agriculture and Agri-Food Canada, "Government of Canada Announces Investment in Dairy Farmers of Canada to Support Sustainability," *Newswire* (11 July 2023), online: <https://www.newswire.ca/news-releases/government-of-canada-announces-investment-in-dairy-farmers-of-canada-to-support-sustainability-831554475.html> [https://perma.cc/M38L-BGS8].

72 Brooks Animal Law Digest: Canada Edition, "Ontario Invests $300,000 to Expand Dairy Herdsperson Apprenticeship Program" (10 August 2023), online: <https://thebrooksinstitute.org/animal-law-digest/canada/issue-49/ontario-invests-300000-expand-dairy-herdsperson-apprenticeship> [https://perma.cc/WHE3-GLEL].

73 *Ibid*.

74 See Omanjana Goswami, "As the USDA Invests in 'Climate-Smart' Agriculture, It's Hard to Follow the Money," *Union of Concerned Scientists* (8 December 2022), online: <https://blog.ucsusa.org/omanjana-goswami/in-climate-smart-agriculture-its-hard-to-follow-the-money/> [https://perma.cc/45WY-QGHJ].

75 *Ibid*.

76 *Ibid*. See also American Society for the Prevention of Cruelty to Animals, *Building a More Humane Food System through the 2023 Farm Bill* (New York: ASPCA, 2023), online (pdf): <https://www.aspca.org/sites/default/files/2023_farm_bill_policy_platform_final_digital_v5_1523_1.pdf> [https://perma.cc/2WYR-E3ZB].

77 Annette Manusevich, "What Is the Farm Bill and Why Does It Matter?," *World Animal Protection* (12 May 2023), online (blog): <https://www.worldanimalprotection.us/latest/blogs/what-farm-bill-and-why-does-it-matter/> [https://perma.cc/3H4Q-92XS].

78 Nationally Determined Contributions (NDCs) are non-binding national plans that include policies and measures governments aim to implement in response to climate change and as a contribution to achieve the global targets set out in the Paris Agreement. In the Food and Agriculture Organization of the United Nations' (FAO) latest global update report on NDCs, they concluded that only 36 per cent of countries included livestock-related mitigation interventions in their recent NDC and only 55 per cent indicated livestock systems as a priority area for adaptation measures in the agricultural sector. In response, the FAO launched a new initiative to help countries better integrate livestock adaptation and mitigation interventions in their national climate action. The initiative aims to improve countries' understanding and analysis of their policy environment to better incorporate livestock development objectives with climate actions. It targets both countries that already have livestock-specific interventions included in their NDCs and those that still need to start integrating them. See K. Crumpler et al, "2021 (Interim) Global Update Report: Agriculture, Forestry and Fisheries in the Nationally Determined Contributions" (2021), Food and Agriculture Organization of the United Nations, Working Paper No 9, online: <https://openknowledge.fao.org/server/api/core/bitstreams/f628b91f-f387-42a2-9e96-d7805d82eee5/content> [https://perma.cc/38RW-SK6K]. See Jutta Brunnée, "Between Stability and Change: International Climate Change Law in Precarious Times" in this volume.

79 See The Leaflet, "Global Stocktake at COP 28 Ignores Food, Responsible for 1/3rd Global Emissions, Say Leading Organisations" (12 December 2023), online: <https://theleaflet.in/global-stocktake-at-cop-28-ignores-food-responsible-for-1-3rd-global-emissions-say-leading-organisations/> [https://perma.cc/RK5C-P2VL]; World Animal Protection, Press Release, "COP28 Fails to Address Animal Agriculture" (13 December 2023), online: <https://www.worldanimalprotection.ca/news/cop28-fails-address-animal-agriculture> [https://perma.cc/VW7F-SKK8]; Neel Kamal, "Cop 28 Closes with Food System Action Omitted: Food Experts," *Times of India* (13 December 2023), online: <https://timesofindia

.indiatimes.com/india/cop28-closes-with-food-system-action-omitted-ipes-food/articleshow/105966489.cms> [https://perma.cc/QN88-CB4N]; Leah Douglas, "COP28 Summit: Cow Burps, Food Waste in Focus on Agriculture Day," *Reuters* (2 December 2023), online: <https://www.reuters.com/world/cow-burps-food-waste-take-spotlight-cop28-agriculture-day-2023-12-02/> [https://perma.cc/CDM5-UG8U].

80 Kitty Block, "Commit to Meat Reduction in 2024 for the Sake of Animals, People and the Planet," *The Humane Society of the United States* (10 January 2024), online: <https://www.humanesociety.org/blog/commit-meat-reduction-2024-sake-animals-people-and-planet> [https://perma.cc/9E78-A695].

81 Eden Villalovas, "Beef Served at COP28 while UN Prepares to Release Report Calling for Reduced Meat Consumption," *Washington Examiner* (8 December 2023), online: <https://www.washingtonexaminer.com/news/2448168/beef-served-at-cop28-while-un-prepares-to-release-report-calling-for-reduced-meat-consumption/> [https://perma.cc/56YE-63FJ].

82 Phoebe Weston & Jonathan Watts, "The Cow in the Room: Why Is No One Talking about Farming at Cop26?," *The Guardian* (9 Nov 2021), online: <https://www.theguardian.com/environment/2021/nov/09/the-cow-in-the-room-why-is-no-one-talking-about-farming-at-cop26-aoe> [https://perma.cc/D897-CVJR].

83 The idea is that politicians can only recommend a range of policies once a social issue has hit "acceptability," otherwise they risk looking too extreme (specifically prior to "acceptability" when ideas are still considered to be "too radical" or even "unthinkable"). "Acceptability," however, shifts the window to an idea seeming "sensible," becoming "popular," and then, if politicians take it up, becoming "policy." See "Overton Window," *Wikipedia* (last updated 8 February 2023), online: <https://en.wikipedia.org/wiki/Overton_window> [https://perma.cc/HXZ9-RF3X].

84 But see Tristram Stuart, *The Bloodless Revolution: A Cultural History of Vegetarianism from 1600 to Modern Times* (New York: W.W. Norton, 2008) (examining the influence of vegetarianism from India on England).

85 Mackinac Center for Public Policy, "The Overton Window" (17 April 2023), online: <https://www.mackinac.org/OvertonWindow#overview> [https://perma.cc/ZB26-NUAV].

86 Plant-Based Foods of Canada, News Release, "Plant-Based Foods of Canada Announces the Launch of the First Annual Plant-Based Food Week," *Cision* (21 March 2022), online: <https://www.newswire.ca/news-releases/plant-based-foods-of-canada-announces-the-launch-of-the-first-annual-plant-based-food-week-874293665.html> [https://perma.cc/Q8F2-DTNG].

87 *Ibid.*

88 Brooks Animal Law Digest: Canada Edition, "Poll Finds That the Majority of GTA Residents are Interested in Exploring More Plant-Based Foods" (19 Oct 2022), online: <https://thebrooksinstitute.org/animal-law-digest/canada/issue-28/poll-finds-majority-gta-residents-are-interested-exploring-more> [https://perma.cc/D2FE-TAN3].

89 Dan Howe, "Toronto Residents Want Laws to Protect Farmed Animals," *Animal Justice* (19 Oct 2022), online: <https://animaljustice.ca/blog/toronto-residents-want-laws-to-protect-farmed-animals> [https://perma.cc/KF2Y-BBPC].

90 Angus Reid Group, *BC Plant-Based Lifestyle Survey: Prepared for the Vancouver Humane Society* (Vancouver: Angus Reid, 2023) at 3, online: <https://plantuniversity.ca/wp-content/uploads/2020/05/BC-plant-based-lifestyle-study-factum.pdf> [https://perma.cc/4E8A-2DPV] [Vancouver Humane Society Survey].

91 Steinfeld et al, *supra* note 12; Gerber et al, *supra* note 6; See also Goodland & Anhang, *supra* note 6 cited in David Robinson Simon, *Meatonomics: How the Rigged Economics of Meat and Dairy Make You Consume Too Much – and How to Eat Better, Live Longer, and Spend Smarter* (Newburyport, MA: Conari Press, 2013) at xvii (described as two World Bank scientists identifying the animal agriculture system as "the single greatest cause of climate change on the planet").

92 *An Inconvenient Truth*, DVD (Hollywood, CA: Paramount Vantage, 2006). It was based on Al Gore's 1992 book *Earth in the Balance*. See Jamieson, *supra* note 35 at 38.

93 The film won an Academy Award and was the fifth highest grossing documentary in American movie history. Gore was awarded (jointly with the IPCC) the Nobel Peace Prize in 2007. Jamieson, *ibid* at 50–52.

94 *Cowspiracy: The Sustainability Secret*, DVD (Santa Rosa, CA: AUM Films, 2014) at 16:30 (interview with Kirk R. Smith, University of California, Berkeley, Professor of Global Environmental Health).

95 See Viveca Morris, "The Cow-Shaped Hole in Biden's Methane Plan," *Politico* (16 Nov 2021), online: <https://www.politico.com/news/agenda/2021/11/16/methane-emissions-cows-agriculture-climate-change-522550> [https://perma.cc/2TJ5-4T9H], cited in Fisher, *supra* note 15.

96 *#ForNature – A Film by Greta Thunberg* (2021), Gripping Films, *Vimeo*, online: <https://vimeo.com/552829226> [https://perma.cc/J6FE-NU8X].

97 See Fisher, *supra* note 15.

98 See Catherin C. Ivanovich et al, "Future Warming from Food Consumption" (6 March 2023) 13 Nat Clim Chang 297 at 300, 301, online at <https://doi.org/10.1038/s41558-023-01605-8>. The high-methane foods focused on were ruminant meat, dairy, and rice.

99 IPCC, *An IPCC Special Report on Climate Change, Desertification, Land Degradation, Sustainable Land Management, Food Security, and Greenhouse Gas Fluxes in Terrestrial Ecosystems* (New York: Cambridge University Press, 2019), online: <https://www.ipcc.ch/srccl/>.

100 Although there are still significant barriers related to people's inability to respond to statistical information, data and other forms of rational argument, as well as "implicatory denial," whereby people accept the facts, evidence, and consequences of climate change but deny nonetheless the psychological, political, or moral implications" for a variety of reasons. This challenge applies to both climate change and animal suffering in animal agriculture. See Núria Almiron, "The 'Animal-Based Food Taboo.' Climate Change Denial and Deontological Codes in Journalism" (2020) 5 Frontiers in Communication 1 at 1, online: <https://doi.org/10.3389/fcomm.2020.512956> [https://perma.cc/9VQG-U9CV].

101 See Brooks Animal Law Digest: Canada Edition, "Leaked Draft of Latest IOC Report Reveals Meat Industry Blocked Attempt to Recommend a Plant-Based Diet" (24 March 2023), online: <https://thebrooksinstitute.org/animal-law-digest/canada/issue-39/leaked-draft-latest-ipcc-report-reveals-meat-industry-blocked> [https://perma.cc/L55M-X8NJ].

102 Rachel Sherrington, "Plans to Present Meat as 'Sustainable Nutrition' at Cop28 Revealed," *The Guardian* (29 November 2023), online: <https://www.theguardian.com/environment/2023/nov/29/plans-to-present-meat-as-sustainable-nutrition-at-cop28-revealed> [https://perma.cc/6GQZ-LMGJ].

103 Gibbs & Cappuccio, *supra* note 52.

104 See for example recent stories about the growth and development of the cultivated meat industry: Brooks Animal Law Digest: Canada Edition, "Cultivated Meat" (2022 & 2023), online: <https://thebrooksinstitute.org/animal-law-digest/search?f%5B0%5D=digest_edition%3A505&f%5B1%5D=digest_key_terms%3A525> [https://perma.cc/KC78-VFMX].

105 Gibbs & Cappuccio, *supra* note 52.

106 See Brooks Animal Law Digest: Canada Edition, "University of Guelph Researchers Develop More Sustainable Plant-Based Meat" (20 August 2023), online: <https://thebrooksinstitute.org/animal-law-digest/canada/issue-47/cop28-presidency-commits-serving-plant-based-options-after-youth> [https://perma.cc/RM79-LQS2].

107 Government of Canada, "Canada's Food Guide" (last modified 14 March 2023), online: <https://food-guide.canada.ca/en/> [https://perma.cc/SE9W-T2QE].

108 *The Game Changers*, Netflix (United States: Refuel Productions, 2018).

109 See Brooks Animal Law Digest: Canada Edition, "New Book Reveals Olympic Athletes' Secrets to Enhanced Performance and Recovery with

Plant-Based Diets" (4 August 2023), online: <https://thebrooksinstitute.org/animal-law-digest/canada/issue-48/new-book-reveals-olympic-athletes-secrets-enhanced-performance> [https://perma.cc/H9Q5-TDRB].

110 Michael Greger, *How Not to Die: Discover the Foods Scientifically Proven to Prevent and Reverse Disease* (New York: Flatiron Books, 2015).

111 Jonathan Epstein, "Preventing Future Pandemics with Jonathan Epstein" (webinar delivered at the Yale Law School, Law, Ethics and Animals Program's One Health Speaker Series, 17 February 2021). See also Matthew Hutson, "Can We Predict Which Viruses Will Spread from Animals to Humans," *The New Yorker* (2 Sept 2022), online: <https://www.newyorker.com/science/annals-of-medicine/can-we-predict-which-viruses-will-spread-from-animals-to-humans> [https://perma.cc/6HUH-S8BP].

112 Sebo, *supra* note 7 at 58–65.

113 Quoted in John S. Mackenzie & Martyn Jeggo, "The One Health Approach – Why Is It So Important?" 4:2 Trop Med Infect Dis at 2, online: <https://doi.org/10.3390/tropicalmed4020088>.

114 The conference was held in New York City, and the priorities set to combat human and animal health threats were known as "the Manhattan Principles." There was a focus on epidemic/epizootic diseases such as Ebola and Avian Influenza. Meetings in the first decade of the 2000s continued to focus on avian and pandemic preparedness. The Centers for Disease Control and Prevention in the United States established a One Heath office in 2009. In 2011 the United Nations and the World Bank recommended adoption of One Health approaches and the European Union reaffirmed its commitment to operate under the One Health umbrella. See Centers for Disease Control and Prevention, "One Health Basics: History" (accessed 15 March 2023), online: <https://www.cdc.gov/one-health/about/one-health-history.html> [https://perma.cc/K23U-U4LC].

115 Mackenzie & Jeggo, *supra* note 113.

116 See Centers for Disease Control and Prevention, Media Statement, "Importance of One Health for COVID-19 and Future Pandemics," *CDC Newsroom* (3 Nov 2021), online: <https://archive.cdc.gov/#/details?url=https://www.cdc.gov/media/releases/2021/s1103-one-health.html> [https://perma.cc/NVW5-52KY] [CDC]; World Health Organization, "One Health" (3 Oct 2022), online: <https://www.who.int/news-room/fact-sheets/detail/one-health> [https://perma.cc/BT3S-48MF]; The World Bank, "One Health Approach Can Prevent the Next Pandemic," *World Bank* (24 Oct 2022), online: <https://www.worldbank.org/en/news/feature/2022/10/24/one-health-approach

-can-prevent-the-next-pandemic> [https://perma.cc/E6GZ-U37P] [World Bank].

117 See *ibid.*

118 World Bank, *supra* note 116.

119 CDC, *supra* note 116.

120 For images, see McArthur & Wilson, *supra* note 57 and summary in Angela Fernandez, "Exemplary Legal Writing 2022, Books, Four Recommendations" (2023) Green Bag Almanac & Reader 56 at 63–4. See also Episode 763, "Will We Ever Know Covid-19's Origin Story," *The Big Story* (20 March 2023), online: <https://thebigstorypodcast.ca/2023/03/20/will-we-ever-know-covid-19s-origin-story/> [https://perma.cc/74JV-7X4T]. On the animal theory, see Katherine J. Wu, "The Strongest Evidence Yet That an Animal Started the Pandemic: A New Analysis of Genetic Samples from China Appears to Link the Pandemic's Origin to Raccoon Dogs," *The Atlantic* (16 March 2023), online: <https://www.theatlantic.com/science/archive/2023/03/covid-origins-research-raccoon-dogs-wuhan-market-lab-leak/673390/>.

121 Sebo, *supra* note 7 at 199.

122 One Welfare, "About One Welfare" (accessed 15 March 2023), online: <https://www.onewelfareworld.org/about.html> [https://perma.cc/KE5A-MQLL]. We encountered it in the context of a report by the Vancouver Humane Society aimed at reducing trauma when interacting with at-risk humans. See Celeste Morales & Rochelle Stevenson, *Helping People and Animals Together: Taking a Trauma-Informed, Culturally Safe Approach Toward Assisting Placed-at-Risk People with Addressing Animal Neglect* (Vancouver: Vancouver Humane Society, June 2021), online (pdf): <https://vancouverhumanesociety.bc.ca/wp-content/uploads/2021/06/Helping-people-and-animals-together-VHS.pdf> [https://perma.cc/DT8P-MCAJ]. It is important to remember that there are other public policy lenses. For criticisms of One Heath, see e.g., Maneesha Deckha, "The One Health Initiative and a Deeper Engagement with Animal Health and Wellbeing: Moving Away from Animal Agriculture" in Irus Braverman, ed, *More-than-One Health: Humans, Animals, and the Environment Post-COVID* (London: Routledge, 2023) 157 at 157–70, online: <https://doi.org/10.4324/9781003294085-12>.

123 Email to Angela Fernandez from Sareeta Lopez, Program Manager, Vancouver Humane Society (17 February 2023).

124 US, AB 1289, *An act to amend Section 239 of the Food and Agricultural Code, relating to the Agriculture Trust Fund*, 2023, Reg Sess, Cal, 2023.

125 UK, *Agriculture Act 2020*, c 21, s 1.

126 AEL Advocacy, *supra* note 29 at 35 citing to McLeod-Kilmurray & Chalifour, *supra* note 69. See Claire Carlile, "Sowing Doubt: How Big Ag

Is Delaying Sustainable Farming in Europe," *DeSmog* (21 December 2022), online: <https://www.desmog.com/2022/12/21/sowing-doubt-how-big-ag-is-delaying-sustainable-farming-in-europe/> [https://perma.cc/LDW9-S6GY] (on how 20 million euros spent on lobbying by the agrochemical industry and others in the intensive farming sector since 2020 is seriously undermining the EU Farm-to-Fork strategy).

127 AEL Advocacy, *supra* note 29 at 63.

128 See Simon, *supra* note 91 at 77 ("we all […] incur the costs of animal food production in one way or another"), 78 ("Vegetarians and vegans experience the externalized costs of animal foods at the same rate as the rest of society"), 79–89 (explaining the US farm subsidy system, who gets these subsidies, how they harm small producers, those in less developed countries, and domestic consumers and taxpayers); 88 (putting the total annual bill of externalized costs put on American consumers and taxpayers by US producers of meat, fish, eggs, and dairy at $414 billion).

129 Andrea Polanco & Jo Anderson, "Reforming Animal Agriculture Subsidies: A Guide for Advocates," *Faunalytics* (January 2023), online: <https://osf.io/kpuah> [https://perma.cc/PCL4-SVET].

130 See Vancouver Humane Society Survey, *supra* note 90 at 6.

131 The European Union livestock farmers received 1200 times more public money and the US was 800 times more. See Damian Carrington, "'Gigantic' Power of Meat Industry Blocking Green Alternatives, Study Finds," *The Guardian* (2023), online: <https://www.theguardian.com/environment/2023/aug/18/gigantic-power-of-meat-industry-blocking-green-alternatives-study-finds> [https://perma.cc/G6XD-6SWJ].

132 *Ibid*. See also Simona Vallone & Eric F. Lambin, "Public Policies and Vested Interests Preserve the Animal Farming Status Quo at the Expense of Animal Product Analogs," *One Earth* (18 August 2023), online: <https://www.cell.com/action/showPdf?pii=S2590-3322%2823%2900347-0> [https://perma.cc/K2MN-PSC6].

133 See *Interest and Curiosity in Cellular Food Continues to Grow*, (Guelph, ON: Canadian Food Innovation Network, 2023), online: <https://www.cfin-rcia.ca/viewdocument/interest-and-curiosity-in-cellular> [https://perma.cc/A469-EV2S].

134 See Joe Fassler, Inside Big Beef's Climate Messaging Machine: Confuse, Defend, and Downplay," *The Guardian* (3 May 2023), online: <https://www.theguardian.com/environment/2023/may/03/beef-industry-public-relations-messaging-machine> [https://perma.cc/H3Z6-WWSW].

135 See Kenny Torrella, "The Aubrey Plaza Ad for Big Dairy That May Have Violated Federal Law, Explained," *Vox* (31 May 2023), online <https://www.vox.com/future-perfect/2023/5/5/23709822

/milk-dairy-plant-based-meat-soy-almond-fake-processed> [https://perma.cc/J4H4-DX2D].

136 See e.g., "The Meat and Dairy Industries Peddle Misinformation. It's Time for Plant-Based Food Brands to Fight Back," *Fast Company* (2 May 2023), online: <https://www.fastcompany.com/90895172/plant-based-meat-fight-meat-dairy-misinformation> [https://perma.cc/8JQ9-EPZU].

137 Vesanto Melina, Winston Craig & Susan Levin, "Position of the Academy of Nutrition and Dietetics: Vegetarian Diets" (2016) 116:2 J Acad Nutr Diet 1970, online: <https://doi.org/10.1016/j.jand.2016.09.025>. See also Joanne Schepers & Lieven Annemans, "The Potential Health and Economic Effects of Plant-Based Food Patterns in Belgium and the United Kingdom" (2018) 48 Nutrition 24, online: <https://doi.org/10.1016/j.nut.2017.11.028>.

138 The USDA defines a CAFO as an agricultural facility that houses and feeds over 1,000 "animal units" in a confined area for 45 days of more in a twelve-month period, where a unit is the equivalent of "live" animal weight. This would be 1,000 meat cows but 10,000 pigs weighing more than fifty pounds, 55,000 turkeys or 125,000 chickens. See "Concentrated Animal Feeding Operation," *Wikipedia* (last updated 7 March 2023), online: <https://en.wikipedia.org/wiki/Concentrated_animal_feeding_operation> [https://perma.cc/CQQ6-YASD].

139 Sebo, *supra* note 7 at 97; US, Bill S2332, *Farm System Reform Act of 2021*, 117th Cong, 2021.

140 Cory Booker, "Booker Introduces Package of Bills to Reform US Farm System" (2 February 2023), online: <https://www.booker.senate.gov/news/press/booker-introduces-package-of-bills-to-reform-us-food-system> [https://perma.cc/XM8Y-6NQL].

141 US, AB2764, *An Act to add* Chapter 4 *(Commencing with Section 16600) to Part 1 of Division 9 of the Food and Agricultural Code*, relating to animals, 2022, Reg Sess, 2022.

142 US, SB85–1, *Relating to confined animal feeding operations*, Reg Sess, 2023.

143 Food & Water Watch, Press Release, "At Public Hearing, Oregonians Decry Last-Minute Effort to Gut Factory Farm Moratorium Bill" (22 March 2023), online: <https://www.foodandwaterwatch.org/2023/03/22/at-public-hearing-oregonians-decry-last-minute-effort-to-gut-factory-farm-moratorium-bill/> [https://perma.cc/X4V7-2B4T]; Food & Water Watch, Press Release, "At Public Hearing, Oregonians Urge Passage of Factory Farm Moratorium Bill" (6 March 2023), online: <https://www.foodandwaterwatch.org/2023/03/06/at-public-hearing-oregonians-urge-passage-of-factory-farm-moratorium-bill/>.

144 Vegetarian Society, "Default veg – Your Easy Way to More Sustainable Choices" (accessed 15 March 2023), online: <https://vegsoc.org/defaultveg/> [https://perma.cc/X4DL-PMFN].

145 Greener by Default, "About Us" (accessed 15 March 2023), online: <https://www.greenerbydefault.com/about-us> [https://perma.cc/SN4D-QQB2].

146 The Monday Campaigns, "Meatless Monday" (accessed 15 March 2023), online: <https://www.mondaycampaigns.org/meatless-monday/resources> [https://perma.cc/2PTR-N7LM].

147 Plant-Powered Fridays were introduced in New York City Public Schools in February 2022 after the successful introduction of Meatless Mondays in 2019 and Meatless Fridays in 2021. See Karen Asp, "Vegan Fridays Come to New York City Public Schools," *Forks Over Knives* (8 February 2022), online: <https://www.forksoverknives.com/wellness/vegan-fridays-nyc-public-schools/> [https://perma.cc/J8XY-KWGX]; The New York City Public Schools website uses the term "Plant-Powered Friday." See NYC Public Schools, "Plant-Powered Meals" (accessed 30 April 2024), online: <https://www.schools.nyc.gov/school-life/food/school-meals/plant-powered> [https://perma.cc/9VSV-UG6Y].

148 "Preserving choice" is the phrase often used in this context. See Green, *supra* note 3 at 201–2; Maya Mathur, "Nudges to Reduce Meat and Animal Consumption: The State of the Scientific Evidence," Scholars' Track, North American Animal Law Conference (29 September 2023) (reviewing the scientific evidence around "nudges").

149 Greener by Default, "Sustainability" (accessed 15 March 2023), online: <https://www.greenerbydefault.com/sustainability> [https://perma.cc/YU5J-HH7C].

150 See Vancouver Humane Society Survey, *supra* note 90 at 6.

151 Adalene Minelli et al, *Towards Plant-Forward Diets: A Toolkit for Local Policymakers* (New York: Centre for Environmental & Animal Protection, 2021), online (pdf): <https://guarinicenter.org/wp-content/uploads/2022/11/2021-10-04-Guarini-CEAP-Towards-Plant-Forward-Diets.pdf> [https://perma.cc/WGL5-UENX].

152 Vancouver Humane Society, *Increasing Plant-Based Purchasing at the Municipal Level: A Cost-Benefit Analysis* (Vancouver: Vancouver Humane Society, June 2021), online (pdf): <https://vancouverhumanesociety.bc.ca/wp-content/uploads/VHSCostBenefitAnalysis_Vancouver_June22.pdf> [https://perma.cc/3UN6-XQSD].

153 Minelli et al, *supra* note 151.

154 Maya Mathur et al, "Interventions to Reduce Meat Consumption by Appealing to Animal Welfare: Meta-Analysis and Evidence-Based Recommendations" (2021) 164 Appetite at 13, online: <https://doi

.org/10.1016/j.appet.2021.105277> (citing Jonathan van't Riet et al, "The Importance of Habits in Eating Behaviour: An Overview and Recommendations for Future Research" [2011] 57:3 Appetite 585, online: <https://doi.org/10.1016/j.appet.2011.07.010>).

155 Suzanne Higgs, "Social Norms and Their Influence on Eating Behaviors" (2015) 86 *Appetite* 38–44, online: <https://doi.org/10.1016/j.appet.2014.10.021> (cited in Mathur et al, *ibid*).

156 Green, *supra* note 3 at 17, 196–207.

157 Nicolas Delon, Zoe Griffiths & Courtney Dillard, "Social Norms: What They Are and How They Help and Hinder Farmed Animal Advocacy," *Mercy for Animals* (2022) at 2, online (pdf): <https://nicolasdelon.com/resources/Social-norms-and-eating-meat.pdf> [https://perma.cc/8UQD-LV6T].

158 *Ibid* at 3.

159 *Ibid.*

160 *Ibid* at 4. See Sarah B. Schindler, "Banning Lawns," 82 Geo Wash L Rev at 418–22 (discussing norms and explaining that "movement away from an entrenched norm might occur more naturally when the historic norm is shown to be harmful in contemporary settings").

161 Delon at al, *supra* note 157 at 3.

162 On carrots and sticks see Chalifour & McLeod-Kilmurray, *supra* note 69; Robinson, *supra* note 1 at 175, 188. For example, in Toronto refusing to use a green box for compost will leave a person dealing with two weeks of worth of garbage, as weekly collection alternates between trash and recycling, with green bin collection every week, creating a pretty serious "stick," as that garbage will include wet organic matter and not just dry items.

163 McArthur, *supra* note 57 at 299.

164 Jack P. Hughes et al, "Impact of Pictorial Warning Labels on Meat Meal Selection: A Randomised Experimental Study with UK Meat Consumers" (2023) 190 Appetite 1, online: <https://doi.org/10.1016/j.appet.2023.107026> [https://perma.cc/5ZZL-9PK4].

165 *Ibid.*

166 *Ibid.*

167 For a more in-depth discussion of how countries can ensure a just transition to a plant-based food system, see e.g., The Vegan Society, *Planting Value in the Food System – Part One: Our Vision* (Birmingham: The Vegan Society, 2021), online (pdf): <https://assets.website-files.com/60c75dd8ff810b2330162245/60e8425ed2c2b229c9b3e2fb_TVS_Planting_Value_in_our_Food_System_Our_Vision.pdf> [https://perma.cc/39VW-U66Z]; The Vegan Society, "Planting Value in the Food System – Part Two: The Research" (2021), online: <https://perma.cc/2SGM-EYEN>;

The Vegan Society, *Policy Brief: Achieving Climate Goals through Plant-Based Agriculture and Food* (Birmingham: The Vegan Society, 2021), online (pdf): <https://assets.website-files.com/60c75dd8ff810b2330162245/60e878daf334145ee5853880_Planting%20Value%20in%20the%20Food%20System%20-%20Part%202.pdf> [https://perma.cc/LTT8-GVQT]; Cleo Verkuijl et al, *A Just Transition in the Meat Sector: Why, Who and How?* (Stockholm: Stockholm Environment Institute, 2022), online: <https://doi.org/10.51414/sei2022.046> [https://perma.cc/JB82-ZDN9].

168 For example, if there were to be a Royal Commission as recommended in Iacobucci & Trebilcock, *supra* note 59.

169 See Q&A *supra* note 49 at approximately 1 hour, 22 minutes (in response to a question about litigation around failures to reach emissions reduction targets).

170 *References re Greenhouse Gas Pollution Pricing Act*, 2021 SCC 11, online: <https://decisions.scc-csc.ca/scc-csc/scc-csc/en/item/18781/index.do> [https://perma.cc/AJU5-ME8A]. See Green, *supra* note 3 at 167, 165 (explaining that "[t]he provinces can still do more if they want or do different things; the federal government is just setting the floor").

171 The litmus test Iacobucci & Trebilcock invoked for inclusion in the Royal Commission they propose. See Q&A *supra* note 49 at approximately 1 hour, 26 minutes. See also Green, *supra* note 3 at 45.

172 UofTAnimalLaw, "University of Toronto Faculty of Law Climate Change Conference to Serve Plant-Based Foods," *Instagram* (3 March 2023), online: <https://www.instagram.com/p/CpVFI32OGAI/> [https://perma.cc/X3QQ-BS5V]. The 2023 Vancouver Humane Society Survey, *supra* note 90 at 3, found that 73 per cent of respondents put taste in the top five factors that had a "strong influence" on food choice.

173 Q&A, *supra* note 49 at approximately 1 hour, 9 minutes.

7 Climate Change, Vulnerability Theory, and the BC Heat Dome: From Inclusion to Responsive Government

GABRIELLE PETERS AND TRUDO LEMMENS

I. Introduction

The shifting paradigm from "climate change *will* affect future generations" to "climate change *is* affecting us now" seemed to catch many by surprise. In 2021, the Working Group I of the Intergovernmental Panel on Climate Change (IPCC) stated that "[h]uman-induced climate change is already affecting many weather and climate extremes in every region across the globe." The level of confidence in their claims has increased since the IPCC's last report in 2013.[1] We are increasingly witnessing this impact in Canada, where warming is, on average, double the magnitude of global warming and is projected to continue at this accelerated rate in the future.[2] The consequences of climate change are upon us, and the speed and severity are worse than has been predicted.

Moreover, just as the effects of climate change do not follow borders, neither are its impacts so neatly siloed that they can be discussed in isolation of one another. The IPCC has highlighted the concurrence of climate change with non-climatic factors as well as the concurrence of different climate events happening simultaneously and repeatedly in the same region.[3] A recent report found that while the risk of death on days of extreme heat or days with high levels of air pollution increased by 6.1 per cent or 5 per cent, respectively, on days where there was both extreme heat and air pollution (as was the case during the BC heat dome, which we discuss further), there was a 21 per cent increase in the risk of death.[4] Yet governments who have been informing us about the extreme dangers of climate change have so far put almost no effort into climate change adaptation.[5] Surely the role of government should involve more than making announcements.[6]

Climate change must be considered by governments and society within the context of broader inequity and historic and ongoing injustice in Canada. As Kimberely Thomas et al. frame it, "Populations are not uniformly vulnerable to climate change. The reasons for vulnerability are largely social and economic, not merely a matter of different exposure to climate-related and environmental hazards."[7] Among the most impacted by these hazards are disabled people. Emphasizing how specific components of climate change threaten the right to health of disabled persons, Penelope Stein et al. point out that "The global mortality rate of people with disabilities in natural disasters is up to four times higher than people without disabilities due to a scarcity of inclusive planning, accessible information, early warning systems, transportation, and discriminatory attitudes within institutions and among individuals."[8]

In response, many have called for "inclusive" climate change adaptation and mitigation and emergency response planning.[9] For example, the 2019 UN Human Rights Council resolution on climate change and the rights of persons with disabilities called on governments to "adopt a comprehensive, integrated, gender-responsive and disability-inclusive approach to climate change adaptation and mitigation policies" and "strengthen and implement policies aimed at increasing the participation of persons with disabilities in climate change responses at the local, national, regional and international levels."[10]

But the lack of implementation of these in practice has created cynicism and frustration.[11] "Inclusion" has always conveyed a sense that disabled or other marginalized people are allowed to participate – with conditions – in a system and structure that intentionally restrained the type and degree of input possible. Inclusion is presented as a gift bestowed upon us, disabled persons, and the assumption is that any value we bring is limited. Such inclusion is not transformative.[12]

This is not to say that being present and involved in decision-making capacity is not important. Disabled people, particularly those most marginalized and facing the greatest threat from the impacts of climate change, have knowledge that is essential for saving lives. Thomas et al. emphasize how "[K]nowledge and information intersect with vulnerability to climate change in myriad ways, directly and indirectly shaping people's adaptive capacity, exposure, and sensitivity. Knowledge and information arise from within situated contexts."[13]

The rationale behind these calls for inclusion appears to be twofold: first, that current failures in policy reflect a lack of awareness and understanding among those involved in planning; second, that the "inclusion" of disabled people in the process will change the outcome for the better.

We agree wholeheartedly with the first part. Due to positionality in society and the broad exclusion of our knowledge and needs, disabled people have unique insights and analysis and have developed a subculture that includes adaptation "hacks" and specialized expertise. On the second point, however, we argue that "inclusion" fails to result in substantially better policy and outcomes in the timely manner that climate change adaptation and mitigation demands. Implied within inclusion is that it will add to and enhance, but not fundamentally challenge or alter, the structure, principles, and values of what one is being included into.

"Inclusion" into a neoliberal process where the approach is largely premised on the state playing only a limited role is tokenistic and performative. "Inclusion" does not even meet the bar of belonging. This chapter argues that without a more fundamental recognition of and emphasis on the essential role of the state, these efforts will ultimately fall short of their intended goals.

Martha Fineman's vulnerability theory offers a good basis for a better approach. It asserts that universal vulnerability and resilience created by a responsive state is a prerequisite for building genuinely inclusive adaptation, mitigation, and emergency response measures. Fineman argues that universal vulnerability is an essential component of the human condition. As she puts it:

> The fundamental realization of vulnerability theory is that the individuals and groups described as "vulnerable populations" should not be labeled vulnerable, nor should they be sequestered in discrete categories for the purposes of law and policy… [I]t is an argument that "vulnerability" is the wrong concept to use to define and isolate these groups, or any other specific group, from the whole of humanity. Human vulnerability is universal and constant, inherent in the human condition.[14]

Moreover, Fineman provides us with a framework for discussing and understanding the role of the state in this context. Her analysis explains current failures and provides a path towards future success. To mitigate and adapt to climate change and the resulting change in needs, and particularly to do so comprehensively, equitably, and with the speed necessary to prevent unnecessary suffering and loss of life, Fineman argues, the state must shed the myth of the independent, autonomous legal subject:

> It must be made clear that the choice is *not* one between an active state on one hand versus an inactive state on the other. Rather, the choice is

> whether or not the state is going to act to fulfill a well-defined responsibility to implement a comprehensive and just equality regime that ensures access and opportunity for all consistent with a realistic conception of the human subject. Our present insistence that the state need be constrained underestimates or even ignores the many ways in which the state – through law – shapes institutions from their inception to their dissolution, and the ways in which those institutions produce and replicate inequalities. We must show how these institutions operate to produce systems of privilege. To this end, it is imperative to recognize that no one is an autonomous, independent individual.[15]

Our chapter will discuss current understandings of inclusion and vulnerability in policymaking and consider better solutions for disabled persons and the broader society in the context of climate change.

II. Climate Change, Vulnerability, and "Inclusion" as Solution

A review of thirty-four papers about events associated with climate change, including droughts, floods, heat waves, hurricanes, and wildfires, found that disabled people are at greater risk from climate change largely due to multidimensional inequalities and their exclusion from adaptation and mitigation efforts.[16] Other examples illustrate that disabled people and older adults made up 77 per cent of Camp Fire victims in Paradise, California; nearly 50 per cent of Superstorm Sandy victims; and approximately 71 per cent of Hurricane Katrina victims.[17]

There is a broader context to the concerns about the impact of climate change on disabled persons. Before discussing the BC heat dome more concretely as a case study, we first want to briefly explore here the following issues: the idea of "harvesting" of "the vulnerable" in these discussions; the concept of ableism; and the link with neoliberalism.

1. Harvesting and Vulnerability

The BC heat dome occurred over a year into the COVID-19 pandemic, a time when it became more broadly recognized and visibly apparent how prevalent and endemic eugenic attitudes and beliefs remain in our society. A key example is the way in which clinical triage policies were introduced which deprioritized some disabled persons from access to potentially life-saving ventilators, reflecting stereotypical and false perceptions of their likelihood of survival and quality of life.[18]

In both the pandemic and the heat dome, "vulnerability" was raised in relation to the cause of death. It intentionally or otherwise contributed to minimizing the ways in which policy failed to create the necessary conditions for human survival. Frances Ryan, a disabled journalist, described the way "vulnerable" became a synonym for "acceptable death" during the pandemic. Referring to the failure to implement testing in long-term care homes, he argued the deaths were the result of a system that devalued the lives of disabled and elderly people.

> [The term vulnerable] implies that the mass deaths of disabled and old people were inevitable, and conveniently exonerates the state from responsibility. [...] The truth is, disabled and older people were not "vulnerable" to the virus simply because of their health or age: they were vulnerable because the government did not bother to keep them safe.[19]

Part of the inaction may be explained by an analysis of the causes of deaths that can be characterized as "harvesting" or "mortality displacement." In heat events – as in the pandemic – a number of deaths are ascribed to a group deemed to be vulnerable. Who is vulnerable can vary, but it is generally used to signify weakness, illness, deprivation, age (either young or old), and sometimes oppression. In this way, the entire concept of vulnerability is not a means to identify areas where policy is needed to support resilience, but becomes rather an excuse for not changing policy at all.

> Some heat-related deaths may occur in people whose health is already compromised, resulting in a decrease in the expected number of deaths following an initial increase, a phenomenon referred to as mortality displacement or "harvesting" [...]. It is important to understand mortality displacement because if heat-related deaths occur only in already frail individuals with a short life expectancy, the heat impact would have less public health importance [...].[20]

"Harvesting" ignores the value of a single moment, let alone weeks, months, or year(s) of human life, and the degree of error that is known to occur in prognosis while a person is still alive, let alone speculating on their lifespan postmortem. In a study that examined the rate of error among 343 doctors of 468 terminally ill patients, the prognosis was accurate in 20 per cent of cases.[21]

In the case of heat domes and poor outdoor air quality, the deflection from government culpability for not ensuring resources and access to adaptation measures is particularly striking: no one dies of heat illness or acute complications from outdoor air pollution in a mechanically cooled building with proper air filtration.

Research by a group of psychologists in the United States during the pandemic raises the possibility of unintentional consequences that can result from disaggregating data and highlighting disproportionate impact. Their "findings suggest that alerting the public to racial health disparities (such as those observed with COVID-19) has the potential to perpetuate systemic racial inequalities – by reducing White U.S. residents' concerns about public health issues and support for policies aimed at protecting public health."[22]

It is reasonable to wonder if a similar dynamic is involved in the lack of public urgency and demands for accountability and the resulting lack of political will and government inaction following the deaths during the heat dome that we discuss later. Invoking vulnerability explains away the problem.

The current use of vulnerability absorbs and expects preventable death and assigns and offloads any blame or responsibility that might exist onto individuals. At the same time, it has become increasingly popular in some activist circles to try to counter this by using vulnerable as another word for discrimination and oppression, suggesting that vulnerability is not intrinsic to our humanity and is strictly a consequence of injustice. But disability justice encourages us to celebrate our vulnerable, imperfect bodies and minds, not deny them.[23] Denying our vulnerability as humans is ableist; it is also difficult to imagine how doing so would lead to the adaptation and mitigation disabled and non-disabled humans require especially during climate change. Rather than denying vulnerability, it makes sense to extend it to all of humanity and deny the existence of invulnerability.

2. *Ableism*

Disabled people remain largely unconsidered as a demographic, nor are we given decision-making roles in research, funding, policy, or planning.[24] Ableism, specifically modern Western ableism, creates a hierarchical ranking and method of categorizing. It places conditionality on being human and operates structurally, systemically, consciously, and unconsciously to regulate and act as a means of exerting power and controlling access to resources based on a socially constructed, inconsistently applied, arbitrary, and politically motivated definition of a normal human. Fiona Kumari Campbell explains ableism as "[a] network of beliefs, processes and practices that produces a particular kind of self and body (the corporeal standard) that is projected as the perfect, species-typical and therefore essential and fully human. Disability then is cast as a diminished state of being human."[25]

Ableism establishes a framework for dehumanization and creating "other." Because it comes wrapped in a veneer of science-sounding common sense, and because being non-disabled confers privilege, it remains largely unexamined and unchallenged. Ableist rhetoric and ideas have proven difficult to penetrate. James Cherney argues that

> passing laws challenging discriminatory action can serve a valuable function, but these have historically not done much to challenge ableist culture. When people interpret such laws and their application in a context predominantly shaped by ableist rhetoric, the meaning of the legislation becomes an extension of ableist thinking.[26]

Even if anti-discrimination human rights approaches successfully addressed, in specific circumstances, some disabled people's adaptation needs to a limited degree, such approaches would ignore the fact that heat does not just put disabled people at risk. Ultimately, as the planet warms every human will require adaptations like mechanical cooling. Already, infants, children, older people, pregnant people, poor and working class people, people working outdoors, in factories, in kitchens and fast-food counters, as well as people likely unaware they are taking one or more medications that impact heat tolerance, and a myriad of others already face heightened risk to heat events. The adaptation needs of disabled people are fundamentally human needs. Schools built as recently as two years ago in BC lack air conditioning, with students sweltering inside them.[27] Mechanical cooling may be another example of what is known as the "curb cut effect," which is when a policy or design responds to advocacy of a marginalized group and ends up benefitting many others as well.[28]

A principle of disability justice is to leave no one behind and to engage in cross-movement solidarity. By virtue of making vulnerability and interdependence a universal quality, vulnerability theory eradicates the false division maintained about normal versus disabled – that one is independent and invulnerable, while the other has special needs that makes them dependent and vulnerable.

> The idea that some of us are not vulnerable or that some of us are uniquely so, operates on the individual level to disadvantage both those deemed vulnerable and those excluded from that category. It also works to "narrow and confine our vision for social justice" on the societal level which serves to "ultimately diminish the well-being of the collective community.[29]

3. *Neoliberalism*

In examining how neoliberalism has prevented necessary action on climate change, Anders Fremstad and Mark Paul list three core components of neoliberalism: decentralize democracy; defund public investments; and deregulate the economy.[30] A thorough discussion on the role of neoliberalism is beyond the scope of this chapter, but the second point is particularly relevant to the potential impact of "inclusion" alone to create policy necessary for equitable adaptation to, and mitigation of, climate change. If the overriding ideology is that government spending on public investments is to be avoided or significantly limited, how useful is it to bring in disabled people for "inclusion" in policy discussion when recommendations will require increased funding and expansion of public services?

Glen Fieldman argues that neoliberalism produces vulnerability to climate change impacts and simultaneously incapacitates collective social responses, linking survival to personal wealth. He suggests that "While rich and poor alike will confront climate-induced changes, those with accumulated assets and/or adequate earnings potential are likely to cope better than those without, as was demonstrated by the different fates of rich and poor New Orleans during and after [the] Katrina [huricane]."[31]

III. Martha Fineman: The Vulnerable Subject, Disability Justice, and the Responsive State

Fineman's theory of the role of the democratic state also targets neoliberalism. Fineman argues that "in a world in which vulnerability is resisted and autonomy and independence define the legal subject individuals are bound to fail. And we see that around us today in the neoliberal dystopia that has been created. The abdication of state responsibility has resulted in distinctive harms, poverty, deprivation, and inequality for many in society."[32]

As we will see in the example of the BC heat dome and the response to it, the individual harms caused "by the profound neglect or callous indifference and disregard on the part of the state to the realities of the human condition."[33] But, as Fineman also points out, the harm extends beyond that which is done to the individual: "Such profound neglect is a violation of the very rationale for the existence of government and law. A rejection of the responsibility and principles that legitimate the constitution of the state in the first place."[34]

Because, as Fineman explains, our "embodied vulnerability is not the foundation for the norms, laws, values and aspirations we have established for our society and its institutions,"[35] it does not inform our understanding of individual or collective responsibility. Instead, we base our norms, laws, and understanding on "abstract notions of equality, freedom and autonomy as though these were desirable and attainable human qualities."[36]

Inclusion within a framework of universal embodied vulnerability would be qualitatively different because everyone's needs are acknowledged, and variation is expected and not considered extraordinary.

For Fineman, recognizing our "fundamental, universal, and perpetual human vulnerability reveals the fallacies inherent in the ideals of autonomy, independence, and individual responsibility that have supplanted an appreciation of the social." She posits in contrast, that "we need to develop a robust language of state or collective responsibility, one that recognizes that social justice is realized through the legal creation and maintenance of just social institutions and relationships."[37]

For Fineman, the concept of the liberal subject as bearer of rights is intrinsically connected to a view of the restrained state. State intervention is restricted by a libertarian notion of freedom which provides protection only where actions clearly discriminate or interfere with the rights of other liberal subjects. It reflects a "veneration of state non-intervention."[38] This approach is incapable of addressing the social and economic disparities connected with and augmented by disasters such as climate change. Such crises strain different societal institutions and their provision of societal assets. When the state does not consider itself responsible for maintaining these institutions' resiliency and effectiveness, their vulnerability is realized, as it results in institutional decay and a subsequent lack of effectively and fairly distributed societal assets. This ultimately leads to the exacerbation of social and economic disparities. Climate change thus augments already existing inequities and failures of the state, and disproportionally affects those already disadvantaged. A responsive state is therefore needed to address the social and economic disparities that exist as well as those created by climate crises. Direct, positive intervention by the state is necessary to build and maintain societal institutions that are resilient against such external forces and that apportion societal assets equally among individuals, regardless of the strain climate crises put them under. This response is needed before climate crises happen, not after. By redefining vulnerability, Fineman invites us to discuss the role of social institutions; to decentre the individual; and to focus on collective social organization and develop a universal social justice project that extends beyond discrimination and disaster.[39]

In our opinion, vulnerability theory is also particularly powerful to address ableism at a more foundational level, precisely because it is not focused exclusively on addressing disability itself, or disability-related policy interventions. This may sound counter-intuitive, but we will elaborate: Ableism informs the cultural, economic, political, and social structure and institutions of our society, and therefore, it affects everyone, not just disabled people. By creating a mythical "normal," defining and controlling its boundaries and making full membership in society conditional on a performance of non-disabledness, ableism molds disabled and non-disabled people alike. Robert McCruer discusses in Crip Theory what he terms to be "compulsory able-bodiedness," which he argues produces disability.[40]

Addressing ableism at a policy level typically involves an anti-ableist unpacking of whatever exists or is being built. It is therefore always reactive and conflict-based. It involves trying to convince people operating from and informed by ableism, working within an ableist structure, and using ableist tools, theory, and practice that the thing they are designing, creating, suggesting, or planning is ableist. It puts the burden of proof, to use a legal concept, on those being oppressed. It is exhausting and has a high rate of failure.

Like vulnerability theory, disability justice, a social justice movement that considers the way ableism and other oppressions intersect, emphasizes interdependence. Universal vulnerability and interdependence exist within the same paradigm. As disability justice leader Mia Mingus explains,

> With disability justice, we want to move away from the "myth of independence," that everyone can and should be able to do everything on their own. I am not fighting for independence, as much of the disability rights movement rallies behind. I am fighting for an interdependence that embraces need and tells the truth: no one does it on their own and the myth of independence is just that, a myth.[41]

Disabled people, whose right to live in the community is often predicated on meeting socially satisfactory levels of independence,[42] are likewise frequently referred to as dependent, that is, "the vulnerable." This has become a defining binary for dividing humanity – dependent or independent – and effectively eliminated any discussion about interdependence.

Embedded in the concept of the vulnerable subject is the notion that people are fundamentally connected, exist in webs of relationships and contexts, and are in a constant state of potential vulnerability. As embodied beings, we are all submitted to the inevitability of developmental, environmental, and social change and their implications for our social and physical well-being. We are all faced with "the ever-present possibility of harm, injury, and misfortune from mildly adverse to catastrophically devastating events, whether accidental, intentional, or otherwise."[43]

Vulnerability theory moves us away from one of the main sources of conflict in the design of policy and recurring failures with "inclusive" planning by asserting that everyone is vulnerable. By eliminating the categorization of some people as vulnerable, and the implication that "normal" people are not vulnerable, a different discussion for development of policy emerges. If everyone is vulnerable and the role of the state is to actively work to create and support resilience directly or via its support of other societal institutions, then the question becomes about how to do so rather than whether to do so.[44]

To survive climate change, we must abandon our myths about independence and embrace our interdependence and mutually supportive resilience. The 2021 BC heat dome illustrates this aptly.

IV. The 2021 BC Heat Dome

1. Heat Dome in Numbers: Impact on Disabled Persons

For one week, from 25 June to 1 July 2021, a heat dome set in on BC.[45] The term heat dome was coined in 2011 to describe what happens when a high pressure system traps hot air at the surface. During a heat dome, temperatures do not cool at night and the air quality worsens over time. The danger and threat heat poses to human health and life particularly to certain populations was well known. And yet 619 people died that week because of the heat. Heat deaths are preventable, and the mass death event reflects an enormous failure in planning and policy. Of those deaths, 91 per cent were people with comorbidity, which is often another way of saying disabled people; 90 per cent were aged 60 years or older; 98 per cent of the deaths occurred inside; 56 per cent lived alone; and 61 per cent lived in neighbourhoods that were mostly materially or socially deprived.[46] It should be noted that only 22 per cent of the BC population at the time was disabled. The then BC premier John Horgan infamously said that they were trying to get the message out and that people had "personal responsibility" and "fatalities are part of life."[47]

Remarkably, the word disability never appears in the BC Coroners report on the heat dome. It refers only to people with chronic health conditions. This is strikingly at odds with calls from organizations like the UN, the World Bank,[48] the WHO,[49] and journals such as The Lancet,[50] the British Medical Journal,[51] and others, which identify both the heightened risk faced by disabled people and the need to identify and include disabled persons in the development of mitigation and adaptation strategies and emergency response. Moreover, these mortality statistics should not be understood to be a comprehensive reflection of the health and other harm that results from heat minus means for adaptation and mitigation. Other research has noted the increase of overdose deaths, acts of self-harm, and accidents during heat waves.[52] As well, disabled people, especially those with chronic conditions, often experience worsening of their conditions, and people who survive heat illness can be left with long-term health effects.

The BC heat dome's disproportionate impact on certain populations illustrates the essential role of the various societal institutions that Fineman identifies as promoting resilience. It is the combined failure of those social institutions that explains the serious impact of the heat dome on disabled and/or older persons, especially at the low-income level. Addressing these on a case-by-case individual human rights claims cannot compensate for these structural failures.

The BC Human Rights Code may provide some protection against landlords who deny tenants the right to install and use air conditioning and those who may be guilty of discrimination. For a tenant to assert rights in this situation, they must: prove that mechanical cooling is essential for medical reasons, purchase the air conditioner themselves, be denied the right to use it, and file a human rights complaint. At every stage of this process, it benefits fewer and fewer people and becomes increasingly inaccessible and less useful to some of the most in need of mechanical cooling.[53] In some cases, landlords have prohibited and threatened to evict a tenant from installing a window or portable air conditioner in their unit.[54] While there are fewer and less onerous barriers involved in filing a Human Rights complaint compared to other legal actions, a lower barrier is not no barrier. Almost a million people in BC do not have a primary care physician,[55] and those who do may face cost barriers in acquiring the necessary documentation. Likelihood of having a primary care physician is also negatively impacted by having a lower income[56] and living outside of major cities. In Ontario, Black women are three times less likely to have a family doctor than non-racialized women.[57] Use of specialists who might better understand the impact of heat on a specific health condition is also affected by income and region.[58]

The rate and nature of the change that is needed makes the issue by issue, case by case, province by province incremental snail-pace approach to change, which is typical for disabled people in Canada,[59] particularly unsuited for climate change adaptation. We also need to do more than create an "inclusive" disaster and emergency response. We need to look upstream. Given that we know that poor people are significantly more likely to die in extreme weather events, would the solution not be to end poverty?

For an article for The Maple, one of us (GP) interviewed disabled people following the heat dome. One man, who had three friends dying that week, credited his survival and those of others he knew with deciding to sleep outside.[60] Significantly, the government seemed to consider its nearly exclusive role to be "informing citizens" of what they should do – without providing them with the means to do so. But even then, there was no government alert or health authority recommendation advising people to sleep outside, the one measure that likely saved their lives.

Of those who died, 73 per cent were inside private residences: 39 per cent in multi-unit buildings and 34 per cent in detached buildings); 10 per cent occurred in social housing, single room occupancy (SRO), or supportive housing; 7 per cent occurred in trailer homes, mobile homes, RVs, or campers; and 7 per cent occurred in senior or long-term care homes, while 56 per cent lived alone.

2. *Official Heat Dome Review: How Inclusion Became Exclusion*

Of the two authors of this chapter, one (GP) lived directly through the heat dome and participated in the official Coroner's review of the crisis. The following is GP's account of her experience and some of the correspondence she wrote at the time. It is written in the first person for clarity of the nature of what is being shared (personal account and reflection of direct experience). This brief autoethnographical insert is aided by notes and documents from the time.

> As a disabled person living in social housing that lacks mechanical cooling and with numerous health conditions that cause me to be at particular risk from the effects of heat, I developed heat stroke during the heat dome. In the midst of the heat dome and while dealing with its effects, I and a fellow Commissioner on the Vancouver City Planning Commission, Amina Yasin, wrote a memorandum from the Commission to the City outlining what needed to be done at the municipal level. The following year I was asked to be a member of the BC Coroners Panel reviewing the deaths during the heat dome. I requested an accessibility accommodation (remote participation) and while this was reluctantly eventually agreed

to, the Coroner's office made no arrangements for that to actually happen. On the day of the panel one of the staff members who I reached by phone offered to put his cell phone on a table so I could "listen in" to the meeting. Eventually that was upgraded to a laptop placed on the table. This allowed me to hear most of the proceedings but see only fractions of it. Nonetheless I contributed my thoughts which were not well received. I further followed-up with eight recommendations:

1. Where the page 6 of the Draft states: "By December 1, 2022, the Ministry of Health will review including cooling devices as medical equipment accessible to persons most at risk of dying during an extreme heat event." [As of June 2023 the report still has yet to be completed and released.]

   I recommend the date be changed from December 2022 to June 30, 2022. Further that the language be changed to: The Province immediately establish a short-term trial project for funding for air conditioners and air purifiers under the BC Medical program in order to lessen the likelihood of preventable heat deaths this summer. The viability of a permanent program be researched and a report completed by December 2022.
2. Bring BC in line with international research and leadership on extreme heat and disaster research and policy requires collecting and analysing data and crafting policy, using a disability lens. Disabled people must be named.[61]
3. Apply an anti-oppression lens to the development of all extreme heat policy, preparedness and response. We now know that simply saying "everyone" has the effect of planning and prioritizing a select few, reinforces existing privilege and entitlement and fails to address systemic and discriminatory causes of risk.[62]
4. Vulnerability Theory. There are various theoretical approaches to the concept of vulnerability. What has become apparent during the pandemic is that naming of vulnerability, which was originally intended under human rights to be a means to ensure the state provided specific protections and took additional measures, has instead become an excuse for the state's inability to safeguard certain human lives. I recommended to use Martha Fineman's Vulnerability Theory, because it emphasizes that vulnerability is a universal human trait.[63]
5. Planning for and emergency response for extreme heat events be included as part of the emerging BC Accessibility Act standards.[64]
6. Nothing about Us without Us.

The essential role of disabled people in crafting policy response.[65] To this end, the province will form a Lived Expertise Advisory Council for Extreme Heat, Poor Air Quality and Climate Change Related Disaster Preparedness and Response Work Group. Further, that the Province provide funding for local governments to establish similar groups.
7. Cooling in summer be understood under the same framework as heating in the winter. Namely that all housing must include cooling of indoor air and that Landlord and Tenant law be altered to reflect a date and/or temperature by which air conditioning is turned on.
8. Emphasis on interdependence, and avoiding the paternalism of suggesting vulnerable people need to be "checked on" but rather that they be consulted as to their well-being and supported."

All of my recommendations were rejected. I requested that my name be listed as dissenting from rather than endorsing the final report but instead it was removed entirely. In short, my experience of "inclusion" was one of exclusion. It resulted in no policy change.

3. *Vulnerability Applied: Role of State Institutions in Creating Resilience to Climate Change*

Fineman recently provided a schematic representation of the various systems through which the state creates resilience (figure 7.1).

It is in our view striking how, in the context of a concrete climate change disaster as the heat dome, failures in various social institutions overlap with particular ways in which the heath dome impacted on disabled persons. It illustrates the value of vulnerability theory, with its emphasis on systemic state action to create resilience, for addressing complex issues such as climate change. Here we want to briefly illustrate the interaction between failures of our institutions, and the impact of climate change on disabled persons.

1. "FAMILY" AS A SOCIAL INSTITUTION

The year 2021 broke the record for the number of people living alone in Canada, describing the living circumstances of 15 per cent of people over the age of 15. The percentage was higher for disabled people, with 20.8 per cent of disabled people living alone. Likewise, it varies by age, with 42 per cent of people 85 years and older living in private residences alone. In contrast, only 7 per cent of people aged 20–24 live alone.[66] Disabled people who live alone and/or are single parents are also more likely to live in poverty than other disabled people, who as

Figure 7.1. Resilience and Universal Vulnerability: The State and Social and Legal Institutions and Relationships

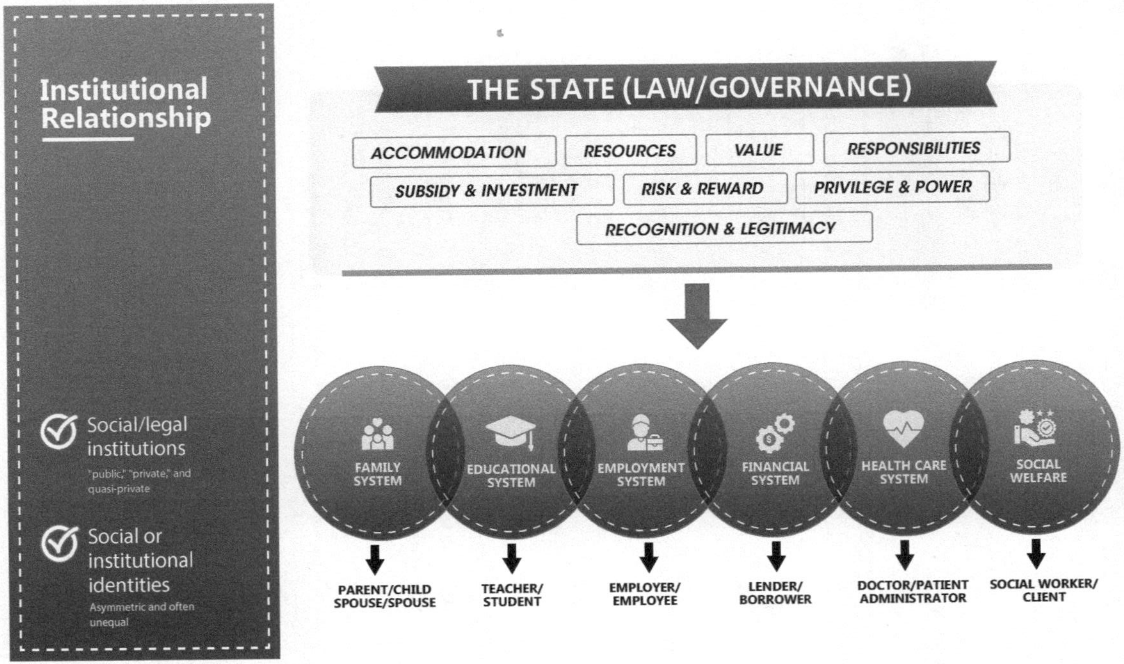

Source: Martha Albertson Fineman. Used with permission.

a group overall already experience double the poverty rate of non-disabled people. Non-disabled people who live alone are also more likely to live in poverty, and BC has a higher than national average poverty rate.[67] Disability benefit clawbacks are barriers to disabled people's ability to live with someone else and may be a contributing factor to the higher rates of living alone as well as the higher rate of poverty and isolation.[68] The limited range of accessible options available in housing, particularly at the lower income level, also create restrictions on the type of living situations possible for disabled people. For example, sharing a house with friends may not be possible due to the presence of stairs or other barriers. Disabled people are more likely to have core housing needs, to live in housing in need of major repairs, and to be spending more than 30 per cent of their income on housing.[69] Disability benefits can also be a barrier to acquiring housing both due to their low amount and as a source of income. While it is illegal to discriminate on this basis, it does not mean that landlords follow the law.[70]

2. EMPLOYMENT/INCOME AS A SOCIAL INSTITUTION

The issue of participation of disabled people in the capitalist workforce is not as straightforward as awareness campaigns calling for inclusion in the workforce suggest. The social construction of disability and modern Western ableism is rooted in and intertwined with colonialism,[71] enslavement[72] and scientific racism,[73] the emergence of capitalism,[74] and the industrial revolution. In the present, while there is discussion about making workplaces more accessible, this discussion is largely limited to things like installing ramps or providing captions in meetings. Some disabled people will not be able to participate in the workforce under any circumstances, and the decision has been made by our society that punishment for this is deep poverty.

According to Statistics Canada, persons with disabilities between the age of twenty-five and sixty-four are less likely to be employed (59 per cent) than those without disabilities (80 per cent). People with severe disabilities experience a higher likelihood of being unemployed. People with more severe disabilities in the same age bracket are more likely to be living in poverty (28 per cent) than those without disabilities (10 per cent) or those with milder disabilities (14 per cent). Disabled persons are twice as likely to live in poverty, accounting for 41 per cent of those who do.[75]

The official number of disabled people living in poverty in Canada is damning. But the number is artificially low because the poverty line itself has an ableist bias, reflecting the structural, institutional, and systemic nature of ableism.[76] Disabled people often refer to this difference between the cost of living as a disabled versus a non-disabled person in Canada as a "crip tax." Researchers have recently documented what disabled people long knew and discussed: it simply costs more to live as a disabled person, particularly in a society that was not designed for us to live in or be a part of. Further, because so many programs of additional support in Canada, such as ones that might provide funding for wheelchairs or other equipment, are means-tested, the inaccuracy of the poverty line cuts some disabled people off from essential resources.[77]

The incidence of disability increases with age, which means many people become disabled *after* having left the capitalist workforce at a time in their life when incomes go down. While poverty among seniors has typically been lower in Canada than elsewhere, there is an upward trend explained partly by the decline in coverage by workplace pensions.[78]

3. EDUCATION AS A SOCIAL INSTITUTION

Disabled people experience multiple barriers to all levels of education.[79] Only 14 per cent of disabled people 25–64 years old have a bachelor's degree or higher, compared with 27 per cent of non-disabled people. Lack of education is correlated with poverty. As with all else, racialized disabled people face additional and disproportionate discrimination within the school system.

4. HEALTH CARE AS A SOCIAL INSTITUTION

The majority of people who died during the heat dome had some contact with health care in their last month. Many were found dead during wellness checks or died after. Yet wellness checks and contact via registries were the solutions offered by the BC Coroners report. This identifies multiple flaws in treating this as a medical rather than a social policy issue. Disabled people with those same health conditions who lived inside air-conditioned homes and had proper support did not die. By focusing on the individualistic and flawed definition of vulnerability and the medical model definition of disability, the BC Coroners report falsely locates the problem and solution within individual bodies instead of the society they exist in.

5. SOCIAL WELFARE SYSTEM AS AN INSTITUTION

Disability benefits have been maintained at a level of deep poverty, with some provinces hovering around the 40 per cent poverty line, which has not been corrected for ableist bias – meaning deeper poverty and more disabled people than statistics represent. Poverty is also a cause of disability, which means the same lack of institutional resilience that may have caused an individual to face greater risk of morbidity or mortality during heat also denies them the means to survive it.

6. HOUSING AS A SOCIAL INSTITUTION

Building codes and design standards are not adjusted to the challenges posed by climate change. Indoor air temperatures are strongly influenced by the design, materials, size, construction, and other aspects of the building. The impacts of climate change were predicted long before the devastating loss of life occurred in BC. The government shared a considerable amount of information over decades about the fact that climate change was taking place. Yet this was not reflected in changes to building codes or requirements for retrofitting of existing housing. Following the heat dome deaths, the City of Vancouver passed a motion requiring that as of 2025, all new multi-family buildings require cooling systems as part of their design. However, due to the phenomena known as "filtering" whereby new housing tends to be the most expensive housing on the market leaving the existing buildings to be more affordable options, it is likely to be a long time before this results in society-wide air-conditioned housing that includes disabled people at lower income levels.

There were reports of landlords banning tenants from installing air conditioners. The province's crown corporation, BC Housing, that oversees non-market and owns and operates public housing was found to have earlier turned off the cooling in multiple buildings that had it available. This was discovered by the then chair of the Vancouver City Planning Commission while doing her graduate research.[80]

Heating is identified in the housing code as a necessity, while cooling is identified as a luxury. This clearly fails to protect those particularly vulnerable to the impacts of heat and makes surviving heat conditional on financial privilege. Laws that mandate maximum indoor temperatures, similar to laws that mandate minimum indoor temperatures, would eliminate areas of conflict and provide protection to ensure proper adaptation to climate change. The Ontario Human Rights Commission has called for such laws.[81]

Vancouver and other cities have "visitable" standards for housing. Non-disabled people visit friends and relatives in their homes throughout their lifetimes, but inaccessibility has prevented disabled people from doing the same. This has resulted in disabled children being left out of birthday parties and other events, and may contribute to isolation, and even unemployment for disabled adults. Such a standard should surely include mechanical cooling.[82]

V. Conclusion

The only way to effectively safeguard the lives of those most affected by heat and most at risk of dying is to standardize mechanical cooling for everyone. Cooling must be an opt out (where one can choose to not turn it on if one does not require or desire it), just like heating in our housing and all built environments. Vulnerability theory teaches us to begin with our embodied nature, with the body, and understand that, as embodied beings, we are necessarily vulnerable. Vulnerability to heat is universal among embodied beings. Every human body is vulnerable to heat. The only thing that varies among people is at what point the temperature and humidity become fatal to an individual person.

The window for variation is remarkably narrow: it is not the case that people who die of heat illness do so under conditions that are not understood as hot for other humans. The planet is warming and those who died during the heat dome and who have died during other heat waves, do not possess any singular characteristic. As well, deaths due to heat is only one measure of the impact of heat on human mortality. Moreover, mortality itself is only one measure of human suffering because of heat.

We need to understand heat-related deaths as an inevitable result of the social institutions of our society failing to create necessary resilience for human survival, particularly in the face of climate change. If someone dies inside an unheated building during a period of extreme cold in the winter, we understand the problem to be the lack of heating in the building. We understand that humans in Canada should not be housed in buildings with no source of heat. How the body responds to heat varies depending on multiple internal and external factors. How we respond as a society to climate change depends not on our bodies but on our willingness to act as a society. This is why vulnerability theory offers such a valuable approach to dealing with climate change. If applied consistently, it can help us to address the problematic and dramatic impact of climate change on disabled persons in the immediate future, but in doing so also the implications for all. While vulnerability theory begins from the body, it does not end there. Instead, it gives us a path to a better future for all.

Acknowledgments

The authors would like to thank Catherine Frazee, Martha Fineman, and Ramona Coelho for detailed suggestions and comments on earlier versions of this chapter and for sharing presentation material included in this chapter (MF); Jutta Brunee and Brenda Cossman for content and editing suggestions; Troy Klassen for background research; and Madison Regan for diligent work on the references.

NOTES

1 IPCC, *Climate Change 2021: The Physical Science Bias. Working Group I Contribution to the Sixth Assessment Report of the Intergovernmental Panel on Climate Change*, Valérie Masson-Delmotte et al, eds (Geneva: IPCC, 2021).

2 Elizabeth Bush et al, *Canada's Changing Climate Report in Light of the Latest Global Science Assessment* (Ottawa: Government of Canada, 2022).

3 Hans-Otto Portner et al, eds, *Climate Change 2022: Impacts, Adaptation and Vulnerability. Working Group II Contribution to the Sixth Assessment Report of the Intergovernmental Panel on Climate Change* (Geneva: Intergovernmental Panel on Climate Change, 2022).

4 Mostafijur Rahman et al, "The Effects of Coexposure to Extremes of Heat and Particulate Air Pollution on Mortality in California: Implications for Climate Change" (2022) 206:9 Am J Respir Clin Care Med 1117, online: <https://doi.org/10.1164/rccm.202204-0657OC>.

5 Tapan K. Dhar & Luna Khirfan, "Climate Change Adaptation in the Urban Planning and Design Research: Missing Links and Research Agenda" (2017) 60:4 J Environ Plan Manage 602, online: <https://doi.org/10.1080/09640568.2016.1178107>.

6 Portner et al, *supra* note 3.

7 Kimberely Thomas et al, "Explaining Differential Vulnerability to Climate Change: A Social Science Review" (2019) 10:2 WIREs Clim Chang, online: <https://doi.org/10.1002/wcc.565>.

8 Penelope J.S. Stein & Michael Ashley Stein, "Climate Change and the Right to Health of People with Disabilities" (2022) 10:1 Lancet Glob Health 24, online: <http://doi.org/10.1016/s2214-109x(21)00542-8>. See also Sebastien Jodoin, Nilani Ananthamoorthy & Katherine Lofts, "A Disability Rights Approach to Climate Governance" (2020) 47:1: Ecology LQ 73 at 76, 81–94 and references, online: <https://doi.org/10.15779/Z38W37KW48>. For an earlier warning about the disproportionate impact of climate change on persons with disabilities, see Gregor Wolbring & Verlyn Leopatra, "Climate Change, Water, Sanitation and Energy Insecurity Invisibility of People with Disabilities" (2012) 66 Can J Disab Studies 1, online: <https://doi.org/10.15353/cjds.v1i3.58>.

9 See e.g., International Disability Alliance, "Disability Inclusive Climate Action" (accessed 05 November 2024), online: <https://www.internationaldisabilityalliance.org/climate-change>; Emma Calgaro, "Climate Disaster Risk, Disability, and Resilience" (2021) 120:829 Curr Hist

320, online: <https://doi.org/10.1525/curh.2021.120.829.320>; Jodoin, Ananthamoorthy & Lofts, *supra* note 8.

10 *Human Rights and Climate Change*, UNHRC, 41st Sess, 2019, UN Doc A/HRC/RES/41/21, HRC Res 41/21.

11 HPOD, "COP26 Climate Change Summit Inaccessible to Wheelchair Users" (7 November 2021), online (blog): <https://hpod.law.harvard.edu/news/entry/cop26-incident-shines-light-on-impact-of-climate-change-on-disabled>.

12 Mia Mingus, "Access Intimacy, Interdependence and Disability Justice" (12 April 2017), online (blog): <https://leavingevidence.wordpress.com/2017/04/12/access-intimacy-interdependence-and-disability-justice/>.

13 Thomas et al, *supra* note 7 at 10 [reference omitted].

14 Martha Albertson Fineman, "Universality, Vulnerability, and Collective Responsibility" (2021) 16:1 Ethics For 1, online: <https://doi.org/10.7202/1083648ar >.

15 Martha Albertson Fineman, "The Vulnerable Subject and the Responsive State" (2010) 60:2 Emory LJ 251, online: <https://scholarlycommons.law.emory.edu/elj/vol60/iss2/1/>.

16 Cadeyrn J. Gaskin et al, "Factors Associated with the Climate Change Vulnerability and the Adaptive Capacity of People with Disability: A Systematic Review" (2017) 9:4 Weather Clim Soc 801, online: <https://doi.org/10.1175/WCAS-D-16-0126.1>.

17 Valeria Novack "Centering the Disability and Aging Communities in Federal Emergency Response Efforts" (16 June 2020), online: <https://www.americanprogress.org/article/centering-disability-aging-communities-federal-emergency-response-efforts/>.

18 Samuel R. Bagenstos, "The New Eugenics" (2021) 71:3 Syracuse L Rev 751, online: <https://repository.law.umich.edu/articles/2690/>; Trudo Lemmens & Roxanne Mykitiuk, "Disability Rights Concerns and Clinical Triage Protocol Development During the COVID-19 Pandemic" (2020) 40:4 Health L Can 103; Jackie Leach Scully, "Disability, Disablism, and COVID-19 Pandemic Triage" (2020) 601 J Bioethical Inquiry 601, online: <https://doi.org/10.1007/s11673-020-10005-y >.

19 Frances Ryan, "During Covid, to Be 'Vulnerable' Is to Be Told Your Life Doesn't Matter," *The Guardian* (24 June 2021), online: <https://www.theguardian.com/commentisfree/2021/jun/24/covid-vulnerable-life-death-toll-old-disabled>.

20 Zhen Qiao et al, "Assessment of Short- and Long-Term Mortality Displacement in Heat-Related Deaths in Brisbane, Australia 1996–2004" (2015) 123:8 Environ Health Perspect 766, online: <https://doi.org/10.1289/ehp.1307606>.

21 Nicholas A. Christakis & Elizabeth B. Lamont, "Extent and Determinants of Error in Doctors' Prognoses in Terminally Ill Patients: Prospective Cohort Study" (2000) 320 BMJ 469, online: <https://doi.org/10.1136/bmj.320.7233.469>.

22 Allison L. Skinner-Dorkenoo et al, "Highlighting COVID-19 Racial Disparities Can Reduce Support for Safety Precautions Among White U.S. Residents" (2022) 301 Soc Sci Med 114951, online: <https://doi.org/10.1016/j.socscimed.2022.114951>.

23 Chanelle Gallant, "Let's Celebrate Our Vulnerable, 'Imperfect' Bodies," *Xtra Magazine* (17 May 2021), online: <https://xtramagazine.com/power/sex-disability-justice-201022>.

24 Aleksandra Kosanic, "An Inclusive Future: Disabled Populations in the Context of Climate and Environmental Change" (2022) 55 Curr Opin Env Sust, online: <https://doi.org/10.1016/j.cosust.2022.101159>.

25 Fiona A.K. Campbell, "Inciting Legal Fictions: 'Disability's' Date with Ontology and the Ableist Body of the Law" (2001) 10:1 Griffith L Rev 42 at 44.

26 James L. Cherney, *Ableist Rhetoric: How We Know, Value, and See Disability*, Kindle ed (University Park: Pennsylvania State University Press, 2019) at 172–3.

27 Julie MacLellan, "How Hot Is Too Hot? New West Schools Baking in Heat Wave," *New Westminster Record* (18 May 2023), online: <https://www.newwestrecord.ca/local-news/how-hot-is-too-hot-new-west-schools-baking-in-heat-wave-7022744>.

28 Angela Glover Blackwell, "The Curb-Cut Effect" (2017) 15:1 Stanford Soc Innov Rev 28, online: <https://ssir.org/articles/entry/the_curb_cut_effect>.

29 Martha A. Fineman, "Vulnerability, Justice, and the Human Condition: Reasoning from the Body" (2022), Trinity Lectures: Vulnerability, Justice and the Human Condition by Prof. Martha A. Fineman, Trinity College Dublin, at 05:00–05:30, online (video): <https://vimeo.com/showcase/9966989/video/763436327> [Fineman, "Vulnerability, Justice, and the Human Condition"]; Martha Albertson Fineman, "Reasoning From the Body: Universal Vulnerability and Social Justice" (2022) Emory University School of Law Research Paper No 22–18, online: <https://papers.ssrn.com/sol3/papers.cfm?abstract_id=4100709>.

30 Andres Fremstad & Mark Paul, "Neoliberalism and Climate Change: How the Free-Market Myth has Prevented Climate Action" (2022) 197 Ecol Econ, online: <https://doi.org/10.1016/j.ecolecon.2022.107353>.

31 Glenn Fieldman, "Neoliberalism, the Production of Vulnerability and the Hobbled State: Systemic Barriers to Climate Adaptation" (2011) 3:2 Clim Dev 159, online: <https://doi.org/10.1080/17565529.2011.582278>.

32 Fineman, "Vulnerability, Justice, and the Human Condition," *supra* note 29 at 17:25–18:00.
33 *Ibid.*
34 *Ibid.*
35 *Ibid* at 14:50–15:10.
36 *Ibid* at 15:15–15:30.
37 Martha Albertson Fineman, "Vulnerability and Social Justice" (2019) 53:2 Val U L Rev 341 at 342.
38 Martha A. Fineman, "The Vulnerable Subject: Anchoring Equality in the Human Condition" (2008) 20 Yale JL & Feminism 1, online: <https://hdl.handle.net/20.500.13051/6993> [Fineman, "The Vulnerable Subject"].
39 Emily Zarychta & Laura Track, "Human Rights in Heat Waves" (16 June 2022), online: <https://bchrc.net/human-rights-in-heat-waves/>.
40 Robert McRuer, *Crip Theory: Cultural Signs of Queerness and Disability*, Kindle ed (New York: New York University Press, 2006) at 9.
41 Mia Mingus, "Changing the Framework: Disability Justice" (12 February 2011), online (blog): <https://leavingevidence.wordpress.com/2011/02/12/changing-the-framework-disability-justice/>.
42 Lillian Roy & Angela MacKenzie, "'I Can't Live that Way': Montreal Man Seeking Medically Assisted Death Due to Home Care Conditions," *CTV News Montreal* (29 September 2022), online: <https://montreal.ctvnews.ca/i-can-t-live-that-way-montreal-man-seeking-medically-assisted-death-due-to-home-care-conditions-1.6090165>.
43 Fineman, "The Vulnerable Subject," *supra* note 38.
44 It should be noted that international human rights law, particularly as promoted by the International *Convention on the Rights of Persons with Disabilities*, increasingly emphasizes the duty of States to enhance resilience and ensure the effective realization of rights. See e.g., *Human Rights and Climate Change*, UNHRC, 41st Sess, 2019, UN Doc A/HRC/RES/41/21, HRC Res 41/21 at 4–5 calling on States to "support the resilience and adaptive capacities of persons with disabilities … to respond to the adverse impact of climate change." This appears compatible with a universal vulnerability approach. Yet, recognizing universal vulnerability and the need to promote resilience for all avoids the problems we identified with singling out disabled persons as being in need of 'inclusive' measures; measures which tend to be isolated, at times haphazardous, and not easily addressing a universally shared need for building resilience. For a good discussion of the use of international human rights claims in relation to disability and climate change, see Jodoin, Ananthamoorthy & Lofts, *supra* note 8. The authors also explicitly recognize how promoting disability rights in relation to climate change can contribute to interventions that benefit all (see e.g., at 110–11 "Given

the knowledge, resources, and communities that persons with disabilities have developed for resilience in the face of natural disasters as well as the structural barriers that they must confront on a daily basis, their roles as knowers and makers should be especially valued in a future where life will likely be much more challenging due to the impacts of climate change. That knowledge has the potential not only to improve the lives of people with disabilities, but also the lives of society at large"). Yet they appear to put more trust in individual rights claims and in measures that put responsibility on individual disabled persons (see e.g., their recommendations to ensure the provision of "information," and to consult, whereas we emphasize, informed by vulnerability theory, the need for broad, strong state intervention that benefits all). On the interaction of vulnerability theory and human rights law, see Ani B. Satz, "Disability, Vulnerability, and the Limits of Antidiscrimination" (2008) 83 Wash Law Rev 513.

45 Spencer Weart & American Institute of Physics, "The Discovery of Global Warming (Timeline)" (accessed 11 November 2024), online: <https://history.aip.org/climate/timeline.htm>.

46 Chief Coroner of British Columbia, *Extreme Heat and Human Mortality: A Review of Heat-Related Deaths in B.C. in Summer 2021* (Victoria: BC Coroners Service, 2022).

47 Denise Wong, "B.C. Premier Walks Back Comments about Heatwave Deaths," *CityNews Vancouver* (29 June 2021), online: <https://vancouver.citynews.ca/2021/06/29/bc-premier-heatwave-deaths/>.

48 World Bank, *Disability Inclusion in Disaster Risk Management – Assessment in the Caribbean Region* (Washington, DC: World Bank, 2022), online: <https://hdl.handle.net/10986/37173>.

49 Lindsay Lee et al, "WHO Functioning and Disability Disaggregation (FDD11) Tool: A Reliable Approach for Disaggregating Data by Disability" (2022) 80 Arch Pub Health, online: <https://doi.org/10.1186/s13690-022-01001-2>.

50 Stein & Stein, *supra* note 8.

51 Pauline Castres, "Climate Policy and Activism Need to Make Space for Disabled People" 379 (2022) BMJ 1, online: <https://doi.org/10.1136/bmj.o2387>;

52 Fernando Florido Ngu et al, "Correlating Heatwaves and Relative Humidity with Suicide (Fatal Intentional Self-Harm)" (2021) 11 Sci Rep, online: <https://doi.org/10.1038/s41598-021-01448-3>; Robin Cooper, "The Impacts of Extreme Heat on Mental Health" (30 July 2019), online (blog): <https://www.psychiatrictimes.com/view/impacts-extreme-heat-mental-health>; Rahini Mahendran et al, "Interpersonal Violence Associated with Hot Weather" (2021) 5:9 Lancet Planet Health e571, online:

<https://doi.org/10.1016/S2542-5196(21)00210-2>; Christopher Ingraham, "Two New Studies Warn That a Hotter World Will be a More Violent One," *The Washington Post* (16 July 2019), online: <https://www.washingtonpost.com/business/2019/07/16/two-new-studies-warn-that-hotter-world-will-be-more-violent-one/>; Connor Y.H. Wu, Benjamin F. Zaitchik & Julia M. Gohlke, "Heat Waves and Fatal Traffic Crashes in the Continental United States" (2018) 119 Accid Anal Prev 195, online: <https://doi.org/10.1016%2Fj.aap.2018.07.025>; Christopher Flavelle, "Work Injuries Tied to Heat Are Vastly Undercounted, Study Finds," *The New York Times* (17 July 2021), online: <https://www.nytimes.com/2021/07/15/climate/heat-injuries.html>.

53 Jihan Abbas & Sonia Alimi, *A Qualitative Look at Serious Legal Problems for People with Disabilities in Central Canada* (Montreal: DAWN-RAFG Canada, 2021); Zarychta & Track, *supra* note 39.

54 Charlie Carey, "Surrey Man Facing Eviction After Installing Air Conditioner Without Permission," *CTV News Vancouver* (28 June 2021), online: <https://vancouver.citynews.ca/2021/06/28/surrey-man-eviction-air-conditioner/>.

55 Jon Azpiri, "Nearly 60% of British Columbians Find It Difficult to Access a Doctor of Have no Access at All: Poll," *CBC News* (8 September 2022), online: <https://www.cbc.ca/news/canada/british-columbia/angus-reid-institute-doctor-access-bc-1.6575386>.

56 Carmen Chai & Beatrice Politi, "Can't Find a Family Doctor? Well-Off More Likely to Secure Appointments, Canadian Research Suggests," *Global News* (25 February 2013), online: <https://globalnews.ca/news/397670/looking-for-doctor-well-off-may-do-better-than-poor-getting-appointments-study-4/>.

57 Nan DasGupta et al, "The Pervasive Reality of Anti-Black Racism in Canada," *Boston Consulting Group* (14 December 2020), online: <https://www.bcg.com/en-ca/publications/2020/reality-of-anti-black-racism-in-canada>.

58 Jeremiah Hurley & Michel Grignon, "Income and Equity of Access to Physician Services" (2006) 174:2 CMAJ 187, online: <https://doi.org/10.1503/cmaj.051214>; Nicole Ineese-Nash, "Disability as a Colonial Construct: The Missing Discourse of Culture in Conceptualizations of Disabled Indigenous Children" (2020) 9:3 Can J Disabil Stud 28, online: <https://doi.org/10.15353/cjds.v9i3.645>.

59 Brendon D. Pooran & Cara Wilkie, "Failing to Achieve Equality: Disability Rights in Australia, Canada, and the United States" (2005) 20 J L & Soc Pol 1, online: <https://doi.org/10.60082/0829–3929.1017>.

60 Gabrielle Peters, "Alone in the Dome: Disabled People, Many Poor, Struggled to Survive B.C.'s Fatal Heat Wave," *The Maple* (5 September

2021), online: <https://www.readthemaple.com/alone-in-the-dome-disabled-people-many-poor-struggled-to-survive-b-c-s-fatal-heat-wave/>.

61 Gaskin et al, *supra* note 16.

62 Gregor Wolbring, "A Culture of Neglect: Climate Discourse and Disabled People" (2009) 12:4 M/C Journal, online: <https://prism.ucalgary.ca/server/api/core/bitstreams/153dd32b-c444–4f20-b09b-a3e6651b2665/content>; Stein & Stein, *supra* note 8.

63 Martha A. Fineman, "Understanding Vulnerability Theory" (26 August 2019), online (blog): <https://scholarblogs.emory.edu/vulnerability/2019/08/26/understanding-vulnerability-theory/>.

64 I cited "Emergency planning for PWDs presents challenging legal questions because it poses an extreme test of the meaning of accessibility": Adrien A. Weibgen, "The Right to be Rescued: Disability Justice in an Age of Disaster" (2015) 124:7 Yale LJ 2202, online: <https://www.yalelawjournal.org/note/the-right-to-be-rescued>.

65 Calgaro, *supra* note 9; International Disability Alliance, *supra* note 9.

66 Statistics Canada, "Home Alone: More Persons Living Solo Than Ever Before, but Roomies the Fastest Growing Household Type," *The Daily* (13 July 2022), online (pdf): <https://www150.statcan.gc.ca/n1/en/daily-quotidien/220713/dq220713a-eng.pdf?st=sreNVeRq>.

67 Gillian Petit & Lindsay Tedds, "Poverty in British Columbia: Income Thresholds, Trends, Rates, and Depths of Poverty" Munch Personal RePEc Archive Working Paper No 104002, online: <https://mpra.ub.uni-muenchen.de/104002/>.

68 Jeff Rock, "Twenty Years of Marriage Equality? No, Not for Disabled Ontarians," *Toronto Star* (13 January 2021), online: <https://www.thestar.com/opinion/contributors/2021/01/13/twenty-years-of-marriage-equality-no-not-for-disabled-ontarians.html>.

69 Jeff Randle & Zachary Thurston, *Housing Experiences in Canada: Persons with Disabilities* (Ottawa: Statistics Canada, 2022), online: <https://www150.statcan.gc.ca/n1/pub/46-28-0001/2021001/article/00011-eng.htm>.

70 The Saint John Human Development Council, *Serious Problems Experienced by People with Disabilities Living in Atlantic Canada* (Ottawa: Department of Justice Canada, 2021) at 19.

71 Ineese-Nash, *supra* note 58.

72 Stefanie Hunt-Kennedy, *Between Fitness and Death: Disability and Slavery in the Caribbean*, Kindle ed (Champaign: University of Illinois Press) at 70, 128.

73 Jenifer L. Barclay, *The Mark of Slavery: Disability, Race, and Gender in Antebellum America*, Kindle ed (Champaign: University of Illinois Press, 2021) at 141–4.

74 Marta Russell, "Capitalism and Disability: Selected Writings by Marta Russell" (Haymarket Books, Kindle Edition) at 17–22

75 Katherine Wall, *Low Income Among Persons with Disability in Canada* (Ottawa: Statistics Canada, 2017), online: <https://www150.statcan.gc.ca/n1/pub/75–006-x/2017001/article/54854-eng.htm>.

76 Craig W.M. Scott et al, "Disability Considerations for Measuring Poverty in Canada Using the Market Based Measure" (2022) 163 Soc Indic Res 389, online: <https://doi.org/10.1007/s11205–022–02900–1>.

77 *Ibid.*

78 HOOPP, *Seniors and Poverty – Canada's Next Crisis* (Toronto: Healthcare of Ontario Pension Plan, 2017), online (pdf): <https://hoopp.com/docs/default-source/newsroom-library/research/hoopp-research-article-senior-poverty-canada-next-crises.pdf>; "Older Adults," *Poverty Hub* (accessed 11 November 2024), online: <https://povertyhub.ca/topic/diversity/older-adults/>; Justin Chandler, "By the Numbers: The Rising Rate of Senior's Poverty," *TVO Today* (3 November 2022), online: <https://www.tvo.org/article/by-the-numbers-the-rising-rate-of-seniors-poverty>.

79 Ontario Human Rights Commission, "Main Barriers to Education for Students with Disabilities (Fact Sheet)" (accessed 11 November 2024), online: <https://www.ohrc.on.ca/en/main-barriers-education-students-disabilities-fact-sheet>.

80 Penny Daflos, "BC Housing Disabled Cooling Devices at Some Sites Over Costs," *CTV News Vancouver* (21 July 2022), online: <https://bc.ctvnews.ca/bc-housing-disabled-cooling-devices-at-some-sites-over-costs-1.5997284>.

81 Ontario Human Rights Commission, News Release, "OHRC Statement on Human Rights, Extreme Heat Waves and Air Conditioning" (19 August 2022), online: <https://www.ohrc.on.ca/en/news_centre/ohrc-statement-human-rights-extreme-heat-waves-and-air-conditioning>.

82 VisitAble Housing Canada & Canadian Centre on Disability Studies, "Introduction to VisitAble Housing" (September 2014), online (pdf): <https://med-fom-learningcircle.sites.olt.ubc.ca/files/2015/04/PPP-Introduction-to-VisitAble-Housing.pdf>.

PART THREE

Governance

8 The Most Dangerous Branch?

ANDREW GREEN AND ALBERT YOON

I. Introduction

Climate change is an existential risk. If we fail to limit the increase in temperatures, we face rising sea waters, more flooding, more droughts, worse storms, mass displacement of people, loss of species, and more.[1] Unfortunately the complexity of climate change hinders action at all levels – by individuals in their daily lives, by governments seeking to limit domestic emissions, and by the international community trying to set global targets. At its most basic level, climate change raises a tragedy of the commons problem because those who benefit from emitting greenhouse gases do not bear the costs. As Garrett Hardin noted, "Ruin is the destination towards which all men rush, each pursuing his own best interest in a society that believes in the freedom of the commons."[2] Failure to see beyond our immediate self-interest is leading us towards climate ruin.

A significant focus of action to move us off this deleterious path has been the courts. Those facing harms from climate change have tried to use private law causes of action such as nuisance or public nuisance to sue those who are responsible for greenhouse gas (GHG) emissions. Individuals or groups have raised constitutional or human rights claims against governments for failing to take sufficiently strong action. Other parties bring administrative law challenges to try to force governments to act (just as some challenge government action that imposes economic costs). Courts are increasingly being called upon to actively respond to the perceived existential climate threat through expanding legal doctrines to shape policy more forcefully. As legal scholar and former senior climate advisor to the US Environmental Protection Agency, Lisa Heinzerling notes, "departures from the legal status quo are exactly what we need in order to defend aggressive future action on climate change."[3]

Advocates for a strong judicial role in addressing climate change often assume that actions taken by a court in one country are easily transferable across countries. Yet law and legal institutions are place-based – the history, constitutional structure, administrative law principles, and even norms both limit and provide openings for courts in particular countries to take greater or less action. A move towards a greater role of courts within and across countries to address climate change requires careful consideration of both the normative and positive dimensions. The former asks what role courts should take on in the face of an existential crisis such as climate change. The latter asks what role courts and judges can play given their constraints. These two questions are evidently related – courts can shape some of the constraints they face. Both vary across jurisdictions.

In this chapter, we discuss these normative and positive questions in the context of administrative law challenges to climate action or inaction in Canada and the United States. The supreme courts have taken divergent approaches to such challenges recently. The US Supreme Court, for example, has taken space away from the executive in dealing with issues such as climate change, most notably in *West Virginia v EPA* where the majority rejected a move by the Biden administration to use the *Clean Air Act* to increase reliance on cleaner energy sources.[4] Conversely, the Supreme Court of Canada seemed to endorse the delegation of broad, almost open-ended, policy space to the federal government in the context of a challenge to federal carbon pricing legislation.[5]

We focus on the interplay between the courts, legislatures, and the executive to discuss the nature of such challenges. We use a simple model to frame the contours of the constraints that varying institutional structures place on the power of courts to address climate change. To set up the model, section II describes some of the key (related) institutional and legal differences that may impact how courts act, including the separation of powers, the nature of administrative law, and the structure of the supreme court. Section III then uses these institutional elements to ground the model of how judges may be constrained in acting on climate change under different conditions. Section IV applies this model to the role of courts recently in the United States and Canada. Section V discusses the implications of this analysis.

II. Institutional Constraints

Many aspects of a country's institutional structure can impact its climate decisions, including the courts.[6] We focus on three key elements to make our point: the separation of powers generally, the nature of administrative law in the jurisdiction, and the structure of the country's supreme court. In so doing, we recognize that we put in the background other important elements, such as a country's electoral system (such as first-past-the-post systems versus proportional representation). The three broad elements are related but we begin by addressing each in turn.

1. Separation of Powers

A major structural feature that may influence the role of the courts is the presidential versus the parliamentary system. A presidential system, as in the United States, has a wide range of actors who can hinder the passing of legislation, including at the most basic level, the House of Representatives, the Senate, and the president but also others such as various Congressional committees.[7] The result is that legislation must satisfy the preferences of these actors either directly or through logrolling on other issues.

Parliamentary systems have fewer barriers, particularly when there is a majority government as the legislature and principal executive actors are largely controlled by the same party.[8] A minority government faces greater risk of vetoes as the party leading the government must obtain agreement from some other party to pass any legislation. They may also need formal support from a second body, such as the Senate in Canada, which can pose an additional constraint, depending on its structure, composition and norms.

Under both systems, democratically elected officials in the legislature pass laws, but the institutional structure may alter the ultimate path of law-making and the nature of the laws. The greater number of vetoes in the presidential system in theory makes it more difficult to pass new legislation. Enacted legislation necessarily reflects greater compromise, and existing legislation should be difficult to change.[9] A majority in a parliamentary system can enact stronger legislation, although there remain the constraints due to the need for re-election. There may be greater costs from delay and weaker legislation under a presidential system than a majority parliament, though the differences will be less where there is a minority parliament.[10]

From a positive perspective of these vetoes, they may mean that more interest groups can impact legislation through these vetoes and that there is greater deliberation.[11] The division of political power at any given time, however, will influence these differences. Again, a minority parliament may bring similar benefits. The structure of the government in general, and the division of political power in any particular government, will then impact the majoritarian nature of the resulting legislation.

What does this mean for the role of the courts? An important consideration is what Bickel noted as the counter-majoritarian difficulty.[12] The court can decide in ways that are non-majoritarian – that cut against the decisions of the legislature. Hamilton, in the Federalist Papers in the United States, saw a limitation in the role of the courts. He argued that, while the legislature sets rules and allocates spending and the executive holds the "sword," the courts have "no influence over either the sword or the purse; no direction either of the strength or of the wealth of the society, and can take no active resolution whatever. It may truly be said to have neither FORCE nor WILL, but merely judgment" (emphasis in original).[13] The result in the structure of the US system is "that the judiciary is beyond comparison the weakest of the three departments of power; that it can never attack with success either of the other two; and that all possible care is requisite to enable it to defend itself against their attacks."[14]

Yet courts do wield power. They can both negate existing laws or create new rights. They can also invalidate decisions of the executive or, in some cases, force executive action. It is in part the relationship between the courts' ability and willingness to take activist positions and the structure of government that is central to our concerns about the role of the courts – especially supreme courts – in the context of climate change.

2. *Administrative Law and Deference*

The structure of the three principal institutions – legislative, executive, and judiciary – can influence the power or room for courts to either force or hinder action by the executive and to interpret the wishes of the legislature. The role of judges in addressing government action is also limited by the general structure of judicial review. This structure is in many ways endogenous. Judges are subject to but also help set this structure. The structure can and has changed over time in both countries.

Courts can take a range of stances when reviewing a challenge to a climate change decision by the executive. At one extreme, they may *always defer* to the choice of the executive – either the interpretation of a statute or the exercise of discretion. Conversely, a judge may *never defer* – that is, always decide in accordance with their own views. In the latter case, they may decide in accordance with what they think is most in line with the legislature's choice – how they think the legislature meant the statute to be interpreted or the discretion to be exercised in the circumstances. On the other hand, they may decide based not on the legislature's views but their own preferred policy outcomes.[15] Between these extremes of judicial deference is a spectrum of closer or lighter forms of review, requiring for example, the executive's decision to be "reasonable" in some sense (*sophisticated deference*).[16]

3. The Structure of the Supreme Court

One last group of broad factors that may influence how a court will decide relates to the structure of the Supreme Court in a particular country. Supreme Courts differ in a wide variety of ways.[17] The particularly important factors in our discussion of the activism of courts are the method of appointment, the norms of judicial decision-making, and the way cases come before the court.

In terms of appointments, the manner and norms around appointments can mean judges are split along ideological grounds. In some countries such as the United States, the process of appointing judges is political, drawing in elected officials across different bodies. For others, politically independent or representative bodies may select judges. Specific processes may mix these elements such as where an independent body provides a list for a political body to choose from or where judges sit with others on the selecting body.

The norms of decision-making also matter. Particularly for our concerns, judges may be more or less comfortable with choosing according to their own political or policy preferences. Policy differences of judges appointed under a relatively political system may be dampened where judges commit to, or understand their role as, requiring them not to decide cases politically. Conversely, a relatively non-political system can still result in political decisions if the judicial norm is to decide in accordance with one's own policy preferences. Magill and Ortiz speculate that "judicial culture" may be an important factor in differences across administrative law systems.[18]

The final factor we will discuss is how cases come before the courts. For example, standing may make a difference to the nature and extent of judicial activism. If there are limited standing grounds, such as where an individual must be personally impacted by executive action, the range of challenges may be narrow. Broad standing to bring challenges in the public interest opens avenues for judicial action. Further, the form of approval to get to the court – that is, the number of judges needed to agree to hear a decision and the threshold for importance - may also be important to the range and nature of decisions heard.

III. A Simple Spatial Model

We can think initially of two broad factors that influence how activist a court can or may wish to be. First, the structural limits on the judges – including not only the structure of the court but also the general structure of the government and of administrative law – may constrain judges in how they can decide. Second, judges decide cases in the context of the relative preferences of the different actors.[19]

As a way to think of the scope for judicial activism, consider two broad structural dimensions, as illustrated by figure 8.1. First, as noted earlier, governments may vary in the number of veto points. The greatest number of veto points exists in the case of the presidential system where power is split across political parties. Similarly, the number of vetoes will be larger in a parliamentary system under a minority government. The size of the policy space open for judges in such situations will depend on the scope of differences in policy views across parties. At the other end of the spectrum, the fewest number of legislative veto points exists under a majority parliament and, relatedly, where the same political party controls the different actors under a presidential system. This range is depicted on the horizontal axis, with an increasing number of vetoes as you move to the right. Second, the level of deference accorded by the courts to executive decisions under administrative law is important. The range of deference is shown on the vertical axis, with no deference at the bottom and complete deference at the top.

These two dimensions are interdependent. McGill and Ortiz, for example, note that judicial review, at least in theory, should be less strict in a parliamentary system as the unification of legislative and key executive functions means that there is less likely to be "drift" – or a principal–agent problem in which the courts need to rein in the executive if it departs from the wishes of the legislature.[20] In practice, they argue, there may not be a large difference.

Further, these institutional features are not fixed. Supreme Courts can (and, as we will discuss, do) alter their level of deference over time. Similarly, the number of veto points can be increased or decreased through, for example, increasing the power or remit of committees or individuals within different branches of government.[21]

These two dimensions provide a structure for thinking about the constraints on judges wishing to act on climate change – either to foster greater climate action by the executive or to hinder such action. The least scope for judicial action exists in Quadrant II, where there are few vetoes (such as where there is a majority parliament or a unified government), meaning that legislation is easier to pass and is subject to

Figure 8.1. Vetoes and Deference

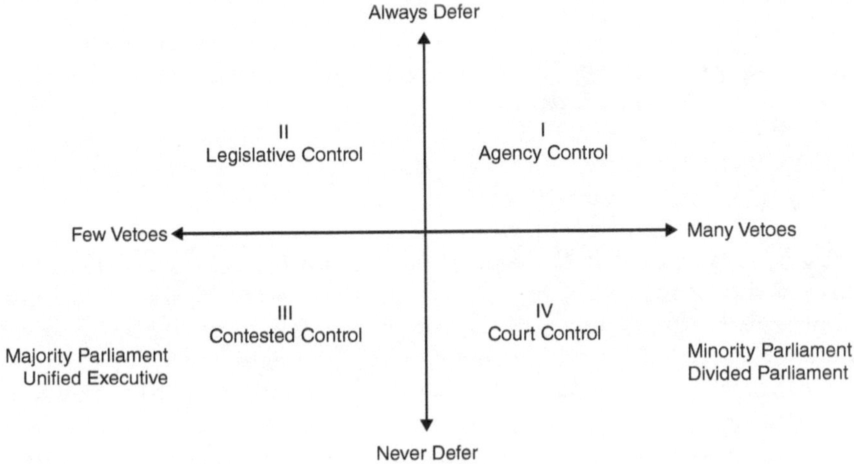

Notes: The horizontal axis is the number of vetoes in a legislative system, increasing from left to right. The vertical axis is the level of deference granted by a court under administrative law, ranging from the court never deferring to an executive decision-maker at the bottom to always deferring at the top.

less compromise, and can more easily override any judicial or executive action contrary to legislative wishes. Moreover, in this quadrant, judges are constrained by a deferential approach to judicial review. In such a context, the current legislature emerges as the dominant body.

The greatest scope for judicial action occurs in Quadrant IV. In that case, judges are less bound by, or even unbound by, a deferential approach. Moreover, the divided presidential government or minority parliament means that legislation will be subject to compromise, and therefore, it will be much harder to pass legislation that overrides judicial decisions. This difficulty of override becomes even greater (and affords judges even more policy space) to the extent that the ideological positions of the parties controlling the different branches are more varied. In this quadrant, then, there is maximum judicial control.

The other two quadrants are more nuanced in terms of judicial control. In Quadrant I, the executive tends to be more dominant as judges are subject to a norm of deference to executive decisions, and the existence of numerous veto points means legislative overrides of executive decisions that depart from the wishes of the legislature will be more difficult to enact. Finally, in Quadrant III, judicial power is heavily contested. The judges are less subject to the requirement of deference and so are better able to follow their own views. However, the fewer veto points means that the legislature can more tightly supervise the exercise of power by the executive and activism of the court. Judges in this circumstance have to be the most strategic in thinking about how legislators will react to their decisions.

Figure 8.1 illustrates that political structure constrains the level of judicial activism, even in the face of an existential threat like climate change. As noted, the courts or the legislature can potentially alter these constraints and move the system into a different quadrant. Courts may alter norms of deference on principle relating to a belief in the proper role of the courts or for instrumental reasons to aid in reaching some substantive policy goal. However, the effect of doing so depends on a second set of constraints – the relative preferences of the different actors, including legislators, the executive, the judges, and the public.

Judges may consider the preferences of the other actors such as the legislature when deciding whether to uphold or invalidate executive decisions. Similarly, legislators and the executive may consider the judicial response when deciding, for example, how much power to delegate or whether to adopt an expansive or novel interpretation of a statute.[22]

Consider two forms of judicial activism, both relative to the status quo. For the first, the court may decide in a way that alters the status quo. For example, the court may force the executive to decide in a manner that fosters greater climate action. For the second, the court may hinder moves from the status quo, such as where a court invalidates executive action that attempts to take stronger climate action. In either case, the court is trying to decide what is the appropriate outcome in light of the decision by a (former) legislature to enact a particular statute.

The court may be active ways that are beneficial or problematic. A court may properly believe, for example, that, on the best interpretation of the statute, the actions of the executive do not fit with the wishes of the enacting legislature or with the best interpretation of the statute given its purposes. It may believe that the executive is mistaken or that it is captured in some form. A more problematic reason would be that a court misinterprets the wishes of the enacting legislature or the purposes of the legislation. A still more problematic reason would be that the judges decide not on jurisprudential grounds but in accordance with their own personal policy preferences.

Courts take a risk when deciding each case. Their decisions may provoke a backlash by the legislature – the legislature may enact a law that either eliminates the effect of the court's decision or possibly even creates legislation that takes permissible executive action even further away from the court's preferred position.[23] From a democratic viewpoint, new legislation is beneficial if it truly reflects the public interest as opposed to special interests. To the extent judges account for these reactions, judicial review shifts decisions towards the wishes of the current legislature (as opposed to the enacting legislature).[24] If judges are concerned with particular policy outcomes (as opposed to what the legislation requires), they should account for such reactions. Further, if the legislature and the executive ignore or circumvent the court's decisions, the court can appear to be powerless. Relatedly, a court that decides in a manner that is blatantly political may lose public trust or legitimacy in the long run.[25]

How do the relative preferences play into this decision? Suppose environmental groups challenge the climate policies formulated by the executive but which they deem inadequate. A court may wish to allow the challenge if it believes that the stronger action fits with the enacting legislature's statute or if the court wants to follow its own policy preferences for stronger action. It may be constrained not only by the structure of government and the nature of the deference but by the preferences of the current legislature and the public. If both the current legislature and the public support the status quo (weak climate policy), the court will face its greatest risk in allowing the challenge where the government is unified as the legislature can override the judicial decision more easily. On the other hand, in the context of a divided government, the legislature cannot react as easily. The power then shifts away from the sitting legislature.[26] Who gets that power depends on the deference regime and how judges decide. In a deferential system (Quadrant I), the agency will have the power (and can either attempt to follow its view of the wishes of the enacting legislature or its own policy preferences). In a non-deferential regime (Quadrant IV), the courts have greater sway to either push their view of the wishes of the enacting legislature or their own policy preferences. Of course, if the legislature and the public oppose the status quo, the risk to the court is low and the deference regime becomes more important (the more deferential the court has to be, the less scope there is for activism).

Conversely, suppose the existing climate policy is weak and the executive implements stronger policy action (that is, attempts to alter the status quo). If industry challenges this action, a court wishing to uphold the status quo (and negate the executive action) will face a low risk of backlash where the legislature and the public support the status quo, but will be more constrained by the deference regime. If the existing legislature and the public is against the status quo, the court

Figure 8.2. Judicial Risk Relative to Attitudes of Legislature and Public Towards the Status Quo

		Legislature	
		Supports SQ	Opposes SQ
Public	Supports SQ	(1) High Risk to Change; Low Risk to Stop Change	(2) Medium Risk
	Opposes SQ	(3) Medium Risk	(4) Low Risk to Change; High Risk to Stop Change

will face the greatest risk in the context of a unified government. If the government is divided, power shifts away from the existing legislature. The court faces less risk of backlash, and the power again shifts to either the executive (in a deferential regime) or the court (in a non-deferential regime).

The likelihood of these two types of challenges is influenced by the nature of the legislation as well as the process for cases to come before the court. For example, it is easier (and in some cases only possible) to challenge an actual decision made – such as to impose a requirement to limit emissions. It is much more difficult to challenge the lack of a law; it is difficult to achieve standing, and in some legislative regimes, such challenges are specifically not permitted.

We can then think of attitudes of the legislature and the public relative to the status quo. It is important to remember that given the timing of policy decisions and the advent of new information or issues, the legislature that enacted the governing statute is not likely to be the same as the legislature that is in power.[27] In figure 8.2, the court faces different risks of activist positions depending on the attitudes of the legislature and the public. There are four states of the world:

1. Both the public and legislature support the status quo: A court decision changing the status quo (such as by mandating action by the executive) here poses the highest risk to the court, because the court will have support from neither group. Conversely, the court faces a low risk where it negates action by the executive to alter the status quo (such as where the executive tries to take stronger climate action).
2. Public supports the status quo, but legislature opposes it: A court altering the status quo or negating executive action faces a medium

risk, as the court may be able to find safe haven in the split. The public and legislature may differ where, for example, the public is mistaken as a risk or firms with particularized benefits gain from change but the public faces diffuse costs from the change.
3. Public opposes the status quo, but the legislature supports it: This also carries medium risk, as the court may find safe haven in the split. There may, for example, be particularized costs from the change to firms but diffuse benefits to the public.
4. Both public and the legislature oppose the status quo: A court decision altering the status quo poses a low risk in general to the court, although it raises the issue of why – given this unity – the legislature did not pass a law to change the status quo (as we discussed, possibly because of vetoes that hinder action). A court decision negating executive action would face a high risk because it would be opposed by both.

The size of the risk depends at least in part on the probability of backlash. With a more unified legislature, the power shifts to the current legislature, and the courts incur more risk from taking a view different than that current legislature. The more divided the legislative branch, the more the power shifts to the executive or the court (depending on the deference regime) and to the enacting legislature (to the extent the executive or the court attempts to faithfully fulfill the wishes of the enacting legislature as opposed to their own policy preferences). The more divided the legislature (the more vetoes), the greater is the policy space for the courts (and the executive) to act. The more deferential the administrative law regime, the more scope there is for the executive's choices to prevail. There are of course limits even with a divided legislature – a court cannot produce a stable outcome, even an outcome faithful to the enacting legislature, that both parties agree is worse than they could get from enacting new legislation. The policy space for the court is not unbounded, only larger if there is a unified government. Courts may consider this range, whether they are interested in furthering their own policy choices or concerned about fulfilling the wishes of the enacting legislature to the maximum extent possible.

Of course, courts can play different roles even where their decisions are ultimately overridden by the legislature. They can signal the importance of the issue. More importantly, a move that forces new legislation requires the legislature to be clear about its position. Where the legislature and the public are aligned, the courts (and the enacting legislature) give way to a new democratic decision. Where the legislature and the public are at odds over the right policy, it forces the legislature to make its position clear. Judicial review therefore can be a key element in fostering democratic decision-making depending on its structure.

Lastly, regarding the judiciary's constrained preferences, these choices appear sequential: the legislature enacts a law, the executive decides how to implement it, someone challenges the law, the court decides, and then the legislature reacts. This process is an important part of how we need to think about the potential role of the court. However, these structural elements can be changed. The legislature may change its structure to hinder reactions and therefore give greater power to the enacting legislature (over future legislatures) such as by creating more veto points.[28] Further, if a court wishes to enhance its power relative to either the executive or potentially the existing legislature, it can reduce the deference given by courts to the executive.

IV. Two Paths

1. The United States: Taking Space

The United States of course has a presidential system, which is sharply divided politically. The range of policy differences across veto actors when the system is divided is particularly large at the moment. As a result, it has been difficult to pass climate legislation, and the path of legislation tends to involve considerable compromise (even within an existing party).

In terms of administrative law, the United States has seen fierce battles over the role of the court in reviewing administrative action. The form of judicial review has varied over time. US administrative law, as with the Canadian counterpart, is convoluted. A central element for our discussion is the court's approach to challenges to the executive's interpretation of a statute. The key precedent is *Chevron, U.S.A. Inc. v. National Resource Defence Council, Inc.*,[29] which requires a reviewing court first to decide if the statute is ambiguous. If it is not, the court must apply the clear meaning. If it is, *Chevron* deference requires judges to defer to the agency interpretations of the statute where it is reasonable. *Chevron* arose at a time when conservatives were wary of the courts' attempts to limit rollbacks of regulatory constraints.[30]

A key decision involving *Chevron* on the scope of the federal power to address climate change is the 2007 US Supreme Court decision in *Massachusetts v EPA*.[31] The EPA had refused to regulate GHG emissions from motor vehicles under the *Clean Air Act* on the grounds that the Act did not give it power to do so, and even if it did, the EPA did not want to exercise that power. The court held that the Act was not ambiguous and clearly covered GHGs. It "nudged the federal government into action on the most consequential regulatory question of the day."[32] The court found executive power to deal with the issue under the broad language of the Act, even where the executive did not want to act. In one sense, it gave power to the enacting legislature (or, depending on one's view, the judges' policy preferences) and found space for the executive to act.

However, *Massachusetts* was close: a 5–4 split with very strong dissents arguing that the scope should be given to the EPA not to act. The US Supreme Court has become more conservative since that decision, with additional Republican-appointed justices. More recently there has been pushback by conservatives against deference, including against the *Chevron* doctrine.[33] The Supreme Court has moved in a "more formalist, less pro-agency direction," with a shift in power away from agencies and towards the legislature (and in some ways the courts).[34] In that vein, the *West Virginia* decision, along with others also dealing with the "major questions" doctrine, requires Congress to speak clearly before agencies are permitted to make broad-ranging moves into new areas. In *West Virginia*, the issue was whether the EPA could adopt essentially a cap-and-trade system that covered existing power plants. The court used a new major questions doctrine to find that it could not, because the legislature had not clearly delegated it the power to deal with an issue of such "economic and political significance."

Under this new major questions doctrine, the court must determine if the issue raises major economic or political questions and, if so, whether Congress has clearly delegated the executive the power to address that question. The result is to limit the space for the executive and to enhance the power of the courts. A whole realm of decisions is taken out of the executive's power (that is, seen as not delegated to it), unless the court finds that the issue is either not a major question of economic and political significance or, if it is, the legislature has clearly delegated the power to address that question. The use of the major questions doctrine is biased against action as Congress must expressly give power to make major economic and social decisions but not to avoid those questions.[35] In the context of a divided government, the court's view of the preferences of the enacting legislature prevail. In the context of a unified government, the matter shifts to the current legislature, and the court must pay particular attention to the policy preferences of the existing legislature to avoid a backlash.

In terms of our conceptual framework, the court is pushing the system from Quadrants I and II towards Quadrants III and IV and, given the divided government, in particular towards Quadrant IV where the courts have significant power. The result of this move away from deference may mean the executive is less likely to engage in big "boundary-pushing regulation projects."[36] The law is steered away from large-scale solutions to climate change and towards small, incremental steps.[37] Further, the likelihood of the courts playing a significant role in climate policy depends on the preferences of existing judges, which currently are relatively conservative. As Heinzerling notes in reference to the US Supreme Court "[t]he conservative justices' approach to statutory interpretation, agency discretion, and access to courts favors passivity over action, and small steps over big steps, on problems like climate change."[38]

Finally, the ability of courts to be sources of change in the climate area depends on cases coming before the courts. The United States has particularly narrow standing doctrines. By requiring an injury-in-fact, standing in the United States "tends to disfavor plaintiffs who suffer from widespread, future-oriented harm that comes from many sources," all key characteristics of the harm from climate change.[39]

2. *Canada: Holding Space*

In Canada, with its parliamentary system, the move in many ways has been the opposite to that of the United States. The Supreme Court of Canada has, on the substantive review side, created a system largely based on deference not only on factual issues and discretionary choices by the executive but also on questions of statutory interpretation in many cases. While there is some debate about whether the Supreme Court hindered this move somewhat in its most recent big decision on substantive review, deference remains a key element of administrative law in Canada.[40] The result has been a move, over time, towards power of the executive (that is, towards Quadrants I and II in our framework).

In administrative law challenges, judges primarily determine whether the government decision is reasonable as opposed to deciding if it is correct. Reasonableness review for the court is "robust."[41] It starts with the reasons given by the decision-maker. The challenger has the burden of showing that the decision is unreasonable. The court is to determine if there are any logical errors and, perhaps more importantly for the majority of appeals, whether the decision fits within any factual and legal constraints. To determine the latter question, the court examines whether the decision fits with the statutory language, accords with other law (such as the common law), accounts for the evidence and for the submissions of the parties, and is (somehow) consistent with the principles of statutory interpretation. The decision-maker has an added justificatory burden where the impact of the decision is particularly large or the decision departs from prior decisions. This review for reasonableness covers most questions of law and fact and discretion. However, for questions of law, there remain some questions on which the court has the final say, including most controversially where the legislature has specified a statutory right of appeal.

The court has noted that reasonableness "takes its colour from context."[42] In some contexts the court demands a fair amount from the decision-maker. In others, ones that are key to climate determinations, it demands quite little. In a way, such review is a mix of a court-centred and deferential approach. The courts are to look at the reasoning process – the reasons and how they relate to the basic structure of the law, facts, and history. Such a review could be at one extreme quite intense, with a court not only ensuring that the decision-maker considers the law and the facts but also examining whether the actual choices made accord with the relevant law and facts. At the other extreme, the review could be quite light on the actual decision – that is, giving large scope for the decision-maker not only in the choices on the merits but also in explaining its reasoning. For example, in the context of decisions by Cabinet, the courts have at times noted that making technical determinations and value judgments is beyond the ken of the courts and at the same time required little of Cabinet in the way of explanation.[43] The review of these decisions seems to push the system towards Quadrants I and II of our framework.

The Supreme Court recently dealt with a key federal act relating to climate change – the *Greenhouse Gas Pollution Pricing Act (GGPPA)*.[44] The GGPPA was challenged on the basis that it intruded too heavily on provincial powers – that is, it was challenged on federalism grounds. However, part of the decision dealt with the broad discretion granted under the Act to Cabinet to determine the coverage of the Act as well as its stringency. Not only was the language granting regulatory power extremely broad, the Act included a "Henry VIII" clause, which stated that in the event of a conflict between the regulations and the Act, the regulation prevails.[45]

Cote J, in dissent, strongly objected to this broad grant of discretion noting that the power was essentially "boundless" as there was "no meaningful limit to the power of the executive."[46] She saw this power as essentially legislative in nature and as such not in accordance with the constitutional separation of powers in Canada. In her view, it allows the executive to effectively override the preferences of the legislature. The majority, however, had no difficulty with such a broad grant of discretion.[47] It noted that "even broad or important powers may be delegated to the executive, so long as the legislature does not abdicate its legislative role,"[48] which the legislature did not do in this case even with the Henry VIII clause. The majority noted that any use of this power was limited by the purposes of the GGPPA and the guidelines in the Act, as well as by the principles of administrative law as the use of power is subject to judicial review.[49]

The breadth of the delegation, and the willingness of the court to allow the executive to wield such power, further pushes the system towards Quadrants I or II. The effect of this decision partly depends on whether there is meaningful judicial review of the use of discretion.[50] The majority clearly believed that judicial review could cabin overly broad uses of this power. Cote J. was not as sanguine. Even regulations that decimated specific high-emitting industries would "fulfill the statutory purpose of reducing GHG emissions through GHG pricing and therefore be a valid use of the executive's regulatory powers accorded by the GGPPA. This cannot be so."[51] Of course, although the concern raised in the GGPPA decision was about using the discretion to institute overly stringent regulation, it could just as easily be about overly lax regulation.

Unlike in the United States, then, where power seems to have moved towards the courts and the legislature, and away from the executive, power in Canada seems to have moved from the courts towards the executive and the current legislature. Courts seeking to alter the decisions of the executive face a much more difficult structure in terms of the deference system. Moreover, with a majority government, the risk is even higher for an activist court. If the executive or the existing legislature do not want action, the courts will be hard pressed to bring about change regardless of their preferences. Of course, the converse is also true – in the face of a strong executive and legislative move towards climate action, the courts have less ability to stand in the way.

V. Courts in the Era of Climate Change

Courts seem like a natural place to focus resources to bring about greater action on climate change. In a first-best world, the legislature makes broad value choices, a strong executive uses broad powers to fulfill these choices in an evidence-based fashion, and the judiciary defers to these decisions except where there are obvious mistakes. Further, if either the executive or the courts do not follow the script, the legislature can seamlessly readjust the legislation. However, in the absence of such a cleanly functioning system, the courts play a central role in rational climate policy. Heinzerling states, "while legislative action is necessary if we to meet the full scale of the climate threat, it is not sufficient. Any legislative changes will still be filtered through the political and ideological predispositions of the courts. The courts, too, must change their legal approach in order to make way for regulatory action that is as ambitious as the climate threat is dire."[52]

However, the key to understanding the role of the courts is to understand "that legislatures, executives, and courts act within an interconnected system; and that it is impossible to assess the actions of one constitutional actor without contemplating the reactions of the others."[53] The courts may be the most dangerous branch in some circumstances – depending on the structure of the government, the nature of the administrative law regime, and the preferences of the various actors. It can, however, be dangerous not only for those trying to hinder climate action but for those seeking stronger action. In other cases, the courts may indeed, in accordance with Bickel, be the least dangerous branch for all involved.[54]

Your view of the proper role of the courts may involve institutional considerations.[55] You may, for example, view courts as independent, free (mostly) from the pull of political preferences, and able to competently deal with the technical issues relating to climate change relative to a captured executive swayed by concentrated interests or the vagaries of public attention. Such a view would favour a stronger role for the courts. On the other hand, you may see judges as self-interested maximizers of their own preferences, prone to making errors on the science and economics of climate change relative to an executive that has the technical ability to make rational policy decisions.

A supporter of strong climate action would want a deferential regime if they feel (i) the courts are liable to make mistakes (that is, expertise matters); (ii) accountability helps – that is, the relevant parties (such as legislators and the public) want climate action and accountability matters; and (iii) the courts are more conservative than the executive. Deference would mean that in the case of a unified government, the courts would not forestall action or if they did, then at least in the case of a unified government, the legislature could react. On the other hand, they would want a less deferential regime where (i) courts can make scientific determinations (error costs are low); (ii) accountability does not help (that is, the legislature or the public do not want climate action – or the executive is captured by powerful interests that do not want action); and (iii) judges are more liberal than the executive or the legislature.

The courts have altered the deference regime in some ways politically. In the United States, for example, as the courts have become more conservative, there has been a shift away from deference – exacerbated in the context of a divided government as there can be no legislative reaction. In Canada, the shift has been towards deference with a less clear political emphasis. The result is that in Canada the accountability aspects have greater emphasis. For a unified government, it really matters whether the public cares or legislators care. For a minority government, the executive under a parliamentary system may face fewer constraints on its action.

Central to calibrating the role of the court is to think about the form of review and the potential remedies for the court. The United States' move away from *Chevron* deference, including through the major questions doctrine, takes whole matters away from the executive at discretion of court, especially where there is a divided government. The effect is moderated where there is unified government but the move shifts decisions towards the courts, with concerns about errors and political preferences. The Canadian approach, which allows broad, almost formless grants of discretion is problematic because it could be akin to a blank cheque if the courts, as they do at times, take an extremely light-handed review of the exercise of discretion. The decision in the *GGPPA Reference* looks like, and is, a win for broad powers in the executive to take strong climate action, but it also opens the door for continued weak climate policy.

The solution then is to find a way to allow the executive the flexibility to act in light of changing concerns and the existential threat of climate change while tying it to the exercise of expertise and accountability for its decisions. Part of the answer lies in the courts ensuring that there is adequate reasoned justification for the decision and the power of the courts to send decisions back to the executive to reconsider and provide such adequate justification. As Heinzerling states "No good can come of empowering the Supreme Court to pronounce upon hugely consequential scientific questions."[56] Administrative law remedies of sending the decision back to the executive to do over or give a better explanation make sense in this regard. It is central to both the US and Canadian systems of judicial review and can foster better, more deliberative decision-making.[57]

A further element relates to political accountability, though not necessarily through elections. In the Canadian context, Daly argues that the "best remedies for this evil [of extremely broad delegation] are political in nature" though he recognizes more debate is needed.[58] Cote J, on the other hand, notes "the meaningful check on the legislation ought to be the separation of powers analysis, not simply a further delegation to the ballot box."[59] However, both Daly and Cote J point to earlier work by David Mullan that emphasizes a further option. Mullan would "condemn the use of Henry VIII clauses and, indeed, in at least some circumstances, the conferral of unstructured, broad discretion unless accompanied by an obligation to engage in broadly-based notice and comment procedures in the development of policy under the terms of such delegations.[60] This tie to the publicness of the decision-making process can allow some greater public control on broad decision-making power and is also an element of arbitrariness review in the United States.[61]

Sunstein argues that review by US courts focusing on reason-giving and public participation should help ensure that decision-makers seriously engage with scientific and economic considerations and different perspectives.[62] Such accountability both reduces arbitrary decisions and mitigates large swings in policy that do not accord with the underlying science or other relevant factors. It is in this sense potentially "expertise-forcing."[63] It also limits the scope for imposition of judges' own views or mistaken assumptions.

While this chapter has been broadly about Supreme Courts, judicial power implicates the court system as a whole. The Supreme Court sets the structure for lower courts where many of the battles over climate change will play out. The Supreme Court has the power to set deference regimes, which shifts power away from or towards lower courts in reviewing the myriad of administrative law decisions in the context of climate change. The concern about preferences and mistakes may in this regard be particularly acute as review is spread across a wide variety of courts.

Courts may indeed be the most dangerous branch, but climate change does not alter the basic structure of the problem underlying administrative law. Like most other matters, it just makes it seem more extreme. The solution for obtaining better climate policy is not to tear down the basic foundations of administrative law but to ensure that the key features of fostering rational policy are preserved and strengthened.

NOTES

1 UNFCCC, *AR6 Synthesis Report: Climate Change 2023 Summary for Policymakers* (Geneva, IPCC, 2023), online (pdf): <https://www.ipcc.ch/report/ar6/syr/downloads/report/IPCC_AR6_SYR_SPM.pdf>.

2 Garrett Hardin, "The Tragedy of the Commons" (1968) 162 Science 1243 at 1244, online: <https://doi.org/10.1126/science.162.3859.1243>.

3 Lisa Heinzerling, "The Rule of Five Guys" (2021) 119 Michigan LR 1137 at 1142, online: <https://doi.org/10.36644/mlr.119.6.rule>.

4 *West Virginia v EPA*, 142 S. Ct. 2587 (2022).

5 *Reference re Greenhouse Gas Pollution Pricing Reference*, 2021 SCC 11.

6 Andrew Green, *Picking Up the Slack: Law, Institutions, and Canadian Climate Policy* (Toronto: University of Toronto Press, 2022), online: <https://doi.org/10.3138/9781487553319>.

7 William N. Eskridge Jr., "Vetogates and American Public Law" (2015) 31:4 JL Econ & Org 756, online: <https://doi.org/10.1093/jleo/ews009>. Eskridge, relying on earlier work by McNollgast, calls these potential barriers to legislation "vetogates."

8 See Eskridge, *supra* note 7 and M. Elizabeth Magill and Daniel R. Ortiz, "Comparative Positive Political Theory and Empirics" in Blake Emerson, Peter L. Lindseth & Susan Rose-Ackerman, *Comparative Administrative Law* (Cheltenham, UK: Edward Elgar, 2017) 71.

9 Eskridge, *supra* note 7 and Magill & Ortiz, *supra* note 8.

10 Eskridge, *supra* note 7.

11 Eskridge, *supra* note 7 at 762.

12 Alexander M. Bickel, *The Least Dangerous Branch: The Supreme Court at the Bar of Politics* (New Haven, CT: Yale University Press, 1962).

13 Federalist Papers no. 78.

14 *Ibid.*

15 There is an extensive literature seeking to determine the extent to which judges decide in accordance with their own policy preferences. See, for example, Jeffrey A. Segal & Harold J. Spaeth, *The Supreme Court and the Attitudinal Model Revisited* (Cambridge: Cambridge University Press, 2002), online: <https://doi.org/10.1017/CBO9780511615696>; Lee Epstein & Jack Knight, *The Choices Justices Make* (Washington, DC: CQ Press, 1998); Richard Posner, *How Judges Think* (Cambridge MA: Harvard University Press, 2008); and Kent Barnett, Christina L. Boyd, & Christopher J. Walker, "Administrative Law's Political Dynamics" (2018) 71:5 Vand L Rev 1463; Kent Barnett, Christina L. Boyd and Christopher J. Walker, "The Politics of Selecting Chevron Deference" (2018) 15 J Empirical Leg Stud 597, online: <https://doi.org/10.1111/jels.12187>. For a comparative view across high courts, see Benjamin Alarie & Andrew Green, *Commitment and Cooperation on High Courts* (New York: Oxford University Press, 2017), online: <https://doi.org/10.1093/oso/9780199397594.003.0001>.

16 John Ferejohn & Barry Weingast, "Limitation of Statutes: Statutory Interpretation" (1992) 80 Geo LJ 565 at 268 in the context of straight statutory interpretation assumes three stances of judges: a "[n]aive textualist" will interpret legislation as close as possible to what she believes the enacting legislature would want; a "[p]olitically sophisticated honest agent" will instead focuses on the outcome she believes the legislature would have wanted; and an "[u]nconstrained policy advocate" will attempt to maximize her own preferences, taking into account whether the outcome is politically viable.

17 See Alarie & Green, *supra* note 15 for an analysis of institutional differences in supreme courts across a range of countries and their connection to how judges decided cases.
18 Magill and Ortiz, *supra* note 8.
19 This is slightly broader than Jacobi who points to two conditions of Positive Political Theory (i) "judges are constrained not only by their self-imposed limits but also by their institutional limitations" and (ii) judges act strategically: Tonja Jacobi, "The Impact of Positive Political Theory on Old Questions of Constitutional Law and the Separation of Powers" (2006) 100:1 Nw UL Rev 259 at 260.
20 Magill & Ortiz, *supra* note 8.
21 Eskridge, *supra* note 7.
22 Jacobi, *supra* note 19 notes such interaction of the different branches is a key insight of positive political theory.
23 William Eskridge, "Reneging on History? Playing the Court/Congress/President Civil Rights Game" (1991) 79 Cal L Rev 613, online: <https://doi.org/10.2307/3480831>.
24 Ferejohn & Weingast, *supra* note 16.
25 For example, Jacobi, *supra* note 19 at 260 notes that "being overturned by Congress is institutionally costly to the courts, as overrides make the courts appear weak, lower their legitimacy, and waste judicial resources."
26 Ferejohn & Weingast, *supra* note 16 discuss the shift between the preferences of the enacting legislature and the sitting legislature in the face of judicial review.
27 Ferejohn & Weingast, *supra* note 16 at 566.
28 Ferejohn & Weingast, *supra* note 16 arguing that a sitting legislature can seek to enhance the future impact of its laws by altering structural features such as the power of committees.
29 467 U.S. 837 (1984).
30 See, for example, Kristin E. Hickman and Aaron L. Nielson, "Narrowing Chevron's Domain" (2021) 70:5 Duke LJ 931.
31 549 U.S. 497 (2007).
32 Jody Freeman & Adrian Vermeule, "Massachusetts v EPA: From Politics to Expertise" (2007) 1 Sup Ct Rev 51 at 51, online: <https://doi.org/10.1086/655170>. They note that the decision also has important implications for forcing executive action refusing to act where the refusal would be contrary to the purposes of the act (53). According to the court, the exercise of discretion not to act was reviewable under the arbitrary and capricious standard and the EPA needed to provide more fulsome reasons tied to the act for its decision not to exercise its discretion to regulate in this case.

33 See, for example, Cass Sunstein, "Zombie Chevron: A Celebration" (2021) 82:4 Ohio St LJ 565.
34 Kristen E. Hickman, "The Roberts Court's Structural Incrementalism" (2022) 136 Harvard L Rev For 75 at 78.
35 Heinzerling, *supra* note 3 at 1147, noting that the Court's decisions in this area mean that "If Congress wishes to deprive an agency of regulatory power over a question of great economic and political significance, it need not say so in clear terms, and an agency renouncing that power deserves deference."
36 Hickman, *supra* note 34 at 86.
37 Heinzerling, *supra* note 3 at 1147.
38 Heinzerling, *supra* note 3 at 1143 (writing before the *West Virginia* decision was handed down but taking into account the trend in the major questions doctrine).
39 Heinzerling, *supra* note 3 at 1153.
40 *Canada (Minister of Citizenship and Immigration) v. Vavilov*, 2019 SCC 65.
41 *Ibid*. For a discussion of *Vavilov* and its impact, see Paul Daly, "*Vavilov* and the Culture of Justification in Contemporary Administrative Law" (2021) 100 Sup Ct L Rev (2d) 279, online: <https://doi.org/10.60082/2563-8505.1422>.
42 *Ibid* at 89.
43 See, for example, *Portnov v. Canada (Attorney General)*, 2021 FCA 171.
44 *Reference re Greenhouse Gas Pollution Pricing Act*, 2021 SCC 11 ("*Reference re GGPPA*").
45 GGPPA s 168(4) "If a regulation made under this Part in respect of the fuel charge system states that it applies despite any provision of this Part, in the event of a conflict between the regulation and this Part, the regulation prevails to the extent of the conflict."
46 *Reference re GGPPA*, para 236.
47 See Paul Daly, "The Administrative State After the Carbon Tax Reference" (2022) 20:1 Rev Const Stud 33 for a strong defence of the majority's decision on this issue and the difficulties in policing a non-delegation doctrine.
48 *Reference re GGPPA*, para 85.
49 *Reference re GGPPA*, paras 73–4.
50 Green, *supra* note 6; Daly, *supra* note 47.
51 *Reference re GGPPA*, para 238.
52 Heinzerling, *supra* note 3 at 1143.
53 Ferejohn and Weingast, *supra* note 16 at 566.
54 Bickel, *supra* note 12.
55 Green, *supra* note 6 and Cass Sunstein, "Arbitrariness Review and Climate Change" (2022) U Penn LR 991.

56 Heinzerling, *supra* note 3 at 1153.
57 Cass Sunstein, *supra* note 55, for example, has defended "aggressive" procedural review of reasoning as fostering deliberation and reducing arbitrariness. See also Daly, *supra* note 47 arguing that Canadian reasonableness review can fulfill this function.
58 Daly, *supra* note 47 at 40.
59 *Reference re GGPPA*, at para 239.
60 David Mullin, "The Role of the Judiciary in the Review of Administrative Policy Decisions: Issues of Legality" in MJ Mossman and G. Otis, eds, *The Judiciary as Third Branch of Government: Manifestations and Challenges to Legitimacy* (Montreal: Canadian Institute for the Administration of Justice, 1999) 313 at 378.
61 Sunstein, *supra* note 55.
62 Sunstein, *supra* note 55.
63 Freeman & Vermeule, *supra* note 32 at 52.

9 Who Is Paying for the Costs of Climate Change? The InsuResilience Global Partnership as an Institutional Bypass

MARIANA MOTA PRADO AND PATRICIA GALVÃO FERREIRA

I. Introduction

In November 2022, the Parties to the United Nations Framework Convention on Climate Change (UNFCCC) reaffirmed their commitment to keeping the global average temperature increase to well below 2°C, preferably 1.5°C, above pre-industrial levels.[1] The recommitment happened seven years after this temperature goal was originally established in the Paris Agreement (2015), a legally binding treaty. Yet, insufficient reductions of greenhouse gases (GHGs) emissions still leave the world on a path towards a temperature rise far above 2°C.[2] Unless all countries, but especially large emitters, adopt much greater "systems transformations,"[3] achieving the Paris temperature goal will be impossible. Most concerning is the fact that the global average temperature has already increased by 1.1°C above pre-industrial levels.[4] This means that even if the world managed to achieve net-zero global GHGs emissions and gradually reversed global mean temperatures, some impacts would continue in their current trajectories for centuries.[5] The negative impacts of the current concentrations of GHGs in the atmosphere are already being felt around the world and include extreme weather events, prolonged heatwaves, rising sea levels, desertification and crop failures.

These negative impacts of climate change are not evenly distributed, raising several questions related to distributive justice.[6] Many developing countries are incurring significant costs due to climate change. For instance, in 2022, Pakistan had unusually heavy monsoon rains, which caused more than US$30 billion in damages and financial losses (equivalent to 9 per cent of the country's GDP).[7] A multi-agency report coordinated by the World Meteorological Organization (WMO) in 2023 showed that lack of adequate climate action is undermining virtually all sustainable development goals.[8] Vulnerable nations, such as Small Island Developing States (SIDS), are more frequently, intensively, and severely affected by the unavoidable risks of climate change; some SIDS are threatened by extinction due to rising sea levels.[9] Who should pay for climate-related loss and damage in vulnerable developing countries? Developing countries have argued that it is unfair to expect the most vulnerable developing countries that contributed the least to the climate problem (and many of which have very limited financial resources) to bear these costs. But this argument has been disputed for decades in climate negotiations. These disputes involve a series of issues: should developed countries have the legal obligation to pay for such costs? Should that be through bilateral channels or a dedicated fund? Should contributions be mandatory? Which financial instruments and funding mechanisms should be in place to channel payments? Who will manage the funds and determine how the money is used?[10] The distributive justice questions related to how to allocate loss and damage costs include both the costs of insuring developing countries for the increased climate-related risks and compensating for damages after they have already occurred.

This chapter explores the institutional arrangements related to some of these questions. More specifically, we will analyse two initiatives related to climate insurance: one inside the UN system and one outside. In 2013, after decades of disagreement, an official mechanism to address loss and damage was incorporated in the UNFCCC through the Warsaw International Mechanism on Loss and Damages associated with Climate Change Impacts (WIM). At the time of writing (summer 2023), WIM had not advanced concrete measures regarding funding for loss and damage. In the meantime, some alternatives have been created, including one focused on insurance finance, founded in 2015. Spearheaded by the G7, the InsuResilience Global Partnership ("IGP") is a global multi-stakeholder initiative to facilitate insurance mechanisms in climate-vulnerable developing countries. Despite being created by the world's seven richest nations, it is touted to be a collaboration between the G7, the G20, and the V20 (the group of most climate-vulnerable countries).[11] It also involves insurance companies, research institutes, multilateral organizations, and high-profile individuals.

The creation of IGP follows a well-known pattern in international governance and international relations, which is the creation of multiple governance structures performing similar and often overlapping functions. The specialized literature has coined myriad terms to describe this phenomenon (e.g., fragmentation, institutional choice, regime shifting, forum shopping), but none of these terms fully captures the relational dimension of this phenomenon, that is, how the new institution is designed or used as an alternative to the pre-existing one. This relational dimension is specifically focused on how the coexistence of institutions with overlapping functions may change incentives and create behavioural change among the stakeholders that operate within this particular system of norms. To describe such a phenomenon, one of the authors of this chapter has articulated, in previous work, the concept of "international institutional bypass."[12] Our main claim in this chapter is that IGP is operating as an international institutional bypass of the multilateral mechanisms adopted within the UN framework (WIM) when it comes to the creation of an international mechanism to finance insurance for loss and damage in vulnerable countries. Both IGP and WIM are promoting insurance pools and other financial instruments related to management of climate risks, but IGP has features that try to overcome some of the shortcomings of WIM. This in turn raises questions about the impact that IGP may have on insurance finance for climate-vulnerable developing countries through the multilateral system.

While at first sight IGP looks like a promising innovation, it is unclear what specific role it may play in helping address the distributive concerns related to insurance mechanisms for climate loss and damage. As an institutional bypass, its impact will partly depend on how it interacts with WIM, the multilateral mechanism. One possibility is that IGP will compete with the current multilateral arrangement, reducing incentives for countries to strengthen WIM for providing financial support for insurance mechanisms in vulnerable developing states. Alternatively, it may perform a complementary function to WIM, creating a more robust set of global institutional arrangements in this realm of climate insurance finance. Being outside the UN Framework, IGP does not need to abide by the common but differentiated responsibilities principle (CBDR-RC),[13] raising equity concerns if it weakens WIM insurance schemes. For example, it is unclear what percentage of the funds for insurance mechanisms supported by IGP are coming from developed countries and what percentage is coming from V20 countries (directly or in the form of loans).[14] Moreover, IGP seems to reinforce the voluntary nature of the financial support given by developed countries, raising apprehensions that developed countries may be using the initiative to help evade their legal obligation to provide predictable and additional climate finance to vulnerable countries.

While IGP may be addressing existing gaps in the UN Framework, it is possible that improvements to UN system will continue to occur, and these may include funding mechanisms for climate insurance schemes for vulnerable developing countries. The 2022 Conference of the Parties

(COP 27) ended with an announcement about the creation of a separate Loss and Damage Fund to support countries that are especially vulnerable to the negative impacts of the climate crisis.[15] A group of developed countries have committed to contributing €255 million (US$262 million) to this fund.[16] Not many details had been revealed at the time of writing (summer 2023). Representatives from twenty-four countries are still working together to determine the form the fund will take. While the COP 27 Loss and Damage Fund will certainly fill some gaps in the current climate finance institutional structure, it is still unclear whether – and to what scale – it will include insurance mechanisms.[17] The potential inclusion of insurance in the Fund raises yet another possibility: reforms in the existing multilateral system outside of WIM. Nevertheless, it remains to be seen if such reforms will address the distributive concerns of vulnerable nations. It is also unclear what form funding will take, including insurance, and if the Fund will compete with or complement other existing initiatives, such as the IGP.

II. Loss and Damage in Climate Change Policy

Climate change policies can be organized around three pillars: mitigation, adaptation, and loss and damage.[18] While these are often discussed in silos, they are highly interconnected and interdependent. Reducing GHG emissions in the atmosphere and increasing carbon sinks (mitigation) would limit the increase in the global average temperature, lessening the need to adjust to the actual or expected effects of climate change (adaptation), and preventing costs related to extreme weather events, forest fires, sea level rise, and other climate-induced effects (loss and damage).[19] The more we decrease the global average temperature rise above pre-industrial levels, and the more we reduce the severity of these negative impacts, the smaller will be the need to address loss and damage.[20] Yet, it is clear that current mitigation and adaptation efforts are unlikely to prevent harm resulting from residual climate impacts.[21] This raises the stakes for the design of effective financial mechanisms to cover climate-related loss and damage costs, which is the focus of our chapter.

"Loss and damage" is a relatively recent addition to over thirty years of history of climate policy under the UN climate regime. The UN Framework focused first on mitigation and then on adaptation.[22] At COP 20 in 2013, parties to the UN climate regime finally agreed to the creation of WIM as an official mechanism for "loss and damage."[23,24] WIM was designed to perform three functions: enhance knowledge of risk management approaches to address loss and damage; strengthen dialogue and coordination among stakeholders; and enhance action and support to address loss and damage.[25] The third function, which includes climate finance for loss and damage, is what we will analyse in this chapter.

Climate finance is a broad term with different meanings depending on the context.[26] The UNFCCC uses international climate finance to refer to the obligation of developed countries to provide financial support to developing countries, and more generally to the commitment all parties undertook to "making finance flows consistent with a pathway towards low greenhouse gas emissions and climate-resilient development."[27] Climate finance encompasses public and private capital via a variety of products, including grants or loans through official UN financial mechanisms such as the Green Environmental Fund (GEF) and the Green Climate Fund (GCF), official development assistance (e.g., "green aid," disbursed via bilateral or multilateral channels), bonds (e.g., green bonds), tradable offsets, and climate insurance.[28] These financial instruments are deployed to address the three pillars of climate policy: mitigation, adaptation, and loss and damage.

Within the context of loss and damage, a series of financial products have been developed, including those to compensate for actual losses and damages (e.g., incurred after an extreme weather event such as a typhoon) and those to address the costs of managing risks. The latter are often referred to as disaster risk finance (DRF) or Climate and Disaster Risk Finance and Insurance (CDRFI).[29] CRDFI beneficiaries may include sovereign and sub-sovereign governments, as well as individuals, households, and corporations, including micro and small enterprises. At the sovereign and sub-sovereign levels, financial products include reserves, contingent credit, shock-resistant loans, sovereign risk pools, catastrophe (cat) bonds, budget reallocations, and post-disaster borrowing.[30] While all these financial mechanisms are relevant to deal with loss and damage, this chapter will focus exclusively on insurance finance mechanisms within (WIM) and outside (IGP) the UN framework.

Climate risk insurance at the sovereign, sub-sovereign, individual, or corporate level can perform a number of important functions, including creating incentives for mitigation and adaptation to climate change.[31] In the context of loss and damage, insurance can pay for human and material losses, provide post-disaster relief, and reduce potential long-term negative impacts of the disaster (such as reduced growth and poverty).[32] It does so by creating mechanisms to manage risk that can be related to risk pooling,[33] risk transferring,[34] or both.

III. Loss and Damage Finance within the UN Framework

Since the inception of the UNFCCC, developed countries have accepted a general legal obligation to provide financial support for climate action to developing countries, which is grounded on the equity principle of common but differentiated responsibilities and respective capabilities (CBDR-RC).[35] Yet, the exact contours of this obligation have remained extremely vague, including how much each developed country should contribute, as well as when and how.[36]

The dispute between developed and developing countries has also been long-lasting and acute regarding loss and damage finance. In 1991, in the lead up to the UNFCCC, the Alliance of Small Island States (AOSIS) proposed an international insurance pool to compensate victims of sea level rise,[37] with "mandatory contributions from industrialized countries based on GNP and on relative greenhouse gas (GHG) emissions; that is, contributions to the fund would be based on ability to pay as well as responsibility for impacts."[38] The AOSIS proposal also included a multilateral governance structure that gave equal voice to developing nations.[39] It was never incorporated in the UN Convention, primarily due to resistance from developed countries, who have also resisted any reference to the term "loss and damage" in international policy instruments.

Even when the concept of "loss and damage" was officially acknowledged as part of international climate policies in 2013 with the creation of the WIM, the disputes continued. Developed countries rejected the idea that a loss and damage mechanism meant they were accepting liability for climate change costs and the legal duty to compensate vulnerable countries for loss and damage.[40] In line with this, the 2015 UNFCCC decision adopting the Paris Agreement stated that its Article 8, concerning loss and damage, does not involve liability or compensation. The inclusion of this statement was a red line for developed countries in the Paris Agreement negotiations.[41] Some argue that the strong political opposition by developed nations to any form of liability mechanisms may be driven by the fear that reparations for past climate harms may then evolve to extend to claims for reparations for other harms (e.g., slavery, colonialism).[42] There may also be a concern with the scale of the potential compensation, particularly without significant investment in risk management and adaptation and mitigation efforts.

This stance by developed countries has significantly slowed down the development of loss and damage finance mechanisms within the UNFCCC system. Although the WIM provisions refer to finance generally, the clear priority has been finance for risk insurance and management of risk, rather than compensation for actual loss and damage.[43] Regarding climate insurance finance, the WIM has focused on collecting and disseminating information and pooling expertise, rather than on creating actual insurance finance mechanisms that would ease the premium load on developing countries. Until 2023, there had been no significant advances in WIM's mandate on "enhancing action and support, including finance" apart from informational initiatives.[44] As we will discuss later, the creation of a new loss and damage fund in COP 27 could play an important role on climate insurance for loss and damage in the future. However, details were still being negotiated at the time of writing (summer 2023).[45] Therefore, our analysis focuses on the fact that most of the international action currently takes place outside the UN framework.

IV. Loss and Damage Finance Outside the UN Framework

As described in the previous section, developed countries have accepted to provide financial support for climate action to developing countries, although the details of how much finance, when to disburse it, and to which projects remain undefined.[46] Moreover, despite repeated calls from developing countries for financial support from developed countries to flow through UN financial mechanisms, climate finance remains highly decentralized. Developed countries have disbursed most of their support outside the UN channels, via bilateral or multilateral mechanisms or other initiatives.[47] For a long time, most of their financial contributions went to a select number of developing countries (many of them emerging economies) and were primarily for mitigation. After much pressure, these contributions were timidly extended to adaptation.[48] Despite these initiatives, there has always been uncertainty around exactly how much climate finance developed countries were to provide or to mobilize for climate action in developing countries. Only in 2009, developed countries made a pledge to mobilize US$100 billion annually by 2020[49] (later extended through 2025),[50] and to balance their contributions between adaptation and mitigation. However, this pledge has yet to be totally fulfilled: the largest amount in one single year was US$83 billion in 2021.[51] Loss and damage finance has not been explicitly a part of these pledges, with WIM being the only mechanism with the mandate to address this type of finance within the UNFCCC system.

Instead of relying on the slow-moving WIM and considering the challenges of increasing climate finance under the UN framework, developing countries have established their own risk-pooling mechanisms outside the UN framework, which includes insurance for climate related disasters alongside other types of catastrophes.[52] These mechanisms are used in the context of climate change "to spread risks over larger geographical areas by aggregating risks sub-nationally, nationally or regionally."[53] Examples of international risk pooling for climate-related loss and damage include the Caribbean Catastrophe Risk Insurance Facility, the European Solidarity Fund, and the Pacific Catastrophe Risk Assessment and Financing Initiative. These initiatives have adopted catastrophe risk insurance, which provides coverage for low-probability, high-cost disasters, disbursing rapid payouts after a catastrophe.[54] This means that these insurance schemes may not provide a robust and system-wide response, as they are not well-equipped to deal with high-frequency or slow onset disasters, with a high degree of certainty of occurrence, such as sea levels rising, ocean acidification, and desertification.[55] Thus, as climate change intensifies, the frequency of some disasters may increase, and others will become more certain, thus making it harder to insure against losses through risk pooling.[56]

While insurance mechanisms based on risk pooling have grown in importance in recent years, they have important limitations. Significantly, insurance mechanisms are inadequate to deal with the costs of slow onset events such as sea level rise. Three other limitations are worth mentioning. First, the responsibility for the premiums is primarily bore by developing nations, with occasional voluntary financial support from developed countries either bilaterally or via multilateral institutions.[57] Thus, these pooling mechanisms transfer the costs of climate change to vulnerable nations, raising distributive concerns.[58] Second, by requiring developing countries to shoulder the costs of such schemes, insurance schemes may be depriving these nations from funding for other valuable and pressing human needs.[59] Third, the sheer cost of climate-related loss and damage is likely to be staggering and will quickly surpass the capacity of existing insurance schemes.[60] Even if these limitations could be overcome, it is uncertain if such risk-pooling schemes will trickle down to the most vulnerable individuals and legal persons: there are significant upfront investments (education, information, infrastructure, etc.) to create low-cost, affordable insurance for the most vulnerable households and micro and small enterprises in developing countries.[61]

In summary, while existing risk management and insurance mechanisms have provided developing nations with some protection against the costs of unavoidable climate change risks, they have not helped to overcome the disputes over fair allocation of climate costs, or broader distributive concerns. Developed and developing nations are still disputing how to structure these insurance mechanisms, as one form of loss and damage finance, and who should pay the premiums for climate risk insurance for vulnerable countries.

V. The InsuResilience Global Partnership ("IGP") as an Institutional Bypass

To address some of the aforementioned issues, IGP was announced in a G7 Summit in 2015[62] and launched in 2017, at a side event at the UN Climate Change Conference in Bonn, Germany. It was spearheaded by the group of rich countries (G7) but touted as a partnership between the G20 and V20. IGP is self-described as a global initiative with a mission to strengthen people's ability to deal with climate shocks, especially in developing countries.[63] In line with the decision of the COP not to embrace liability and compensation (see section 2 *supra*), IGP focuses specifically on insurance solutions.[64] As a multistakeholder initiative, the IGP has over 120 members, including countries, multilateral institutions, civil society organizations, private sector actors, academia and think tanks, implementing partners and programs, and initiatives and networks.

At the apex of its governance structure is a high-level executive body, the High-Level Consultative Group (HLCG), which does strategic planning and ensures coordination and information sharing. The members of the HLCG are from all IGP's member groups, and it is led by two co-chairs who each represent V20 and G20+ members. Another body on its governance structure is the Program Alliance. This "delivery vehicle" of IGP provides a set of services to aid the delivery of CDRFI, including research, technical assistance, solution design, and financial assistance.[65]

Unlike WIM, IGP is largely focused on concrete action, which is structured around a concrete set of targets. Some of its targets for 2025[66] are to ensure that 500 million vulnerable people are covered against climate disaster shock; 80 vulnerable countries have CDRFI strategies in place; 60 vulnerable countries have new or enhanced (sub-) sovereign pre-arranged risk financing and insurance mechanisms[67]; and 15 per cent of climate and disaster losses that vulnerable populations face are covered by pre-arranged CDRFI solutions.[68] To achieve these, in 2017, IGP was supporting the expansion of "sovereign risk pools," among their other insurance schemes.[69] For this purpose, it has partnered with the African Risk Capacity (ARC) and Caribbean Catastrophe Risk Insurance Facility (CCRIF).[70] In the case of ARC, IGP is developing a mechanism to match insurance disbursements with UN and other humanitarian agencies that may be providing funding in the aftermath of a disaster.[71]

Another important difference between WIM and IGP is that the latter has a dedicated fund. The InsuResilience Solutions Fund (ISF) was created to help implement CDRFI solutions. It was set up by KfW Development Bank on behalf of Germany, represented by the Federal Ministry for Economic Cooperation and Development (BMZ). The ISF began its activities in 2018 and its funding operations in 2019. It is funded by the BMZ.[72] IGP also aims to "crowd in" private capital, mindful that government funding is unlikely to be enough to cover the ever-increasing costs of climate change.[73] Private capital may be particularly important to reduce high insurance premiums in developing nations.[74]

As IGP seems to be addressing some of the shortcomings of WIM, it could be classified as an international institutional bypass. International institutional bypass (IIB) is a concept used to describe the creation of a parallel institution in global governance that performs at least part of the same function of a pre-existing institution.[75] Despite the high level of fragmentation and overlap in the international sphere, only a select number of international institutions can be classified as IIB. An IIB has six characteristics[76]:

(1) It keeps the dominant institution in place;
(2) It creates an optional alternative pathway through which to discharge functions performed by the dominant institution;
(3) It has at least one distinctive feature that aims at addressing a perceived dysfunction in the dominant institution;
(4) It has effects in the same international regimes or domestic legal orders of the dominant institution;
(5) It is compatible with the requirements of the international regimes or domestic legal orders within which the bypass is operating; and
(6) It is separated from the dominant institution's governance structure.

IGP has all six characteristics. Both WIM and IGP are designed to facilitate the development of climate insurance and other financial mechanisms for vulnerable countries, and to provide support for such mechanisms. Yet, IGP does not seek to intentionally modify or reform WIM, currently the dominant institution in loss and damage finance. Therefore, both initiatives operate in parallel: IGP leaves WIM in place, at least for the time being. IGP was created independently of WIM and outside the UN framework (although it was launched in a side event of a COP).

Until today, WIM has not advanced significantly on its mission related to financial support, lacking especially engagement with concrete action. It has limited itself to performing a rather technical and detached informational role regarding insurance schemes.[77] In contrast, IGP has engaged in action, providing financial assistance, technical support, and advice to developing countries. As a result, IGP has created an alternative pathway that V20 countries are using to strengthen their climate insurance mechanisms. There is some overlap between the two institutions as both IGP and WIM invest in knowledge mobilization and support for insurance schemes. However, IGP has distinguished itself by being able to establish partnerships with V20 countries and to concretely support specific initiatives financially, with capacity building and/or technical assistance.

IGP's governance structure is independent from the UN framework (and thus separated from WIM). This allows it to bring a new set of non-state actors to the table, including organizations from the private sector and civil society. This governance structure may have allowed IGP to bypass the political divide among developing and developed countries that has hampered the ability of WIM to progress faster in providing concrete action (especially financing) for insurance mechanisms for loss and damage in the climate regime. As a multistakeholder initiative, IGP has been able to creatively engage with private insurance companies and multilateral banks, attracting new forms of investments to climate insurance and, consequently, increasing the pool of resources available to address the issue. It has done so without being forced to confront the thorny questions about developed countries' contributions.

VI. The Potential Impact of IGP as an International Institutional Bypass

The creation of multiple governance structures performing similar and often overlapping functions is a common phenomenon in international governance, and has been described by the specialized literature as fragmentation, institutional choice, regime shifting, or forum shopping, among others. By labelling the phenomenon an international institutional bypass, we are emphasizing its relational dimension: our analysis focuses on how this coexistence of institutions with overlapping functions may modify incentives and create behavioural change among the stakeholders that operate within this system of norms.[78]

While IGP may be offering an alternative to vulnerable countries in the short term, it is unclear what will be the impact of this IIB in the long term. In many cases, by creating an alternative option, institutional bypasses allow for stakeholders to "exit" the pre-existing system and end up reducing the pressure for its reforms. This exodus, especially if it includes powerful actors, may result in a continuous decay until the system becomes obsolete.[79] Therefore, one of the risks associated with the creation of IGP is that powerful countries would stop to press for improvements in the WIM. However, this does not seem to have happened yet. V20 countries are actively using IGP programs, but they also continue to engage with WIM and to press for more specific financial mechanisms for loss and damage under the UNFCCC and through international litigation.[80] The announcement of a new loss and damage fund at COP 27 is a result of this pressure. This may suggest that the possibility to use alternatives has not disempowered or discouraged stakeholders to press for changes in the dysfunctional system.[81]

It is possible that IGP will not evolve to replace WIM but will instead complement it and the UNFCCC financial mechanisms. In fact, the V20 countries' support to IGP seems to suggest that they do not see it as a threat to WIM or to loss and damage finance at the UN. The same may be said about Germany, which has been the main force behind the creation of IGP and has also provided significant support for loss and damage finance within the UN framework.[82] One could speculate if all these actors currently supporting IGP see it as venue for experimentation and innovation, which will pilot innovative financial mechanisms and tools. Whenever successful, these financial mechanisms could then become a permanent fixture of the slow-moving and risk-averse WIM. In this case, IGP would have a complementary role to WIM: only after being tried and tested by IGP, mechanisms would be supported under the UNFCCC regime.

Another possibility is that IGP is serving as a temporary solution, and it would be discontinued if an international insurance pool is eventually created under the UN framework. In such case, IGP would not have a complementary role to WIM; rather, it would be serving as a competitor (or simply a backstop) that will cease to perform its function if WIM eventually starts to perform the functions demanded by V20 countries. This possibility may explain why the participation of these vulnerable countries in IGP does not seem to have reduced their pressure for measures that will strengthen loss and damage responses under the UNFCCC.

VII. Conclusion

The current UN framework for loss and damage finance has a series of limitations and has accomplished little to date as it relates to risk insurance finance. Our main claim is that IGP has been developed as an international institutional bypass of the WIM, an alternative pathway for vulnerable countries to develop or strengthen climate insurance outside the UN Framework. We argue that considering IGP as an institutional bypass facilitates a critical assessment of how this mechanism will impact the creation and evolution of insurance-related loss and damage finance mechanisms within the UN multilateral climate framework. While IGP may not be intended to replace insurance mechanisms for loss and damage in the UN framework, the institutional bypass concept suggests that creating institutional alternatives may have unintended consequences. One of these could be that IGP will reduce the incentives for stakeholders to continue to engage with and press for reforms in the multilateral system. Although there are yet no indications that this is happening with insurance finance, vulnerable developing countries and the members of IGP should be attentive to this possibility.

Despite having accomplished very little in loss and damage finance to date, the role and significance of the UN framework on this issue may be about to change. At COP 26 in Glasgow, Scotland pledged £2 million (US$2.7 million) as a one-off payment for loss and damage. Shortly before COP 27, Denmark pledged a US$13 million contribution to developing countries that have suffered damage from climate change.[83] COP 27 ended with the announcement of a separate loss and damage fund, based on significant pledges by developed nations, spearheaded by a strong commitment by Germany (€170 million, out of a total €255 million pledged).

While the announcement of a UN loss and damage fund at COP 27 potentially revamps the role of UNFCC financial mechanisms in addressing loss and damage in vulnerable countries, it is still unclear what form funding will take, whether the fund will include insurance mechanisms (or will be focused on compensation mechanisms), and if it will compete with or complement other existing initiatives, such as the IGP. The little information available so far seems to suggest that the developed/developing country divide persists: while developed countries want to have autonomy on how to use their pledges, developing countries are pushing for a common pool of resources, where pledges would go to a single fund under the auspices of the UN that would be managed according to a democratic structure with participation of developed and developing countries.[84]

In summary, it is unclear what the future holds regarding climate insurance. There are many roles this new fund could play in strengthening insurance within the UN Framework. The new fund can also interact in multiple ways with existing initiatives (being a complement or a substitute to IGP, for instance). Perhaps the new Loss and Damage Fund and IGP are both opening the way for the creation of an international insurance pool under the UNFCCC regime, with developed countries paying the premiums as part of their obligation to provide climate finance to vulnerable developing countries, as AOSIS proposed in 1991. Either way, one can only hope that robust financial mechanisms will be in place soon, as climate related loss and damage will not wait.

Acknowledgments

We are deeply grateful for detailed comments and insightful suggestions by Benjamin Alarie, Sarah Riley Case, Andrew Green, and the participants of the Climate Change Conference at the University of Toronto, Faculty of Law in March 2023. We are also in debt to Robert Halperin for research assistance. Any remaining errors are ours.

NOTES

1 UNFCCC, *Second Periodic Review of the Long-Term Global Goal Under the Convention and of Overall Progress Towards Achieving it*, UNFCCC, 27th Sess, UN Doc FCCC/CP/2022/L.17 (2022) at para 5.
2 UNEP, *Emissions Gap Report 2022* (Nairobi: United Nations Environment Programme, 2022), online: <https://www.unep.org/resources/emissions-gap-report-2022>.
3 UNFCCC, *supra* note 1 at para 13.
4 *Ibid* at para 5.
5 IPCC Working Group I, "Summary for Policymakers" in *Climate Change 2021: The Physical Science Basis. Working Group I Contribution to the Sixth Assessment Report of the Intergovernmental Panel on Climate Change*, Valérie Masson-Delmotte et al, eds (Geneva: Intergovernmental Panel on Climate Change, 2021) (the IPCC states, with high confidence, that "it would take several centuries to millennia for global mean sea level to reverse course even under large net negative CO_2 emissions" at para D.1.6).
6 Simon Caney, "Climate Change" in Serena Olsaretti, ed, *The Oxford Handbook of Distributive Justice* (Oxford: Oxford University Press, 2018) 664, online: <https://doi.org/10.1093/oxfordhb/9780199645121.013.23>.
7 Sharm El-Sheikh, "Should Rich Countries Pay for Climate Damage in Poor Ones?," *The Economist* (24 November 2022), online: <https://www.economist.com/international/2022/11/20/a-new-un-fund-for-loss-and-damage-emerges-from-cop27>.
8 United Nations Environment Programme, Press Release, "Climate Change Undermines Nearly All Sustainable Development Goals," (14 September

2023), <https://www.unep.org/news-and-stories/press-release/climate-change-undermines-nearly-all-sustainable-development-goals>.

9 IPCC Working Group II, "Summary for Policymakers" in *Climate Change 2022: Impacts, Adaptation and Vulnerability. Working Group II Contribution to the Sixth Assessment Report of the Intergovernmental Panel on Climate Change* (Geneva: Intergovernmental Panel on Climate Change, 2022) at para B.2.5. See also IPCC Working Group II, "Small Islands" in *Climate Change 2014: Impacts, Adaptation, and Vulnerability. Part B: Regional Aspects. Contribution of Working Group II to the Fifth Assessment Report of the Intergovernmental Panel on Climate Change* (Geneva: Intergovernmental Panel on Climate Change, 2014).

10 For a careful and detailed historical map of these disputes, see Sarah Riley Case, *Climate Change, Anticolonial International Law, and the Universality of the Commons* (SJD Dissertation, University of Toronto Faculty of Law, 2023).

11 It is interesting to note that most of the members are from G7 (under the leadership of Germany) and V20. Some key emerging economies from G20, such as China and Brazil, are not part of the Initiative.

12 Mariana Mota Prado & Steven J. Hoffman, "The Promises and Perils of International Institutional Bypasses: Defining a New Concept and its Policy Implications for Global Governance" (2019) 10:3–4 Transnat'l Leg Theory 275, online: <https://doi.org/10.1080/20414005.2019.1686866>.

13 Lavanya Rajamani, "The Principle of Common but Differentiated Responsibilities and Respective Capabilities in the International Climate Change Regime" in Rosemary Lyster & Robert R.M. Verchick, eds, *Research Handbook on Climate Disaster Law* (Cheltenham, UK: Edward Elgar, 2018) 46, online: <https://doi.org/10.4337/9781786430038.00009>.

14 The IGP announced the Global Shield Against Climate Risks as its successor initiative. This is a joint initiative of the Vulnerable Twenty (V20) Group of Finance Ministers and the G7. The Global Shield claims to add a robust governance structure and a larger funding base to bolster the response to climate loss and damage, but there is still no clarity on who is making the contributions. Insuresilience Global Partnership Vision 2025 Update, online: <https://www.insuresilience.org/knowledge/annual-reports/> (Accessed October 29 2024).

15 United Nations Environment Programme, News Release, "COP27 Ends with Announcement of Historic Loss and Damage Fund" (22 November 2022), online: <https://www.unep.org/news-and-stories/story/cop27-ends-announcement-historic-loss-and-damage-fund>.

16 El-Sheikh, *supra* note 7.

17 United Nations Environment Programme, News Release, "What You Need to Know about the COP27 Loss and Damage Fund" (29 November 2022),

online: <https://www.unep.org/news-and-stories/story/what-you-need-know-about-cop27-loss-and-damage-fund> ("[i]t is important that a Loss and Damage Fund tackles the gaps that current climate finance institutions such as the Green Climate Fund do not fill"). Details on the operationalization of the Loss and Damage fund, its scale, and access modalities remained unclear in October 2024 (at the time when this chapter was in the final stages of the production process). Liane Schalatek, "One Year in, New Loss and Damage Fund Has Met Deadlines, but Decisions on its Vision, Scope, and Scale Are Still to Come" (9 October 2024), online: <https://us.boell.org/en/2024/10/09/one-year-new-loss-and-damage-fund-has-met-institutional-deadlines-decisions-elaborating>).

18 *Cf* UNFCCC, "Key aspects of the Paris Agreement", online: <https://unfccc.int/most-requested/key-aspects-of-the-paris-agreement> (another possible organization is around the three formal goals of the Paris Agreement: mitigation – "to strengthen the global response to the threat of climate change by keeping a global temperature rise … well below 2 degrees Celsius above pre-industrial levels and [preferably at] 1.5 degrees Celsius; adaptation – "to increase the ability of countries to deal with the impacts of climate change;" and finance – "making finance flows consistent with a low GHG emissions and climate-resilient pathway"). See also Daniel Klein et al, eds, *The Paris Agreement on Climate Change: Analysis and Commentary* (Oxford: Oxford University Press, 2017), online: <https://doi.org/10.1093/law/9780198789338.001.0001>.

19 Meinhard Doelle & Sara L. Seck, eds, *Research Handbook on Climate Change Law and Loss & Damage* (Cheltenham, UK: Edward Elgar, 2021) at 2, online: <https://doi.org/10.4337/9781788974028>.

20 UNFCCC, *supra* note 1 at para 7.

21 Veera Pekkarinen, Patrick Toussaint & Harro van Asselt, "Loss and Damage After Paris" (2019) 13:1 Carbon & Climate L Rev 31, online: <https://doi.org/10.21552/cclr/2019/1/6>.

22 Saleemul Huq, Erin Roberts & Adrian Fenton, "Loss and Damage" (2013) Nature Clim Change 947, online: <https://doi.org/10.21552/cclr/2019/1/6>. See also UNFCCC, *Decision 1/CP.13: Bali Action Plan*, UNFCCC, Add 1, FCCC/CP/2007/6/Add.1 (2007) at 3 (loss and damage was actually a provision included under adaptation measures during COP 13 in 2007).

23 See generally Doelle & Seck, *supra* note 19.

24 UNFCCC, *Decision 3/CP.18: Approaches to address loss and damage associated with climate change impacts in developing countries that are particularly vulnerable to the adverse effects of climate change to enhance adaptive capacity*, UNFCCC, Add 1 FCCC/CP/2012/8/Add.1 (2012) at 21; UNFCCC, *Decision 2/CP.19: Warsaw international mechanism for loss and damage*

associated with climate change impacts, UNFCCC, Add 1, FCCC /CP/2013/10/Add.1 at 6. Please note that in 2015 the Paris Agreement was the first legal instrument to include a dedicated provision (Article 8) on loss and damage.

25 "Warsaw International Mechanism for Loss and Damage Associated with Climate Change Impacts (WIM)," *UNFCCC* (accessed 29 October 2024), online: <https://unfccc.int/topics/adaptation-and-resilience/workstreams/loss-and-damage/warsaw-international-mechanism>.

26 Nina Araneta-Alana, "Climate Finance and Governance", in Ruth Buchanan, Luis Eslava, & Sunhya Pahuja, eds, *The Oxford Handbook of International Law and Development* (Oxford University Press, 2023) 581, online: <https://doi.org/10.1093/oxfordhb/9780192867360.013.42>.

27 "Introduction to Climate Finance" *UNFCCC* (accessed 29 October 2024), online: <https://unfccc.int/topics/introduction-to-climate-finance>.

28 Liane Schalatek & Charlene Watson, "Climate Finance Fundamentals 2: The Global Climate Finance Architecture," *Heinrich Böll Stiftung North America* (February 2019), online (pdf): <https://us.boell.org/sites/default/files/cff2_2018_eng-digital_8.pdf>.

29 InsuResilience Global Partnership, *From Innovation to Learning: A Strategic Evidence Roadmap for Climate and Disaster Risk Finance and Insurance* (Bonn: Deutsche Gesellschaft für Internationale Zusammenarbeit, 2022) at 10.

30 See Durand et al, *Financing Options for Loss and Damage: A Review and Roadmap* (Bonn: German Development Institute, 2016).

31 Vanessa Lueck, *Governing Climate Change Adaptation through Insurance: Complexity, Risk, and Justice Concerns?* (PhD Dissertation, Arizona State University, 2020).

32 Pekkarinen, Toussaint & van Asselt, *supra* note 21 at 42.

33 Durand et al, *supra* note 30 at 6 (risk pooling refers to risk holders aggregating their assets in a collective reserve fund with contributions from a diverse group; losses affecting some members of the group should be offset by unaffected members).

34 *Ibid* at 6 (risk transfers refers to mechanisms that allow "risk holders to pass some of their high exposure to risk over to actors with relatively stable financial bases in exchange for a premium").

35 Jorge Gastelumendi & Inka Gnittke, "Climate Finance" in Daniel Klein et al, *supra* note 18; Patrícia Galvão Ferreira, "Against the Headwind: Innovative Sources of Loss and Damage Finance" in Doelle & Seck, *supra* note 19.

36 Patrícia Galvão Ferreira, "Arrested Development: The late and Inequitable Integration of Loss and Damage Finance into the UNFCCC" in Doelle & Seck, *supra* note 19; Case, *supra* note 10. See also Sarah Riley Case & Julia Dehm, "Redressing Historical Responsibility for the Unjust Precarities of

Climate Change in the Present" in Benoit Mayer & Alexander Zahar, eds, *Debating Climate Law* (Cambridge: Cambridge University Press, 2021) 170, online: <https://doi.org/10.1017/9781108879064.014>.

37 At the time there was some science linking extreme weather events to climate change, but it was not as developed as today. See Michael Burger, Jessica Wentz & Radley Horton, "The Law and Science of Climate Change Attribution" (2020) 45:1 Colum J Envtl L 57.

38 Linda Siegele, "Loss and Damage under the Convention" in Doelle & Seck, *supra* note 19 ("[p]erhaps the strongest remnant of the AOSIS proposal for an insurance pool can be found in Article 4.8 of the Convention, where Parties are obliged to 'give full consideration' to the actions necessary, including insurance, to 'meet the specific needs and concerns of developing country Parties arising from the adverse effects of climate change'" at 76–7).

39 Case, *supra* note 10.

40 Elisa Calliari, "Loss and Damage: A Critical Discourse Analysis of Parties' Positions in Climate Change Negotiations," (2018) 21:6 J Risk Res 725, online: <https://doi.org/10.1080/13669877.2016.1240706>; Lisa Vanhala & Cecilie Hestbaek, "Framing Loss and Damage in the UNFCCC Negotiations: The Struggle over Meaning and the Warsaw International Mechanism," (2016) 16:2 Glob Environtl Pol 111, online: <https://doi.org/10.1162/GLEP_a_00379>.

41 Siegele, *supra* note 38; Linda Siegele, "Loss and damage under the Paris Agreement" in Doelle & Seck, *supra* note 19.

42 See Case, *supra* note 10.

43 Ferreira, *supra* note 36.

44 *Ibid.*

45 Schalatek, *supra* note 17.

46 Ferreira, *supra* note 36. *Ibid.*

47 *Ibid.*

48 In March 2022, the COP 27 Glasgow Pact decision included a section on Adaptation finance where Parties noted "with concern that the current provision of climate finance for adaptation remains insufficient to respond to worsening climate impacts in developing countr[ies]". See UNFCCC, *Decision 1/CP.26: Glasgow Climate Pact*, UNFCCC, Add 1, FCCC/CP/2021/12/Add.1 (2021) at 3.

49 UNFCCC, *Decision 2/CP.15: Copenhagen Accord, UNFCCC,* FCCC/CP/2009/11/Add.1 (2009); UNFCCC, *Decision 1/CP.16: The Cancun Agreements: Outcome of the work of the Ad Hoc Working Group on Long-term Cooperative Action under the Convention*, UNFCCC, Add 1, FCCC/CP/2010/7/Add.1 (2010).

50 "OECD Confirms: Rich Countries Broke the $100-Billion Promise," *German Climate Finance* (10 August 2022), online: <https://www.germanclimatefinance.de/2022/08/10/oecd-confirms-rich-countries-broke-the-100-billion-promise/>.

51 "There Is a Better Way to Help Poor Countries Fight Climate Change," *The Economist* (17 November 2022), online: <https://www.economist.com/leaders/2022/11/17/there-is-a-better-way-to-help-poor-countries-fight-climate-change> ["Help Poor Countries"]. See also Lorena Gonzalez, "Where Do We Go from the $100 Billion Goal? Procedural Options to Enhance Climate Finance Ambition at COP26," *WRI* (22 October 2021), online: <https://www.wri.org/technical-perspectives/where-do-we-go-100-billion-goal-procedural-options-enhance-climate-finance>.

52 One example is the Caribbean Catastrophe Risk Insurance Facility (CCRIF). See Durand et al, *supra* note 30, which describes the CCRIF as "the first multi-country catastrophe risk insurance instrument. Formed in 2007, the Facility draws upon a regional fund jointly financed by Caribbean governments to quickly provide financial liquidity to respond promptly and limit the fiscal impact of hurricanes and earthquake" at 8).

53 *Ibid* at 6.

54 *Ibid* at 8.

55 Sofya Matteoni & Olga Nartova, "Climate Change: Implications for the (Re) Insurance Industries" (2012) 10 NZ J Pub & Internat'l L 107; "MCII 2012: The Role of Insurance in Loss & Damage," *Munich Climate Insurance Initiative* (2012), online: <https://climate-insurance.org/publications/mcii-2012-the-role-of-insurance-in-loss-damage/>.

56 Durand et al, *supra* note 30 at 7.

57 *Ibid* at 6 ("[f]or example, at COP21, the United States pledged US$30 million towards climate risk insurance in vulnerable countries. Most of this funding contributes to existing risk pools and risk transfer efforts such as the PCRAFI [Pacific Catastrophe Risk Assessment and Financing Initiative], the African Risk Capacity program and the expansion of the CCRIF to cover Central American countries. In addition, in June 2015, the G7 announced a goal to increase insurance coverage in the world's most vulnerable developing countries by up to 400 million people by 2020 in order to help these nations cope with climate risks" [citations omitted]).

58 Pekkarinen, Toussaint & van Asselt, *supra* note 21 at 41.

59 Durand et al, *supra* note 30 at 11.

60 "Help Poor Countries," *supra* note 51.

61 Kati Kulovesi et al, *Results of the COP 21 Paris Negotiations* (Helsinki: Ministry of the Environment, Finland, 2016).

62 UNFCCC, News Release, "G7 Climate Risk Insurance Initiative – Stepping Up Protection for the Most Vulnerable" (8 October 2015), online: <https://

newsroom.unfccc.int/news/g7-climate-risk-insurance-initiative-stepping-up-protection-for-the-most-vulnerable>.

63 "Vision & Mission," *InsuResilience Global Partnership* (accessed 29 October 2024), online: <https://www.insuresilience.org/about-us/vision-mission/#vision> (IGP's vision is to "strengthen the resilience of developing countries and to protect the lives and livelihoods of poor and vulnerable people from the impacts of climate shocks and disasters by enabling faster, more reliable and cost-effective responses").

64 InsuResilience Global Partnership, *supra* note 29 at 10. For a detailed list of the financial instruments IGP works with, see "Programmes & Projects," *InsuResilience Global Partnership* (accessed 29 October 2024), online: <https://www.insuresilience.org/implementation/programmes-projects/#projects>.

65 "Governance" *InsuResilience Global Partnership* online: <https://www.insuresilience.org/about-us/about-the-igp/#governance>.

66 InsuResilience Global Partnership, "Background Note on Targets and Indicators for Vision 2025: A Refined Monitoring & Evaluation Framework for the InsuResilience Global Partnership" (2021) ["IGP Background Note"]. The "IGP Background Note" outlines the Partnership's monitoring and evaluation framework (M&E). In this document, they outline six result areas that the M&E covers, their lead indicators (LI) and the headline target for 2025.

67 *Ibid* at 7.

68 *Ibid* at 9.

69 UNFCCC, News Release, "'InsuResilience' to Provide the Poor with More Financial Protection Against Climate Risks" (14 November 2017), online: <https://unfccc.int/news/insuresilience-to-provide-the-poor-with-more-financial-protection-against-climate-risks>.

70 "InsuResilience Global Partnership" (accessed 29 October 2024), online: *UNFCCC* <https://unfccc.int/topics/adaptation-and-resilience/resources/S-N/IRGP>.

71 "ARC Replica," *African Risk Capacity* (accessed 29 October 2024), online: <https://www.arc.int/arc-replica>.

72 "About ISF," *InsuResilience Solutions Fund* (accessed 29 October), online: <https://insuresilience-solutions-fund.org/about/about-isf>.

73 "Making Impact Visible: Development of a Holistic M&E Framework," *InsuResilience* (2020), online: <https://annualreport.insuresilience.org/development-of-a-holistic-me-framework/>. See also "Help Poor Countries," *supra* note 51.

74 Durand et al, *supra* note 30 at 21.

75 Mariana Mota Prado & Steven J. Hoffman, "The Concept of an International Institutional Bypass" (2017) 111 AJIL Unbound 231, online: <https://doi.org/10.1017/aju.2017.61>.

76 Prado & Hoffman, *supra* note 12.

77 Ferreira, *supra* note 36.

78 Prado & Hoffman, *supra* note 12.

79 Mariana Mota Prado & Michael J. Trebilcock, *Institutional Bypasses: A Strategy to Promote Reforms for Development* (Cambridge: Cambridge University Press, 2018).

80 César Rodríguez-Garavito, ed, *Litigating the Climate Emergency: How Human Rights, Courts, and Legal Mobilization Can Bolster Climate Action* (Cambridge: Cambridge University Press, 2022), online: <https://doi.org/10.1017/9781009106214>; Joana Setzer & Lisa C. Vanhala, "Climate Change Litigation: A Review of Research on Courts and Litigants in Climate Governance" (2019) 10:e580 WIREs Clim Chang, online: <https://doi.org/10.1002/wcc.580>.

81 This seems to be contrary to Albert Hirschman's original prediction in his book *Exit, Voice and Loyalty*, but seems aligned with his later writing. Albert O. Hirschman, "Exit, Voice, and the Fate of the German Democratic Republic: An Essay in Conceptual History" (1993) 45:2 World Pol 173 at 177, online: <https://doi.org/10.2307/2950657>.

82 "Germany, Belgium Pledge Funds to Tackle Climate 'Loss and Damage,'" *EURACTIV* (8 November 2022), online: <https://www.euractiv.com/section/climate-environment/news/germany-belgium-pledge-funds-to-tackle-climate-loss-and-damage/>.

83 "What Is Climate 'Loss and Damage'?," *The Economist* (3 October 2022), online: <https://www.economist.com/the-economist-explains/2022/10/03/what-is-climate-loss-and-damage>.

84 Interview with Dr. Saleemul Huq by Nick Breeze & ClimateGenn, "Dr Saleemul Huq: The Long Game of Loss & Damage (#COP27)," *YouTube* (17 November 2022), online (video): <https://youtu.be/jxs40xamxIc>.

10 Climate Anxiety and Youth Activism

BRENDA COSSMAN

The American Psychological Association has recognized "eco-anxiety" – the fear of environmental damage, climate change, and ecological disaster – as a growing threat to mental health.[1] The APA defines eco-anxiety as "a chronic fear of environmental doom."[2] The emerging area of climate psychology has demonstrated that individuals are experiencing a range of mental health problems associated with climate change, including post-traumatic stress disorder, depression, substance abuse, and anxiety.[3] Climate anxiety is described as acute or chronic anxiety due to an individual's inability to control climate change and its destructive impacts.[4] I have previously considered the role of anxiety in contemporary systems of governance, arguing that anxiety could be productively analysed through the register of self-governance, a mode of governance in which individuals are called on to govern themselves through the choices they make.[5] I explored some of the ways that free-floating discourses of anxiety produce anxious subjects, who with the help of experts then undertake a range of self-governing projects to manage, mitigate, and reduce the unpleasant emotion. Eco-anxiety produced self-governing, responsible eco-subjects, who sought to take individual responsibility for climate change by engaging in various carbon reduction behaviours.

Building on this earlier work, in this chapter I return to eco-anxiety and reconsider its role in political engagement with climate change, focusing on the impact on youth. In the intervening years, the impacts of climate change have intensified, as has attention to its mental health impacts. Severe weather events, from catastrophic storms and floods to wildfires to heat domes, are bringing the here and now of climate change in our backyards. A survey done by the APA in 2020 found that two thirds of all American adults experienced at least some eco-anxiety.[6] But the impact on young adults is heightened: half of those between 18 and 30 stated that the stress they feel about climate change is affecting their daily lives.[7] Emerging studies support the finding that young people are disproportionately burdened by the mental health impacts of climate change, including climate anxiety.[8]

Some studies have considered the impact of climate anxiety on young persons' attitudes towards governments and their failure to prevent climate change. A study published in September 2021 observed that government failure is "experienced as betrayal and abandonment, not just of the individual but of young people and future generations generally."[9] Climate anxiety is created not only by ecological destruction but also by government failure: "the failure of governments to adequately reduce, prevent, or mitigate climate change is contributing to psychological distress, moral injury and injustice."[10]

In this chapter, I revisit the role of eco-anxiety in governance. I consider youth eco-anxiety in relation to regulatory failure: how government failure to prevent climate change has produced eco-anxiety and how eco-anxiety is shaping the political engagement/disengagement of youth. In my earlier work, I argued that eco-anxiety was producing individualizing and depoliticizing approaches to environmental issues. The impact of regulatory failure on youth is contradictory. Many of the proposed solutions to the mental health problems of climate change remain individualizing, with individuals encouraged to develop resiliency and personal responsibility. At the same time, however, there is a more political response, with youth being more politically engaged in response to the eco-anxiety produced by previous generation's regulatory failure. I consider recent legal challenges brought by young activists as examples of the transformation of eco-anxiety and a pervasive sense of regulatory failure into collective political action. I argue that climate anxiety is now animating a generation of youth climate activists, whose political and legal actions for meaningful government intervention include a recognition of the mental health impacts of the existential threat of climate change. But the outcomes of litigation on the very anxiety that animates the cases remains ambivalent at best.

I. Anxiety, Eco-Anxiety, and Solutions

Anxiety is generally used to describe an unpleasant emotional state experienced in anticipation of some uncertain risk, threat, or danger. Anxiety theorists have long connected anxiety with freedom. Kierkegaard famously described "anxiety is the dizziness of freedom."[11] Others have connected anxiety with modernity and its individualization.[12] Ulrich Beck describes a radical shift in the late-twentieth century in which meaning and identity that was once based in loyalty to institutions and structures increasingly became based in the self. Individuals must make more decisions about their own lives and choose their own path. Yet these choices are to be made against the backdrop of what he calls the risk society. Risk, he argues, has become increasingly central to society. Individuals must make their life decisions, which include a calculation and management of risk, at a moment when the consequences of risk can no longer be adequately measured or controlled. According to Beck, these processes produce "the commonality of anxiety" in a risk society.[13] Others address the prevalence of "free-floating anxiety," of the perception of being at risk as a pervasive mood in society.[14] These free-floating anxieties can attach, detach, and reattach to more specific concerns and experiences, animating what he calls a culture of fear.[15] This literature tells us about the pervasiveness of anxiety in the current age and suggests that its pervasiveness is related to the risk society in which we live.

Through the concept of anxiety governance, I connected anxiety with the project of self-governance. More specifically, that anxiety could help explain how and why individual subjects undertake projects of self-governance. Self-governance is a form of governance associated with neo-liberalism. With the decline of the welfare state and the emergence of a neo-liberal state, governments retracted from the provision of social goods and services, and individuals were called upon to become responsible for themselves and their families.[16] As responsibility is shifted from the state to privatized market institutions and individual market actors, individuals are to become enterprising, responsible selves and to take primary responsibility for themselves and their families.[17] While this shift to self-governance and responsibilization has been documented across multiple areas of social life,[18] less attention had been paid to the psychic or emotional processes that animate individual subjects to do so. Anxiety and the need to mitigate it, I argued, animates individuals towards self-governance. Generalized anxiety can attach itself to an almost limitless number of specific issues, from terrorism to gun violence to illness to environmental degradation. Once attached, individuals will then focus their anxiety or fears on a set of more specific concerns and undertake some action to address these anxieties.

Enter eco-anxiety. Eco-anxiety arrived as a buzzword in the early 2000s, described as an overwhelming concern for environmental degradation. Early eco-anxiety therapists both identified the problem and then advocated taking action as a way to mitigate it.[19] Action, however, was often highly individualized: individual actions of "greening" and reducing one's carbon footprint particularly through making better consumer choices. The message was largely one of self-care and responsibilization. As mentioned, the field of climate change psychology has grown significantly in the intervening years, as has expertise on eco-anxiety in particular. Climate-informed therapy has given rise to multiple therapeutic interventions for eco-anxiety. While the term "eco-anxiety" implies the presence of anxiety, the literature recognizes the range of emotions, including fear, anger, powerlessness, and grief. Climate-informed therapists are also cautious in not pathologizing eco-anxiety, recognizing that it as a reasonable response to the climate crisis, but they are seeking ways to mitigate the extreme anxiety and paralysis that it may bring.

At the therapeutic level, the solutions for eco-anxiety and other climate change-related mental health issues often remain focused, almost by definition, on individual mental health and consider what individuals can do to manage their anxiety. Many of the proposed solutions track the earlier recommendations: individuals are encouraged to acknowledge their emotions, reduce their carbon footprint, and connect with nature. A study of emerging interventions for the treatment of eco-anxiety tracked these themes: fostering individual reliance, promoting social connections, taking action (individually and collectively, by reducing carbon footprints, and developing action plans, mitigation, and adaptation), and connecting with nature.[20] There is often an emphasis on overcoming paralysis. A climate-informed therapist quoted in the *Washington Post* states, "The key to addressing eco-anxiety at any age, says psychiatrist Haase, is getting 'unstuck,' losing that feeling of paralysis in the face of the problem's magnitude."[21] The article elaborates this:

> The emphasis, doctors say, should be on personal responsibility and empowerment. For an overwhelming problem like climate change, being able to take some action – whether eating less meat or switching to an electric vehicle – can help fight paralysis and get patients to recognize that the worst of climate change is not a fait accompli and that some progress can be made.[22]

Taking responsibility through taking action continues to be a theme, although what is meant by action varies from consumer choices to community engagement.

Building resilience is another common theme. The APA recommends building resilience, defined as "the ability of a person to cope with, grow through, and transcend adversity."[23] For individuals, it recommends building belief in one's own resilience, fostering optimism, cultivating active coping and self-regulation, finding a source of personal meaning, boosting preparedness (such as emergency kits), and building strong social support networks.[24] Moving beyond the individual, the APA report also discusses the promotion of community resilience. These include recommendations for community support and planning, disaster relief, and community action. But community action is envisioned largely as engagement in "advance planning and capacity building and continuing through disaster management and recovery."[25]

Perhaps due to the nature of the mental health literature, there is rather less emphasis on political action. Scholars have observed the depoliticizing nature of much contemporary climate change discourse.[26] In the context of mental health, there is a tendency to focus on assisting individuals to cope with and adapt to climate change, rather than to engage in political action. Some of the mental health scholarship, however, has begun to explore the behavioural impacts of eco-anxiety, and whether it motivates individuals to take action or leads to "eco-paralysis."[27] Some have begun to distinguish between adaptive and maladaptive anxiety, with the former motivating individuals to address climate change and the latter potentially debilitating. Yet even appropriate levels of anxiety can lead some people to despair:[28]

> The overarching threats of a changing climate can also incite despair and hopelessness as actions to address the "wicked problem" of climate change seem intangible or insignificant in comparison to the scale and magnitude of the threats.[29]

This scholarship is beginning to consider, then, the ways in which climate anxiety may – or may not – produce political action.[30]

Some studies on the impact of climate change on mental health have also begun to observe that failure of government action is a factor in eco-anxiety. Scholars of children's mental health caution against the prevailing individualizing narratives, suggesting that instead of individuals taking action, responding to the mental health of children and youth requires government action. The global survey demonstrated that large numbers of young people see governments as having failed to acknowledge and act on the climate crisis.[31] Young people speak of being let down by prior generations and the heavy responsibility that now lies on them.[32] They express feelings of betrayal and distrust in government.

I argued in my earlier work that regulatory failure was contributing to eco-anxiety and anxiety governance. Government failure to protect against the environmental degradation and pervasive toxins perpetuated the cycle of anxiety governance. The cycle begins with identifying a problem/toxin that the government has failed to regulate. Not only must individuals now do it themselves, but the perception of regulatory failure reinforces the generalized anxiety that encourages self-governance. We cannot trust our governments; we must do it ourselves. Regulatory failure continues to play an important role, but one that has shifted slightly. Youth articulate a generational failure, which includes governmental failure, but for many, the eco-anxiety produced by regulatory failure is producing individual subjects who are demanding more from their governments. The anxious subjects are not content with self-governance, with individual or even collective responsibilization. Rather, their eco-anxiety is becoming a powerful motivator to engage in political and legal action.

II. Youth Taking Legal Action

Leading youth climate change campaigner Greta Thunberg has given voice to the eco-anxiety of her generation. In interviews, she expresses her own eco-anxiety and how she deals with it:

> It's a quite natural response, because, as you see, as the world is today, that no one seems to care about what's happening, I think it's only human to feel that way.
>
> When you take action, you also get a sense of meaning that something is happening. If you want to get rid of that anxiety, you can take action against it.[33]

Like Thunberg, for many young people, taking action is not about green consumerism or simply reducing their own carbon footprint. Taking action has become about political activism. A youth climate movement has emerged as an informal international network of local, national, and regional organizations, aimed at mobilizing young people to take action against climate change.[34] The activism is taking many forms. Some have engaged in strikes and political protests, like Fridays for the Future, a global youth movement holding regular school strikes. Other have taken a more radical angle, from throwing soup at masterpieces of Western art[35] to locking themselves to roadways and speaker's chairs,[36] some have taken to a kind of civil disobedience designed to attract public attention.

While less high profile and certainly less sensationalistic, there has also been a rise in legal actions by and on behalf of children and youth.

Legal actions against climate change are becoming more common in general,[37] but it is notable that many high-profile cases have been brought by children and youth. Elizabeth Dong has noted that "By the end of 2020, 33 youth-led cases had been filed across 21 countries and supranational forums, representing 26 per cent of the 126 rights-based climate cases initiated during that time."[38]

Youth climate litigation raises a host of complicated legal, ethical, and strategic questions.[39] There are questions about the efficacy of these challenges. Setzer and Byrnes have observed that although there has been an increased use of these challenges to try to influence government policy on climate change, there remains "insufficient evidence of the impacts of climate change litigation."[40] Many cases have been unsuccessful in the courts, because they do not raise a justiciable issue, or because the plaintiffs not having standing, or simply on the merits of the constitutional arguments. Even in cases where the courts have decided in favour of the plaintiffs, it remains difficult to evaluate the impact of the litigation.

For example, in 2018, twenty-five children and youth, with the support of the advocacy organization Dejusticia, brought an action against the Colombian government demanding that it take action against the deforestation of the Colombian Amazon, and to guarantee public participation in the creation of an intergenerational plan to protect the Amazon. Supreme Court of Justice of Colombia granted the petition and ordered the Presidency and the Ministries of Environment and Agriculture to create an "intergenerational pact for the life of the Colombian Amazon." The court specifically recognized the failure of the government to take action: "It is clear, despite numerous international commitments, regulations, and jurisprudence on the matter, that the Colombian State has not efficiently tackled the problem of deforestation in the Amazon."[41] This would seem like a significant victory. Yet Dejusticia has pointed out many of the government failures in the aftermath of the decision, and the fact that the deforestation of the Colombian Amazon continues.[42]

In Germany, youth activists brought a legal challenge to the Federal Climate Protection Act, arguing that the government's emission targets were insufficient and violated their fundamental rights under Germany's Basic Law.[43] The German Constitutional Court agreed.[44] In a potentially far-reaching decision, the court held that state's duty to protect life and physical integrity under the Basic Law included the duty to protect life and health against risks posed by climate change. The court ordered the government to expand a 2019 law to set clear provisions for reduction targets. The government immediately initiated a review of the law, and within two months, the parliament approved significant amendments, introducing more ambitious emission reduction targets. The new targets – 65 per cent reduction by 2030 – have been in effect since 31 August 2021, along with the target of making Germany carbon-neutral by 2045.

Closer to home, youth have brought climate change challenges in Canada, though with limited success.[45] In Ontario, seven young people brought an action against the Ontario Government, alleging that it violated their constitutional rights in abdicating its responsibility to address climate change. In *Mathur v. Ontario*, the first climate change legal action in Canadian courts, the plaintiffs argued that the government has violated their rights to life and security of the person under section 7 of the charter, as well as their equality rights under s.7, since climate change disproportionately affects children and youth, who are more vulnerable to its health effects and will live more of their lives in an era of climate crisis.

The litigants themselves explicitly link their actions with eco-anxiety. Alex Neufeldt, one of the litigants in Mathur says:

> Being a part of this case has had a really positive impact on my life because action breeds hope. Inaction breeds despair. I find I have less climate anxiety now than I used to. The problem is getting worse, and yet I've felt more hope and more optimism [by doing something about it]. I hope our case inspires other young people around the world to step into their power.[46]

The applicants included the impact of climate change on mental health as part of their pleadings. They argued that the many catastrophic impacts of climate change on current and future generations include "an increase in serious psychological harms and mental distress arising from the impacts of climate change."[47]

In April 2023, the Ontario Superior Court rejected the constitutional challenge, holding that neither section 7 nor section 15 were violated.[48] While the court found against the applicants, it did find that the matter was justiciable and, in very strong language, recognized the existential threat of climate change. The court quoted the Supreme Court of Canada, with approval, that "climate change is an existential challenge. It is a threat of the highest order to the country, and indeed to the world... The undisputed existence of a threat to the future of humanity cannot be ignored."[49]

Significantly, the court's review of the negative impact of climate change specifically included its mental health impacts that had been argued by the applicants:

> The various impacts caused by climate change have been shown, through strong evidence, to be leading to a range of serious and wide-ranging negative mental health impacts within Canada. These mental health impacts can range from mild to severe, and include: emotional reactions; psychosocial outcomes such as depression, *anxiety*, and post-traumatic stress disorder (PTSD); grief and loss; increased drug and alcohol use; social and family stress; increased suicide ideation and suicides; loss of cultural knowledge and continuity; and deterioration and loss of place-based connection.[50] (emphasis added)

Climate anxiety is specifically recognized by the court as a serious mental health consequence of climate change.[51] The court further observed the disproportionate impact of climate change on young people, including on their mental health:

> Climate change may also differentially impact the mental health of children and youth through adverse experiences and post traumatic distress following climate related emergencies, the psychosocial impacts of watching family members suffer, or due to a general sense of environmental hopelessness and fears over future security.[52]

Assessing the impact of the litigation is not straight forward. On the one hand, the plaintiffs lost. On the other hand, it was a very high-profile case, which raised awareness about youth taking action against climate change and resulted in some potentially helpful judicial findings about the harms of climate change. An appeal was heard by the Ontario Court of Appeal in January 2024.

Many, if not most, of the court challenges brought by youth to the inaction of government on climate change have not produced judicial victories. Yet, we cannot assess the impacts in terms of wins and losses in courts alone. Strategic litigation involves a consideration of the costs and benefits beyond winning or losing in courts. Strategic climate litigation may help raise awareness about climate change and mobilize further support for taking action, regardless of the outcome in the courts. Judicial opinions may contain language that recognizes the multiple harms of climate change, even where the case is unsuccessful, on which future litigation or political action could build. In *Mathur*, the court specifically recognized the mental health harms being brought about by climate change.

While we might find victories within defeat, the continuing losses in court also raise significant questions about managing the expectations of the litigants, particularly so because they are children and youth. Lawyers arguing on behalf of children and youth must manage the expectations of their clients to ensure they understand the many possibilities and limitations of this litigation. Loss in the courts is the most obvious. Even wins in the courts have come with costs and disappointments, as seen in the Colombian case. Without managing these expectations, losses could cause further mental health harms. In other words, climate litigation, while motivated by anxiety and seeking to mitigate anxiety by taking action, could also lead to more climate anxiety.

Each case is based on the claim that governments have failed to take sufficient action to protect their populations against climate change. They are each based on the idea of regulatory failure: that government regulatory initiatives to address climate change have failed in both design (insufficient action and targets) and implementation (inadequate regulatory enforcement). The cases reflect the opinion of youth that governments have failed to acknowledge and act on the climate crisis. Despite a prevalent sense of being let down by governments, and this generation's feelings of betrayal and distrust, the perception of regulatory failure is, in each of these cases, animating youth to take action against government. In contrast to the potential depoliticizing effects of eco-anxiety and regulatory failure, these legal challenges reflect a form of collective political action.

Climate anxiety is one of the motivators of the litigation. More specifically, it is experienced by youth as taking action against climate change, which helps alleviate climate anxiety. The litigation is also leading to at least some legal recognition that climate anxiety – and other mental health challenges – are real and serious consequences of climate change. However, this litigation is not without its risks, including the same mental issues that have given rise to the litigation. As Dong has observed, youth bringing these challenges may be "exposed to significant levels of criticism and bullying in physical and digital spaces. The level of public scrutiny and opposition generated by these climate cases can be high, potentially taking a toll on these plaintiffs in a similar way."[53] She further observes that "the legal process itself can disempower or generate cynicism," noting that timelines are long, remedies are limited, and any actual impact on their lived experience is remote.[54] As Greta Thunberg said, after a court loss in Norway, the decision "just proves that the climate and ecological crisis cannot be solved within today's systems. There are no tools, no laws nor regulations that keep us from destroying the living conditions for life on this planet as we know it."[55] Legal losses could produce a further sense of regulatory despair and in turn increased climate anxiety.

III. Conclusion

In my earlier work, while arguing that eco-anxiety was producing self-governing and depoliticized subjects, I gestured towards the contradictory possibilities of anxiety, wondering whether it was possible to reclaim anxiety in the service of democratic projects and political engagement. I asked whether anxiety might be embraced and reclaimed for a more collective politics, whether we might "self-govern in more subversive directions? We do have a dizzying array of choices; can we reclaim anxiety as a condition of our freedom in negotiating those choices?" In the intervening years, the deployment of anxiety by young environmental activists suggests it is indeed possible. Many young people now speak of being animated into action by what was a potentially paralysing emotion. Political action is seen by many young activists as a way of mitigating anxiety. Similarly, despite the overwhelming sense that youth have of regulatory failure, youth activists are demanding state action. The existential threat of climate change has become more and more acute and is no longer seen as a dystopian distant future but experienced in here and now, as heat domes, wildfires, droughts, and floods emerge as the new normal. From that perspective, the mental health impacts of climate change have emerged as the new normal as well. Climate anxiety is no longer exclusively the province of individualizing therapeutic interventions and its self-governing approaches like green consumerism. Rather, climate anxiety is animating political and legal action, which in turn is recognizing the mental health impacts of climate change. A question that needs to be further explored is why climate anxiety motivates some to political action, while others remain paralysed and despairing. It is not simply that we all need a little more anxiety; presumably many of us have plenty. The question is how that anxiety can be harnessed and directed towards meaningful political action.

NOTES

1 American Psychological Association, *Mental Health and Our Changing Climate: Impact, Implications, and Guidance* (Washington DC: American Psychological Association, 2017), online (pdf): <https://www.apa.org/news/press/releases/2017/03/mental-health-climate.pdf>.

2 *Ibid* at 68.

3 See for example Joseph Dodds, "The Psychology of Climate Anxiety" (2021) 45:4 BJPsych Bulletin 222 at 1–5, online: <https://doi.org/10.1192/bjb.2021.18>. Robert J. Ursano, Joshua C. Morganstein & Robin Cooper,

APA Resource Document Resource Document on Mental Health and Climate Change (Washington, DC: American Psychiatric Association, 2017); Climate Psychology Alliance, *Handbook of Climate Psychology* (St David, UK: Climate Psychology Alliance, 2020); British Psychological Society, "Psychology Has an Important Role in Combating Climate Change," (*BPS News* (7 May 2019), archived online: *Wayback Machine* <https://web.archive.org/web/20211017223635/https://www.bps.org.uk/news-and-policy/psychology-has-important-role-combating-climate-change>.

4 The terms "climate anxiety" and "eco-anxiety" are used interchangeably. While "eco-anxiety" was more common as a buzzword in the early 2000s, the literature studying the mental health impacts of climate change has tended to use both words.

5 Brenda Cossman, "Anxiety Governance" (2013) 38:4 Law & Soc Inquiry 892, online: <https://doi.org/10.1111/lsi.12027>.

6 "Majority of US Adults Believe Climate Change Is Most Important Issue Today," *American Psychological Association* (6 February 2020), online: <https://www.apa.org/news/press/releases/2020/02/climate-change>.

7 *Ibid*.

8 See Jason Plautz, "The Environmental Burden of Generation Z: Kids Are Terrified, Anxious, and Depressed about Climate Change: Who's Fault Is That?," *The Washington Post* (3 February 2020), online: <https://www.washingtonpost.com/magazine/2020/02/03/eco-anxiety-is-overwhelming-kids-wheres-line-between-education-alarmism/>; Laura Holson, "Climate Change Is Scaring Children: Here's How to Talk to Them," *The New York Times* (27 June 2019), online: <https://www.nytimes.com/2019/06/27/science/climate-change-children-education.html>; Caroline Hickman et al, "Young People's Voices on Climate Anxiety, Government Betrayal and Moral Injury: A Global Phenomenon" (September 2021) [preprint], online <https://doi.org/10.2139/ssrn.3918955>; Susan Clayton, "Climate Anxiety: Psychological Responses to Climate Change" 74 J Anxiety Disord 102263, online: <https://doi.org/10.1016/j.janxdis.2020.102263>.

9 *Ibid*. See also Caroline Hickman et al, "Climate Anxiety in Children and Young People and their Beliefs about Government Responses to Climate Change: A Global Survey" 5:12 Lancet Planet Health e863, online: <https://doi.org/10.1016/S2542-5196(21)00278-3>.

10 *Ibid*.

11 Søren Kierkegaard, *The Concept of Anxiety*, Howard Vincent Hong and Edna H. Hong, trans and ed (Princeton, NJ: Princeton University Press, [1844] 1980) 61.

12 Eric Fromm, *The Escape from Freedom* (New York: Rinehart, 1941); Ulrich Beck, *Risk Society: Towards a New Modernity* (London: Sage, 1992).

13 Beck, *supra* note 12 at 49; see also Anthony Giddens, *Modernity and the Self-Identity: Self and Society in the Late Modern Age* (Cambridge: Polity Press, 1991).

14 Frank Furedi, *The Culture of Fear: Revisited* (London: Continuum Press, 2007) 28 [Furedi, *Culture of Fear*]; Frank Furedi, *The Politics of Fear: Beyond Left and Right* (London: Continuum Press, 2005) [Furedi, *Politics of Fear*].

15 Furedi, *Culture of Fear, supra* note 14.

16 Nikolaus Rose, *Powers of Freedom: Reframing Political Thought* (Cambridge: Cambridge University Press, 1999), online: <https://doi.org/10.1017/CBO9780511488856>; Alan Hunt, *Governing Morals: A Social History of Moral Regulation* (Cambridge: Cambridge University Press, 1999).

17 Thomas Lemke, "The Birth of Bio-Politics: Michel Foucault's Lecture at the College de France on Neo-Liberal Governmentality" (2001) 30 Econ Soc 190, online: <https://doi.org/10.1080/03085140122085>; Nikolaus Rose, *Inventing Ourselves* (New York: Cambridge University Press, 1994). Peter Miller & Nikolas Rose, "On Therapeutic Authority: Psychoanalytic Expertise Under Advanced Liberalism" (1994) 7:3 Hist Human Sci 29, online: <https://doi.org/10.1177/095269519400700302>; Janine Brodie, "Reforming Social Justice in Neo-Liberal Times" (2007) 1:2 Stud Soc Just 93, online: <https://doi.org/10.26522/ssj.v1i2.972>.

18 Nikolaus Rose "Community, Citizenship, and the Third Way" (2000) 43:9 *Am Behav Sci* 1395, online: <https://doi.org/10.1177/00027640021955955>.

19 See Thomas Doherty, "Nurturing the Sustainable Self: Talking to Clients about Environmental Issues" (2006) Oregon Psychol (accessed 19 June 2012), online (pdf): https://selfsustain.com/wp-content/uploads/2012/06/nurturing_sustainable_self.pdf.

20 Paul Baudon & Liza Jachens, "A Scoping Review of Interventions for the Treatment of Eco-Anxiety" (2021) 18:18 Int J Env Res Pub Health 9636, online: <https://www.ncbi.nlm.nih.gov/pmc/articles/PMC8464837/>.

21 Plautz, *supra* note 8.

22 Plautz, *supra* note 8.

23 APA, *supra* note 1 at 40.

24 *Ibid* at 44.

25 *Ibid* at 50.

26 Anabela Carvalho, Margit van Wessel & Pieter Maeseele, "Communication Practices and Political Engagement with Climate Change: A Research Agenda" (2017) 11:1 Envtl Comm 122. The authors describe: "Depoliticization stands for a discursive logic that frames climate change in terms of a social consensus about how it should be understood and what should be done about it.... This literature has revealed different strategies of depoliticization, such as scientization, economization and moralization, as well as a higher order strategy of naturalization of the

capitalist system." These discourses operate to demobilize, discourage, and delimit citizen political engagement. See also Erik Swyngedouw, "Apocalypse Forever? Post-Political Populism and the Spectre of Climate Change" (2010) 27:2–3 Theor Cult Soc 213, online: <https://doi.org/10.1177/0263276409358728>.

27 See e.g., Clayton, *supra* note 8. Clayton notes that the word "eco paralysis" was coined in Glenn Albrecht, "Chronic Environmental Change: Emerging 'Psychoterratic' Syndromes" in Inka Weissbecker, ed, *Climate Change and Human Well-Being: Global Challenges and Opportunities* (New York: Springer, 2011) 43, online: <https://doi.org/10.1007/978-1-4419-9742-5_3>.

28 Steven Taylor, "Anxiety Disorders, Climate Change, and the Challenges Ahead: Introduction to the Special Issue" (2020) 76 J Anxiety Disord 102313, online: <https://doi.org/10.1016/j.janxdis.2020.102313>; Marianne Hrabok, Aaron Delorme & Vincent I.O. Agyapong, "Threats to Mental Health and Well-Being Associated with Climate Change" (2020) 76 J Anxiety Disord 102295, online: <https://doi.org/10.1016/j.janxdis.2020.102295>.

29 Katie Hayes et al, "Climate Change and Mental Health: Risks, Impacts and Priority Actions" (2018) 12:1 Int J Ment Health Syst art 28, online: <https://doi.org/10.1186/s13033-018-0210-6>.

30 Others have also explored the question of why in the face of overwhelming evidence of catastrophic climate change, individuals are not changing behaviours. Some have argued that inaction is based in the limitations of human's psychological nature, most famously argued by Robert Gifford (Robert Gifford, "The Dragons of Inaction: Psychological Barriers That Limit Climate Change Mitigation and Adaptation" (2011) 66:4 Am Psychol 290, online: <https://doi.org/10.1037/a0023566>). Others are more critical of the psychological barriers explanation, arguing for a broader consideration of social factors and inequalities to explain the inaction. See Michael T. Schmitt et al, "The Perils of Explaining Climate Inaction in Terms of Psychological Barriers" (2020) 76:1 J Soc Iss 123, online: <https://doi.org/10.1111/josi.12360>.

31 Hickman et al, *supra* note 9.

32 Plautz, *supra* note 8.

33 Natalie Thomas, Barbara Lewis & Jonathan Shenfield, "Guilt, Grief and Anxiety as Young People Fear for Climate's Future," *Reuters* (22 October 2021), online: <https://www.reuters.com/business/cop/guilt-grief-anxiety-young-people-fear-climates-future-2021-10-22/>. See Karin Andrea Stephan, "Eco-Anxiety: Great Thunberg Is One of Many Suffering from It" (11 June 2022), online (blog): *Earkick* <https://blog.earkick.com/eco-anxiety-greta-thunberg-suffers-from-it/>.

34 See generally Noah Herfort et al, "Mapping the Global Youth Climate Movement: Towards a Green Economic Mandate," *Green Coalition Economy* (February 2023), online (pdf): <https://www.greeneconomycoalition.org/assets/reports/GEC-Reports/YCM-2023/Mapping-the-Global-YCM-March23-FINAL.pdf>. Joost De Moor et al, "New Kids on the Block: Taking Stock of the Recent Cycle of Climate Activism" (2021) 20:5 Soc Move Stud 619, online: <https://doi.org/10.1080/14742837.2020.1836617>.

35 Shannon Gibson, "Throwing Soup on a Van Gogh and Other Ways Young Climate Activists Are Making Their Voices Heard," *The Conversation* (16 November 2022), online: <https://theconversation.com/throwing-soup-on-a-van-gogh-and-other-ways-young-climate-activists-are-making-their-voices-heard-193210>.

36 See e.g., Bryn Stole, "Hanging Out with the German activists Who Glue Themselves to Things," *Mother Jones* (8 February 2023), online: <https://www.motherjones.com/environment/2023/02/german-climate-activists-gluing-themselves-letzte-generation-civil-disobedience/>. Damien Gayle, "Eight Arrested After Climate Activists Glue Themselves Around Commons Speaker's Chair," *The Guardian* (2 September 2022), online: <https://www.theguardian.com/environment/2022/sep/02/extinction-rebellion-activists-superglue-themselves-commons-chamber-speaker-seat>.

37 See "Climate Change Litigation Databases," *Columbia University* (accessed 15 October 2024), online: <https://climatecasechart.com/>.

38 Elizabeth Dong, "Children and Youth in Strategic Climate Litigation: Advancing Rights through Legal Argument and Legal Mobilization" (2022) 11:2 Transnat'l Envtl L 263 at 270, online: <https://doi.org/10.1017/S2047102522000218>, citing César Rodríguez-Garavito, "Litigating the Climate Emergency: The Global Rise of Human Rights-Based Litigation for Climate Action" in César Rodríguez-Garavito, ed, *Litigating the Climate Emergency: How Human Rights, Courts, and Legal Mobilization Can Bolster Climate Action* (New York: Cambridge University Press, 2021) iii, online: <https://doi.org/10.1017/9781009106214>.

39 See e.g., Cheryl Milne, "Vulnerable Litigants and Radical Lawyering" in this volume.

40 Joana Setzer & Rebecca Byrnes, *Global Trends in Climate Change Litigation: 2019 Snapshot* (London: Grantham Research Institute, 2019), online (pdf): <https://www.lse.ac.uk/granthaminstitute/wp-content/uploads/2019/07/GRI_Global-trends-in-climate-change-litigation-2019-snapshot-2.pdf>.

41 Dejusticia, "Climate Change and Future Generations Lawsuit in Colombia: Key Excerpts from the Supreme Court's Decision," *Dejusticia* (13 April 2018),

online: <https://www.dejusticia.org/en/climate-change-and-future-generations-lawsuit-in-colombia-key-excerpts-from-the-supreme-courts-decision/>.

42 Dejusticia, "The Colombian government has failed to fulfill the Supreme Court's landmark order to protect the Amazon," *Dejusticia* (5 April 2019), online: <https://www.dejusticia.org/en/the-colombian-government-has-failed-to-fulfill-the-supreme-courts-landmark-order-to-protect-the-amazon/>.

43 Federal Constitutional Court, Karlsruhe, 24 March 2021, *Neubauer, et al v. Germany*, BvR 2656/18/1, BvR 78/20/1, BvR 96/20/1, BvR 288/20 (Germany).

44 *Ibid.* The challenge had been brought by youth in Germany, Nepal, and Bangladesh. The decided not to consider the responsibility of the German State with respect to the rights of the children of Nepal and Bangladesh, but focused exclusively on the German youth, who were protected by the German Basic Law. For further information on the case in English, see "Neubauer et al. v Germany, Case No BvR 2656/18/1, BvR 78/201/1, BvR 96/201/1, BvR 288/20 – Germany," *ACRISL*, online: <https://www.acrisl.org/casenotes/m2ll8m8skjpglk8-83mk2-k5yza-dcafy-x5ztr-bjfxk-c9y55-5ryfp>; Melissa Eddy "German High Court Hands Youth a Victory in Climate Change Fight," *The New York Times* (29 April 2021), online: <https://www.nytimes.com/2021/04/29/world/europe/germany-high-court-climate-change-youth.html>.

45 For a review of the challenges in Canada, see Jennifer Earle Chalifour & L. Macintyre, "Coming of Age in a Warming World: The Charter's Section 15 Equality Guarantee and Youth-Led Climate Litigation" (2021) 17 JL & Equality 17. See also Milne, *supra* note 39.

46 Mitchell Beer, "Ontario Youth Court Case Makes Climate a Charter of Rights Issue," *The Energy Mix* (5 September 2022), online: <https://www.theenergymix.com/2022/09/05/ontario-youth-court-case-makes-climate-a-charter-of-rights-issue/>.

47 *Mathur et al v. The Queen* (25 November 2019), Ontario, ONSC CV-19–00631627–0000 (application) at para 46(1).

48 *Mathur et al v. This Majesty the King in Right of Ontario* 2023 ONSC 2316 [*Mathur*]. On section 7, the Court held that if positive obligations could be imposed under section 7 in the special context of climate change (a question it decided not to decide), "the Applicants' rights to life and to the security of the person are engaged in this case as a result of Ontario's failure to set a higher Target." However, the Court held that it did not do so in a violation of the principles of fundamental justice. On section 15, the Court rejected the applicants' argument that the government target discriminated on the basis of age. While it accepted that climate change

will have a disproportionate impact on young people, the Court was not prepared to conclude that this was caused by the government's target, plan, or legislation.

49 *References re Greenhouse Gas Pollution Pricing Act*, 2021 SCC 11 at para 167, cited in *Mathur, supra* note 48 at para 17.

50 *Mathur, supra* note 48 at para 23(g).

51 The Court further noted in relation of climate disasters, including increased flooding that "Individuals exposed to floods are significantly more likely to develop mental health issues, including depression, phobias, and generalized anxiety disorder." *Mathur, supra* note 48 at para 23(d).

52 *Ibid* at para 25(d). The Court further noted that Indigenous youth are even more seriously impacted: "Indigenous youth face particular mental health challenges due to their strong ties to the land." (at para 25(e)); "Indigenous peoples are particularly vulnerable to the mental health impacts of climate change. Climate impacts are leading to anxiety, depression, grief, family stress, loss of identity, increased likelihood of substance usage, and suicide ideation among Indigenous individuals" (at para 25(h)).

53 Dong, *supra* note 38 at 283.

54 *Ibid* at 284.

55 Citing Henrik Pryser Libell & Derrick Bryson Taylor, "Norway's Supreme Court Makes Way for More Arctic Drilling," *The New York Times* (22 December 2020), online: <https://www.nytimes.com/2020/12/22/world/europe/norway-supreme-court-oil-climate-change.html>.

PART FOUR

Lawyering in Times of (Climate) Change

11 Vulnerable Litigants and Movement Lawyering in Climate Justice Litigation

CHERYL MILNE

I. Introduction

As the climate crisis continues to accelerate, activists and concerned citizen alike are looking to creative, even radical, ways to bring attention to the issue in the hopes of changing the dismal outlook for the future. Litigation has always been one method for seeking to change the behaviour of government or private actors regarding environmental issues, along with legislative advocacy and public protest. Analysis of the impact or success of public interest litigation has demonstrated that multi-pronged approaches that do not simply rely on remedies achieved through the courts tend to produce enduring and more meaningful results.[1]

Given the time frame within which action on climate change must be conducted, reliance on litigation to change behaviour cannot be the main strategy. Litigation is slow, costly, and too often produces conservative results that would, in today's climate crisis, make little impact on the immediate or distant future.[2] Indeed, despite the high profile of decisions such as *Urgenda*[3] and ongoing cases such as *Juliana v United States*,[4] questions remain about the whether the outcomes actually have had any meaningful affects.[5] So, then why do it? Are more innovative strategies derived from movement lawyering warranted?[6]

Litigation is often a tactic of last resort – when protest and other forms of advocacy have failed to garner change despite growing acceptance of the merits of the cause.[7] Climate change is no longer a debatable topic among scientists and world leaders. Yet incremental measures and outright stalling on limits to greenhouse gas (GHG) emissions seem to be the status quo. The last ten years has seen a shift in public concern and acceptance of the environmental movement. What was once the purview of environmental activists has become a social movement, with children and youth as major voices for change. Inspired by Greta Thunberg, youth have engaged in worldwide climate strikes and "Fridays for the Future" protests over the past several years. Thunberg's consistently alarmist message that dramatic action needs to happen now or else children will face a catastrophic future[8] has helped to foster climate change awareness among children and youth, many of whom have become increasingly anxious about their futures.[9]

A current trend in climate justice litigation has been to harness the distress being expressed by children and young people about the type of environmental future they are facing, and to frame potential impacts in terms of rights infringements for existing children, young people, and future generations.[10] As Elizabeth Donger recently noted, 26 per cent of rights-based climate cases filed globally prior to 2021 have involved children or children's organizations as claimants.[11] This growing use of legal arguments on behalf of children within strategic climate litigation comes at a time when child rights are gaining stronger support more generally.[12] In a recent three-year project analysing the practice of child rights strategic litigation (CRSL) globally, researchers noted that "Children have moved to the front of litigation efforts in the environmental protection context with a sharp upward trend in this area of CSRL noted in the last ten years."[13]

Set within this context, this chapter seeks to examine the strategic and ethical elements of climate change litigation with children as the subjects or litigants primarily in the Canadian context, where this litigation has begun to grow, but also in reference to the international movement that has inspired this methodology for change. It draws upon the literature respecting movement lawyering generally and both climate justice and child rights strategic litigation more specifically. People under the age of eighteen face systemic barriers within court systems in Canada and worldwide, including lack of standing, the need for adult litigation guardians, and paternalistic attitudes that make full engagement with the litigation difficult. Legal arguments that place children at the centre of the negative impacts of climate change often emphasize the vulnerability and lack of political agency of people under the age of eighteen, potentially stereotyping children or overstating their democratic influence for the sake of the cause. This chapter posits that lawyers and organizations supporting children within this litigation best serve their clients and the cause when they take a child rights focused approach and engage in reflective practice that critically examines the power dynamics at play and the realistic impact of the litigation more broadly. It also draws from the literature on movement lawyering to suggest that litigation may not be the right fit for our rapidly changing circumstances.

II. Litigation to Effect Social and Political Change

Despite the academic debate on the effectiveness of court action to effect social change,[14] public interest lawyering remains a distinct area of legal practice and a major advocacy strategy on behalf of specific marginalized groups or in relation to distinct legal or social causes. In Canada, with the advent of the *Charter of Rights and Freedoms*, much of the litigation practice has focused on upholding those rights, but there has been little study of its overall impact.[15] Even less studied is the role of litigation within a broader strategy that seeks legislative and social change, although there is comparative literature on its impacts elsewhere.[16] It is within this broader context, and with reference to the international literature, that this chapter seeks to situate the discussion of lawyers' professionalism, ethics, and accountability when engaged in strategic litigation for climate justice on behalf of children and youth.

The type of legal practice that seeks to effect social change or move government to better protect rights has been given many names: movement lawyering, cause lawyering, public interest lawyering, social justice lawyering – or in the context of the courts, public interest litigation – or strategic litigation. There is also definitional variance and development. Susan Carle and Scott Cumming describe the historical transition from mainly top-down public interest litigation in the 1970s to more client-centric community lawyering as a response to criticism of the former and the limits of the court-centric approach.[17] Lani Guinier and Gerald Torres, lamenting the court-centric approach to the analysis of legal change, propose an approach they call *demosprudence* that is the study of the dynamic equilibrium of power between lawmaking and social movements that integrates lawyers as fellow advocates.[18] They seek to acknowledge the work of other social movement actors as sources of lawmaking. According to Josephine Balzac-Arroyo, "Movement lawyers start with the belief that systemic social change comes from social movements, rather than courts or heroic lawyers or impact litigation."[19] Scott Cumming defines more contemporary movement lawyering as

> the mobilization of law through deliberately planned and interconnected advocacy strategies, inside and outside of formal law-making spaces, by lawyers who are accountable to politically marginalized constituencies to

> build the power of those constituencies to produce and sustain democratic social change goals they define.[20]

In the climate justice movement, this more recently means these constituencies are children and young people, not simply as the object of protection-oriented legal arguments but as leaders and activists.[21]

Much more study of the relationship between lawmaking/lawyers and social movements has been made internationally, and more specifically, in the United States, than has taken place in Canada. Michael McCann notes that while most traditional legal scholars have focused on litigation campaigns and judicial actions in a court-centred analysis of legal mobilization in the furtherance of social movements, considerable study points to litigation and other legal actions as most effective when used as a supplementary or secondary strategy.[22] At the very least, public interest litigation is seen as part of a broad and multifaceted approach to effecting change within the blanket concept of movement lawyering. An evaluation of public interest litigation in South Africa identified a number of successful strategies to achieve social change, of which litigation was only one aspect,[23] and an Open Society Justice Initiative that looked at strategic litigation worldwide found that "a broad, holistic, multi-stakeholder strategy is ultimately more determinative of positive impact than the legal strategy alone."[24] The positive contributions that litigation can make include helping to build the movement through judicial victories that impart legitimacy to rights-based claims and exposing vulnerabilities in the system or of opponents to the claims.[25] The experience in the United States has been that litigation can succeed in building the movement when the mass media is responsive to the rights claims, but that legal action can fail without such favourable social conditions.[26] Even if litigation has succeeded, at times its modest wins have failed to improve the overall conditions of those most affected. Gerald Rosenberg, for example, is critical of "elite, well-educated, and comparatively wealthy lawyers" who uncritically believe that rights trump politics and that success in court is equivalent to effecting real social change.[27]

It is beyond the scope of this chapter to examine the literature on the overall effectiveness of public interest litigation to produce desired outcomes. The Open Society report states that "assessing the impact of strategic litigation is a complex undertaking in which multiple factors, including timeframe, causality, and individual perspective, can shape perceptions of strategic litigation's impact or lack thereof."[28] However, some lessons can be drawn from the limited research available, along with the scholarly critiques of litigation as a strategic methodology for change. Douglas NeJaime summarizes the competing theories found in the US legal mobilization and cause lawyering literature to conclude that even litigation losses can produce wins, but even he acknowledges that social movement lawyers use litigation as merely one tactic among many,[29] and therefore, its impact is difficult to isolate. Lawyers ought to use their skills, knowledge, and expertise to support the building of the movement with the appropriate humility to acknowledge that the legal tactics for which their skills are needed are not necessarily central.[30] Faye Faraday et al. caution that dabbling in public interest litigation can be dangerous,[31] and they advocate for consciously critical reflection by legal practitioners engaging in movement lawyering.[32] Essential to this reflection is the acknowledgment that the litigation ought not be the only or central methodology for change.[33]

Another significant point of reflection is the power relationship between lawyers and the clients and communities with whom they work. Guinier and Torres's concept of *demosprudence* depends upon a "participatory power-sharing process within the lawyer/client relationship."[34] Cumming's definition of movement lawyering is premised on lawyers responding to the legal liberal critiques of lawyer accountability and legal efficacy through collaborations that seek "to deepen the *participation* of marginalized communities in movement activities and the *impact* of those activities over time."[35] Regarding accountability, he asks the rather obvious question, "who decides?" to interrogate what the lawyer-client relationship looks like and who drives the legal strategies.[36] Derrick Bell's reflection on school desegregation litigation in the United States is an often-cited example of how the cause, as defined by the organizations and movement lawyers, can lose sight of the individual clients in ethically suspect ways.[37] Concerns included the conflicts between the idealism of the organizations and lawyers representing them with individual families and children,[38] funding and funders driving the class actions rather than the class members,[39] remedies that furthered narcissistic goals of the lawyers over the clients,[40] and unprofessional solicitation of clients.[41] The heart of the conflict was the ideal of desegregation over the desires of parents for better educational resources regardless of racial separation.[42] Martha Matthews, writing twenty years later, laments the lack of commentary on the unique and troubling ethical issues that arise in what she calls structural reform litigation involving children.[43]

To address these concerns, Carle and Cummings note that scholars have advocated "a client-centred approach, in which lawyers deferred to their clients' aims, articulated after active dialogue and counselling."[44]As a check on the ethical issues, they cite the principles of movement lawyering that centres the work of lawyers in sync with the desires and interests of the constituents within the movement and suggest that ethical rules are not sufficient:

> Their success in doing so comes not from standard ethical rules but from training in self reflection and prudence. Such training involves cultivating skills, which may be first taught in law schools, in areas such as close listening, consultation, collaboration, mindfulness, fair-mindedness, and sensitivity to context and nuance. All of these qualities are part of the ethical apparatus that movement lawyers should bring to bear on their work. [p 464]

Guinier and Torres discuss social change movements integrating lawyers into the enterprise of change as fellow advocates, not as leaders, thereby transforming the lawyer-client relationship through participatory power-sharing processes.[45]

Examining whether these principles of movement lawyering are being applied to climate justice litigation, Camila Bustos sees many of the same concerns expressed by Rosenberg, Bell, and Cumming about past public interest litigation being repeated. Factors include the diverse and marginalized circumstances of those affected by climate change, the "end justifying the means" rationale based on the urgency of the cause, the power hierarchies of the lawyer-client relationship, and the highly technical nature of the evidentiary basis for the litigation.[46] Methods of recruiting and engaging individual clients in the litigation, challenged on the grounds of legal ethics in the US school desegregation cases due to claims of solicitation,[47] are now fueled by technology resulting in crowdsourcing, not just funding for litigation, but claimants as well.[48] A key question arises as to how and whether such movement lawyering is conducted differently, and to the extent that these concerns are replicated or intensified, when the focus of legal advocacy is on the rights of children and when the clients themselves are children.

III. Child Rights Strategic Litigation

A three-year international research collaboration examined the manner in which strategic litigation involving child rights had been conducted in a number of countries.[49] Child rights strategic litigation (CRSL) was defined as "litigation that seeks to bring about positive legal and/or social change in terms of children's enjoyment of their rights."[50] They noted that child rights had not been generally used as a framework by which to assess and critique the conduct of the litigation other than as part of the legal arguments or its impact.[51] They observed that

> The research indicates that strategic litigators engaging in litigation who focus on children's rights as their general everyday work are more likely to apply a child rights-consistent approach in selecting their themes for litigation, than those that have a general human rights orientation or are more centred on another human rights issue.[52]

Why is this important? Lawyers or organizations standing in for children run the same risks articulated by the critiques of public interest litigation more generally. Failure to be reflective of the power imbalances and the views of their client group perpetuate the marginalization that children as a group experience in the legal system and society. Catherine Hartung, in her book examining theories and practices of child participation, suggests that any participatory work with children needs to also reflect on theory to better interrogate humanistic assumptions about agency, voice, competence, and change in order to acknowledge the "messiness of context and complex power relations underpinning participatory work."[53]

Litigation can alienate those who would have otherwise benefited. Litigation can also set precedents that make further gains on behalf of children's rights elusive when children are instrumentalized or essentialized for a cause defined by adults. Conducting test case litigation on behalf of children but not with children perpetuates the power structures or narratives that continue their marginalization. A key aim of the researcher's examination of CRSL was to strengthen efforts to advance children's rights by "clarifying what child rights-consistent practice looks like" and "to support practitioners in improving their work by putting children's rights at the heart of their practice."[54] The principles developed to make CRSL more child rights-centred are largely focused on participatory and expressive rights that are consistent with the client-centred approach, that is advocated by Cummings for ethical movement lawyering,[55] with one added aid – the application of the United Nations Convention on the Rights of the Child (UNCRC).[56]

The UNCRC is key to establishing child rights standards for advocacy on behalf of children. Article 12 states that a child who is capable of forming their own views has the right to express them freely in all matters affecting the child and that they be given due weight in accordance with age and maturity.[57] While lawyers acting for children are arguably not duty bearers under the UNCRC, Article 12(1) clarifies that the child shall in particular be provided the opportunity to be heard in any judicial or administrative proceedings affecting the child directly or indirectly. Article 12 is the basis for arguments in favour of child participation more generally and is the starting point for Hart's ladder of participation developed at the request of UNICEF to facilitate children's participation and the realization of their rights under the UNCRC.[58] An adaptation of Arnstein's 1969 ladder of adult participation,[59] Hart's eight-rung ladder places child-initiated, adult-shared decisions at the top rung and manipulation, decoration, and tokenism on the lower rungs.[60] Hart's approach is conceptually useful in relation to children's civic engagement and in relation to environmental causes.[61] It also sparked considerable scholarship on child participation particularly in the field of education focused on how to meaningfully engage children. For example, Lundy's proposal for implementation of article 12 in education requires consideration of four factors helpful in the justice context:

> SPACE: Children must be given the opportunity to express a view.
> VOICE: Children must be facilitated to express their views.
> AUDIENCE: The view must be listened to.
> INFLUENCE: The view must be acted upon, as appropriate.[62]

Similarly, the Canadian Bar Association's Child Rights Toolkit instructs lawyers to "(1) Prepare the child; (2) Hear the child's views; (3) Assess the child's capacity; (4) Give due weight to the child's views and explain the decision to the child; and, (5) Address complaints, remedies and redress: be accountable to the child."[63] These approaches are consistent with the UN Committee on the Rights of the Child General Comment on participation rights,[64] and form a strong foundation for engagement with child litigants in legal practice that is client-focused.

In litigation involving children, there are systemic issues that act as barriers to participation, including the standing requirements that place adult representatives between the child and litigation decision-making,[65] and the conduct of collective actions, whether class actions or systemic cases, where the possibility of divergent perspectives among a group of children can lead to a disconnect between the lawyer and the children's views.[66] In a review of the literature on general child participation over a thirty-year period, Christine McMellan and Kay Tisdall found that despite Hart's seminal work, "the practice of participation can often be tokenistic, decorative participation and not move beyond consultation" and that "adult attitudes, adult-child power dynamics and adults systems" can diminish participation opportunities.[67] The ACRiSL report also noted that there is a growing tendency to "talk about 'child-led' or 'youth-led' litigation" but found few examples in which children brought a theme or issue to adult CRSL practitioners who then acted on that basis.[68]

With meaningful participation by children in CRSL comes responsibility for the lawyer to "do no harm." This can apply to the lawyer's role in two distinct ways. First, a client-centred approach to representation requires the maintenance of an ethical and humane relationship with clients, "no matter how numerous, how young, how inarticulate, or how powerless."[69] For example, Matthews believes that children's lawyers have an ethical duty to educate themselves about children, including child and adolescent development, and to avoid using their position as lawyers to silence or coerce the child into passive compliance with the lawyer's views.[70]

Client-centred legal practice in many areas of law involving children also requires a trauma-informed approach.[71] For practitioners using trauma-informed practices, much of the client engagement centres around empowerment of the client because a significant aspect of trauma is a feeling of helplessness or experiences of disempowerment.[72] Trauma can also be caused by the litigation itself. As noted in the ACRiSL Report,

> The risk of harm can take different forms, including stress or trauma caused by having to think about or to repeat accounts of earlier harm. The risk of harm could also be in the form of impact on the children's time, their home life, their education and their right to rest and leisure. Physical harm or bullying may also be a risk in certain circumstances. These harms and attacks have become more prevalent in cyberspace, where the children can be trolled and subjected to many types of abuse and threats for being part of particular advocacy, movements or cases.[73]

In the climate justice context, attention ought to be paid to the effect on children of placing the burden on them of educating the planet and motivating governments and corporate entities to change practices: "Not only is this unrealistic but also it is unfair. The over responsibility placed on this generation of youth has led to anger, frustration, sadness, and nervousness."[74] It is a delicate balance with some young people engaged in climate justice litigation finding that the experience has lessened their climate anxiety by giving them a sense of agency,[75] while the conclusion of a recent study of children and youth cautions against over-individualizing the response to climate change when action needs to be taken by those in power.[76] Experienced practitioners of CRSL in the climate justice field have provided ongoing support to the young people involved in the litigation going so far as to provide experienced psychologists to conduct sessions on climate anxiety and grief, along with other interventions to support their clients through the litigation.[77]

The second area that requires special attention to ensure no harm is done focuses on the substantive and remedial implications of the litigation. Aoife Nolan and Ann Skelton point to the UN Committee's General Comment No. 3, which views the child's best interests as a procedural rule requiring decision-makers to consider and evaluate the possible impact on the child's best interests of engagement in the litigation more generally.[78] Applying this to CRSL would require a holistic view of both the legal argumentation and remedial goals of the litigation with all of the child's rights under the UNCRC being considered where applicable. Strategic litigation within the concept of movement lawyering should also be considered a process rather than a single legal intervention where various stages of the litigation can have significant implications,[79] or each particular piece of litigation builds towards bigger outcomes.[80] While much scholarship on the role of litigation in social movements expresses optimism about the impact of defeat on the movement,[81] less is known where, as in the case of climate justice litigation, one movement seeks to adopt the perspectives and rights arguments that might have broader implications for a particular marginalized group, in this case children, in other areas of their lives.

From the perspective of child rights advocates, care must be taken to ensure that arguments that support the goal in one area of child rights do not frustrate other legitimate rights claims. For example, overemphasis on children's vulnerability or powerlessness to make a point in climate change litigation can essentialize children as passive victims,[82] thus undermining arguments that support their right to participation in many other decisions affecting them. In Canada, equality rights claims on behalf of children must contend with a contentious area of law[83] that has proven unhelpful for children facing discrimination on the basis of age primarily because the Supreme Court is quick to excuse differential treatment on the basis that it is responding to the needs and capacities of children as less mature and in need of protection.[84] Advocacy that seeks to obtain remedies in the climate change context through the exaggeration of children's otherness can thus inadvertently perpetuate discrimination in other legal situations.

Kent Roach notes that judges do not find cases justiciable or consider whether rights have been violated without considering remedies, and cautions that demands for extensive remedies can lead to findings of non-justiciability.[85] Referring to structural reform on behalf of children, Matthews describes remedies as complex forms of injunctive relief with indeterminate choices requiring years of persistence and sophisticated knowledge of bureaucracy to achieve compliance.[86] She could have been referring to the types of remedies sought in the current climate justice litigation on behalf of children. The ACRiSL report found that while the design of remedies was considered important by legal practitioners, they offered few examples of child participation and tended to overlook the right of the child to be heard and have their views considered.[87] Even where remedies have been ordered in such cases that have found that the rights of children and future generations are implicated, the enforcement of those rights can remain elusive.[88]

The management of expectations where the litigation involves novel and complex legal arguments with catastrophe being the outcome of a loss, is critical to supporting the child litigant. NeJaime's optimistic view of loss is premised on the work of "savvy advocates" who can "configure the loss in ways that result in productive social movement effects."[89] The ACRiSL report describes positive stories that demonstrated that if children are well prepared with adequate information and an opportunity to express their views, they seem better able to deal with the losses.[90] Failure to manage expectations and support child litigants following a negative outcome can cause harm to the child and is potentially exploitative.[91] However, engaging children and youth more directly through input in the design of remedies, and through frank discussions about reasonable outcomes, respects their roles as activists and provides space for the other modes of social change that is child rights-respecting.

IV. Climate Justice Litigation

Since the movement towards rights-based climate change litigation, advocacy has begun to focus on the rights of children as particularly powerful arguments to enforce government accountability and more impactful climate governance. Children are well-placed to represent the disproportionate effects of climate change on younger and future generations.[92] Yet despite compelling arguments, the results have been underwhelming to date. Donger's review of youth-led climate justice cases up to 2020 worldwide concluded that courts have been unwilling to define enforceable obligations relating to children's rights.[93] The few cases that have not been summarily dismissed have made little headway in respect of the rights-based arguments[94] or meaningful change.[95] Jacqueline Peel at al., in a review of the literature on the impacts of climate litigation, reinforce this theme of incremental, often only modest, change or impact with the evidence of impacts mostly anecdotal.[96]

Roach would say that such incremental gains are all that can be expected from the courts[97] – a view that reinforces the need for a broader, more radical strategy when the need for change is urgent. Those other strategies are found within the principles of movement lawyering and the recognition that litigation is only one tactic among many.

The small gains made internationally from a rights-based approach that centres on the impact on children and future generations has inspired recent cases in Canada. Until now, public interest litigation in respect of the environment in Canada has been based on a diverse range of legal theories and a wider range of legal contexts.[98] That is partly because there is no specifically applicable *Charter* protection. With the movement towards a more rights-based approach internationally, the *Charter* has taken a more prominent role domestically in the fight to effect change and hold governments to account for its commitment to reducing emissions at the provincial and national levels – and children, youth, and future generations have been central in the litigation.

Since late 2018, five separate climate cases have been filed in Canada on behalf of children and youth.[99] For the most part, the *Charter* arguments are based on section 7, the right to life, liberty and security of the person, and section 15(1), the right to equality for young people under a specified age and future generations, not yet born. As acknowledged by Nathalie Chalifour at al., the "Canadian youth climate equality claims are no slam dunk."[100] Neither are the section 7 claims when one examines the remedies sought and the justiciability of the claims overall. Two of the five cases that have raised age-based arguments have failed; one might say completely in respect of that ground. Two others have failed at a preliminary stage and are currently under appeal. The fifth has failed at the court of first instance on the merits but is also currently under appeal.

The first to fail was an attempt to judicially review a decision to approve the Trans Mountain Pipeline's expansion in Western Canada. Twelve separate applications were consolidated in the proceedings of which only one referenced the *Charter* grounds of age-based discrimination, an application by four teenagers aged 13 to 18 from the group Youth Stop TMX. The Federal Court of Appeal dismissed all *Charter*-based applications as being unsupported by the evidence.[101] The second case, *Environnement Jeunesse v Canada (Attorney General)*,[102] was an attempt at a class action on behalf of all young people in Quebec under the age of thirty-five, based on the claim that the Canadian government had breached their rights under section 7 by not setting appropriate GHG emissions targets. It failed on the grounds that the age cut-off of thirty-five was arbitrary and not objective, and that the claims were not justiciable because they were an attempt to compel legislative action. While all children in the province were included in the proposed class, the upper age limit of thirty-five takes this case outside the realm of CRSL.

Of the three remaining cases, two are under appeal by the claimants having failed at the initial stage of justiciability,[103] with only *Mathur* having been argued on its merits, but it too was dismissed at first instance.[104] *Misdzi Yikh v Canada* is an application brought by two hereditary chiefs on behalf of two Wet'suwet'en House groups of the Likhts'amisyu (Fireweed) Clan: the Misdzi Yikh (Owl House) and Sa Yikh (Sun House). The section 15 claim is based on the denial to younger and future generations of equal protection and benefit of the law due to the failure of the government to adhere to international agreements to lower GHG emissions. *La Rose v Canada* presents a more child rights-focused set of arguments on behalf of a group of children and youth ranging in age from 13 to 18 at the time the application was filed. The claims are based upon the young people's rights under sections 7 and 15 of the *Charter* and the UNCRC and reference the impact on future generations.[105]The Federal Court of Appeal upheld the Federal Court's decision to strike the claims based on section 15 but permitted the claimants in each case to file amended applications based on the section 7 claims only.[106]

In contrast, *Mathur v Ontario* survived a similar motion to strike primarily because the claim was more clearly focused on a particular government plan, which had the force of law and was considered reviewable and subject to the *Charter*.[107] Given the ages of the claimants ranging from 15 to 27, the section 15 equality claim reaches beyond children to a less defined group of youth and future generations. In the applicants' arguments on the merits, youth were defined as under thirty years of age and included children, while noting that young people under the age of eighteen were particularly vulnerable.[108] While emphasizing the vulnerability of young people under the age of eighteen might perpetuate their disempowerment, the arguments advanced in *Mathur* instead asserted that the actions of the government, which force young people and future generations to inhabit a world without their input, instead propagate these patterns of powerlessness and paternalism.[109] The decision on the merits dismissed the application, finding that there was no breach of the *Charter*. The Court specifically rejected the argument that adverse effects to be experienced by the applicants was an age-based distinction, instead finding that it was temporal in nature such that the impacts will be experienced by everyone eventually, discounting the argument that children and youth will be disproportionately impacted.[110]

Chalifour et al. provided an in-depth albeit optimistic analysis of the section 15 claims in the Canadian climate justice challenges to date given the decision in *Mathur*.[111] They suggested that the current inconsistency and confusion in the section 15(1) jurisprudence makes the claims on behalf of children and young people difficult to evaluate, and suggest that the cases present a novel way of looking at the ground of age, as a cohort rather than a numerical designation.[112] This might prove problematic for child rights advocates relying upon the UNCRC to bolster their claims on behalf of children because of its application only to children under the age of eighteen. Children as a distinct group are the holders of rights defined in the UNCRC, but as a cohort, they do not carry those rights forward into adulthood. Donger also warns that an overemphasis on age-based discrimination does not account for the discrimination between children on the basis of other intersecting factors such as gender, economic status, and ethnic background.[113] Chalifour at al. further suggest tying the definition of the cohort to voting qualification at the time government decisions were made, but this perhaps overstates the influence that marginalized minority groups have in democratic decision-making. Despite the uncertain judicial interpretation of equality rights for children or youth, they argue that courts may see a compelling case that the government's conduct is discriminatory in its effects on them given the urgency of the climate change crisis.[114] Unfortunately, all of these arguments were rejected by the court in *Mathur*.[115]

Most of the cases involving children and youth as litigants tend to merge their rights with those of future generations of people not yet born. Three successful cases – *Future Generations v Ministry of the Environment et al* in Colombia,[116] the trial level decision, *Urgenda v State of the Netherlands*,[117] and the German Constitutional Court decision, *Neubauer v Germany*[118] – have recognized the interests of future generations raised by young people. However, as noted by Donger, children are not interchangeable with future generations and a focus on the future can obscure the impacts in the present on children and their rights, especially when child rights arguments are not raised in the cases.[119] Strategies that focus on the impact of climate change on future generations through claims by children risk instrumentalizing children in the process, unless child rights form part of the claims.[120] In one South Korean case awaiting decision, the organization Youth4Climate Action defined future generation as children under eighteen rather than those not yet born. They asserted that one effect on this particular cohort was a lower life expectancy than adults and argued that the situation was going to get exponentially worse for this generation in the future.[121]

However, with the effects of climate change becoming more immediate, children may soon drop out of the picture as a distinctly vulnerable group as more people, except the most privileged, experience significant harms.[122]

Donger notes that while children's involvement in climate litigation has the potential to further their procedural rights, there are risks.[123] Further, the lack of empirical knowledge about the experience of the young people involved in the many cases commenced on their behalf potentially obscures any negative impacts.[124] Given the ongoing nature of the *LaRose* and *Mathur* cases, it is not possible to assess the overall experience of the child and youth litigants without interfering in the lawyer-client relationship.[125] However, a search of Canadian news media suggests that the claimants in *Mathur* have taken a lead role as the spokespeople for the case.[126] Guidelines for ethical and competent legal practice require self-reflection and education to ensure the best possible strategies for both the individual clients as well as the climate justice cause. Realistic expectations of possible outcomes require respectful client relationships and appropriate supports than meet the needs of children affected. Litigation that is not conducted in a child rights-focused manner risks setting legal precedents that impact other areas of law that might have profound impacts on particular groups of children.[127] It also requires lawyers to reflect on their role as legal advisors, not just in the litigation, but as part of the larger movement led by their young clients and in furtherance of the goals of both climate justice and children's rights.

V. Future Directions

The benefits of involving children directly in climate justice litigation are numerous. Children's activism in respect of climate change is a global reality that is growing, and ought to grow given their stake in the future as well as the present. Their role as claimants gives meaning to their right to be heard in matters affecting them in accordance with article 12 of the UNCRC. Litigation is a powerful platform for storytelling to mobilize the public and influence decision-making, and the impact on children is a compelling part of this narrative.[128] The incremental nature of litigation as a strategy requires coordination with broader strategies that also centre children as activists in the cause. While climate justice litigation has not always been faithful to either child rights or movement lawyering principles, there are recent positive developments and guidance that lawyers and environmental activists can draw upon to ensure full engagement. First, ACRiSL has developed a set of principles for climate justice litigation involving children, which provides clear expectations for meaningful engagement with child litigants that is consistent with a child rights approach and arguably the principles of movement lawyering.[129] It is designed for lawyers representing children and youth, but it could prove particularly helpful for those who might have more expertise in environmental causes and less experience with young clients.

Second, citing Guinier and Torres, Jha argues that climate litigation is increasingly taking on *demosprudential* characteristics by engaging the public across jurisdictions through transnational advocacy networks involving individuals, state actors, and civil society.[130] These networks are significant for climate change "because of their particular mix of contentious strategies. By operating transnationally, using the rhetoric of catastrophe, and relying on mass mobilisation, these networks seek to change the environment in which formal legal rules are made."[131] These networks, including Fridays for the Future, increasingly involve children at the grass roots. In one internationally focused case, a group of 16 children, including Greta Thunberg, brought a complaint before the UN Committee on the Rights of the Child against Argentina, Brazil, France, Germany, and Turkey.[132] While the Committee ruled the claim inadmissible because the claimants had failed to exhaust domestic remedies, it left the door open for future claims and made findings regarding the impact of climate change on children, the extraterritorial nature of the states' obligations, and the individual responsibility of states due to their effective control over emissions.[133]

Third, many young people engaged in litigation through various organizations are viewing their involvement as a catalyst for further actions that move beyond the remedial limits of litigation. Some of those actions are disruptive, illegal, and therefore controversial. School strikes started by Greta Thunberg are arguably at the least controversial end of the spectrum of such actions, with soup cans thrown at works of art and pipeline blockades resulting in criminal law responses featuring at the other end. Balzac-Arroyo observes, "It is clear that the climate movement has embraced both civil disobedience and law through social innovation to challenge the oppressive system that governments are supporting."[134] Thunberg, through her Fridays for the Futures Fund, supports litigation but at the same time expresses realistic expectations about the law's influence and the need to dramatically change the world's economic system. She has expressed forcefully the need to take action that is outside the law:

> If we look through history, people who were advocating for example for social justice, if they had only used the legal methods then we wouldn't

be where we are today for example when it comes to racial rights and women's voting, etcetera. So we need to think outside the box because this is an existential crisis.[135]

There is a consistent theme from experiences with movement lawyering and climate change litigation that litigation is no "silver bullet"[136] to effect the change necessary during this climate emergency. Bustos attributes this to a lack of imagination that creates a barrier to innovation. Balzac-Arroyo sees this innovation in coordinated efforts by organizations like the US-based Climate Defence Project, which legally defends activism that showcases more assertive strategies, including non-violent civil disobedience.[137] Obligations to protect children and to act in their best interests seem anathema to these approaches, yet children have frequently taken part in protests at times with highly detrimental impacts.[138] Acknowledging this reality and children's right to freedom of peaceful assembly, UNICEF has published guidance on how to enable this right.[139] Alternatively, Trott suggests that while children are engaged in highly visible activism through global protest, they are simultaneously experimenting with ways to live more sustainably, particularly in the global South, making changes in their own lives that represent a broader and potentially long-term cultural shift.[140] Lawyers and activists seeking to work with children and young people need to understand that they often prefer youth-led or youth-controlled activities within their own communities.[141]

VI. Conclusion

In 1996, Sharon Stephens commented that it was "extraordinary how little attention [had] been given in environmental justice literature to the vulnerabilities of children" attributing that to the widespread assumption that "children could be *objects* of environmental inequalities," but not "*actors* and *participants* in grass roots activism."[142] Today we are seeing children take on those activist roles in the proliferation of climate justice litigation involving children as parties, but perhaps more importantly, in activism that does not rely on courts and lawyers. Perhaps not surprisingly, the lessons gleaned from the critique of movement lawyering have not been consistently applied to climate change litigation involving children. But there have been clear steps in that direction. Organizations such as ACRiSL have stepped in to provide resources to lawyers to foster a child rights-respecting approach and a community of practice that includes children's voices. The call for reflective legal practice within the social justice context is being heeded by those analysing the impact of climate justice litigation more generally, while the expectation that such practice be client-focused has led to analysis that is especially applicable to children as the clients. Seeing beyond litigation, lawyers must also consider supporting the non-legal means of effecting radical change that children and youth are advocating to avoid the professional self-deception of seeing litigation tactics as the only meaningful solution.

NOTES

1 Stephen Budlender, Gilbert Marcus SC & Nick Ferreira, *Public Interest Litigation and Social Change in South Africa: Strategies, Tactics and Lessons* (Bermuda: The Atlantic Philanthropies, 2014), online (pdf): <https://www.atlanticphilanthropies.org/wp-content/uploads/2015/12/Public-interest-litigation-and-social-change-in-South-Africa.pdf>; Michael McCann, "Law and Social Movements: Contemporary Perspectives" (2006) 2 Ann Rev Law Sci 17 at 28, online: <https://doi.org/10.1146/annurev.lawsocsci.2.081805.105917>; Basil Alexander, "Pragmatic Assorted Strategies: How Canadian Cause Lawyers Contribute to Social Change" in Cheryl Milne & Kent Roach, eds, *Public Interest Litigation in Canada* (Toronto: LexisNexis, 2019) 3; Faye Faraday, Tracy Herrernan & Helen Luu, "Winning the Right to Housing: Critical Reflections on a Holistic Approach to Public Interest Litigation" in Cheryl Milne & Kent Roach, eds, *Public Interest Litigation in Canada* (Toronto: LexisNexis, 2019) 31.

2 McCann, *supra* note 1; *Strategic Litigation Impacts: Insights from Global Experience* (New York: Open Society Justice Initiative, 2018), online: <https://www.justiceinitiative.org/publications/strategic-litigation-impacts-insights-global-experience> [Open Society Justice Initiative].

3 The Hague District Court of Appeal, 2015, *Urgenda Foundation v State of the Netherlands (Ministry of Infrastructure and the Environment)*, C/09/456689/HA ZA 13–1396 (Netherlands) [*Urgenda*].

4 *Juliana v United States*, 947 F (3d) 1159 (9th Cir 2020) at 5.

5 Jacqueline Peel, Alice Palmer & Rebekkah Markey-Towler, *Review of literature on impacts of climate litigation*, (Melbourne: Children's Investment Fund Foundation, 2022).

6 Scott L. Cummings, "Movement Lawyering" (2017) U Ill L Rev 1645; Josephine Balzac-Arroyo, "Movement Lawyering: A Social Innovation to Achieve Climate Justice" (2021) 21 J L Soc Dev 1; Carlie D. Trott, "What Difference Does It Make? Exploring the Transformative Potential of Everyday Climate Crisis Activism by Children and Youth" (2021) 19:3 Child Geogr 300, online: <https://doi.org/10.1080/14733285.2020.1870663>.

7 Lydia Slobodian, "Defending the Future: Intergenerational Equity in Climate Litigation" (2020) 32:3 Geo Envtl L Rev 569 at 588. This was also

the consensus of a group of practitioners who agreed that litigation is a "last resort" and that courts are no more than "second best" to resolve climate issues: British Institute of International and Comparative Law, "The Role of Science in Climate Change Litigation: International Workshop Report" (London: British Institute of International and Comparative Law, 2021), cited in Peel at al, *supra* note 5 at 15.

8 Greta Thunberg, "Greta Thunberg on the Climate Delusion: 'We've Been Greenwashed Out of Our Senses. It's Time to Stand Our Ground,'" *The Guardian* (8 October 2022), online: <https://www.theguardian.com/environment/2022/oct/08/greta-thunberg-climate-delusion-greenwashed-out-of-our-senses>.

9 Linda Goldman, *Climate Change and Youth: Turning Grief and Anxiety into Activism* (New York: Routledge, 2022) at 13, online: <https://doi.org/10.4324/9781003051770>; Brenda Cossman, "Climate Anxiety and Youth Activism," in this volume. The UN Committee on the Rights of the Child cited child activism as a key motivation for its development of *General Comment No. 26 (2023) on Children's Rights and the Environment, with a Special Focus on Climate Change* (United Nations, CRC/C/GC/26, 2023).

10 The definition of child is that found in the UN Convention on the Rights of the Child, being under 18 years. In the litigation in Canada and internationally, the age range for youth varies considerably from under 25 to under 35 as discussed below. While future generations can refer to children not yet born, some litigation has defined future generations to be current children (see Constitutional Court of Korea, *Do-Hyun et al. v South Korea* (Republic of Korea), 13 March 2020, online: <https://climatecasechart.com/non-us-case/kim-yujin-et-al-v-south-korea/>.)

11 Elizabeth Donger, "Children and Youth in Strategic Climate Litigation: Advancing Rights through Legal Argument and Legal Mobilization" (2022) 11:2 Transn'l Envtl L 263 at 264, online: <https://doi.org/10.1017/S2047102522000218>.

12 Aoife Nolan & Ann Skelton "'Turning the Rights Lens Inwards': The Case for Child Rights-Consistent Strategic Litigation Practice" (2022) 22:4 HRLR 1, online: <https://doi.org/10.1093/hrlr/ngac026>.

13 Aoife Nolan, Ann Skelton & Karabo Ozah, *Advancing Child Rights-Consistent Strategic Litigation Practice* (Nottingham: ACRiSL, 2022) at 6, online: <https://www.acrisl.org/s/DRAFT-06_ACRiSL-Report.pdf> [ACRiSL Report].

14 Micheal W. McCann & Helena Silberstein, "Rethinking Law's 'Allurements': A Relational Analysis of Social Movement Lawyers in the United States" in Austin Sarat & Stuart Scheingold, eds, *Cause Lawyering: Political Commitments and Professional Responsibilities* (Oxford: Oxford University Press, 1997) 261, online: <https://doi.org/10.1093

/oso/9780195113198.003.0009>; Gerald N. Rosenberg, *The Hollow Hope: Can Courts Bring about Social Change?* (Chicago: University of Chicago Press, 1991).

15 Cheryl Milne & Kent Roach, "Introduction" in Milne & Roach, *supra* note 1 at xxxi.

16 Budlender, Marcus & Ferreira, *supra* note 1; Open Society Justice Initiative, *supra* note 2.

17 Susan D. Carle & Scott L. Cummings, "A Reflection on the Ethics of Movement Lawyering" (2018) 31:3 Geo J Legal Ethics 447 at 455–6.

18 Lani Guinier & Gerald Torres, "Changing the Wind: Notes Toward a Demosprudence of Law and Social Movements" (2014) 123:8 Yale LJ 2740 at 2749.

19 Balzac-Arroyo, *supra* note 6 at 2.

20 Cummings, *supra* note 6 at 1690.

21 Trott, *supra* note 6 at 304.

22 McCann, *supra* note 1 at 17, 22.

23 Budlender, Marcus & Ferreira, *supra* note 1.

24 Open Society Justice Initiative, *supra* note 2 at 19.

25 McCann, *supra* note 1 at 26–7; See also Douglas NeJaime, "Winning through Losing," (2010–2011) 96 Iowa L Rev 941, in which he analyses the progress that can also be made through court losses.

26 *Ibid* at 26–7; It should be noted that the conditions include the country in which the litigation is taking place, a contextual point that is often missing from the American scholarship, which was noted by Charles R. Epp in relation to human rights litigation in Charles R. Epp, *The Rights Revolution: Lawyers, Activists and Supreme Courts in Comparative Perspective* (Chicago: University of Chicago Press, 1998).

27 Gerald N. Rosenberg, "Courting Disaster: Looking for Change in All the Wrong Places" (2006) 54 Drake L Rev 795 at 797.

28 Open Society Justice Initiative, *supra* note 2.

29 NeJaime, *supra* note 25 at 968–969.

30 Jim Freeman, "Supporting Social Movements: A Brief Guide for Lawyers and Law Students" (2015) 12 Hasting Race Poverty LJ 191 at 195–203; Faraday, *supra* note 1 at 35.

31 Faraday et al, *supra* note 1 at 35.

32 *Ibid* at 34.

33 Guinier & Torres, *supra* note 18; McCann, *supra* note 1 at 23; Open Society Justice Initiative, *supra* note 2.

34 *Ibid* at 2753.

35 Cummings, *supra* note 6 at 1697.

36 *Ibid* at 1716.

37 Derrick A. Bell Jr., "Serving Two Masters: Integration Ideals and Client Interests in School Desegregation Litigation" (1975–6) 85 Yale LJ 470, online: <https://doi.org/10.2307/795339>.

38 *Ibid* at 488.

39 *Ibid* at 490–1.

40 *Ibid* at 493.

41 *Ibid* at 494–5.

42 *Ibid* at 494; Bell's article is often cited by other scholars examining movement lawyering in the United States. See e.g., Carle & Cummings, *supra* note 17 and NeJaime, *supra* note 25.

43 Martha Matthews, "Ten Thousand Tiny Clients: The Ethical Duty of Representation in Children's Class Action Cases" (1996) 64:4 Fordham L Rev 1435 at 1436.

44 Carle & Cummings, *supra* note 17 at 455, citing Gerald P. Lopez, *Rebellious Lawyering: One Chicano's Vision of Progressive Law Practice* (Boulder, CO: Westview Press, 1992).

45 Guinier & Torres, *supra* note 18 at 45–6.

46 Camila Bustos, "Movement Lawyering in the Time of the Climate Crisis" (2022) 39 Pace Envtl L Rev 1 at 24–6, online: <https://doi.org/10.58948/0738-6206.1854>.

47 Bell, *supra* note 37 at 494–5. The methods used by the NAACP to recruit clients were challenged on the basis of state solicitation laws, although the Supreme Court dismissed the claims stating that the methods were consistent with political expression and in the public interest.

48 Ketan Jha, "Networked Public Interest Litigation: A Novel Framework for Climate Claims?" in Jolene Lin & Douglas A. Kysar, eds, *Climate Change Litigation in the Asia Pacific* (Cambridge: Cambridge University Press, 2020) 38 at 65, online: <https://doi.org/10.1017/9781108777810.004>.

49 ACRiSL Report, *supra* note 13.

50 *Ibid* at 5.

51 *Ibid* at 17, 31.

52 *Ibid* at 42.

53 Catherine Hartung, *Conditional Citizens: Rethinking Children and Young People's Participation* (Singapore: Springer Nature, 2017) at 113, 123, online: <https://doi.org/10.1007/978-981-10-3938-6>.

54 ACRiSL Report, *supra* note 13 at 4.

55 Cummings, *supra* note 6.

56 *Convention on the Rights of the Child*, 28 May 1990, Can TS 1577 No 3.

57 *Ibid*, art 12.

58 Roger Hart, *Children's Participation: From tokenism to citizenship*, Innocenti Essays No 4 (Florence: International Child Development Centre, 1992).

59 Sherry R. Arnstein, "A Ladder of Citizen Participation" (1969) 35:4 J Amer Planning Assoc 214, online: <https://doi.org/10.1080/01944366908977225>.
60 Hart, *supra* note 58.
61 Roger A. Hart et al, *Children's Participation: The Theory and Practice of Involving Young Citizens in Community Development and Environmental Care* (London: Earthscan, 1997). The model has its limitations and has been criticized for not reflecting the complexity of children and young people's participation: Hartung, *supra* note 53.
62 Laura Lundy, "Voice is not enough: conceptualizing Article 12 of the United Nations Convention on the Rights of the Child" (2007) 33:6 Br Educ Res J 927 at 933, online: <https://doi.org/10.1080/01411920701657033>.
63 "The CBA Child Rights Toolkit," *Canadian Bar Association* (accessed 28 February 2023), online: <https://www.cba.org/Publications-Resources/Practice-Tools/Child-Rights-Toolkit/theChild/Child-Participation>. The toolkit references the United Nations Committee on the Rights of the Child, General Comment No 12.
64 *General Comment No. 12 (2009): The Right of the Child to be Heard*, UNCRC, 51st Sess, UN Doc CRC/C/GC/12 (2009) General Comment.
65 See e.g., in Ontario, *Rules of Civil Procedure* RRO 1990, Reg 194, s 7.01.
66 Nolan & Skelton, *supra* note 12 at 14; Matthews, *supra* note 43 at 1456. These concerns have also been noted by Carle & Cummings, *supra* note 17, as ethical considerations in movement lawyering more generally, but when the group is made up of children, rather than adult activists, substituting the lawyers' views for the group interests is more common.
67 Christine McMellan & E. Kay M. Tisdall, "Children and Young People's Participation Rights: Looking Backwards and Moving Forwards." (2020) 28 Int'l J Child Rights 157 at 169. Hartung, *supra* note 53 at 107 & 123, also cautions that participatory practices by adults can have the effect of homogenizing children and privileging those who align with the dominant values held by the adults while excluding children who cannot meet the idealistic image of the competent or "agentic" child.
68 ACRiSL Report, *supra* note 13 at 51.
69 Matthews, *supra* note 43 at 1458.
70 *Ibid* at 1458.
71 Katherine Kruse, "Fortress in the Sand: The Plural Values of Client-Centered Representation" (2006) 12 Clin L Rev 369; See also Carolyn Salisbury, "From Violence and Victimization to Voice and Validation: Incorporating Therapeutic Jurisprudence in a Children's Law Clinic" (2005) 17 St. Thomas L Rev 623; Renee DeBoard-Lucas et al, "16 Trauma-Informed, Evidence-Based Recommendations for Advocates Working with Children Exposed to Intimate Partner Violence" (2013) 32:9 Child L Prac

136; Jean Koh Peters, *Representing Children in Child Protective Proceedings : Ethical and Practical Dimensions*, 2nd ed (Newark, NJ: LexisNexis, 2001).

72 Claudia Pena, "Trauma Abounds: A Case for Trauma-Informed Lawyering" (2019) 26:1 UCLA Women's LJ 7 at 9, online: <https://doi.org/10.5070/L3261044345>.

73 ACRiSL Report, *supra* note 13 at 68.

74 Goldman, *supra* note 9 at 13. For a review of the research on the impacts of climate change on child and adolescent health, see Adrienne van Nieuwenhuizen et al, "The Effects of Climate Change on Child and Adolescent Mental Health: Clinical Considerations" (2021) 23:12 Curr Psych Rep 88, online: <https://doi.org/10.1007/s11920-021-01296-y>. Hartung also cautions against democratic discourses of citizenship "whereby children and young people's value is conditional on their functioning in accordance with that which meet the needs of society as a whole." Hartung, *supra* note 53 at 65.

75 Cossman, *supra* note 9.

76 Caroline Hickman et al, "Climate Anxiety in Children and Young People and Their Beliefs about Government Responses to Climate Change: A Global Survey" 5:12 Lancet Planet Health e863, online: <https://doi.org/10.1016/S2542-5196(21)00278-3>.

77 ACRiSL Report, *supra* note 13 at 67; Goldman *supra* note 9 at 264.

78 Nolan & Skelton, *supra* note 12 at 18.

79 Open Society Justice Initiative, *supra* note 2 at 74.

80 Douglas Elliott, "Secrets of the Lavender Mafia: Personal Reflections on Social Activism and the *Charter*" (2006) 5 J L & Equal 97.

81 McCann, *supra* note 1; Open Society Justice Initiative, *supra* note 2; NeJaime, *supra* note 25; Jha, *supra* note 48.

82 Sharon Stephens, "Reflections on Environmental Justice: Children as Victims and Actors" (1996) 23:4 Soc Just 62 at 76; Jonathan Herring, "Vulnerability, Children, and the Law" in Michael Freeman, ed, *Law and Childhood Studies* (Oxford: Oxford University Press, 2012) 243 at 249, online: <https://doi.org/10.1093/acprof:oso/9780199652501.003.0016>.

83 Nathalie Chalifour, Jessica Earle & Laura Macintyre, "Coming of Age in a Warming World: The Charter's Section 15 Equality Guarantee and Youth-Led Climate Litigation" (2021) 17 J L & Equal 17 at 35.

84 See for example, *Canadian Foundation for Children, Youth and the Law v Canada (Attorney General)* [2004] 1 SCR 76, in which the majority of the Court held that the justification of physical punishment of children was not discriminatory because it corresponded to their dependence on parents and the need for guidance and discipline; and *A.C. v Manitoba (Child and Family Services)* [2009] SCC 30, in which the majority of the Court held that a provision that enabled forced medical treatment on any child under 16

was not discriminatory because the decision had to be made in her best interests.

85 Kent Roach, "Judicial Remedies for Climate Change" (2022) 1:17 J L Equal 105 at 105, 116.

86 Matthews, *supra* note 43 at 1462–9.

87 ACRiSL Report, *supra* note 13 at 11, 66.

88 Slobodian, *supra* note 7 at 588.

89 NeJaime, *supra* note 25 at 945.

90 ACRiSL Report, *supra* note 13 at 11.

91 Nolan & Skelton, *supra* note 12 at 19.

92 Donger, *supra* note 11 at 273. The UN Committee on the Rights of the Child acknowledges this is *General Comment No. 26, supra* note 9 at para 11.

93 *Ibid* at 280.

94 *Juliana v. United States, supra* note 4, has been a major impetus for child rights focused litigation despite protracted litigation that has taken eight years since filing the petition with the matter only recently going ahead on the merits on amended pleadings at a date yet to be scheduled.

95 Enforcement has been an issue in the Colombian case, Corte Suprema de Justicia, Bogota, 5 April 2018, *Future Generations v Ministry of the Environment et al*, STC4360–2018, Radicación no. 11001–22–03–000–2018–00319–01 at 18–19 (Colombia).

96 Peel et al, *supra* note 5 at 13–14.

97 Roach, *supra* note 85 at 109; see e.g., in Canada, *R v Sharma*, 2022 SCC 39 at para 65, where Brown and Rowe JJ for the majority state, "Incrementalism is deeply grounded in *Charter* jurisprudence."

98 Chris Tollefson, "Advancing an Agenda? A Reflection on Recent Developments in Canadian Public Interest Environmental Litigation" (2002) 51 UNNLJ 175 at 176–7.

99 Chalifour et al, *supra* note 83 at 4. The most recent report on global trends by the Grantham Research Institute stated that thirty-five climate change cases had been filed in Canada since 1986 (Joanna Setzer & Catherine Higham, *Global Trends in Climate Change Litigation: 2023 Snapshot* [London: London School of Economics and Policy, 2023] at 1).

100 *Ibid* at 6.

101 *Raincoast Conservation Foundation v. Canada (Attorney General)*, 2019 FCA 224 (CanLII), [2020] 1 FCR 362 at para 70 (accessed 28 February 2023), online: <https://canlii.ca/t/j28lp>.

102 *Environnement Jeunesse c. Procureur général du Canada*, 2021 QCCA 1871, (CanLII) (accessed 28 February 2023), online: <https://canlii.ca/t/jl8f5>.

103 *Misdzi Yikh v Canada*, 2020 FC 1059 (CanLII) (accessed 28 February 2023), online: <https://canlii.ca/t/jbn58>, leave to appeal pending; *La Rose*

v. Canada, 2020 FC 1008 (CanLII) (accessed 28 February 2023), online: <https://canlii.ca/t/jb8f7>, appeal heard by the Federal Court of Appeal on 14–15 February 2023.

104 *Mathur v His Majesty the King in Right of Ontario*, 2023 ONSC 2316 [*Mathur v HMK*]. The case is currently under appeal with the decision of the Ontario Court of Appeal on reserve.

105 Notice of Application filed 25 October 2019; Court file No T-1750–19.

106 *La Rose v Canada*, 2023 FCA 241 (CanLII).

107 *Mathur v Ontario*, 2020 ONSC 6918 at paras 67–71.

108 Applicants' Factum para 103.

109 *Ibid* at para 206.

110 *Mathur v HMK*, *supra* note 104 at para 180.

111 Chalifour at al, *supra* note 83.

112 *Ibid* at 57.

113 Donger, *supra* note 11 at 279.

114 *Ibid* at 69–70, 90.

115 *Mathur v HMK*, *supra* note 104 at paras 179–83.

116 *Future Generations v Ministry of the Environment et al*, *supra* note 95 at 18–19.

117 *Urgenda*, *supra* note 3.

118 *Neubauer et al. v. Germany*, 1 BvR 288/20, German Constitutional Court, 29 April 2021.

119 Donger, *supra* note 11 at 280.

120 *Ibid*.

121 *Do-Hyun et al. v South Korea*, *supra* note 10.

122 Slobodian, *supra* note 7 at 579.

123 Donger, *supra* note 11 at 283. See also, Aoife Nolan, Ann Skelton & Karabo Ozah, *Child Rights Strategic Litigation: Key Principles for Climate Justice Litigation* (Nottingham: ACRiSL, 2023): Risks include loss of privacy when children are the face of the litigation; intrusive media attention, including negative social media and the near permanence of information on the internet.

124 Donger, *supra* note 11 at 285.

125 While the ACRiSL study involved interviews of practitioners and child litigants, the researchers did not ask to interview children who were part of these ongoing cases for these ethical reasons [Aiofe Nolan, conversation with author, 3 February 2023].

126 See for example, Nick Boisvert, "Young Ontarians Launch Lawsuit Against Province After Ford Government Scales Back Emissions Targets," *CBC News* (26 November 2019), online: <https://www.cbc.ca/news/canada/toronto/ontario-youth-climate-change-lawsuit-1.5372440>; "'There Can't Be Silence After This': Teens Reflect on COP27 Climate

Conference," *CBC Kids News* (18 November 2022), online: <https://www.cbc.ca/kidsnews/post/there-cant-be-silence-after-this-teens-reflect-on-cop27-climate-conference/>; Mitchell Beer, "Hearings to Begin in 'Historic' Youth Climate Lawsuit Against Ontario Government," *Corporate Knights* (8 September 2022), online: <https://www.corporateknights.com/leadership/hearings-to-begin-in-historic-youth-climate-lawsuit-against-ontario-government/>.

127 Perhaps more problematically from a rights-based perspective, another South Korean case has included a foetus as a claimant along with sixty-one babies and children under the age of 11. See Isabella Kaminski, "Foetus Fronts Legal Challenge over Emissions in South Korea," *The Guardian* (24 June 2022), online: <https://www.theguardian.com/world/2022/jun/24/foetus-heads-legal-challenge-carbon-emissions-south-korea>.

128 Peel et al, *supra* note 5 at 26–7.

129 Nolan et al, *supra* note 123.

130 Jha, *supra* note 48.

131 *Ibid* at 57.

132 *Sacchi, et al. v Argentina, Brazil, France, Germany, and Turkey* (2019) CRC/C/88/D/104/2019, CRC/C/88/D/105/2019, CRC/C/88/D/106/2019, CRC/C/88/D/107/2019, CRC/C/88/D/108/2019.

133 Yusra Suedi, "Litigating Climate Change before the Committee on the Rights of the Child in *Sacchi v Argentina et al.*: Breaking New Ground?" (2022) 40:4 Nord J Hum Rights 549; Aoife Nolan, "Children's Rights and Climate Change at the UN Committee on the Rights of the Child: Pragmatism and Principle in Sacchi v Argentina," *EJIL:Talk!* (21 October 21), online (blog): <https://www.ejiltalk.org/childrens-rights-and-climate-change-at-the-un-committee-on-the-rights-of-the-child-pragmatism-and-principle-in-sacchi-v-argentina/>.

134 Balzac-Arroyo, *supra* note 6 at 13.

135 The View, "Greta Thunberg says Climate Crisis is an 'Existential Emergency'" (17 February 2023), online (video): <https://abcnews.go.com/theview/video/greta-thunberg-climate-crisis-existential-emergency-97292879>.

136 Bustos, *supra* note 46 at 12; Peel et al, *supra* note 5 at 25, 29.

137 Balzac-Arroyo, *supra* note 6 at 3.

138 Sophia Boddenberg & Charis McGowan, "Our Children Are Going to Prison: Chile Holds Scores of Minors Arrested During Protests," *The Guardian* (2 March 2020) online: <https://www.theguardian.com/world/2020/mar/02/chile-protests-minors-held-prison>; "Cuba: Peaceful Protesters Systematically Detained, Abused," *Human Rights Watch* (19 October 2021) online: <https://www.hrw.org/news/2021

/10/19/cuba-peaceful-protesters-systematically-detained-abused>; Reuters, "Five Hong Kong Teenagers Sentenced in First Security Case Involving Minors," *CNN* (10 October 2022), online: <https://www.cnn.com/2022/10/09/china/hong-kong-teenagers-national-security-intl-hnk/index.html>.

139 UNICEF, *Free and Safe to Protest: Policing Assemblies Involving Children* (New York: UNICEF, 2023), online (pdf): <https://www.unicef.org/media/144876/file/%20Free%20and%20safe%20to%20protest%20:%20Policing%20assemblies%20involving%20children%20.pdf>. The UN Committee on the Rights of the Child, *General Comment no. 26, supra* note 9 at paras 29–31, also reiterates the child's right to freedom of expression and peaceful assembly within the climate justice context.

140 Trott, *supra* note 6 at 305.

141 Mark Chou et al, *Young People, Citizenship and Political Participation* (London: Rowman & Littlefield, 2017) at 88, 94.

142 Stephens, *supra* note 82 at 72.

12 Ethical Lawyering and Existential Threats

ABDI AIDID

I. Introduction

Lawyers are deeply implicated in the climate crisis. Yet the mechanisms we have for regulating lawyer behaviour are conspicuously absent from discussions about appropriate responses to global warming's existential threat. This could be because legal ethics regimes – broadly defined as the rules and institutions governing lawyer conduct – are often ineffectual. Indeed, there is a rather large literature devoted to criticizing legal ethics' shortcomings, ranging from critiques of legal ethics' as being abstracted from ordinary morality[1] to critiques of professional regulators as uninterested in the more complex issues that lawyers encounter.[2] The existential threat posed by climate change presents an opportunity to rethink some of legal ethics' approaches and core assumptions.

To that end, this chapter asks whether legal ethics regimes (i.e., the rules and institutions that constrain lawyer behaviour) can play a role in responding to the climate crisis. I explain that because of lawyers' involvement in everything from enabling corporate carbon emissions to pursuing climate justice to drafting environmental legislation, legal-ethical rules are an underexplored lever for climate interventions. Put differently, if legal ethics purports to constrain lawyer behaviour, then it should – with some limitations – be capable of constraining the sort of lawyer behaviour that exacerbates climate harm. I then ask whether the *discipline* of legal ethics is capable of responding to challenges on the scale of the ongoing climate crisis. Here, I argue that challenges of an existential nature should motivate a reconsideration of some of legal ethics' more narrow and provincial frameworks, namely the centrality of the lawyer-client relationship and the constraint of jurisdiction.

II. Lawyers and the Climate Crisis

From the outset, an important clarification should be made: lawyer complicity in climate harms is not a conceptually distinct phenomenon from lawyer complicity in other social harms. The legal profession does not appear to have some special propensity for exacerbating climate change, nor is there a unique mechanism for lawyers to inflict environmental damage. As a result, the case for lawyers being culpable for climate harms is more complicated than, say, the professional responsibility of staff accountants in the event of corporate financial abuses. Moreover, a lawyer's involvement in generating climate harms might be indistinguishable on a task-by-task basis from a lawyer's involvement in an otherwise socially productive activity. Imagine, for instance, a lawyer rendering assistance to a client seeking municipal permits for an obviously harmful project, such as a tobacco manufacturing facility that not only creates public health but also emits harmful toxins into surrounding neighbourhoods. The constituent tasks involved in rendering said assistance – and indeed the ultimate work product – would be the same if the lawyer was seeking municipal permits for a food bank or an infectious disease hospital.

With this established, how do lawyers participate in generating climate harms? Of course, some lawyerly tasks are somewhat attenuated from the environmental harm they bring about. Just as ordinary public morality does not take the caretaking or bookkeeping staff at a toxic polluter as deeply implicated in the climate harms caused by their employer, the lawyer working on reviewing insurance policies or drafting internal codes of conduct might not be either. But lawyers are *proximately* involved in at least three capacities that abet climate crises. First, in their *litigating* capacity, lawyers pursue claims on behalf of clients that exacerbate climate change. For instance, a law firm retained by a petrochemicals company may defend against claims of environmental damage by plaintiffs but may also pursue litigation that enables their client to continue to harmful emissions. Some of this litigation takes the form of direct challenges to environmental legislation.

Here, it is worth noting that environmental litigation is a particularly contested space partly because, as Amy Salyzyn and Penelope Simons observe in the context of extractive industries in particular, "[c]ivil litigation is currently one of the few means available to victims wishing to hold corporations to account and to obtain some form of reparation for the harms they have suffered." Indeed, plaintiffs pursue litigation often for want of more robust legislative and regulatory solutions. This means that claims are often substantial and implicate an accused corporate polluter's *core* operations in ways that could threat their continued existence. This is, of course, precisely the point. But as a result, corporations accused of environmental harms will often deploy the most vigorous defence strategies. Salyzyn and Simons locate this in the predominant "resolute advocacy" approach, wherein lawyers are zealous, partisan advocates who conceive of disputes as mostly zero-sum. In this model – a variant of the "standard conception" I discuss later – lawyers are principally concerned with effectuating their client's interests within the constraints of their professional codes of conduct. But resolute advocacy is also prone to behaviours that could be considered aggressive or untoward outside of the dyadic plaintiff-defendant relationship. One example is the phenomenon of "intimidation lawsuits" that are familiar to environmental advocates. Steven Vaughan observes that lawyers pursue "libel claims and fraud counter-claims against environmental defenders, and racketeering claims against environmental [non-governmental organizations]" cases that draw ethical scrutiny partly because they could be construed as being calculated to harass or intimidate, or at least are targeted towards goals other than a discrete litigation victory. A common form that these intimidation lawsuits take is what is frequently termed a "strategic lawsuit against public participation," or SLAPP.[3] A majority of US states and Canada's three largest provinces – Ontario, Quebec, and British Columbia – have all passed anti-SLAPP legislation. In the case of Ontario's *Protection of Public Participation Act*, the preferred resolution to such lawsuits is distinctly procedural. Ontario's anti-SLAPP provisions, for instance, enables defendants to move the court to "dismiss the proceeding against the person if the person satisfied the judge that the matter arises from an expression made by the person that relates to a matter of public interest." Even with this remedy, anti-SLAPP regimes accept that cynical, speech-chilling litigation will occur but do not contemplate penalties for lawyers.

Second, in their *transactional* capacity, lawyers are enabling climate harms by facilitating transactions and other market activity that burden precarious environments directly. Sometimes, the lawyer's role is dispositive. For instance, lawyers who work on securing approvals for projects with certain risk of ecological damage are necessary interlocutors, particularly in complex regulatory environments wherein approval processes are formal and legalistic. Other times, lawyerly impact is somewhat less direct; for example, lawyers who facilitate a merger or acquisition in extractive industries, which might lead to more efficiency – that is, more economical extraction. Beyond these examples, transactional lawyering is implicated in climate change all the way down. Creators of fracking technologies sought patents or to otherwise have their intellectual property protected, just as setting up oil sands operations likely involved some land transactions.

Third, in their *advisory* capacity, lawyers are consulted to advise on climate-harming activity, such as in the form of compliance advice – or strategic non-compliance advice – regarding environmental rules.

In sum, lawyers are involved – as Vaughan explains, lawyers are "part of the narrative of environmental harms" because "they are in the room where it happened." Yet unlike, say, management at the firms they advise, lawyers are protected by a web of rules and regimes that conspires to inoculate the profession against moral or legal judgment for any outcomes that they might enable. I discuss this next.

III. Legal Ethics' Problem State

Legal ethicists have been remarkably self-reflexive about the state of their chosen field. William H. Simon famously opened the aptly titled "The Trouble with Legal Ethics" with a simple – if cursory – statement: "Legal ethics is a disappointing subject."[4] Since then, a near-consensus has emerged among scholars, the judiciary, and the organized bar that legal ethics enforcement is incapable of responding to the myriad complex issues that the profession faces.[5] Indeed, legal ethicists bemoan the state of their own field so frequently that W. Bradley Wendel calls these works "a burgeoning genre – the 'profession in crisis' jeremiad."[6] A quick glance at the titles of some leading articles tells the story: if not Simon's "The Trouble with Legal Ethics,"[7] then Tanina Rostain's "Ethics Lost,"[8] Patrick J. Schiltz's "Legal Ethics in Decline,"[9] or the two separate articles by former Chief Justice Warren Burger and Rebecca Roiphe, each titled "The Decline of Professionalism,"[10] to name a few. Here, I focus on two problems of legal ethics that account for its ineffectiveness: (1) the "standard conception" of lawyering that informs legal-ethical regulation contemplated a role-differentiated morality that obscures responsibility for outcomes; and (2) legal ethics rules encourage a "minimum compliance" world view rather than an aspirational, ethical one. I discuss these two ideas next.

1. The Standard Conception and Role-Differentiated Morality

Any exploration of lawyers' responsibility for the climate crisis will inevitably result in the sobering realization that legal ethics regimes have been formed and re-formed in a manner explicitly designed to separate professional and moral responsibility. Students of legal ethics will be familiar with the "standard conception" of lawyering, an idea that has pervaded the literature for nearly fifty years.[11] Generally, the standard conception formulates the lawyer's duty as being oriented around two principles: (1) partisanship and (2) neutrality.[12] The principle of partisanship requires lawyers to act exclusively in their client's interest.[13] Taken to its extreme, the partisan lawyer zealously pursues their client's desired outcome in a vacuum that is impervious to competing considerations. To the extent that a partisan lawyer accounts for opposing interests, it is as part of a self-interested calculation about maximizing their client's relative position. The related principle of neutrality means that lawyers' do not invade their clients' decision-making with their own judgment or normative aspiration. In other words, as Sung Hui Kim explains, neutrality "requires lawyers to subordinate their moral concerns to those of the client."[14] Lawyers who act as neutrals, then, can perform representative tasks even where they have profound disagreement with the client's ends.

Scholars have also recognized a third principle embedded in the standard conception: "non-accountability." The principle of non-accountability holds that lawyers dutifully performing their tasks within the bounds of the law are not – in any circumstance – implicated in the outcomes enabled by their representative role. David Luban and W. Bradley Wendel describe non-accountability simply as "being exempt from moral criticism for having helped another act immorally."[15] Murray L. Schwartz argues that the non-accountability principle acts to obscure the moral choices that lawyers make in acting with partisanship and neutrality. A lawyer acting as a zealous advocate may trample on an opposing party's well-founded rights and interests, and a lawyer acting neutrally may self-consciously enable an activity that, but not for their professional role, they might want to distance themselves from. Figure 12.1 provides a simple illustration of the standard conception.

At its most extreme, the standard conception presents the lawyer as the "hired gun": a zealous advocate for their client's interests, who is at once willing to exploit advantages to the detriment of opposing parties, but also recognizes that they are an agent of their client and thus not the story's protagonist, so to speak. Note here the interaction between these three constituent parts of the standard conception: neutrality, partisanship, and non-accountability. Where partisanship and neutrality are principles that the lawyer themself can embrace, non-accountability requires an action on the part of the wider legal-professional and epistemic community: to hold the lawyer blameless. Put differently, a lawyer can choose to be partisan and neutral, but it is up to everyone else to decide that they are not implicated in the

Figure 12.1. Standard Conception of Non-accountability in Lawyering

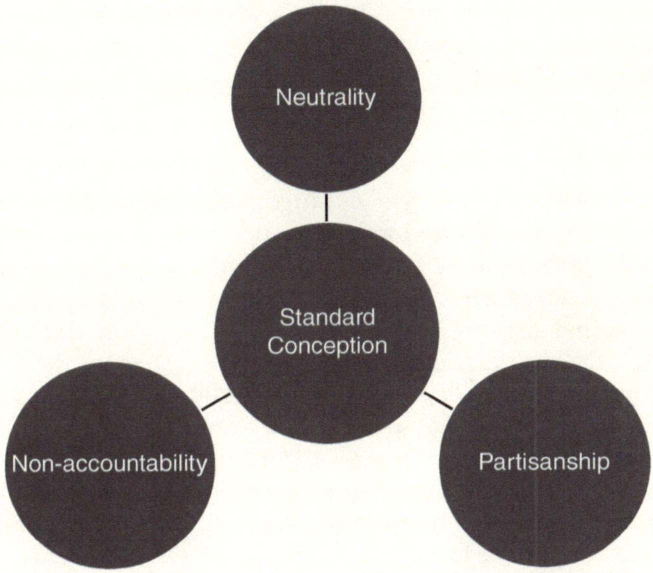

consequences of their representative work. Consider also how non-accountability operates in both professional and moral terms. Lawyers are not generally at risk of criminal or civil liability or advancing their client's ends, save for well-defined instances where lawyers violate an independent positive rule (e.g., committing fraud). In fact, lawyers who do not satisfactorily pursue their clients' interests – whatever those interests might be, as defined and directed by the clients – risk not only discipline by professional regulators but also civil claims of malpractice. Yet non-accountability makes a stronger claim: in addition to being generally protected from institutional consequences for their representation choices, non-accountability aspires to a kind of moral immunity, as well. Murray L. Schwartz likens non-accountability to "the filing of a demurrer, rather than an answer, to the charge of immorality."[16] Put differently, non-accountability is not fixated on bolstering the lawyer's moral case but shielding the lawyer from any moral examination at all.

Here, it bears emphasis that the standard conception is not merely a philosophical construct but the foundation of the entire regulatory scope of legal ethics. Indeed, lawyers who are insufficiently partisan or insufficiently neutral are at risk of professional discipline. The Federation of Law Societies' *Model Rules of Professional Conduct* as well as the American Bar Association's *Model Rules of Professional Conduct* – on which the disciplinary rules of most state bars are based – both have rules requiring lawyers to act resolutely in their clients' best interests and, in all situations, adhere to their client's decisions with respect to the objectives of the representative engagement.[17] With respect to non-accountability, legal-ethical institutions – law societies, state bar organizations, and, to a limited extent, the judiciary – are generally loathe to evaluate, let alone intervene in, outcomes. Taken together, the principles that make up the standard conception limit the scope of lawyers' professional "moral universe" to two questions: first, whether or not the lawyer can exercise their duties within the limits of the law, and second, whether or not the lawyer can exercise their duties without running afoul of professional disciplinary rules. Save for those two sets of constraints, however, lawyers are effectively inoculated by the profession's own regulatory apparatuses from any kind of *moral* judgment. To use the well-worn metaphor, legal ethics regimes permit lawyers to play a role akin to that of a cab driver: get the passenger (e.g., the client) to their chosen destination without scrutinizing where they are going, the reasons they wish to go there, and what they intend to do once there. Like the cab driver, the lawyer performs a distinct function in the division of labour by contributing expertise, but the key choices – and therefore the moral responsibility – rests with the passenger and client.

Critics have derided the standard conception as encouraging lawyers to be "systematically amoral."[18] Too often, these broadsides will obscure the core reasons why the standard conception might be – in some circumstances – preferable. Consider the following two. First, the standard conception is necessary to sustain adversarial legal systems. Lawyers representing clients before adjudicators – be they judges, arbitrators, administrative decision-makers, etc. – are asked to persuade, and effective advocacy in these circumstances demands partisanship. This is especially true in circumstances where the legal dispute presents as a zero-sum contest. Importantly, the web of procedural and substantive rules that govern dispute resolution facilitate partisan and neutral approaches in much the same manner as lawyers' professional norms. Just as importantly, adversarial systems by their very nature offer non-trivial protection against zealous advocacy's extreme effects. The risk of tribunals being misled or improperly briefed by lawyers is at least partially minimized by the presence of opposing parties that are available to contest claims. As Schwartz explains, adversaries are present to "challenge the client's statement of the facts, to sharpen the issues, to seek clarification of positions, or to point to countervailing considerations."[19] Put squarely, the adversarial tradition expressly contemplates zealous advocacy; in fact, it depends on self-interested, partisan lawyers to supply tribunals with the information necessary for lawmaking. In a stylized adversarial litigation model, the courts' inquisitorial research function is effectively outsourced to the litigants who are responsible for supplying and framing the evidence that serves as source material for decision-making.

Second, the standard conception is critical to protecting rights. Take, as one example, a criminal defence lawyer who represents a client accused of committing a murder. Few observers will argue that the lawyer in this case is – if the client is indeed guilty – aiding and abetting a homicide. But in the counterfactual where lawyers share some moral responsibility for their clients' aims and ends, the lawyer would suffer a consequence, reputational or otherwise, for taking on the representative role. This creates a significant disincentive to representing the accused. Indeed, it would also similarly disincentivize lawyers from pursuing cases involving unpopular clients and causes, which can have the long-tail consequences of undermining courts' counter-majoritarian function. Legal ethicists have long pointed to lawyers' role in representing the unpopular clients as part of the profession's *moral* self-justification.[20] By this argument, the salient moral relationship is not the one between the lawyer and the case outcome, nor is it necessarily the one between the lawyer and the client. Instead, the enterprise is justified by the lawyer's critical relationship to the legal system as a whole.

These justifications for the standard conception become considerably less compelling when you consider the modern legal profession in its fuller, more modern scope. In this sense, the standard conception is outmoded. It tends to contemplate a traditional lawyer-client relationship, wherein the lawyer acts as an advocate, typically before a tribunal or in some representative capacity that demands argument. This dramatically underestimates the heterogeneity of lawyer tasks. Lawyers act as advisors, enablers, facilitators, documenters, adjudicators, *and* advocates, among other roles. Sometimes, these tasks are performed outside the narrow strictures of "legal practice," wherein lawyers perform roles that do not demand, but benefit from, their expertise and licensure.[21]

This, of course, challenges legal ethics' already limited institutional reach. The lawyers involved in framing climate change rules and programs, for instance, will tend to escape regulation by legal-ethical regimes because those rules tend to only apply chiefly in lawyer-client contexts. This problem exists beyond the climate change context, of course; legal ethics rules tend not to cover such garden variety lawyer activities as plea bargaining, let alone lawyers' involvement in such large stakes matters as national security and international trade.

2. *Legal Ethics Rules as Minimum Standards*

In addition to resting on the outmoded, amoral standard conception, legal ethics regimes tend to promulgate limited, narrow rules.[22] Indeed, a rather substantial literature rehearses the view that legal ethics adjudication too frequently involves the mechanical application of rules found in professional codes.[23] This phenomenon, which I call here "rule-dominance," is best described by Vincent Johnson, writing:

> As viewed from many perspectives, legal ethics is now focused heavily on uniform compliance with codified rules, rather than on individual decision-making based on moral principles. There are many indicia of the shift. Some of the more visible developments of the current preeminence of codified rules are the continuing revision of codified standards, the widespread use of a standardized professional responsibility exam as a precondition for admission to practice, [and] the proliferation of rule-oriented ethics treatises ...[24]

The choice to emphasize "minimum compliance" may in fact account – at least partially – for the divergence between professional responsibility rules and ordinary morality that is so often bemoaned by legal ethicists. Perhaps by articulating minimum standards of conduct, typically expressed in legalistic terms, the lawyer is discouraged from thinking of herself as a moral agent, particularly where her own judgment counsels a different verdict than the professional rules. As a result, legal ethics becomes an exercise in sanctions avoidance. There is some limited empirical support for these intuitions. In a recent study, Galoob and Li used fact scenarios sampled from the Multistate Professional Responsibility Examination (MPRE)[25] to survey 122 lay participants, finding that the participants' judgments about the proper ethical response frequently differed from the actions demanded by the American Bar Association (ABA)'s *Model Rules of Professional Conduct*, the document that influenced the overwhelming majority of state bar rules.[26]

This was not always the case. Scholars have identified a self-conscious shift on the part of legal ethics institutions from more aspirational rules to highly specific and legalistic rules aimed at contending with the needs of a growing, diversifying, increasingly multi-jurisdictional, and increasingly lucrative profession.[27] Using the United States as an example, consider that early legal ethics codes were designed much more as "aspirational principles for good deportment" than as enforceable disciplinary rules.[28] The ABA's 1908 Canons of Professional Ethics (henceforth the "Canons"), for instance, made clear at the outset of the document that it could not "particularize all of the duties of the lawyer."[29] Subsequently, the 1969 Code of Professional Ethics (or the "Model Code"), was a mixture of the so-called "aspirational principles" of the Canons but included statements that observers would recognize as rules of professional discipline. This combination was often impractical; as Hazard has argued, enforcers of legal ethics rules were sometimes misapprehending the broad, open-ended statements as if they were clear rules.[30] In this key regard, the Model Code was fundamentally imbalanced, as it attempted to hold the profession to the aspirations similar to the Canons, but also hold lawyers to specific ethical commands.

It became readily apparent that the Model Code needed a substantial overhaul[31] The document was revised nine times in the next decade.[32] These revisions happened against the backdrop of a profession undergoing significant change, namely that it was growing, diversifying, and expanding beyond its local origins. Using the United States as an example, consider that the profession experienced sizeable year-on-year growth in the sheer number of active lawyers in just the decade after the Model Code was enacted.[33] Similar growth was observable in Canada, Australia, and New Zealand, among many others. Relatedly, the profession became more diverse. To the extent that the Model Code articulated professional virtues, it articulated the professional virtues of a community with members who were familiar to one another. By the time that the Model Code was being enforced, not only had the demographics of the legal profession meaningfully shifted, but the profession became less fixed to its location: practices crossed state boundaries, and a much broader subset of the population showed an interest in pursuing legal careers.[34] Not only did the Model Code seem more out of step with these demographic realities, but its subject matter was also increasingly limited. A cursory glance at the Model Code reveals that it clearly contemplated traditional litigation – often by smaller law offices or even single lawyers. By 1983, when the Model Rules – which influenced the ultimate Law Society of Ontario's *Rules of Professional Conduct* – were introduced, the legal profession could be more aptly described as lucrative industry than a community. The content of the Model Rules was a radical departure from the Model Code and the Canons that predated it; unlike those documents, the Model Rules were more recognizably "law" in the sense that they prohibited certain conduct, prescribed particularized enforcement, and had more statute-like features. Yet the ambitiousness that characterized the Model Code and Canons was no longer evident; instead, the Model Rules – and many of today's legal ethics codes – articulated conditions for *minimum* compliance.[35]

This "minimum standards" approach has the effect of codifying and institutionalizing the standard conception. This is not to say that such rules are not useful in specific contexts; one can argue that strict rules encouraging minimum standards of conduct are especially helpful for day-to-day, garden variety practice, particularly in settings wherein excessive moral deliberation could lead to unpredictability. Specific rules also have the benefit of optimizing enforcement and error costs: enforcement costs are lowered by the relative ease with which violations of specific rules are proven, and error becomes less likely where the rules offer clear commands.[36]

But even with this established, some consequences flow from the rules as minimum standards. First, the rules do not necessarily demand "ethical deliberation."[37] As Benjamin H. Barton writes:

> Black letter rules trigger a particular mode of thinking-or heuristic-in lawyers: we are trained to read carefully and to analyze rules to find (as precisely as possible) the boundary between legal and illegal behavior. When lawyers apply this same boundary-seeking process to issues of ethics or professional responsibility, the search for the border between permitted and proscribed behavior frequently displaces any consideration of the more general ethical question: "is this the right thing to do?"[38]

Li Feldman makes a related point about "statutory codes of professional ethics," explaining that they encourage lawyers to engage in "technocratic" analyses of rules. To put it simply, lawyers in these quasi-statutory regimes employ a different mode of reasoning than lawyers in aspirational legal-ethical regimes. For example, where the predecessor documents to the Model Rules might have encouraged lawyers to consider the morality of a given action, a minimum statute-like legal ethics rule might instead encourage the lawyer to adopt a course of action that avoids the rule's sanction. Here, modern legal ethics codes "promote a disjuncture between the reasoning processes that make one an effective lawyer, and the reasoning processes that make one an ethical lawyer."[39]

IV. Legal Ethics as a Site for Climate Intervention

Taken together, the enduring influence of the standard conception of lawyering as well as the preference for narrow, minimum standard-style legal ethics rules makes it difficult to conceive of lawyers as a site for climate interventions. Yet legal ethics presents an underexplored lever for climate change efforts. Lawyers are deeply implicated in the climate crisis in at least three distinct roles. First, lawyers serve their traditional function of advocating for the interests of clients who manufacture environmental harm. Here, lawyers cloak themselves in the standard conception's protective imprimatur, even in the face of evidence that their work indirectly exacerbates climate change. A study by the student group Law Students for Climate Accountability examined the Vault 100 list of law firms and found that, in the period from 2017 to 2022, these firms had 420 "total representations" that "exacerbated climate change."[40] Incidentally, pro bono legal representation of environmental organizations and interests declined precipitously; according to the Corporate Pro Bono Institute, "the percentage of pro bono environmental law work within corporate law departments dropped from a paltry 6 per cent in 2012 to an even more startling 2 per cent in 2020."[41]

Notably, some of lawyers' corporate advocacy work involved attempts to actively stymy climate management policy. As one example, consider *Rhode Island v. Chevron*, a 2020 case. There, the state of Rhode Island sued numerous major oil producers alleging

> ... that since the mid-20th century, the production and use of fossil fuel products has directly and substantially contributed to the dramatic rise in emissions of greenhouse gas pollution and increased carbon dioxide (CO2) concentrations in the atmosphere. *Id.* According to Plaintiff, the increase in anthropogenic (human-caused) greenhouse gas pollution, primarily in the form of CO2 emissions, constitutes the dominant cause of global climate change. Plaintiff contends that climate change results in severe damage to the globe, "including, but not limited to, sea level rise, disruption to the hydrologic cycle, more frequent and more intense drought, more frequent and more extreme precipitation, more frequent and more intense heatwaves, and associated consequences of those physical and environmental changes. Plaintiff claims that the main cause of greenhouse gas pollution is the extraction, production, and consumption of coal, oil and natural gas, commonly referred to as fossil fuels products (internal citations omitted).

No fewer than 11 of the Vault 100 firms represented defendants in the case. The study also found that these firms also accepted millions of dollars to lobby on behalf of fossil fuel companies' interests before the government. Only in the peculiar moral universe of the standard conception could an individual work around the clock to undermine climate regulation and still *not* be considered responsible for helping to exacerbate climate change.

In addition to these traditional advocacy relationships, lawyers are also involved in climate change as *facilitators* of environmental harm.

As a simple, factual matter, lawyers assisting with fossil fuel transactions participate in an industry proven to exacerbate the climate crisis. The question remains: have lawyers then behaved unethically? As it stands, legal ethics has little to say about this. In fact, this transactional context poses a distinct challenge. The outer limit of illegality operates on transactional lawyers in the standard conception, too, but the opportunities for strategic unethical behaviour are plenty. This is especially true when contrasted with lawyers engaged in advocacy before a tribunal. In those contexts, lawyers must perform their tasks in plain view of courts, which have the ability constrain unethical behaviour from the bench by imposing sanctions. Moreover, as discussed earlier in this chapter, advocacy in litigation is performed in an adversarial posture, which means there is an opposing party that is present to contest and undermine claims. This adversarial posture often disincentivizes unethical practice, at least in part because it leaves litigants vulnerable to opposing parties who may, in their own strategic wisdom, appraise the tribunal of unethical behaviour. Even where circumstances might not demand a legal sanction, judges have the latitude, in most adversarial systems, to constrain lawyer behaviour by criticizing or reprimanding "from the bench," so to speak, for example, when lawyers engage in unduly sharp strategy or bring frivolous litigation. Of course, such reputational sanctions can have bottom-line consequences; clients can terminate their lawyers, and lawyers can see diminished future engagements. In these contexts, the court operates as an external monitor of lawyer ethicality.[42] Such oversight is unavailable in most transactional contexts.

Finally, in addition to acting as advocates for climate-opposed interests and acting as transactional facilitators for climate-opposed capital, lawyers are also developing significant compliance expertise vis-à-vis the new web of climate-related laws, regulations, policies, and programs. Much like a tax lawyer advising clients about changes to the *Income Tax Act*, lawyers advise clients on environmental regulatory compliance across industries. One large international law firm describes the value of its "Climate Change/Carbon Management" practice as follows: "As climate change law and regulation are rapidly developing, we advise and represent major industry associations and corporations in the transportation, energy, and consumer-product sectors on greenhouse gas (GHG) emissions inventories, control measures, and credit and trading issues arising under domestic and international regulatory regimes."[43] That elite legal service providers are counseling on emissions-reductions efforts does not in and of itself pose an ethical issue, but much as in the transactional context, compliance advising frequently takes the form of sanctions avoidance. At a minimum, these emergent practice areas place lawyers opposite the public interest that regulators – not necessarily legal ethics regimes, but other administrative regulators such as environmental protection agencies – are duty-bound to protect. In ideal circumstances, there is interest convergence. For example, lawyers may advise corporate clients about the appropriate method for fully remediating contaminated worksites, but the lawyer's principal concern under the standard conception is to limit the client's liability and exposure to regulatory scrutiny. Whether the client continues to engage in affirmative business behaviour that creates more contaminated sites is largely besides the point, and perhaps more importantly, beyond a lawyer's traditional remit to constrain.

1. Redrawing the Profession's Boundaries

As it stands, legal ethics' relative impotence vis-à-vis the climate crisis – and, indeed, many complex social phenomena not expressly contemplated by the rules – is well-established but not inevitable. The primary barriers to meaningful lawyer regulation have less to do with the specifics of legal ethics rules or their particular legal content. Instead, they relate chiefly to how legal ethics' regimes are an institutional expression of the profession's antiquated self-image: as being lawyers necessarily representing clients, often before tribunals, in a fixed locale. Even the most casual observer of the legal profession recognizes this is an inapt description, and scholars have since demonstrated substantial diversity among types of lawyers and types of lawyerly tasks. Dana Remus describes this outmoded self-image as the "traditional model," and recognizes it as "eschewed by most scholars but still espoused by bar leaders."[44] The competing "segmented model," Remus explains, contemplates such "specialization and fragmentation" that fundamentally undermines the previous view of the profession as a cohesive whole.[45] This is partly because of the proliferation of non-litigation lawyer roles, but perhaps the more significant challenge to the traditional model is the proliferation of lawyers outside conventional lawyer-client relationships (e.g., lawyers in business or government, exercising roles "for which legal training is valuable but licensure is not required"[46]). These settings tend not to be meaningfully covered by legal ethics rules, especially not with the kind of specificity that can reasonably guide the ex-ante behaviour of lawyers working as advisors, for instance.

One model for holding lawyers to account for their role in exacerbating climate change is to imagine context-specific heightened duties.

Lawyers operating in the environmental domain, for instance, could be subject to duties that required them to engage in ethical deliberation not only as client representatives but also as environmental stewards. This idea is not without precedent; consider, for example, the oft-cited case involving the New York firm Kaye, Scholer, Fierman, Hays & Handler LLP (for these purposes "Kaye Scholer," now Arnold Porter Kaye Sholer LLP).[47] Kaye Scholer lawyers represented the Lincoln Savings and Loan Association. On account of its alleged "failure to disclose problems with the underwriting and investment practices of its client," the Office of Thrift Supervision (OTS) charged the firm and sought to recover hundreds of millions of dollars. The case eventually settled with a substantial payment to the government and two Kaye Scholer partners agreeing to a ban on representing any financial institutions. Along the way, however, OTS took the extraordinary step of freezing Kaye Scholer's assets. Though scholars have observed that the OTS may have been "heavy-handed" in freezing Kaye Scholer's assets (perhaps as a way to encourage speedy settlement), the chief takeaway is that the government considered Kaye Scholer to have a responsibility in the banking context that exceeded what is available in legal ethics codes.[48]

The Kaye Scholer example effectively created an ethical duty to a specific third party: here, the Office of Thrift Supervision. A heightened standard of conduct would not create a specific third-party ethical obligation for lawyers but would mandate that lawyers consider their client's demands in the context of an additional environmental consideration. This approach does not dramatically differ from lawyers' fidelity to the rule of law generally. In that context, lawyers balance client interests against not only the legality of a given course of action but also the extent to which that course of action violates principled community convention or undermines the integrity of the legal system. To the extent that lawyers have a third-party ethical obligation to uphold the rule of law, that obligation is expressed through the lawyer's role as an "officer of the court," but once again rests of a narrow formulation that excludes most lawyers that do not appear before judges. Expressing this heightened standard in terms of a form of "duty to deliberate" would ensure that lawyers who do not practise before environmental regulatory authorities still have to account for climate consequences.

Of course, this need not be adopted as a wholesale obligation to act as a public agent against client interests. The heightened standard of conduct could be more circumscribed depending on the context. Imagine a situation, for instance, where legislatures' examination reveals that large-scale polluters tend to underreport or conceal emissions.

Legislation may specify that lawyers involved in relevant representation have a heightened duty of candour or disclosure in that context. Importantly, any such duty of disclosure would still respect the integrity of the dyadic lawyer-client relationship. For instance, a heightened duty of disclosure about environmental risk, for instance, would require lawyers to advise their clients to share information with the appropriate regulators as necessary. Lawyers still have the option of terminating the representation in situations where they are unable to adequately discharge this duty. In other words, heightened duties do not necessarily demand that lawyers act as whistleblowers. As Wilkins explains, this could be modular: lawyers acting for clients in court would be able to do so zealously without necessarily running afoul of the stronger rules while litigating, whereas lawyers acting for clients in transactional or advisory settings would be more closely scrutinized.[49]

A more forceful expression of this approach would be to consider whether guidelines for lawyer conduct can be expressed in other substantive or procedural laws. Consider, as one example, the US federal law known as the *Sarbanes-Oxley Act of 2002* (Sarbanes-Oxley).[50] The law has the stated purpose of "protect[ing] investors by improving the accuracy and reliability of corporate disclosures made pursuant to securities laws," among other purposes.[51] Recognizing the centrality of lawyers to this objective, section 307 of Sarbanes-Oxley is titled "Rules of Professional Responsibility for Attorneys."[52] It empowers the US Securities and Exchanges Commission (SEC) to require "minimum standards of professional conduct"[53] from lawyers who appear before the SEC, and requires lawyers to report breaches – including of fiduciary duties – to either the most senior legal officer or executive of the corporation.[54] This robust requirement recognizes that lawyers are central to executing the legislation's overarching goal of maintaining the financial system's integrity and, accordingly, places corresponding duties upon them. Future legislation could similarly require that lawyers make regulators aware of any material harms that their client creates in contravention of the applicable environmental rules. More contextually informed legal ethics rules, however, would obviate the need for these sorts of statutory obligations.[55]

V. Conclusion

The case for pulling on legal ethics' available levers in circumstances where lawyers exacerbate climate change is a compelling one, albeit one motivated by a lack of meaningful alternatives. Indeed, the limited reach of legal ethics rules on account of the preference for narrow, minimum standards, coupled with the standard conception's tendency to relieve lawyers of moral culpability, combine to create a situation where lawyer behaviour vis-à-vis climate change is effectively unregulated and even unscrutinized. Lawyers operate in a liminal space here that even bad actor clients do not. A corporation that emits more than its reasonable share of GHGs will risk a regulatory sanction. By contrast, legal ethics cares little about whether a lawyer later advises that same company on techniques for avoiding those sanctions, even if the result in both circumstances is more GHG emissions without recompense.

As it is currently conceived, legal ethics is ineffective at constraining unethical lawyer behaviour that is not obviously illegal and not expressly contemplated by the narrow professional discipline rules. The standard conception of lawyering, which casts lawyers as neutral, partisan, and non-accountable actors prevents the kind of day-to-day moral deliberation that confronting challenges at the scale of climate change will inevitably require.

NOTES

1 Perhaps the most forceful statement about the extent to which legal ethics "depart[s] from ordinary morality" comes from Daniel Markovits: "I claim that lawyers come under professional obligations to display certain characteristically lawyerly vices – to lie and cheat." Daniel Markovits, "Three Issues in Legal Ethics" (2010) 60:4 UTLJ 1003, online: <https://doi.org/10.1353/tlj.2010.0013>. Markovits develops this view in detail in Daniel Markovits, *A Modern Legal Ethics: Adversary Advocacy in a Democratic Age* (Princeton, NJ: Princeton University Press, 2008), online: <https://doi.org/10.1515/9781400828982>. An earlier example of this view was advanced in Gerald Postema, "Moral Responsibility in Professional Ethics" (1980) 55 NYU L Rev 63 ("when professional action is cut off from ordinary moral experience, the lawyer's sensitivity to the moral costs in both ordinary and extraordinary situations tends to atrophy"). It is worth noting that this view has been contested by others. Alice Woolley argues that Markovits underappreciates the extent to which the rules governing lawyers do indeed constrain lawyer behaviour, particularly partisanship, while Tim Dare also argues that lawyers embrace "role-differentiated norms" that allow them to preserve personal integrity while reflecting and indeed grounding their role in ordinary morality; Alice Woolley, "If Philosophical Legal Ethics Is the Answer, What Is the Question?" (2010) 60:4 UTLJ 983, online: <https://doi.org/10.1353/tlj.2010.0012>; Tim Dare, "Philosophical Legal Ethics and Personal Integrity" (2010) 60:4 UTLJ 1021, online: <https://doi.org/10.1353/tlj.2010.0006>.

2 See generally, William H. Simon, "Ethical Discretion in Lawyers" (1988) 101:6 Harv L Rev 1083, online: <https://doi.org/10.2307/1341488>.

3 Chris Tollefson provides a helpful description of what SLAPPs are all about: ""[u]nlike other plaintiffs, a SLAPP filer's main concern is, by definition, not monetary compensation or other legal remedies to correct a wrong or grievance. The decision to proceed with a SLAPP is usually a highly tactical one, forming part of a larger strategy." See Chris Tollefson, "Strategic Lawsuits Against Public Participation: Developing a Canadian Response (1994) 73:2 Can Bar Rev 201 at 206.

4 William H. Simon, "The Trouble with Legal Ethics" (1991) 41 J Leg Educ 65.

5 One need not look very hard to find dozens of articles from lawyers lamenting the so-called decline of professionalism despite the proliferation of rules. See, e.g., Sean P. Ravenel, "The Contagion of Example: Attacking the Root of the Problem in Lawyer Professionalism" (2001) 49 The Federal Lawyer 10 (Explaining that there is "no question" of a crisis of professionalism and noting that "attorneys tend to look at nothing but the rules, and if their conduct meets the minimum standard, their inquiries end"). Also, see generally Don J. Young & Louise L. Hill, "Professionalism: The Necessity for Internal Control" (1988) 61 Temple L Rev 205.

6 *See* W. Bradley Wendel, "Public Values and Professional Responsibility" (1999) 75 Notre Dame L Rev 1.

7 Simon, *supra* note 4.

8 See Tanina Rostain, "Ethics Lost: Limitations of Current Approaches to Lawyer Regulation" (1997) 71 S Cal L Rev 1273 (arguing that regulation is "a poor substitute for legal ethics" and that a "regulatory approach is inadequate to ensure that lawyer-made law serves broader societal purposes").

9 Patrick J. Schiltz, "Legal Ethics in Decline: The Elite Law Firm, the Elite Law School, and the Moral Formation of the Novice Attorney," 82 Minn L Rev 705 (takes the view that lawyers professional lives are "dominated by greed").

10 Warren E. Burger, "The Decline of Professionalism" (1995) 63 Fordham L Rev 949 (describes the conversion to standards of conduct from professional ideals as a "fundamental and more urgent problem facing the legal profession" than the adequacy of legal services or lack of advocacy skills. Chief Justice Burger continues: "The law is not and never has been a 'business.' But we are well on the way to making it less than a profession.") (internal quotations omitted). See also Rebecca Roiphe, "The Decline of Professionalism" (2016) 29 Geo J Leg Ethics 649 (Arguing that the "traditional understanding of the professions was lost as a market ideology took hold in the 1970s" and "professionalism gradually became synonymous with the delivery of services")

11 Sang Hui Kim credits Richard Wasserstrom for starting the debate about the standard conception with his 1975 article "Lawyers as Professionals: Some Moral Issues." Sung Hui Kim, "Economic Inequality, Access to Law, and Mandatory Arbitration Agreements: A Comment on the Standard Conception of the Lawyer's Role" (2020) 88 Fordham L Rev 1665, citing Richard Wasserstrom, "Lawyers as Professionals: Some Moral Issues" (1975) 5 Human Rights 1.

12 Wendel, *supra* note 6 at 8.

13 Kim, *supra* note 11.

14 *Ibid.*

15 David Luban & W. Bradley Wendel, "Philosophical Legal Ethics: An Affectionate History" (2017) 30:3 Geo J Leg Ethics 337, online: <https://doi.org/10.31228/osf.io/fh6ry>.

16 Murray L. Schwartz, "The Zeal of the Civil Advocate" (1983) 8:3 American Bar Foundation Research Journal 543, online: <https://doi.org/10.1086/492024>.

17 See generally Federation of Law Societies of Canada, *Model Code of Professional Conduct* (Ottawa: Federation of Law Societies of Canada, 2022) and American Bar Association, *Model Rules of Professional Conduct* (Chicago: ABA, 2023).

18 Wasserstrom, *supra* note 11.

19 Murray L. Schwartz, "The Professionalism and Accountability of Lawyers" (1978) 66:4 Cal L Rev 669, online: <https://doi.org/10.2307/3479964>.

20 Stephen Jones, "A Lawyer's Ethical Duty to Represent the Unpopular Client" (1998) 1:1 Chap L Rev 105.

21 See, e.g., Barbara A. Spellman, "Reflections of a Recovering Lawyer: How Becoming a Cognitive Psychologist – And (In Particular) Studying Analogical and Causal Reasoning – Changed My Views about the Field of Psychology and Law" (2004) 79 Chicago-Kent L Rev 1185.

22 Here, I largely focus on the "rules" as found in the American Bar Association's *Model Rules of Professional Conduct* and the Federation of Law Societies' of Ontario's *Model Rules of Professional Conduct*.

23 As a preliminary matter, it is worth noting that rule-dominance in legal ethics was not always the norm. In 1969, the American Bar Association promulgated the Model Code of Professional Responsibility which, according to Johnson, "was a milestone in the transformation of principles of legal ethics into enforceable rules of law. State rules patterned on the Code were widely enacted." See Vincent R. Johnson, "The Virtues and Limits of Codes in Legal Ethics" (2000) 14 Notre Dane JL Ethics & Pub Pol'y 25 at 27.

24 *Ibid.*

25 This is a mandatory exam for admission to the bar in all US jurisdictions except Wisconsin and Puerto Rico. As Ariens explains, the test "is based substantially on the model rules." Michael S. Ariens, "The Ethics of Copyrighting Ethics Rules" (2005) 36 U Tol L Rev 235 at 237.

26 See generally Stephen Galoob & Su Li, "Are Legal Ethics Ethical? A Survey Experiment" (2013) 26 Geo J Leg Ethics 481 (finding that "Results from a survey experiment suggest that legal ethics rules about advocacy and confidentiality diverge from lay moral judgments; that lay judgments do not, in general, attribute distinctive moral significance to the lawyer's role; and that norms of professional conduct can change (but do not fully determine) the ordinary moral status of lawyers' actions")

27 See generally Benjamin H. Barton, "The ABA, the Rules, and Professionalism: The Mechanics of Self-Defeat and a Call for a Return to the Ethical, Moral, and Practical Approach of the Canons" (2004) UTK Law Faculty Publications 233.

28 The religious influence on early legal ethics codes cannot be understated. As Ariens notes, the 1908 Canons were based on the professional discipline code for lawyers in the State of Alabama: "Alabama's Code of Ethics, in turn, was based on Judge George Sharswood's 1854 A Compend of Lectures." Sharswood's writing on legal ethics was highly influenced by his reverence for religious institutions. For more on this point, see Bruce A. Kimball, *The True Professional Ideal in America: A History* (Hoboken: Blackwell Publishing, 1992), quoting George Sharswood stating that "[t]here is, perhaps, no profession, after that of the sacred ministry, in which morality is more imperatively necessary than that of the law".

29 "Preamble" in American Bar Association, *Canons of Professional Ethics* (Washington DC: American Bar Association, 1908).

30 Geoffrey C. Hazard Jr., "Legal Ethics: Legal Rules and Professional Aspirations" (1981) 30 Clev St L Rev 571 at 573 ("What has happened is that the Canons and the Ethical Considerations – although supposed to be only aspirational – have been relied on by courts and disciplinary committees as though they were black letter rules").

31 See Young & Hill, *supra* note 5.

32 "Preamble" in American Bar Association, *ABA Model Code of Professional Responsibility* (Washington DC: American Bar Association, 1969): "The Model Code of Professional Responsibility was adopted by the House of Delegates of the American Bar Association on August 12, 1969 and was amended by the House of Delegates in February 1970, February 1974, February 1975, August 1976, August 1977, August 1978, February 1979, February 1980, and August 1980."

33 American Bar Association, "ABA National Lawyer Population Survey: Historical Trend in Total National Lawyer Population, 1878–2022" (2022),

online (pdf): <https://www.americanbar.org/content/dam/aba/administrative/market_research/total-national-lawyer-population-1878-2022.pdf>.

34 Susan Ehrlich Martin and Nancy C. Jurik note that as the number of lawyers grew, the legal profession gradually lost "control over its composition. Restrictions on the training of lawyers prior to 1960 led to a shortage of lawyers, expansion in the number of law schools in the 1960s, and willingness to turn to less expensive women lawyers by the 1970s. Greater demand also led to higher starting salaries that, in turn, made the law a more attractive career option. The civil rights, women's, consumers,' and environmental movements of the 1960s expanded new areas of the law and the demand for lawyers. As racial and sexual barriers to entry into law fell, the number of aspiring lawyers more than doubled, while the number of law schools rose by 25 percent." See Susan Ehrlich Martin & Nancy C. Jurik, *Doing Justice, Doing Gender: Women in Legal and Criminal Justice Occupations* (Thousand Oaks, CA: SAGE Publications Inc, 2007) at 112.

35 Even in the rare cases where old rules from the Canons and Model Code were narrow and specific, the Model Rules turned them into even brighter lines. As one notable example, consider Model Rule 4.2, which bars lawyers from speaking to another lawyer's client in the context of an active litigation. Rule 4.2 is an updated version of Canon 9, which stated that a "lawyer should not in any way communicate upon the subject of controversy with a party represented by counsel; much less should he undertake to negotiate or compromise the matter with him, but should deal only with his counsel." This rule was rather specific for the Canons but was primarily being used as a rule of evidence. When the Model Rules came along, Hazard explains, it became a "prophylactic" rule aimed at protecting opposing clients. See Geoffrey C. Hazard Jr. & Dana Remus Irwin, "Toward a Revised 4.2 No-Contact Rule" (2008) 60 Hastings LJ 797 at 799–800.

36 See William Landes & Richard Posner, "The Economics of Anticipatory Adjudication" (1994) 23 J Leg Stud 683, 684-6, online: <https://doi.org/10.1086/467942>.

37 Heidi Li Feldman, "Codes and Virtues: Can Good Lawyers be Good Ethical Dliberators?" (1996) 69 S Cal L Rev 885 at 885.

38 Benjamin H. Barton, "The ABA, the Rules, and Professionalism: The Mechanics of Self-Defeat and a Call for a Return to the Ethical, Moral, and Practical Approach of the Canon" (2005) 83 NCL Rev 411 at 423–4.

39 Abdi Aidid, "Juridification and Regulating the Modern Lawyer" (2024) 37:3 Geo J L Ethics 457 at 487.

40 Law Students for Climate Accountability, *The 2021 Law Firm Climate Change Scorecard* (Washington DC: Law Students for Climate Accountability, 2021), online (pdf): <https://static1.squarespace.com/static/646e3b899493ae261720e957/t/648bda51d48b0a65991d8430/1686887000203/2021%2BLaw%2BFirm%2BClimate%2BChange%2BScorecard.pdf>.

41 Catherine Rocchi & Camila Bustos, "Lawyers Exacerbate the Climate Crisis: Here's How We Can Help," *American Bar Association* (28 August 2022), online: <https://www.americanbar.org/groups/environment_energy_resources/publications/trends/2022-2023/september-october-2022/lawyers-exacerbate-the-climate-crisis/>.

42 See Aidid, *supra* note 39 at 489.

43 Alston & Bird, "Climate Change/Carbon Management" (last accessed 11 August 2023), online: <https://www.alston.com/en/services/practices/regulatory-specialty/environment-land-use-natural-resources/environmental-compliance-permitting-transactions/climate-change-carbon-management>.

44 Dana A. Remus, "Out of Practice: The Twenty-First-Century Legal Profession" (2014) 63:3 Duke LJ 1243; David B. Wilkins, "Making Context Count: Regulating Lawyers after Kaye, Scholer" (1992–3) S Cal L Rev 1145.

45 Remus, *supra* note 44 at 1255.

46 *Ibid* at 1245.

47 Lawrence J. Fox "OTS vs. Kay, Scholer: An Assault on the Citadel" (1993) 48:4 The Business Lawyer 1521 at 1591.

48 Fred C. Zacharias, "Understanding Recent Trends in Federal Regulation of Lawyers" (2004) University of San Diego Public Law and Legal Theory Research Paper Series, Research Paper No 21. Note that there has been criticism of the OTS' approach as being in tension with lawyers' confidentiality obligations. See e.g., Anthony E. Davis, "The Long Term Implications of the Kaye Scholer Case for Law Firm Management – Risk Management Comes of Age" 35 S Tex L Rev 677 at 682; and Frank Newton, "A Lawyer's Duty to the Legal System and to a Client Drawing the Line" 35 S Tex L Rev 701 at 705.

49 Wilkins, *supra* note 44.

50 *Sarbanes-Oxley Act of 2002*, Pub L No 107–204, 115 Stat 2390 et seq (2002).

51 *Ibid.*

52 *Ibid.*

53 Robert N. Rapp, "Commentary: Sarbanes-Oxley and SEC Standards of Professional Conduct" (2007) 57 Case W Res L Rev 365.

54 Peter J. Henning, "Sarbanes-Oxley Act s.307 and Corporate Counsel: Who Better to Prevent Corporate Crime?" (2004) 8 Buff Crim L Rev 323 at 324, online: <https://doi.org/10.1525/nclr.2004.8.1.323>.
55 David B. Wilkins, "Legal Realism for Lawyers" (1990) 104:2 Harv L Rev 468, online: <https://doi.org/10.2307/1341584>.

PART FIVE

Law, Technology, and Climate Change

13 Markets, Mobilization, and Transformation: Approaches to Innovation in Addressing Climate Change

BENJAMIN ALARIE AND ANDREW GREEN

I. Introduction

We face a huge challenge. Science tells us that we need rapid reduction in the emission of greenhouse gases (GHGs) to keep global temperatures below levels that threaten catastrophe. Even with aggressive action, significant harms are likely to occur and are, in fact, already occurring.[1] We need a massive transformation in how we live, including how we produce energy, how we manufacture goods, how we move around, and how we build our homes. Achieving this transformation requires us to develop and deploy new technologies that enable us to move rapidly towards a "net zero" economy.[2]

While impressive innovations in areas such as renewable energy have already occurred, much more is needed. We are at an important inflection point. Governments are slowly coming to terms with the lack of action in the past. They are developing new plans to reduce GHG emissions while at the same time growing the "green economy." Everyone is trying to "do well by doing good." How we move forward is going to have important implications – for the changes to our climate, for our economic health, for our sense of social trust and fairness.

Two broad but opposing narratives have emerged as contenders for grounding this transformation. The first of these contends that market-driven innovation, entrepreneurship, and competition are best able to foster technological advances and efficiency improvements. It prescribes an incremental and experimental approach based on the incentives and informational advantages of decentralized private markets. The second focuses on large-scale nation-state mobilization. This second approach emphasizes the role of government in coordinating and funding comprehensive efforts to transform energy systems and infrastructure.

These two approaches each have their merits and limitations, which correspond to the strengths and weaknesses of the other approach. The incremental and experimental approach has the potential to foster rapid innovation and adoption of new technologies, as market forces incentivize businesses to develop cost-effective solutions. However, this approach may not be sufficient to address systemic challenges or provide adequate support for the development and deployment of emerging technologies with significant public benefits but long-time horizons and uncertain returns on investment. It may also not bring about transformation as rapidly as would be required to avoid the worst consequences.

In contrast, the large-scale nation-state mobilization approach recognizes the need for coordinated action and investment to achieve transformative change in the face of a global crisis. By marshalling resources and aligning policy objectives, this approach can overcome barriers to innovation and infrastructure development that markets alone may not address and may potentially promote more rapid action. However, such an approach may also be prone to inefficiencies and bureaucratic obstacles, potentially hindering the rapid innovation and adaptation needed to address climate change. Governments on this approach must pick the winning strategy and bet heavily on it.

While the contest between market-based and government-led policies is a long-standing battle in a range of public policy areas, the nature of climate change makes specific elements of the question of the appropriate approach particularly challenging and critical. Section II of this chapter discusses the key features of climate change that make addressing it so difficult and then relates these features to the strengths and weaknesses of these two narratives. Section III uses two examples to highlight how these approaches manifest themselves in current policies: the recent broad policies in the United States and Canada to foster innovation, such as the recent enactment in the United States of the federal *Inflation Reduction Act* and the race to develop fusion as an energy source. Section IV discusses the path forward. Both approaches face significant political challenges. Ultimately a synthesized strategy that combines the strengths of both approaches will be most effective and politically feasible. By fostering public-private partnerships, encouraging innovation through targeted incentives, and leveraging government support to mobilize resources and remove barriers to clean energy deployment, a synthesized approach can harness the power of both market forces and coordinated government action. However, avoiding the weaknesses of each approach will require better institutional structures to allow fairer, more evidence-based decisions.[3]

II. Overview of Incremental and Nation-State Mobilization Approaches

In a contribution in this volume, Edward Iacobucci and Michael Trebilcock lay out the aspects of climate change that make it a "super wicked problem": scientific uncertainty such as around the possibility of catastrophe; technological uncertainty about the path of change; cognitive biases that limit our ability to understand and respond to the crisis; pervasive collective action and coordination problems across time and space; and the polycentric nature of decision-making that implicates trade-offs across contested values.[4] They point to how these features interact to make the choice of the governing institutions central and fraught.

For our purposes, several of these characteristics of climate change are particularly important to discussing these two approaches to transformational change. The first, and perhaps most fundamental, is the tremendous uncertainty about the potential for catastrophic impacts from climate change. As Stern, Stiglitz, and Taylor note, the key question is "how to respond to the deep uncertainty associated with climate change, where we know that we do not know how things may unfold, but we do know that there are scenarios, with not insignificant plausibility or probabilities, that have enormous consequences."[5] The latest report from the IPCC documents the current scientific understanding and brings greater but incomplete clarity.[6] According to Stern, Stiglitz, and Taylor, the residual uncertainty complicates what our ultimate goal of climate policy should be, how fast we need to get there, and potentially the paths that are open to us. They argue that the international community has adopted a "guardrail approach" to avoid most extreme outcomes, setting an objective of limiting global temperature increases to 1.5 °C.[7]

Second, the technological changes required to reduce GHG emissions are daunting. To meet the goals, the international community has set for itself (let alone any more aggressive goals that some say are necessary) "involves nothing less than the wholesale transition of our economy, industry, communities and homes."[8] We need to develop new technologies in areas such as energy generation and production of steel and cement as well as to determine how to deploy many new systems, which will involve seemingly intractable issues such as network effects.

Third, cognitive biases and limited understanding of the crisis hinder our ability to make well-informed decisions and implement effective policies. People tend to prioritize short-term gains over long-term benefits, underestimate the severity of the problem, and suffer from confirmation bias, which leads to the dismissal of information that contradicts their pre-existing beliefs. This makes it difficult to achieve consensus and support for transformational change, as well as to assess the true risks and benefits of potential solutions.[9]

Finally, our choices about the appropriate institutions to use to foster technological change have deep ethical implications. The speed and nature of our response to climate mitigation will have differential effects on present versus future generations as well as on people in different parts of the world.[10]

1. Incremental, Market-Based Approach

Given these challenges at the core of climate change, how can we foster the development and deployment of the technology needed to transform our economy and lives in the time required? The first approach is to lean into what we know has driven innovation and creativity in the past – the market. If, the argument goes, we can just price carbon rather than allow it to be emitted for free, market incentives will lead individuals and companies to invest in and create the technologies we need. The role of government is to make sure that the costs of GHG emissions are imposed on the market but other than that to remain technology neutral. There may be of course some limited role for government in dealing with basic network issues (such as the availability of electric vehicle chargers), but the main institutional player in this view should be the market. Government policies such as the appropriate carbon price or subsidies can be set using market-based mechanisms such as cost-benefit analysis based on the social cost of carbon.[11]

Markets of course have significant benefits. They can aggregate information on both the demand and supply side more efficiently than centralized decision-makers. This information is transmitted through price signals that can provide strong incentives for innovation. Companies and individuals can try different paths, potentially increasing the likelihood that an effective solution will be found. It permits the implementation of small steps and learning from what does and does not work. This method allows for iterative improvement and adaptation while minimizing risks of investing too heavily in any one pathway.[12]

However, this approach also comes with concerns. It rests on markets that properly consider the adverse effects of GHG emissions. A carbon price that is too low would not provide sufficient incentive to change behaviour and induce the proper level of innovation on its own. The price may be too low where, for example, models used to estimate the adverse effects fail to fully account for the nature of the damage from climate change.[13] Moreover, there is a risk for investors from the uncertainty about the carbon price in the future.[14]

Moreover, even if the carbon price could fully account for the harms caused by GHG emissions, there are other market failures that hinder a market-based approach to innovation and new technologies.[15] There are public goods aspects to new technologies, which means that those who develop or deploy the new technology may not be able to reap all the rewards (where, for example, others can appropriate information or where there are positive health co-benefits to reducing emissions), and hence, the technology will be underproduced. There may also be other negative externalities that the new technology creates that are not considered. Failures in related markets, such as capital markets, may also play a role. Further, some aspects of the technology may make reliance on markets alone troublesome. For example, increasing returns to scale can make the race to be first to develop or implement technologies especially important (including features such as network effects). At the same time, the nature of the implementation of such technology, such as the large, "lumpy" nature of investments in some forms of energy generation, can lead to a locking in of particular technologies.[16]

Even if the price system was adjusted and some of these market imperfections could be addressed, there is a risk of timing of this approach. The market approach may be too slow and too marginal to bring about sufficiently rapid changes to address climate change. Seth Klein, for example, argues "So much of our climate-response policies to date can be summarized in four words: incentives, rebates, carbon pricing. We are fiddling at the margins while the planet burns, hoping that market signals can sufficiently alter household consumption and business incentives. They won't."[17] The market models do not adequately account for factors such as the deep uncertainty about the path of climate change with possible long latency periods for effects and unseen tipping points.[18]

Finally, market approaches embrace a single, and controversial, ethical approach to addressing climate change.[19] They imply a market approach to thinking about the trade-offs associated with present versus future generations. Models for setting carbon prices, for example, may incorporate market-based discount rates. Issues of intergenerational trade-offs may not be adequately, or consciously, addressed through an incremental, market-based approach.

2. *Nation-State Mobilization Approach*

A competing approach to addressing the challenge of change in the climate context is to argue that these extensive failures and ethical challenges of markets point to the need for government to decide the path forward. At the least, the concerns with the market-based approach suggest a role for government in seeking to eliminate the market failures. This role would encompass policies such as tax incentives or public support to account for the public goods nature of the development of technology, government lending programs to overcome difficulties in capital markets, or infrastructure spending to account for network effects.[20]

However, the deep uncertainty, non-linearity of effects, and potential for "tipping points"[21] make a slow, marginal approach insufficient, perhaps even if only focused on addressing market failures.[22] Klein, for example, analogizes to the mobilization of resources that occurred during the Second World War and the role of government in taking over production. While being "open to a mixed economy,"[23] he argues that a neoliberalist preference for markets and corporations must give way to a large government role in assessing the scale of electrification needed, coordinating mass production of equipment, investing billions in infrastructure, and creating new Crown corporations to carry the burden. Each sector would get its own plan, and the government must be nimble enough to adapt as new information arises.[24] The government needs to "prioritize and coordinate the use of scarce resources and key inputs for the task of producing what is needed."[25] In part, for Klein, the government can take such a role because it is less about coming up with new ideas than about doing what we know needs to be done.

In a similar, though perhaps less expansive way, Haley argues that Canada needs to move beyond tax measures to leverage public institutions and an "experimental industrial policy approach" to "actively re-shape economic and political environments."[26] Beck, Beugin, and Trottier-Chi also have called for a "sector-by-sector strategy that identifies the priority technologies and pathways that are expected to drive Canada's global competitiveness in a net zero future."[27] In addition, they argue that "high-exposure instruments" (policies that expose the government and the public to greater risk) be applied to "a limited number of high-risk-high reward projects," such as hydrogen fuel.[28]

This top-down, large-scale government mobilization approach has potential benefits. Foremost among them is speed. The government can quickly (though potentially not cheaply) foster action towards reducing emissions. Such speed is especially appealing in this context given the urgent need for action and, it is argued, the fact that we already have solutions needed to hit our targets.[29] Moreover, large public investments can help create new economic growth opportunities (such as allowing countries to take advantage of increasing returns to scale).

Beck, Beugin, and Trottier-Chi note that the government model has shifted from protecting the competitiveness of existing industries to attracting investment in new industries.[30] These investments can also potentially push the economy over a tipping point to a new, fossil fuel-free model and build new constituencies for climate action.[31]

However, this approach also raises concerns. It can lead to subsidizing a useful project more than is needed,[32] such as where some or all of the project would have been undertaken even without public funds. Perhaps more importantly, it can lead to money being spent on projects that are not useful or are less useful than the alternatives. The key concern is that centralized planning lacks the informational and coordination advantages of markets, leading to mistakes. Moreover, the potential for government largesse can lead to wasteful expenditures on lobbying by companies or communities seeking to capture these expenditures.

These opposing approaches to addressing change have strengths and raise concerns that mirror the other. The market-based incremental approach has the potential to leverage incentives and information, but it may also be too slow and subject to market failures. The government-mobilization, central planning approach may be quicker and lead to dramatic transformation, but it may also lead us down a wrong, or at least overly costly, path through government failures. Both are politically difficult to implement fully. The question to which we turn now is this: how much do current government policies look like these different approaches?

III. The Sliding Scale

The previous section set out two potentially stark approaches to transformation. However, while some policies are clearly in one camp or the other, it can be difficult to distinguish clearly between them. The market-based approach can involve considerable government action in attempting to address market failures. The mobilization approach can lean into markets to help foster the industrial strategy goals. In fact, these institutional forms can be placed on a spectrum, as in Figure 13.1. At one end is the market as it has been in the past – that is, without really considering climate change. It is not free of government intervention, of course, but we will take it as not accounting for climate change. As we move to the right, we add more government policies to correct climate-related market failures. The first move, favoured by economists, is to incorporate the harm done by GHG emissions through a carbon price. Even if that carbon price is sufficient to incorporate those harms, there are other forms of market failures tied directly to the development or

Figure 13.1. Spectrum of Institutional Responses

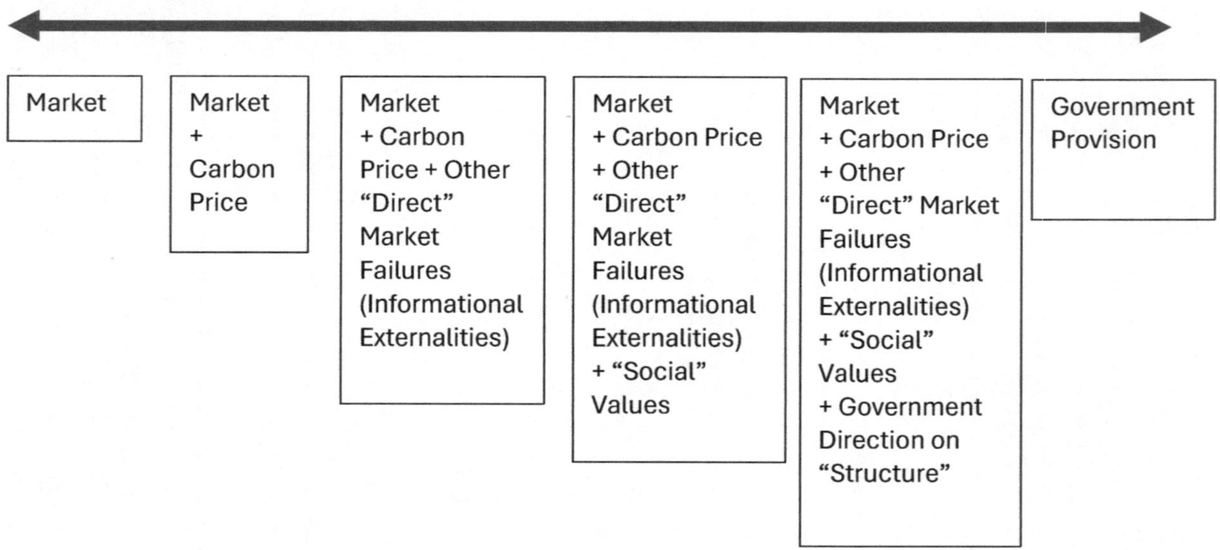

deployment of technology, such as the public goods nature of innovation, which arises because inventors may not be able to capture the entire value of their invention to the reduction of climate change.[33]

Beyond this form of correcting for direct market failures, governments may wish to account for broader social values or benefits that the markets cannot adequately reward. Such benefits include some tied closely to reduction in GHG emissions, such as the health "co-benefits" that come from the improved air pollution from the reduction in the burning of fossil fuels. The government may wish to go further and use climate policy to leverage markets but, at the same time, change aspects of those markets such as inequality through requiring certain labour conditions or wages or Indigenous reconciliation. The last step before the government undertaking the choice of allocation of resources and the production of goods is directing the allocation of resources to or away from specific technologies.

This spectrum of institutional forms can be seen in the recent steps taken by both the United States and Canadian federal governments. The Canadian federal government has instituted a carbon price. The strongest form of the market argument would be that if set correctly, the price will drive innovation and deployment of new technologies through the power of the market. The price, however, is too low presently and is unlikely to ever be sufficient to "solve" climate change on its own.[34] The political constraints on maintaining, let alone raising, the carbon price are daunting.

Both the United States and the Canadian governments have policies that at least in theory could be taken as aiming at eliminating market failures – both direct and more indirect. The US government has taken a massive step in this direction through the *Inflation Reduction Act* (*IRA*), which injects some US$380 billion into climate action.[35] The *IRA* offers tax breaks and financing to businesses and individuals investing in clean energy and technology, much of which is devoted to increasing demand for products ready for the market as opposed to innovation. It is designed to provide incentives for innovation by helping to bring new technologies to market. The United States also has the *CHIPS and Science Act*, which more directly encourages research and commercialization of energy and other green technology.[36] The idea is to use public funds to leverage private investment and drive market-based solutions to climate change and other environmental challenges.

The Canadian federal government attempted to respond in its 2023 budget.[37] The budget brings in broad-based tax credits, some ostensibly not aimed at any specific technology but instead focus on "clean technology," "clean electricity," and "clean manufacturing." There is of course an element of tailoring in specifying eligible equipment. More tailored are the tax credits for "clean hydrogen" (up to a 40 per cent tax credit for investment in specified forms of equipment for producing hydrogen) and for carbon capture, utilization, and storage (CCUS), although these too are defined fairly broadly. The budget also sets up a system of special financing that is meant to account for the risks in undertaking research and deployment in these areas. These subsidies could be seen as accounting for the market failures in innovation and deployment of technologies in this area.

It is, of course, not clear if the subsidies fully address the direct market failures, let alone consider broader social benefits such as the health co-benefits. It is clear, however, that both governments have used these programs to attempt to address other social goals more broadly. Both, for example, condition some of their programs on wage conditions. The Canadian government also in some cases has layered on conditions concerning Indigenous management. In theory, the market still runs but the direction is gently guided.

The US and Canadian governments also take greater steps to encourage specific technologies. The Canadian government, for example, has set up a Canada Growth Fund, is intended to support private investment through better-than-market financing terms. An issue will be how these successful projects will be chosen. Finally, the US and Canadian governments are directly involved in some aspects of clean energy. In Ontario, for example, Crown corporations are largely responsible for electricity production and distribution. The federal government has fostered this use of government direction by providing tax credits to these entities.

The hope would be that the *IRA* and the Canadian budget measures set broad-based market correcting policies at the right level and choose wisely and in a coordinated manner the specific technologies they favour for promotion. Ideally, governments should tailor these institutional choices to the particular contexts in which they are situated. The Canadian government claims that it has taken a "more market-driven approach" than the United States.[38] However, a benefit of each approach is that they use a synthesized strategy, drawing on both the market-driven and mobilization approaches. As we discuss in the next section, the key will be the institutional framework for making these choices.

An example of how such a synthesis may operate is fusion technology. Fusion technology is potentially an excellent example of how a synthesis between market-driven and mobilization approaches can be achieved. As a clean and potentially abundant energy source, fusion has the potential to revolutionize the energy landscape and make significant strides in addressing climate change. However, the technology is still under development, and the path to commercialization is fraught with scientific, engineering, and economic challenges. The aspiration is that private enterprises and governments can work together, potentially even through public-private partnerships, to build on their strengths, share knowledge and technology, and grow a skilled workforce. It could accelerate the development of fusion technology as a viable solution to the world's energy challenges. Again, though, the institutions that govern these relationships will be central to an effective and fair development of technology.

There are numerous privately funded fusion start-ups, such as Commonwealth Fusion Systems, General Fusion, and Helion, racing to develop and commercialize fusion technology. These companies rely on private investment and competitive market forces to spur innovation, bring down costs, and ultimately deliver fusion energy to the market. At the same time, thirty-five nations are collaborating on ITER, which aims to build the world's largest tokamak, a magnetic fusion device designed to demonstrate the feasibility of fusion as a large-scale, carbon-free energy source. These government-supported mobilization approaches are also critical in advancing fusion technology. The ITER project aims to build the world's largest tokamak to demonstrate the feasibility of fusion as a viable energy source.[39] The ITER project exemplifies a massive mobilization effort, harnessing the collective resources, knowledge, and expertise of multiple nations in pursuit of a common goal.

Moreover, the lines between market and government mobilization are blurry, in keeping with the idea of the sliding scale. National governments play a key role in supporting fusion research and development through funding, regulation, and policy. For instance, the US Department of Energy has provided significant funding to private fusion companies through the Advanced Research Projects Agency-Energy (ARPA-E) program.[40] This government support not only helps to mitigate the risks associated with investing in cutting-edge technologies but also accelerates the pace of innovation and commercialization.

To maximize the potential of fusion technology, a balanced synthesis between market-driven and government mobilization approaches is essential. On the one hand, private companies should be encouraged to innovate, compete, and find the most efficient and cost-effective solutions to make fusion energy a reality as quickly as possible within the bounds of safety. On the other hand, governments and international collaborations must provide the necessary support, guidance, and resources to overcome the scientific and engineering challenges that private enterprises alone may not be able to tackle. By strategically leveraging both market-driven and mobilization approaches, fusion technology can be developed more rapidly and efficiently, contributing significantly to the fight against climate change and the transition towards a more sustainable and cleaner future.

IV. Conclusion: The Importance of Both Pedals of the Bicycle

The US and Canadian federal governments have decided to invest heavily in the transition towards a "net zero" economy, an economy where the total amount of GHG emissions produced is balanced by an equal amount of emissions removed from the atmosphere. At least in rhetoric, the governments appear to be attempting to be technology-neutral for the most part, seeking to institute industrial policy without the baggage that that term has accumulated. They do, though, draw on some more tailored policies for some technologies and build in some tilt towards broader goals, such as the focus on ensuring in some cases on specific labour requirements.

Given the complexity and scale of the change that is required, a synthesized approach makes sense. It allows space for the advantages of both approaches and helps mitigate the political risks from attempting either approach in its fullest form. However, the potential for such an approach rests on appropriate institutions – "institutional structures are of the essence both in managing uncertainty and expectations and in system change."[41] Institutions help us mediate the different ideas and interests at play in addressing climate change.[42] For example, the risk that public funding for technologies will be channeled in wasteful or harmful directions may be reduced by ensuring that the decision-makers both have expertise and are politically independent.[43]

Not only do institutions shape the pace and cost of change, they also are key to its fairness. Klein notes that "The true challenge is – can we have more democratic planning?" and "somehow resist the top-down logic of the state."[44] It is a tricky mix, however. The greater the process leans on democratic decision-making, the greater are the risks for quick and possibly even effective decision-making.

The combination of strategies will be controversial. It can drive the innovation needed to find new technologies to address GHG emissions, garner the added benefits, such as to health, and even drive economic growth.[45] Yet how we move will influence equity both across and within generations. It is too important to not to use all our tools.

NOTES

1 IPCC, *Global Warming of 1.5°C: An IPCC Special Report on the Impacts of Global Warming of 1.5°C Above Pre-Industrial Levels and Related Global Greenhouse Gas Emission Pathways, in the Context of Strengthening the Global Response to the Threat of Climate Change, Sustainable Development, and Efforts to Eradicate Poverty* (Cambridge: Cambridge University Press, 2018), online (pdf): <https://www.ipcc.ch/site/assets/uploads/sites/2/2022/06/SR15_Full_Report_HR.pdf>.

2 A "net zero economy" in the context of climate policy refers to an economic system where the total amount of greenhouse gas (GHG) emissions produced is balanced by an equal amount of emissions removed from the atmosphere. In other words, the net emissions of the economy are zero. Achieving a net zero economy is considered a critical goal in mitigating the worst effects of climate change and limiting global warming.

3 Andrew Green, *Picking Up the Slack: Law, Institutions, and Canadian Climate Policy* (Toronto: University of Toronto Press, 2022), online: <https://doi.org/10.3138/9781487553319>.

4 Edward Iacobucci & Michael Trebilcock, "Confronting the Institutional Challenges at the Heart of Climate Change Policy" in this volume.

5 Nicholas Stern, Joseph Stiglitz & Charlotte Taylor, "The Economics of Immense Risk, Urgent Action and Radical Change: Towards New Approaches to the Economics of Climate Change" (2022) NBER Working Paper 28472 at 5, online: <https://doi.org/10.3386/w28472>.

6 IPCC, Sections in *Climate Change 2021: Synthesis Report of the IPCC Sixth Assessment Report (AR6)* (Geneva: IPCC, 2023) 35, online (pdf): <https://www.ipcc.ch/report/ar6/syr/downloads/report/IPCC_AR6_SYR_LongerReport.pdf>.

7 Stern, Stiglitz & Taylor, *supra* note 5 at 5.

8 Seth Klein, *A Good War: Mobilizing Canada for the Climate Emergency* (Toronto: ECW Press, 2020) at 178.

9 See e.g., Robert Gifford, "The Dragons of Inaction: Psychological Barriers That Limit Climate Change Mitigation and Adaptation" (2011) 66 Am Psychol 290, online: <https://doi.org/10.1037/a0023566>.

10 Iacobucci & Trebilcock, *supra* note 4; Stern, Stiglitz & Taylor, *supra* note 5; Green, *supra* note 3; Klein, *supra* note 8.

11 Stern, Stiglitz & Taylor, *supra* note 5 at 2, noting that for some economists "with the right carbon price, the market will take care of it all."

12 For a discussion of iterative, marginal steps for addressing climate change, see e.g., Richard Epstein, "Global Warming: How Not to Respond," *Hoover*

Institution (17 August 2021), online: <https://www.hoover.org/research/global-warming-how-not-respond>.

13 Stern, Stiglitz & Taylor, *supra* note 5.

14 Marisa Beck, Dale Beugin & Calvin Trottier-Chi, *Seven Recommendations to Leverage Public Investment to Help Canada Compete in the Global Energy Transition* (Bobcaygeon: Canadian Climate Institute, 2023).

15 Stern, Stiglitz & Taylor, *supra* note 5; Beck, Beugin & Trottier-Chi, *supra* note 14.

16 Richard Revesz, "Fallacies in the Design of Climate Change Policies: A Response to Richard Epstein" 10:3 Texas A&M L Rev 385, online: <https://doi.org/10.37419/LR.V10.I3.1>.

17 Klein, *supra* note 8 at 171.

18 Revesz, *supra* note 16; Stern, Stiglitz & Taylor, *supra* note 5.

19 There is an extensive literature dealing with how to address intergenerational equity and the benefits and concerns about using market-based discount rates. See e.g., Nicholas Stern, "Ethics, Equity and the Economics of Climate Change Paper 2: Economics and Politics" (2014) 30:3 Econ Philos 446, online: <https://doi.org/10.1017/S0266267114000303>; William Nordhaus, "Climate Change: The Ultimate Challenge for Economics" (2019) 109:6 Am Econ Rev 2003, online: <https://doi.org/10.1257/aer.109.6.1991>; Stern, Stiglitz & Taylor, *supra* note 5.

20 Beck, Beugin & Trottier-Chi, *supra* note 14; Stern, Stiglitz & Taylor, *supra* note 5 at 30.

21 For an explanation of the tipping points concept in the climate context, see T.M. Lenton et al, "Tipping elements in the Earth's climate system" (2008) 105:6 Proc Natl Acad Sci 1786, online: <https://doi.org/10.1073/pnas.0705414105>.

22 Revesz, *supra* note 16.

23 Klein, *supra* note 8 at 205.

24 *Ibid* at 205.

25 *Ibid* at 173.

26 Brendan Haley, "Will the Response to the US Inflation Reduction Act Reveal Canada's Lack of Green Industrial Policy?," *Broadbent Institute* (19 March 2023), online: <https://www.broadbentinstitute.ca/canadas-green-industrial-policy-response>.

27 Beck, Beugin & Trottier-Chi, *supra* note 14 at 26.

28 *Ibid* at 14.

29 Klein, *supra* note 8.

30 Beck, Beugin & Trottier-Chi *supra* note 14.

31 See e.g., Steven Bernstein & Matthew Hoffman, "Climate Politics, Metaphors and the Fractal Carbon Trap" (2019) 9 Nat Clim Chang 919, online: <https://doi.org/10.1038/s41558-019-0618-2>; Jeff Colgan, Jessica

Green & Thomas Hale, "Asset Revaluation and the Existential Politics of Climate Change" (2021) 75:2 Int Organ 586, online: <https://doi.org/10.1017/S0020818320000296>.

32 Beck, Beugin & Trottier-Chi, *supra* note 14.

33 See Niblett paper on the public goods nature of innovation.

34 See Joseph Stiglitz et al, *Report of the High-Level Commission on Carbon Prices* (Washington DC: World Bank, 2017), online: <https://doi.org/10.7916/d8-w2nc-4103>.

35 US Department of Energy, *Inflation Reduction Act of 2022* (Washington DC: US Department of Energy), online: <https://www.energy.gov/lpo/inflation-reduction-act-2022>

36 See Lachlan Carey & Jun Ukita Shepard, "Congress's Climate Triple Whammy: Innovation, Investment and Industrial Policy," *RMI* (22 August 2022), online: <https://rmi.org/climate-innovation-investment-and-industrial-policy>, for an overview of the innovation provisions of the *Inflation Reduction Act* and the *CHIPS and Science Act*.

37 Canada, *Budget 2023: A Made-In-Canada Plan* (Ottawa: Government of Canada, 2023), online (pdf): <https://www.budget.canada.ca/2023/pdf/budget-2023-en.pdf>.

38 Canada, *supra* note 37 at 71.

39 "ITER," *Wikipedia* (last modified 01 October 2024), online: <https://en.wikipedia.org/wiki/ITER>.

40 US Department of Energy, "Advanced Research Projects Agency-Energy (ARPA-E)" (accessed 16 October 2024), online: <https://www.energy.gov/advanced-research-projects-agency-energy-arpa-e>.

41 Stern, Stiglitz & Taylor, *supra* note 5 at 54.

42 See e.g., Iacobucci & Trebilcock, "Confronting the Institutional Challenges at the Heart of Climate Change Policy," in this volume discussing the centrality of institutional choice to progress on climate change.

43 Beck, Beugin & Trottier-Chi, *supra* note 14.

44 Klein, *supra* note 8 at 180.

45 Stern, Stiglitz & Taylor, *supra* note 5.

14 A Cautiously Optimistic View of Innovation and Climate Change

ANTHONY NIBLETT

I. Introduction

Technology makes our lives better. It turns humans into superhumans. Human ingenuity and creativity have enabled today's humans to do things that our ancestors could not even dream of. Technology takes the science fiction of the generation before and transforms it into science fact. We live longer lives and better lives than any other cohort in human history.

But these improvements to the human condition have come at a cost to our planet.[1] The ways in which we generate electricity, produce goods, transport these goods, and transport ourselves has polluted the air we breathe, the water we drink, and the earth we farm. This lack of care and investment in our environment has led us down a path towards climate change that has been described as an "existential threat" to humanity.[2]

To what extent can we rely on technology and innovation to solve the problems of climate change? I am optimistic. History reveals that humans are astonishingly good at finding innovative solutions to existential problems. The twentieth century saw great improvements in the human condition. Famines have been "virtually eradicated from most of the world."[3] Diseases were eliminated. Billions of lives were saved by the innovations of the twentieth century. I am optimistic that the twenty-first century can bear witness to innovations that will help eradicate the ills of climate change.

What role will the law play? Let's be clear: if technology is to play an important role in reducing the harmful effects of climate change, then much of the hard work will be done by engineers, climatologists, geologists, chemists, biologists, and physicists. But the law can play a fundamental role in ensuring that the conditions for innovation are fertile. Law has the power to foster innovation. It can ensure that we have the conditions to stimulate innovative thought and allow human ingenuity to thrive. The law can protect inventors and creators, ensuring they can profit from their ideas. Legal institutions have incentivized the creation of new technologies. This, in turn, spurred economic development and improved human livelihoods by promoting a more dynamic, innovative, and prosperous society. Used in the right way, the law can push humans to use resources more efficiently and effectively.[4] On the other hand, law can also be used to crush innovation. These legal protections can be abused, delaying the implementation of socially beneficial technologies.

The crucial question, therefore, is whether we can use the law to build the right foundation and generate the right conditions to encourage scientists and engineers to find solutions to the problems of climate change. Here is where my optimism is tempered somewhat. My optimism is not blind optimism. It is cautious optimism. There are very good reasons to question the optimistic view. The legal solutions that helped foster so many lifesaving and life-enhancing innovations in the past will likely not work when it comes to climate change. Here, the free rider problem with climate change is pervasive. Trying to overcome one free rider problem creates new free rider problems. Shutting off one leak exposes another.

The traditional legal tools we have used to stimulate innovative behaviour will not work with regards to some of the proposed solutions to climate change. For years, we have assigned property rights over ideas. The market, by itself, fails to offer sufficient incentive to invest in knowledge creation. Because knowledge is a public good, once it is discovered or created, it becomes available to all. Such knowledge is costly to discover or create. Why would anyone invest time and resources if there is little ability to reap the benefits? Patents can help solve this free rider problem. A patent allows the creator to capture some of the social benefit of an innovation, providing an incentive to create knowledge. We have all been the beneficiaries of this legal innovation.

Such legal tools will play a far less crucial role when it comes to finding solutions to climate change. Put simply, private property rights over innovations that serve to remedy climate change are unlikely to offer the appropriate incentive to engage in the types of climate change research that we will need to cool the planet. Patents work well in situations where the inventors can capture part of the social benefits. For example, patents work well with drug discovery, where the beneficiaries of the innovative research pay for the drug. Without ex post capture of profit, the drug would not attract research and would be unlikely to be discovered. This exposes some of the limitations of patents. For example, patents are less likely to spur innovative activity where those who benefit have low ability to pay. In the climate change space, the benefits are too widespread and diffuse. Everyone will benefit from these innovations, but there are few mechanisms for innovators to profit directly from each of us who will benefit. As such, a new free rider problem emerges.

Thus, other means of stimulating innovative activity are required. Increased use of government prizes and research grants appear to be the obvious solutions. With government prizes, the government identifies a specific problem and offers a substantial reward to those who find a solution. They work well in particular situations. Such prizes have historical precedent in situations where a government requires a speedy solution to a pressing, substantial, and easily identifiable problem. There are clear benefits to having prizes rather than property rights. For example, the government can make the knowledge widely and freely available for use by others. This overcomes some of the problems of assigning a monopoly to the inventor.

There are, of course, limitations and challenges with using government prizes when it comes to climate change. Identifying the right set of problems and crafting the optimal contract and reward scheme to generate investment in innovation is not easy. Government grants are essentially prizes for the recipient's *potential* for solving the problems that the government has identified. Compared to ex post prizes (where rewards are only paid out *if* the winner of the prize was successful), a government research grant reduces the risk of those who invest in finding solutions. The government, though, faces greater risk and more substantial monitoring costs.

Government prizes and grants, if used appropriately, offer greater promise than relying on private property rights over innovations when it comes to addressing climate change. Such prizes and grants require governments to be proactive in identifying problems and understanding what solutions look like. But reliance on government prizes and grants gives rise to a different free rider problem. Given that everyone on the planet will benefit if these innovations come to fruition, governments of individual countries may be unwilling to put forward significant investments in prizes and grants if they believe that another country will be investing significant sums to fund these solutions. Governments may free ride and not invest. Given that someone else will pay, no one will end up paying. In short, increased cooperation by governments is required – along with increased commitments to offering rewards to those who find solutions. Climate change necessitates an aggregate effort on the part of governments. International cooperation between governments in creating prizes and rewards is required.

This chapter focuses on how to best encourage new innovations that will cool the earth and reverse the negative consequences of climate change. At this juncture, I wish to make two things clear. First, I am in no way suggesting that these types of solutions are the only ones to mitigate climate change. Indeed, these new innovations are only part of a broad suite of policies and decisions to change the path we are on. Second, I am in no way suggesting that innovations that cool the earth are the perfect solution. Merely because we may be able to develop new technologies to reverse the negative effects does not mean we should stop trying to reduce emissions and change our destructive behaviour. Rather, the innovations that I discuss here are merely part of the solution.

My argument proceeds in four parts:

(1) **There are good reasons to be optimistic.** The arc of progress over the past century has delivered incredible changes that have led to longer lives with much higher quality of living. We have solved devastating problems before. Given the right environment for generating innovations, we will be able to solve the problems of climate change.
(2) **Law has played a crucial role in stimulating innovation.** Innovative solutions do not emerge out of a vacuum. Indeed, law – and its accompanying institutions – can either foster innovation or destroy it. The law can be used to help overcome market failures and generate incentives to uncover scientific solutions and improve the human condition.
(3) **But these legal solutions are unlikely to stimulate innovation that will generate solutions for cooling the earth.** Incentivizing the discovery of solutions to the climate change problem may require different legal instruments to those that have worked in the past. Private property rights over innovations, for example, are unlikely to generate the necessary conditions. The impotency of patents to incentivize research into sustainable technologies has been discussed in the literature.[5] My argument focuses on solutions to cool the earth, such as geoengineering. The cooling of the earth is a global public good. Patents may not solve the problem, because the benefits of reducing the earth's temperature are so diffuse and spread out that it may be difficult for the owner of a property right to reap the rewards of their innovation.

(4) **Other policies, such as government prizes and grants, offer better solutions, but then a different free rider problem emerges.** Prizes and grants do not suffer from the same problem as intellectual property rights incentivizing research into cooling the earth. Governments should offer rewards that are both conditional on *success* (prizes) and conditional on the *potential for success* (grants). But, *even then,* national governments may hold off on incentivizing solutions on the theory that other national governments will invest. Another free rider problem appears. Greater international cooperation and commitment to finding solutions will be required.

II. There Are Good Reasons to Be Optimistic

Life, for the most part, is getting better. Much better. When we think about the "good old days," we need to recognize that they were not that good. At least not for the *average* human. For much of human history, life expectancy of a human hovered around thirty years. This did not change until very recently. In 1900, life expectancy for the average human on earth was a little over thirty-one years. Today, life expectancy for the average human on earth is over seventy-three years.[6] Life expectancy of humans doubled in the twentieth century – and then some. In short, something miraculous happened in the twentieth century.

Many factors correlate with and contribute to increased life expectancy. In 1900, about 75 per cent of the world's population lived in extreme poverty. Until the 1960s, newborn children were more likely to be born into extreme poverty than not. But something incredible has happened in the last fifty years or so. About 1.5 billion people escaped extreme poverty in that time. That's a staggering number of lives that have been improved. Newborn children are far less likely to be born into extreme poverty. This is not to say that poverty has been completely eradicated (recent data suggests about 10 per cent of the world's population still lives in extreme poverty), but the numbers continue to shrink.[7] Indeed, in terms of global living standards for the average human, there is a good argument to make that life is better than it has ever been – and never before has such progress been achieved in such a short period of time.[8]

How did we achieve these miracles in such a short period of time? Innovation and human ingenuity. We have discovered ways to ensure that people have food security. Through technological breakthroughs such as the development of fertilizer and the green revolution, our planet is able to grow food for many more people than before. Food supply is also more consistent. Prior to the twentieth century, it was not unheard of for a bad harvest to result in a famine that killed millions, and life for those who survived was not pleasant. The continued existence of one's life turned on the weather. We have solved most of these problems.

We have also discovered ways to ensure that the world's population has much greater access to clean drinking water and sanitation. Scientists have discovered vaccines and antibiotics that have mitigated the effects of disease and, in some cases, eradicated disease. These measures have saved billions of lives. The benefits have accrued greatly to infants. The reduction in infant mortality over the course of the past two hundred years is staggering. Two hundred years ago, in the richest countries in the world, about one in every three children did not survive until their fifth birthday. Now, that number is about one in three hundred.[9]

Other factors are correlated with better living outcomes. The cost of information transmission has dropped enormously. Solutions can be discovered and instantaneously transmitted to solve problems on the other side on the world. This is particularly true in the age of the internet and smartphones. Furthermore, the true potential of this reduced cost of information transmission emerging from the internet has yet to be realized.

Access to electricity has been a crucial factor. Electricity creates opportunities for those living in poverty to improve their condition. Electricity allows humans to work faster, smarter, and better. Life improves dramatically. Take, for example, lighting technology. The costs of producing light have fallen dramatically. The resources needed to produce a lumen were thousands of times more costly in 1800 than they are now.[10] Nobel Prize winner William Nordhaus described the improvements as "nothing short of phenomenal."[11]

But the way in which many countries generate electricity – through carbon fuels such as gas and coal – has contributed to the problems of climate change. The solution is not to cut back on the supply of electricity. Indeed, there are parts of the world that still require access to electricity to grow. In the poorest countries of the world, about 10 per cent of the population have access to electricity.[12] That number needs to grow to redress global inequality, but we need to provide electricity in ways that do not contribute to climate change.

Innovation and human ingenuity have solved problems that threaten life in the past. It might be tempting, therefore, to simply take the position that new technologies will find a way to solve the problems of climate change. Indeed, this optimism has infected the policy platforms and responses of some governments. In Australia, for example, the previous Liberal government provided a climate change policy with a forecast that 15–20 per cent of the reduction in carbon emissions would come from future (unknown) innovations that had not been invented yet.[13] This illustrates perfectly the problem of free riding. The previous Australian government was essentially banking on benefitting from the hard work exerted by other countries. Who would pay for these future innovations? The thinking goes: if someone else is going to pay, we do not need to. But if everyone thinks that way, then nobody pays. If everybody is a free rider, the innovations never materialize.

III. Law Has Helped Spur Innovation

We cannot guarantee that things will simply continue to improve. The miracles of the twentieth century did not happen simply because scientists and innovators had a desire to improve the human condition. By itself, the desire to help humanity does not generate sufficient incentive to invest time and effort in innovation. An invisible hand fails to produce enough innovation. Help from state institutions is required. The market fails to produce knowledge. This is because free markets do not adequately reward innovators. Knowledge is a public good. As soon as the innovation or new technology is discovered, it is cheaper to imitate than invent. Because imitation is cheap, innovators may not be able to reap the fruits of their labour. It is therefore rational to be an imitator, not an innovator. If everyone thinks this way, a free rider problem emerges.

This is not to say that there would be no innovation without state intervention. Some innovations throughout history have been the result of altruistic behaviour on the part of the innovator.[14] Other innovations arise simply because the innovator has a thirst for knowledge.[15] But altruism and curiosity by themselves are not enough. Some of our greatest inventions have also come about through serendipitous discovery.[16] For example, penicillin was discovered by accident in 1928. Millions of lives have been saved. But the conditions necessary to discover this "serendipitous" finding were put in place by government policy. It was not simply a matter of Sir Alexander Fleming stumbling upon the new knowledge. A scaffolding of research was in place. The fact that the answer was discovered by accident only occurred because Fleming was engaged in active scientific research.

Institutions are crucial for innovation. This includes having the right legal institutions and the right laws.[17] Laws that protect property rights in ideas help incentivize investment in innovation. Such property rights turn the public good of knowledge into a private good. If the innovator invents something that is novel and has utility, the government awards the innovator with a monopoly over the idea. This monopoly allows the innovator the opportunity to reap the benefits of the invention. Currently, this monopoly extends for twenty years in much of the world.

It is not possible to calculate how much of the improvement in the human condition over the past century can be attributed to the assignment of private property rights over inventive ideas. But the life expectancy of the 8 billion people on earth would likely be *far* less than seventy-three years. (Indeed, it is unlikely that we would have eight billion people on earth.) There is little doubt that the research that underpins many of our lifesaving and life-extending advances were incentivized by the promise of a patent.

There are some who question the value of patents. Some historians claim, for example, that many inventions that emerged in the Industrial Revolution were not because of a patent. Indeed, patents are a double-edged sword. They can hinder innovation. After gaining a patent on their improved version of the steam engine, it has been argued that James Watt and Matthew Boulton spent much of their time engaged in battles seeking to quash innovations that built on the idea.[18] It was not until the patent expired that the benefits of their invention began to have an impact on growth. Many commentators have questioned whether the current protections offered through patent law is too strong. If protections are too strong, this can harm innovation. Evidence suggests that moving from no protection to some protection is greatly beneficial. But moving from some protection to strong protection may be counterproductive.[19]

While the legal solutions that promote innovation may have worked in the past, they are unlikely to law to provide the necessary incentives to address the existential problems of climate change.

IV. The Legal Solutions That Worked Well in the Past to Stimulate Innovative Activities Will Likely Fail to Incentivize the Investment Required for Innovations to Help Cool the Earth

What should be done to solve the problems of climate change? How do we do it? The problems can be approached from many different angles, and there is a large patchwork of different policies, each designed to tackle the problem.[20] For example, many governments around the world are wisely imposing a carbon tax. If priced correctly, this policy will be enormously beneficial.[21] Such a tax will force us to pay for the harm that we inflict on the planet and on future generations. Some governments are becoming more proactive by internalizing the external costs of pollutants in more direct ways. The *Inflation Reduction Act of 2022* in the United States, for example, levies additional penalties for the emissions of methane, provides large subsidies for industry and citizens to switch to greener energy sources, and offers incentives to permanently preserve forests.[22]

These policies are good for discouraging emissions and encouraging switching to new technologies that have already been invented. But this will not be enough. The modern world is so entwined with carbon fuels that a sufficient reduction in the reliance on such fuels in the short term seems highly unrealistic.[23] Energy transitions take time. Even if it were easy to switch, there is an argument that the problem of climate change is so encompassing that reducing carbon emissions to zero is not enough. That is, even if we make a wholesale switch to solar, wind, or nuclear in our production of electricity, and even if our factories, ships, cars, and airplanes all switch to cleaner, greener sources of energy in the very near future, the earth will still feel the effects of the temperature increases to date. A movement to green energy sources, *by itself*, may not be enough to reduce temperatures. Such a movement will not put ice back on the poles.

Here, I explore innovations that seek to *reverse* some of the effects of climate change, instead of innovations that reduce emissions or mitigating the adverse effects. I focus on new technologies that can help reduce global temperature and ask how we can incentivize research in this area.

Consider three examples of methods that scientists are currently exploring[24]:

1. *Direct air capture.* The idea here is to directly reduce the amount of carbon in the air.[25] Currently, this is proving to be difficult and inefficient. Carbon dioxide is diffuse. It makes up just 0.04 per cent of the air, and using the current methods of reducing carbon, the cost of employing these methods exceeds the benefit.
2. *Sulfates in the atmosphere.* When a volcano explodes, a cloud of volcanic dust can spread across the earth. The sulfates in the dust cool the planet. This can have devastating effects. The year 1816 was known as the year without a summer because of the global fallout from the explosion of Mount Tambora. Harvests

failed. Millions died. Similar effects were felt after other volcanic explosions, such as Krakatoa and Laki. Scientists now believe that they can harness this cooling effect for good, by artificially placing sulfates in the atmosphere, particularly in the atmosphere above tropical regions.[26]

3. *Marine cloud brightening*. Seeding clouds with sea water can, theoretically at least, cool the earth and the atmosphere by artificially reducing the amount of sun that hits the earth.[27]

These technologies are not without controversy.

First, there is the question of cost effectiveness. But innovations are frequently cost ineffective at first. Take solar energy, for example. The cost effectiveness of solar energy has improved dramatically in the past two decades. If we had refused to keep improving solar energy at the turn of the century merely because it was costly, we would not be able to reap the benefits today.

Second, there are questions of buy-in from communities that may be adversely affected if these technologies fail. They will require buy-in from countries that may be disproportionately affected if these geo-engineering efforts cause harm. For example, seeding the atmosphere above the tropics with sulfates will require countries in the tropics to approve these measures. This buy-in may take time. The governance of geoengineering is an enormous issue – and a hurdle.[28] Regulatory frameworks need to be put in place to ensure these technologies are tested responsibly to reduce the likelihood of disproportionate and massive adverse impacts from these geoengineering efforts.

Third, some claim that geoengineering efforts should be discouraged because such efforts will dull the incentive to undertake other efforts that reduce carbon emissions. These moral hazard arguments are potentially myopic. To my mind, the argument here is analogous to those who wish to discourage seatbelts because it will incentivize people to speed.[29]

Most likely, the best solutions that will work to cool the earth's temperature and prevent the catastrophic effects of climate change have yet to be discovered. Incentivizing research into uncovering new and innovative ways of approaching the problem will be needed. But the patent system, by itself, would likely not provide the necessary incentives. The legal apparatus that was so important for the miracles in the twentieth century will likely not work to create similar miracles in the twenty-first century. The legal solutions that encouraged research in food production, manufacturing, and medicine will likely be impotent when it comes to climate change.

It is not just the knowledge (i.e., a method for lowering temperatures) that is a public good. The very benefit that emerges from the knowledge (i.e., the benefit of lower temperatures) is a public good. If the problem of climate change is as dire as we are led to believe, *everyone* will benefit from lower temperatures. Why would a person pay for lower temperatures when they will receive the benefits of lower temperatures without paying?

Intellectual property rights will not incentivize knowledge production when the diffuse benefits are public goods. Even though the creator has a monopoly on the use of the invention, no one may be willing to pay for it if they think someone else will. This situation can be contrasted to pharmaceuticals, where the patent system is extremely effective at incentivizing research. Inventors of new drugs can easily identify those who benefit from the knowledge they produce. For the most part, the benefits are private and accrue mostly to the patient taking the drug. Of course, this can skew research towards drugs that solve the problems and treat the diseases of richer populations, which may not necessarily align with what is socially optimal. But patents do work to spur innovation where the drug company can reap reward from its investment.

This ability to reap the benefits of the investment in research is less likely when it comes to geoengineering projects or other new innovations that may cool the earth. The prospects for profit are insufficient. But are there other tools in the policy toolkit that *will* work? In the next section, I argue that governments should increasingly turn to prizes and grants to stimulate innovative research activity in this area.

V. Government Prizes and Government-Funded Research Grants Offer a More Fruitful Avenue for Success, but Then a Different Free Rider Problem Emerges

Government prizes may provide a more direct means of solving the problem than patents. With prizes, the government offers a large reward for solving a particular identifiable problem. In essence, it is a unilateral contractual offer with the world. Such an offer encourages research to solve this specific problem. Like a patent, the reward is contingent upon success. But instead of relying on the beneficiaries to ex post pay for the benefits of an invention (patents), the government commits to paying a large sum of money to anyone who can solve a specific problem.

Prizes work well when the government knows exactly what problem they wish to solve. The government can target problems that are not being solved by intellectual property. For example, in 1714, the British government wanted to solve a navigational problem. The government realized there would be great benefit if a ship's longitude could be determined with greater accuracy. The government offered a series of substantial prizes to solve a variety of specific problems. Solutions were soon discovered. Scientists were incentivized to try and solve these specific problems. Many of the prizes went to a watchmaker and part-time scientist, John Harrison, who became both rich and famous as result of his solutions.[30] During the Napoleonic Wars, the French government needed a better solution to the problem of food going rotten. Troops away at war were falling ill because the food they brought with them had gone off. The French government put forward a prize for coming up with solutions. Nicolas Appert found one such solution: canned food.[31]

Literature in law and economics has investigated when prizes outperform patents in incentivizing research and innovation. Steve Shavell and Tanguy van Ypersele argue that, from the perspective of innovators, prizes dominate patents.[32] If the reward is set at a level that incentivizes research, society receives the benefits without the costs of monopoly and deadweight loss that accompany the award of a patent. Nancy Gallini and Susan Scotchmer suggest that prizes work better when the government knows both the value of the solution and the cost of finding it.[33] Gallini and Scotchmer argue that neither intellectual property nor prizes can aggregate the information that is decentralized among firms, and neither will be completely effective at delegating research effort efficiently. Keith Hylton argues that there should not be a choice between rewards and intellectual property, but rather, both should be offered.[34] Other commentators have explored other solutions, such as tax policy or ongoing contracts for research, which can provide incentives to innovate.[35]

When it comes to cooling the earth, prizes likely provide a more fruitful option for governments wishing to incentivize new research. If a government can commit to paying those who solve specific problems, then this will be far more effective at encouraging research. But governments to date have been somewhat reluctant to use these types of prizes to help solve problems related to climate change. Indeed, many of the prizes in this area have been sponsored by wealthy private parties, such as Bill and Melinda Gates, Elon Musk, Jeff Bezos, and Richard Branson.[36] Governments may not know which problems require solving, for example. Further, there is a concern that prizes may be subject to serious lobbying efforts that distort the alignment between private incentives and social benefits.

Prizes may be associated with greater risk for innovators (as compared to patents.) While both patents and prizes are contingent upon success, success is typically defined more narrowly with prizes. With government prizes, the innovation must solve a particular problem. With research that is spurred by patents, even if the intended solution is not found, other patentable innovations may emerge from the research. Governments can bear some of this risk by implementing a different form of prize: government-funded research grants. With research grants, the government funds particular research projects. The risk on the innovator is reduced here because the funding is not contingent upon success (although, subsequent awards may be). Essentially, the government is rewarding ex ante prizes to those who have the *potential* to solve particular problems.

Government prizes and grants are, however, subject to a different free rider problem when it comes to climate change. As Scott Barrett has argued in his excellent book, *Why Cooperate? The Incentive to Supply Public Goods*, free riding is likely to be a large problem when it comes to climate change mitigation.[37] Barrett discusses the incentives to reduce carbon emissions and argues that an "aggregate effort" is required to reduce emissions. This leads to an obvious problem whereby it is optimal for each country to free ride on the reductions of others.

Is the same true for cooling technologies? One might argue that the public good problem with cooling technology is more aligned with the "single best efforts" type of public good. The example Barrett provides is that of an asteroid that will kill billions. Barrett argues that a single intervention from a large country with the means and desire to provide the public good would defend the world by itself. But Barrett argues that climate change does not threaten the survival of the human species in the same way as an asteroid. It is likely that the same "aggregate effort" problem that impacts carbon emissions will also impact the incentive to put forward prizes for new cooling technologies.

Suppose a national government puts forward a substantial prize for inventing a method to cool the earth's temperature. If successful, everyone would benefit. The question, then, becomes *which* national government would offer this prize. Who would bear that burden? Each national government would prefer to free ride on the prizes offered by others. Unless the future, discounted cost is so gravely high, each country in equilibrium will act like the previous Australian government and expect someone else to pay. This will result in too few prizes and too little innovation. What is needed is greater cooperation between countries to offer prizes and grants to help solve the problems of rising temperatures.

National laws and policies on climate change reflect the artificial human-created boundaries between countries. Climate change does not respect these boundaries. Cooperation between different national governments is required. Commitments need to be made by national governments to the rest of the world. To be clear, it is not that all governments need to commit to finding one international solution. Indeed, it is likely better for different governments to commit to rewarding a patchwork of different potential solutions to these problems. This would result in a patchwork of different potential solutions. One hopes that such international cooperation and commitments will provide the sufficient incentive to encourage innovative solution to this global problem in all corners of the globe.

VI. Conclusion

I am optimistic that humans can solve the problem of climate change through innovation and technology. My hope is that, in one hundred years' time, we will be talking about how we eradicated famine in the twentieth century and eradicated the problems of climate change in the twenty-first century. But, as the title of this chapter suggests, my optimism is cautious when it comes to climate change, because the free rider problem rears its head at every turn.

There are many things that need to be done. In this chapter, I focused on one potential part of the solution: generating new breakthroughs to cool the earth. I argue that when it comes to incentivizing such technology, the institution of "law" will likely play a less important role than it has done with other innovations. Overcoming the free rider problem will be difficult here. The benefits from a cooler earth are a public good. Every person will benefit, irrespective of whether they pay for them or not. Potential innovators, therefore, are unlikely to incentivized by the possibility of property rights. The promise of a monopoly only works to incentivize when monopolists can extract payments.

Other policies are therefore needed to cool the planet. Government prizes and grants do not suffer from the same type of free riding problem as intellectual property rights. Innovators will be incentivized to research solutions to cool the earth if a government puts forward a sufficiently large reward. But a different free rider problem emerges. National governments may be incentivized to free ride on the prizes and rewards of others.

A recurring theme in much of my academic work on innovation is that in the long run, the roadblocks to improving the human condition are unlikely to be technological. The roadblocks are likely to be human.[38] Here, too, I sense that the obstacles will be human. I have little doubt that brilliant climate scientists and engineers *can* find the necessary solutions to the problems of climate change. The big question is whether our national governments can develop the right framework to provide sufficient incentives for these scientists and engineers to solve the problem.

NOTES

1 See Gernot Wagner & Martin L. Weitzman, *Climate Shock: The Economic Consequences of a Hotter Planet* (Princeton, NJ: Princeton University Press, 2015), online: <https://doi.org/10.1515/9781400865475>.

2 United Nations Security Council, Press Release, "Climate Change 'Biggest Threat Modern Humans Have Ever Faced', World-Renowned Naturalist Tells Security Council, Calls for Greater Global Cooperation" (23 February 2021), online: <https://press.un.org/en/2021/sc14445.doc.htm>.

3 Joe Hasell & Max Roser, Famine, *Our World in Data* (2013, updated 2024), online: <https://ourworldindata.org/famines>. For data on extreme poverty, see: Joe Hasell, Max Roser, Esteban Ortiz-Ospina & Pablo Arriagada, "Poverty," *Our World in Data* (2022), online: <https://ourworldindata.org/poverty>.

4 See, generally, Douglas C. North & Robert P. Thomas, *The Rise of the Western World: A New Economic History* (Cambridge: Cambridge University Press, 1973), online: <https://doi.org/10.1017/CBO9780511819438>.

5 See, e.g., Reto M. Hilty & Pedro Henrique D. Batista, "Potential and Limits of Patent Law to Address Climate Change," (2023) Max Planck Institute for Innovation and Competition Research Paper No 23–10, online: <https://doi.org/10.2139/ssrn.4424243>.

6 Max Roser, Esteban Ortiz-Ospina & Hannah Ritchie, "Life Expectancy," *Our World in Data* (2019), online: <https://ourworldindata.org/life-expectancy>.

7 For data on extreme poverty, see Hasell et al, *supra* note 3.

8 See, e.g., Matthew Ridley, *The Rational Optimist: How Prosperity Evolves* (New York: Harper, 2010); Charles Kenny, *Getting Better: Why Global Development Is Succeeding – and How We Can Improve the World Even More* (New York, Basic Books, 2011); Steven C. Radelet, *The Great Surge: The Ascent of the Developing World* (New York, Simon & Schuster, 2015); Jonah Norberg, *Progress: Ten Reasons to Look Forward to the Future* (London: Oneworld Publications, 2016); Steven Pinker, *Enlightenment Now: The Case for Reason, Science, Humanism, and Progress* (New York: Viking Press, 2018); Hans Rosling, Ola Rosling, & Anna Rosling Rönnlund, *Factfulness: Ten*

Reasons We're Wrong About the World – and Why Things are Better Than You Think (New York: Flatiron, 2018).

9 See, e.g., Norberg, *supra* note 8, at 45–6. See also, Robert William Fogel, *The Escape from Hunger and Premature Death, 1700–2100: Europe, America, and the Third World* (Cambridge: Cambridge University Press, 2004), online: <https://doi.org/10.1017/CBO9780511817649>; and Max Roser, Hannah Ritchie & Bernadeta Dadonaite, "Child and Infant Mortality," *Our World in Data* (2013), online: <https://ourworldindata.org/child-mortality>.

10 Marian L. Tupy & Gale Pooley, *Superabundance: The Story of Population Growth, Innovation, and Human Flourishing on an Infinitely Bountiful Planet* (Washington, DC: Cato Institute, 2022).

11 William D. Nordhuas, "Do Real-Output and Real-Wage Measures Capture Reality? The History of Lighting Suggests Not" in Timothy F. Bresnahan & Robert J. Gordon, eds, *The Economics of New Goods* (Chicago: University of Chicago Press, 1996) 29.

12 See, e.g., World Bank data showing Chad with 11.3 per cent of the population has access to electricity: Our World Bank Group, "Access to Electricity (% of Population) – Chad" (2023), online: <https://data.worldbank.org/indicator/EG.ELC.ACCS.ZS?locations=TD>.

13 See Sarah Martin, "Australia Commits to 2050 Net Zero Emissions Plan But with No Detail and No Modelling," *The Guardian* (26 October 2021), online: <https://www.theguardian.com/australia-news/2021/oct/26/scott-morrison-says-australia-2050-net-zero-emissions-plan-based-on-choices-not-mandates>.

14 See, e.g., Anumpam Jena, Stephane Mechoulan & Tomas J. Philipson, "Altruism and Innovation in Health Care" (2010) 53:3 JL & Econ 497, online: <https://doi.org/10.1086/648383>.

15 See, e.g., Claire Suddath, "A Brief History of Velcro," *TIME Magazine* (15 June 2010), online: <https://time.com/archive/6916217/a-brief-history-of-velcro/>.

16 Royston M. Roberts, *Serendipity: Accidental Discoveries in Science* (John Wiley & Sons, 1989).

17 See Evan Rosevear, Michael Trebilcock, & Mariana Mota Prado, "The New Progressivism and Its Implications for Institutional Theories of Development" (2021) 39:4 Dev Policy Rev 644, online: <https://doi.org/10.1111/dpr.12517>.

18 Henry Winham Dickenson & Rhys Jenkins, *James Watt and the Steam Engine* (Oxford: Clarendon, 1927); Ben Marsden, *Watt's Perfect Engine: Steam and the Age of Invention* (New York: Columbia University Press, 2002).

19 See, e.g., Michele Boldrin & David K. Levine, "The Case Against Patents" (2013) 27:1 J Econ Perspect 3, online: <https://doi.org/10.1257/jep.27.1.3>.

20 Alessio Terzi, *Growth for Good: Reshaping Capitalism to Save Humanity from Climate Catastrophe* (Cambridge, MA: Harvard University Press, 2022), online: <https://doi.org/10.4159/9780674276338>; Christiana Figueres & Tom Rivett-Carnac, *The Future We Choose: Surviving the Climate Crisis* (New York: Knopf, 2020). For a Canadian perspective on the policies needed, see Andrew Green, *Picking Up the Slack: Law, Institutions, and Canadian Climate Policy* (Toronto: University of Toronto Press, 2022), online: <https://doi.org/10.3138/9781487553319>.

21 Oliver Blanchard, Christian Gollier, & Jean Tirole, "The Portfolio of Economic Policies Needed to Fight Climate Change" (November 2022) PIIE Working Papers 22–18.

22 H.R. 5376 – Inflation Reduction Act of 2022.

23 Vaclav Smil, *How the World Really Works: A Scientist's Guide to Our Past, Present, and Future* (London: Viking Press, 2022).

24 These examples are among the different solutions explored in greater detail in Bill Gates, *How to Avoid a Climate Disaster: The Solutions We Have and the Breakthroughs We Need* (New York: Penguin Random House, 2021).

25 David W. Keith, Geoffrey Holmes, David St. Angelo & Kenton Heide, "A Process for Capturing CO_2 from the Atmosphere" (2015) 2:8 Joule 1573, online: <https://doi.org/10.1016/j.joule.2018.05.006>; John G. Shepherd, Working Group on Geoengineering the Climate (2009) *Geoengineering the Climate: Science, Governance and Uncertainty* (RS Policy document, 10/29) London, Royal Society. The Orca project in Iceland provides an example of a current project seeking to achieve carbon reduction, see Akshat Rathi, "Climeworks Raises $650 Million in Largest Round for Carbon Removal Startup," *Bloomberg* (5 April 2022), online: <https://www.bloomberg.com/news/articles/2022-04-05/climeworks-raises-650-million-in-largest-round-for-carbon-removal-startup>.

26 Paul J. Crutzen, "Albedo Enhancement by Stratospheric Sulfur Injections: A Contribution to Resolve a Policy Dilemma?" (2006) 77 Clim Chang 211, online: <https://doi.org/10.1007/s10584-006-9101-y>.

27 Kate Murphy, Gary Cooper, Sarah Doherty, & Rob Wood, "Here's How We Could Brighten the Clouds to Cool the Earth" (7 September 2021) IEEE Spectrum.

28 Phil Macnaghten & Richard Owen, "Good Governance for Geoengineering" (2011) 479 Nature 293, online: <https://doi.org/10.1038/479293a>.

29 Kateyln Tsipiras & Will J. Grant, "What Do We Mean When We Talk about the Moral Hazard of Geoengineering?" (2022) Envtl L Rev, online: <https://doi.org/10.1177/14614529211069>.

30 See, e.g., Dava Sobel, *Longitude: The True Story of a Lone Genius Who Solved the Greatest Scientific Problem of His Time* (New York: Walker & Company, 1995).

31 See Malcolm Summers, *Nicolas Appert: A Biography of Nicolas Appert 1749–1841* (Reading, UK: Downs Way Publishing, 2015).

32 Steven Shavell & Tanguy van Ypersele, "Rewards Versus Intellectual Property Rights" (2001) 44:2 JL & Econ 525, online: <https://doi.org/10.1086/322811>.

33 Nancy Gallini & Suzanne Scotchmer, "Intellectual Property: When Is It the Best Incentive System?" in Adam B. Jaffe, Josh Lerner, & Scott Stern, eds, *Innovation Policy and the Economy*, vol 2 (Cambridge, MA: NBER, 2002) 51, online: <https://doi.org/10.1086/653754>.

34 Keith Hylton, "A Patent and a Prize" (2023) Boston University School of Law Research Paper Series No 23–7, online: <https://doi.org/10.2139/ssrn.4351974>.

35 Daniel J. Hemel & Lisa Larrimore Ouellette, "Beyond the Patents-Prizes Debate" (2013) 92:2 Tex L Rev 303; Yeon-Kee Che, Elisabetta Iossa, & Patrick Rey, "Prizes Versus Contracts as Incentives for Innovation" (2021) 88:5 Rev Econ Stud 2149, online: <https://doi.org/10.1093/restud/rdaa092>.

36 For example, Bill Gates has invested more than $2 billion towards climate technologies (Katy Daigle, "Bill Gates Upbeat on Climate Innovation, Even If 1.5C Goal Out of Reach," *Reuters* [20 December 2022], online: <https://www.reuters.com/business/environment/bill-gates-upbeat-climate-innovation-even-if-15c-goal-out-reach-2022–12–20>); Elon Musk established the $100 million XPRIZE for carbon removal ("$100M Prize For Carbon Removal," *XPRIZE* [accessed 28 October, 2024, online: <https://www.xprize.org/prizes/carbonremoval>); Jeff Bezos established the $10 billion Bezos Earth Fund, online: <https://www.bezosearthfund.org>; Richard Branson established the Virgin Earth Challenge in 2007, offering $25 million for whoever can discover a commercially viable method for permanent removing greenhouse gases from the Earth's atmosphere (Virgin, "Virgin Earth Challenge" [accessed 28 October 2024], online: <https://www.virgin.com/about-virgin/virgin-group/news/virgin-earth-challenge>).

37 Scott Barrett, *Why Cooperate? The Incentive to Supply Public Goods* (Oxford: Oxford University Press, 2007), online: <https://doi.org/10.1093/acprof:oso/9780199211890.001.0001>.

38 See, e.g., Anthony J. Casey & Anthony Niblett, "A Framework for the New Personalization of Law" (2019) 86 U Chicago L Rev 333.

Contributors

Abdi Aidid is an assistant professor in the Faculty of Law, University of Toronto.

Benjamin Alarie is a professor and Osler Chair in Business Law in the Faculty of Law, University of Toronto.

John Borrows is a professor and Loveland Chair in Indigenous Law, Faculty of Law, University of Toronto, of the Chippewas of the Nawash First Nation.

Jutta Brunnée is a dean, university professor, and James Marshall Tory Dean's Chair in the Faculty of Law, University of Toronto.

Brenda Cossman is a professor, associate dean of research, and Goodman-Schipper Chair in the Faculty of Law, University of Toronto.

David Dyzenhaus is a university professor of law and philosophy and Albert Abel Chair in the Faculty of Law, University of Toronto.

Christopher Essert is an associate professor and associate dean of the JD program in the Faculty of Law, University of Toronto.

Angela Fernandez is a professor in the Faculty of Law and Department of History at the University of Toronto.

Patricia Galvão Ferreira is an associate professor of law at the Schulich School of Law, Dalhousie University.

Andrew Green is a professor and Metcalf Chair in Environmental Law in the Faculty of Law, University of Toronto.

Edward Iacobucci is a professor and TSE Chair in Capital Markets in the Faculty of Law, University of Toronto.

Trudo Lemmens is a professor and Scholl Chair in Health Law and Policy in the Faculty of Law and at Dalla Lana School of Public Health, University of Toronto.

Anthony Niblett is a professor and Canada Research Chair in Law, Economics and Innovation.

Olivia O'Connor is a graduate of the JD program in the Faculty of Law, University of Toronto, and is currently a judicial law clerk at the Court of Appeal for British Columbia.

Gabrielle Peters is a disabled writer, community researcher, and policy analyst living in Vancouver, British Columbia.

Megan Pfiffer is an SJD candidate in the Faculty of Law, University of Toronto.

Mariana Mota Prado is a professor and William C. Graham Chair in International Law and Development in the Faculty of Law, University of Toronto.

Krystal-Anne Roussel is a research associate in animal law in the Faculty of Law, University of Toronto.

Michael Trebilcock is a university professor emeritus in the Faculty of Law, University of Toronto.

Albert Yoon is a professor and Michael J. Trebilcock Chair in Law and Economics in the Faculty of Law, University of Toronto.

FSC
www.fsc.org
MIX
Papier | Fördert
gute Waldnutzung
FSC® C083411

Kolibri 360 GmbH
Ferdinand-Jühlke-Straße 7
99095 Erfurt, Deutschland
produktsicherheit@kolibri360.de